Lecture Notes in Computer Science 2032

Edited by G. Goos, J. Hartmanis and J. van Leeuwen

W0246253

Springer

Berlin
Heidelberg
New York
Barcelona
Hong Kong
London
Milan
Paris
Singapore
Tokyo

Reinhard Klette   Thomas Huang
Georgy Gimel'farb (Eds.)

Multi-Image Analysis

10th International Workshop
on Theoretical Foundations of Computer Vision
Dagstuhl Castle, Germany, March 12–17, 2000
Revised Papers

 Springer

Series Editors

Gerhard Goos, Karlsruhe University, Germany
Juris Hartmanis, Cornell University, NY, USA
Jan van Leeuwen, Utrecht University, The Netherlands

Volume Editors

Reinhard Klette
Georgy Gimel'farb
The University of Auckland
Center for Image Technology and Robotics (CITR Tamaki)
Auckland, New Zealand
E-mail: {r.klette,g.gimelfarb}@auckland.ac.nz

Thomas Huang
University of Illinois, 2039 Beckman Institute
405 N. Mathews, Urbana, IL 61801, USA
E-mail: huang@ifp.uiuc.edu

Cataloging-in-Publication Data applied for

Die Deutsche Bibliothek - CIP-Einheitsaufnahme

Multi-image analysis : revised papers / 10th International Workshop on
Theoretical Foundations of Computer Vision, Dagstuhl Castle, Germany,
March 12 - 17, 2000. Reinhard Klette ... (ed.). - Berlin ; Heidelberg ;
New York ; Barcelona ; Hong Kong ; London ; Milan ; Paris ; Singapore ;
Tokyo : Springer, 2001
    (Lecture notes in computer science ; Vol. 2032)
    ISBN 3-540-42122-X

CR Subject Classification (1998):I.4, I.3, I.5, I.2

ISSN 0302-9743
ISBN 3-540-42122-X Springer-Verlag Berlin Heidelberg New York

Springer-Verlag Berlin Heidelberg New York
a member of BertelsmannSpringer Science+Business Media GmbH

http://www.springer.de

© Springer-Verlag Berlin Heidelberg 2001
Printed in Germany

Typesetting: Camera-ready by author, data conversion by PTP-Berlin, Stefan Sossna
Printed on acid-free paper   SPIN: 10782387   06/3142   5 4 3 2 1 0

Preface

This edited volume addresses problems in computer vision involving multiple images. The images can be taken by multiple cameras, in different spectral bands (multiband images), at different times (video sequences), and so on. Computer vision research has to deal with multi-image or multi-sensor situations in varying contexts such as, for instance,

- *image databases*: representations of similar situations, objects, processes, and related search strategies,
- *3D shape reconstruction*: binocular, trinocular, and multiple-view stereo, structured light methods, photometric stereo, shape from multiple shadows, registration and integration of partial (or single view) 3D reconstructions, and
- *augmented reality*: multi-node panoramic scenes, omniviewing by special cameras, video-to-(still)wide angle image generation, incremental surface visualization, or more advanced visualization techniques.

Recently multi-image techniques have become a main issue in image technology.

The volume presents extended and updated versions of 20 talks given at the 10th International Workshop on Theoretical Foundations of Computer Vision (March 12 - 17, 2000, Schloss Dagstuhl, Germany). Chapters are grouped into four parts as follows: (*i*) 3D Data Acquisition and Sensor Design; (*ii*) Multi-Image Analysis; (*iii*) Data Fusion in 3D Scene Description; and (*iv*) Applied 3D Vision and Virtual Reality. They cover various theoretical, algorithmic, and implementational issues in multi-image acquisition, storage, retrieval, processing, analysis, manipulation, and visualization.

February 2001   Reinhard Klette, Thomas Huang, and Georgy Gimel'farb

Table of Contents

Data Fusion in 3D Scene Description

Applied 3D Vision and Virtual Reality

Modelling and Removing Radial and Tangential Distortions in Spherical Lenses

Steven S. Beauchemin and Ruzena Bajcsy

[1] Department of Computer Science, University of Western Ontario
London, Ontario, Canada, N6A 5B7
beau@csd.uwo.ca
[2] GRASP Laboratory, University of Pennsylvania
Philadelphia, PA 19104-6228, USA
bajcsy@central.cis.upenn.edu

Abstract. Spherical cameras are variable-resolution imaging systems and promising devices for autonomous navigation purposes, mainly because of their wide viewing angle which increases the capabilities of vision-based obstacle avoidance schemes. In addition, spherical lenses resemble the primate eye in their projective models and are biologically relevant. However, the calibration of spherical lenses for Computer Vision is a recent research topic and current procedures for pinhole camera calibration are inadequate when applied to spherical lenses. We present a novel method for spherical-lens camera calibration which models the lens radial and tangential distortions and determines the optical center and the angular deviations of the CCD sensor array within a unified numerical procedure. Contrary to other methods, there is no need for special equipment such as low-power laser beams or non-standard numerical procedures for finding the optical center. Numerical experiments, convergence and robustness analyses are presented.

1 Introduction

Spherical cameras are variable-resolution imaging systems useful for autonomous navigation purposes, mainly because of their wide viewing angle which increases the capabilities of vision-based obstacle avoidance schemes [11]. In addition, spherical lenses resemble the primate eye in their projective models and are biologically relevant [4]. In spite of this, the calibration of spherical lenses is not well understood [10] and contributions to this topic have only recently begun to appear in the literature.

Current standard procedures for pinhole camera calibration are inadequate for spherical lenses as such devices introduce significant amounts of image distortion. Calibration methods such as Tsai's [13] only consider the first term of radial distortion which is insufficient to account for the distortion typically induced by spherical lenses. Other calibration procedures for high distortion and spherical lenses such as Shah and Aggarwal's [9] and Basu and Licradie's [3] have been defined. However, these methods use special equipment such as low-power

R. Klette et al. (Eds.): Multi-Image Analysis, LNCS 2032, pp. 1–21, 2001.

laser beams or ad-hoc numerical procedures for determining the optical center of spherical lenses. We propose a novel method which only requires an adequate calibration plane and a unified numerical procedure for determining the optical center, among other intrinsic parameters.

1.1   Types of Distortion

The calibration of optical sensors in computer vision is an important issue in autonomous navigation, stereo vision and numerous other applications where accurate positional observations are required. Various techniques have been developed for the calibration of sensors based on the traditional pinhole camera model. Typically, the following types of geometrical distortion have been recognized and dealt with [14]:

- **Radial Distortion:** This type of distortion is point-symmetric at the optical center of the lens and causes an inward or outward shift of image points from their initial perspective projection. About the optical center, radial distortion is expressed as

$$\hat{r} = r + \kappa_1 r^3 + \kappa_2 r^5 + \kappa_3 r^7 + \cdots, \tag{1}$$

  where κ_i are radial distortion coefficients, r is the observed radial component of a projected point and $\hat{r}$, its predicted perspective projection [7].
- **Decentering Distortion:** The misalignment of the optical centers of various lens elements in the sensor induces a decentering distortion which has both a radial and a tangential component. They are expressed as

$$\hat{r} = r + 3(\eta_1 r^2 + \eta_2 r^4 + \eta_3 r^6 + \cdots) \sin(\theta - \theta_0)$$
$$\hat{\theta} = \theta + (\eta_1 r^2 + \eta_2 r^4 + \eta_3 r^6 + \cdots) \cos(\theta - \theta_0), \tag{2}$$

  where η_i are the decentering distortion coefficients, θ is the observed angular component of a projected point, $\hat{\theta}$ is its predicted perspective projection and θ_0 is the angle between the positive y-axis and the axis of maximum tangential distortion due to decentering [7].
- **Thin Prism:** Manufacturing imperfections of lens elements and misalignment of CCD sensor arrays from thier ideal, perpendicular orientation to the optical axis introduce additional radial and tangential distortions which are given by

$$\hat{r} = r + (\zeta_1 r^2 + \zeta_2 r^4 + \zeta_3 r^6 + \cdots) \sin(\theta - \theta_1)$$
$$\hat{\theta} = \theta + (\zeta_1 r^2 + \zeta_2 r^4 + \zeta_3 r^6 + \cdots) \cos(\theta - \theta_1), \tag{3}$$

  where ζ_i are the thin prism distortion coefficients and θ_1 is the angle between the positive y-axis and the axis of maximum tangential distortion due to thin prism [7].

1.2   Related Literature

The need for foveated visual fields in active vision applications has motivated the design of special-purpose spherical lenses [4] and catadioptric sensors [2]. These imaging systems introduce significant amounts of radial and possibly tangential distortions (see Figure 2) and traditional methods that only calibrate for the perspective projection matrix and neglect to compensate for these distortions are inadequate [12].

The calibration methods designed for high-distortion lenses typically model the radial and tangential distortion components with polynomial curve-fitting. Examples of such methods are Shah and Aggarwal's [10] and Basu and Licardie's [3]. Both of these methods calibrate the optical center by using procedures that are not elegantly integrated into the curve-fitting procedure which recovers distortion coefficients. For instance, Basu and Licaride's method consists of a minimization of vertical and horizontal calibration-line curvatures whereas Shah and Aggarwal's requires the use of a low-power laser beam based on a partial reflection beam-alignment technique.

Other, similar methods perform minimizations of functionals representing measures of the accuracy of the image transformation with respect to calibration parameters [6,14]. These methods rely on the point-symmetry of radial distortion at the location of the optical center onto the image plane to reduce the dimensionality of the parameter space [6] or to iteratively refine calibration parameters initially obtained with a distortion-free pinhole camera model [14].

In addition to these calibration techniques, Miyamoto [5] defined mappings relating the world plane angle θ_1 to the image plane angle θ_2. One such mapping is given by $\theta_2 = \tan \theta_1$ (see Figure 1). Alternatively, Anderson *et al.* [1] defined a similar mapping this time based on Snell's law of diffraction. Unfortunately, the accuracy of these models is limited to the neighborood of the optical center [10]. Basu and Licardie also proposed alternative models for fish-eye lenses based in log-polar transformations [3] but, in this case, they demonstrate that the small number of calibration parameters does not permit to accurately model a spherical lens.

2   Standard Procedure for Fish-Eye Lens Calibration

The number of free intrinsic parameters for a typical high distortion lens is large, especially when one considers sources or radial distortions, decentering and thin prism, manufacturing misalignments such as tilt, yaw and roll angles of the CCD sensor array with respect to its ideal position, image center versus optical center, *etc.* We encompass radial and tangential distortions in two polynomials for which the coefficients are to be determined with respect to the sources of distortion emanating from the location of the optical center and the pitch and yaw angles of the CCD sensor. We proceed by describing the least-squares method chosen to perform the polynomial fits for both radial and tangential distortions.

Point in real-world plane

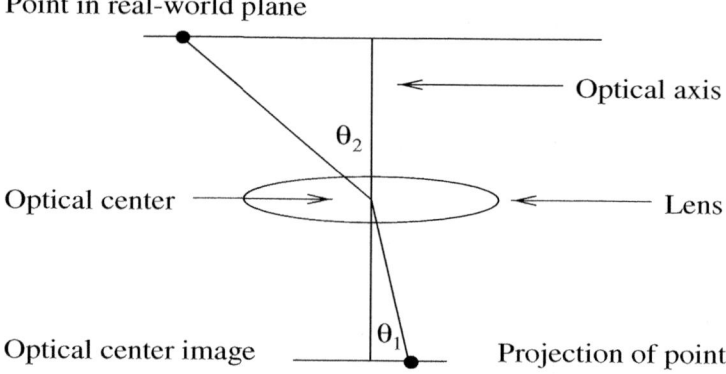

Fig. 1. The image plane and world plane angles θ_1 and θ_2 are the angles formed by the projective rays between the image plane and the world plane, both orthogonal to the optical axis.

2.1   Radial and Tangential Polynomials

Given a set of calibration points and their image locations, the equations describing the transformation from fish-eye to pinhole are

$$\hat{\theta}_{ij} = \sum_{k=0}^{L} a_k \theta_{ij}^k \quad \text{and} \quad \hat{r}_{ij} = \sum_{k=0}^{L} b_k r_{ij}^k \tag{4}$$

where L is the order of the polynomials and $\hat{\theta}_{ij}$ and $\hat{r}_{ij}$ are the corrected polar coordinates of the calibration points. We use a calibration pattern for which the points align into horizontal, diagonal and vertical lines. These n^2 calibration points may be arranged in matrix form consistent with their geometric location on the calibration plane:

$$\begin{bmatrix} \mathbf{P}_{11} & \mathbf{P}_{12} & \cdots & \mathbf{P}_{1n} \\ \mathbf{P}_{21} & \mathbf{P}_{22} & \cdots & \mathbf{P}_{2n} \\ \vdots & & & \\ \mathbf{P}_{n1} & \mathbf{P}_{n2} & \cdots & \mathbf{P}_{nn} \end{bmatrix} \begin{bmatrix} \hat{\mathbf{P}}_{11} & \hat{\mathbf{P}}_{12} & \cdots & \hat{\mathbf{P}}_{1n} \\ \hat{\mathbf{P}}_{21} & \hat{\mathbf{P}}_{22} & \cdots & \hat{\mathbf{P}}_{2n} \\ \vdots & & & \\ \hat{\mathbf{P}}_{n1} & \hat{\mathbf{P}}_{n2} & \cdots & \hat{\mathbf{P}}_{nn} \end{bmatrix} \begin{bmatrix} \mathbf{p}_{11} & \mathbf{p}_{12} & \cdots & \mathbf{p}_{1n} \\ \mathbf{p}_{21} & \mathbf{p}_{22} & \cdots & \mathbf{p}_{2n} \\ \vdots & & & \\ \mathbf{p}_{n1} & \mathbf{p}_{n2} & \cdots & \mathbf{p}_{nn} \end{bmatrix} \tag{5}$$

where $\mathbf{P}_{ij} = (X_{ij}, Y_{ij}, Z_{ij})$ are the 3D calibration points expressed in the coordinate system of the camera, $\hat{\mathbf{p}}_{ij} = (\hat{r}_{ij}, \hat{\theta}_{ij})$ are the 2D projection of $\mathbf{P}_{ij}$ onto the pinhole camera and $\mathbf{p}_{ij} = (r_{ij}, \theta_{ij})$ are projection of $\mathbf{P}_{ij}$ as imaged by the spherical lens.

Various minimization methods may be applied to the polynomials in order to determine their coefficients. For instance, Lagrangian minimzation and least-squares have been used. For our purposes, we adopt a least-squares approach to

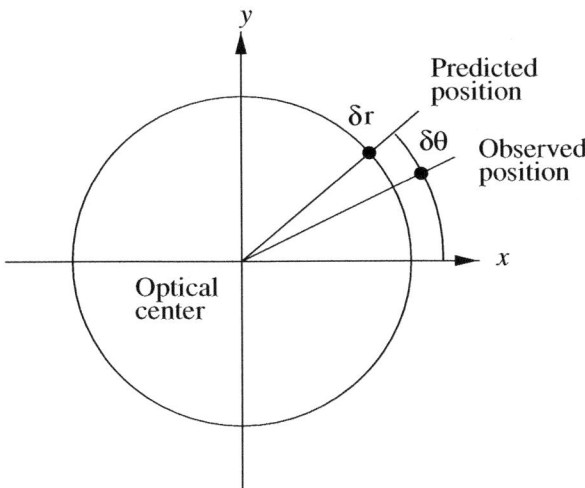

Fig. 2. Radial and tangential distortions. The original point, expressed as (r, θ) is the expected observation. The distorted point as observed, is expressed as $(r + \delta r, \theta + \delta \theta)$, where δr and $\delta \theta$ are the radial and tangential distortions, respectively.

find the polynomial coefficients and perform the correction. This least-squares fit for the radial and tangential distortion polynomial can be expressed as

$$\sum_{i=1}^{n} \sum_{j=1}^{n} \left(\hat{\theta}_{ij} - \sum_{k=0}^{L} a_k \theta_{ij}^k \right)^2 \quad \text{and} \quad \sum_{i=1}^{n} \sum_{j=1}^{n} \left(\hat{r}_{ij} - \sum_{k=0}^{L} b_k r_{ij}^k \right)^2. \tag{6}$$

Deriving the polynomials with respect to coefficients yields the following systems of linear equations

$$\mathbf{a}^T \boldsymbol{\Theta} = \hat{\theta}_{ij} \boldsymbol{\theta}_{ij} \quad \text{and} \quad \mathbf{b}^T \mathbf{R}_{ij} = \hat{r}_{ij} \mathbf{r}_{ij} \tag{7}$$

where

$$
\begin{aligned}
\mathbf{a} &= (a_0, \ldots, a_L)^T \\
\mathbf{b} &= (b_0, \ldots, b_L)^T \\
\mathbf{r}_{ij} &= (r_{ij}^0, \ldots, r_{ij}^L)^T \\
\boldsymbol{\theta}_{ij} &= (\theta_{ij}^0, \ldots, \theta_{ij}^L)^T \\
\mathbf{R}_{ij} &= \mathbf{r}_{ij} \mathbf{r}_{ij}^T \\
\boldsymbol{\Theta}_{ij} &= \boldsymbol{\theta}_{ij} \boldsymbol{\theta}_{ij}^T.
\end{aligned}
$$

We write the general least-squares system of equations in matrix form as

$$\sum_{i=1}^{n}\sum_{j=1}^{n}\sum_{k=0}^{L} b_k r_{ij}^k r_{ij}^0 = \sum_{i=1}^{n}\sum_{j=1}^{n} \hat{r}_{ij} r_{ij}^0$$

$$\sum_{i=1}^{n}\sum_{j=1}^{n}\sum_{k=0}^{L} b_k r_{ij}^k r_{ij}^1 = \sum_{i=1}^{n}\sum_{j=1}^{n} \hat{r}_{ij} r_{ij}^1$$

$$\vdots \qquad \vdots$$

$$\sum_{i=1}^{n}\sum_{j=1}^{n}\sum_{k=0}^{L} b_k r_{ij}^k r_{ij}^L = \sum_{i=1}^{n}\sum_{j=1}^{n} \hat{r}_{ij} r_{ij}^L \tag{8}$$

and

$$\sum_{i=1}^{n}\sum_{j=1}^{n}\sum_{k=0}^{L} a_k \theta_{ij}^k \theta_{ij}^0 = \sum_{i=1}^{n}\sum_{j=1}^{n} \hat{\theta}_{ij} \theta_{ij}^0$$

$$\sum_{i=1}^{n}\sum_{j=1}^{n}\sum_{k=0}^{L} b_k \theta_{ij}^k \theta_{ij}^1 = \sum_{i=1}^{n}\sum_{j=1}^{n} \hat{\theta}_{ij} \theta_{ij}^1$$

$$\vdots \qquad \vdots$$

$$\sum_{i=1}^{n}\sum_{j=1}^{n}\sum_{k=0}^{L} b_k r_{ij}^k \theta_{ij}^L = \sum_{i=1}^{n}\sum_{j=1}^{n} \hat{\theta}_{ij} \theta_{ij}^L \tag{9}$$

The least-squares matrices may be written as

$$\mathbf{A}_r = \begin{pmatrix} r_{11}^0 & \cdots & r_{11}^L \\ r_{12}^0 & \cdots & r_{12}^L \\ \vdots & \vdots & \vdots \\ r_{1n}^0 & \cdots & r_{1n}^L \\ r_{21}^0 & \cdots & r_{2n}^L \\ \vdots & \vdots & \vdots \\ r_{nn}^0 & \cdots & r_{nn}^L \end{pmatrix} \qquad \mathbf{A}_\theta = \begin{pmatrix} \theta_{11}^0 & \cdots & \theta_{11}^L \\ \theta_{12}^0 & \cdots & \theta_{12}^L \\ \vdots & \vdots & \vdots \\ \theta_{1n}^0 & \cdots & \theta_{1n}^L \\ \theta_{21}^0 & \cdots & \theta_{2n}^L \\ \vdots & \vdots & \vdots \\ \theta_{nn}^0 & \cdots & \theta_{nn}^L \end{pmatrix} \tag{10}$$

and we form the least-squares systems of equations as $\mathbf{R}_\theta \mathbf{a} = \boldsymbol{\theta}$ and $\mathbf{R}_r \mathbf{b} = \mathbf{r}$, where $\mathbf{R}_\theta = \mathbf{A}_\theta^T \mathbf{A}_\theta$, $\mathbf{R}_r = \mathbf{A}_r^T \mathbf{A}_r$, $\mathbf{r} = \mathbf{A}_r^T \mathbf{c}_r$, $\boldsymbol{\theta} = \mathbf{A}_\theta^T \mathbf{c}_\theta$ and

$$\mathbf{c}_\theta = \begin{pmatrix} \hat{\theta}_{11} \\ \hat{\theta}_{12} \\ \vdots \\ \hat{\theta}_{nn} \end{pmatrix} \qquad \mathbf{c}_r = \begin{pmatrix} \hat{r}_{11} \\ \hat{r}_{12} \\ \vdots \\ \hat{r}_{nn} \end{pmatrix}$$

The coefficients $\mathbf{a}$ and $\mathbf{b}$ are such that they should minimze $\chi_\theta^2 = |\mathbf{A}_\theta \mathbf{a} - \mathbf{c}_\theta|^2$ and $\chi_r^2 = |\mathbf{A}_r \mathbf{b} - \mathbf{c}_r|^2$. We use Singular Value Decomposition (SVD) to perform the least-squares fits

$$\mathbf{a} = \mathbf{V}_\theta \mathrm{diag}(\mathbf{W}_\theta)(\mathbf{U}_\theta^T \mathbf{c}_\theta) \qquad (11)$$

$$\mathbf{b} = \mathbf{V}_r \mathrm{diag}(\mathbf{W}_r)(\mathbf{U}_r^T \mathbf{c}_r) \qquad (12)$$

where $\mathbf{A}_\theta = \mathbf{U}_\theta \mathbf{W}_\theta \mathbf{V}_\theta^T$ and $\mathbf{A}_r = \mathbf{U}_r \mathbf{W}_r \mathbf{V}_r^T$, and to compute χ_θ^2 and χ_r^2. We use the notation $\mathbf{a}(\mathbf{x}_c, \mathbf{x}_p)$, $\mathbf{b}(\mathbf{x}_c, \mathbf{x}_p, \theta_\mathbf{u}, \theta_\mathbf{v})$, $\chi_\theta^2(\mathbf{x}_c, \mathbf{x}_p)$ and $\chi_r^2(\mathbf{x}_c, \mathbf{x}_p, \theta_\mathbf{u}, \theta_\mathbf{v})$ to indicate that the least-squares solutions for tangential distortion coefficients $\mathbf{a}$ and the residual χ_θ^2 depend on $\mathbf{x}_c$, the location of the optical center with respect to the coordinate system in which the fit is performed and $\mathbf{x}_p$, the translation parallel to the calibration surface, and that the radial distortion coefficients $\mathbf{b}$ and the residual χ_r^2 depend on the optical center $\mathbf{x}_c$, the camera translation $\mathbf{x}_p$ and $\theta_\mathbf{u}$ and $\theta_\mathbf{v}$, the pitch and yaw angles of the CCD sensor array with respect to a plane perpendicular to the optical axis. We further explain and experimentally demonstrate these dependencies in sections 2.3 and 2.4.

2.2   Polynomial Order

The overfit of data, or polynomial orders that exceed the intrinsic order of the data, constitutes our primary motivation for using SVD in the least-squares solutions of the polynomial coefficients. For instance, if any of the singular values is less than a tolerance level of 10^{-5}, we set its reciprocal to zero, rather than letting it go to some arbitrarily high value. We thus avoid overfits of the calibration data when solving for $\mathbf{a}(\mathbf{x}_c, \mathbf{x}_p)$ and $\mathbf{b}(\mathbf{x}_c, \mathbf{x}_p, \theta_\mathbf{u}, \theta_\mathbf{v})$ in (11) and (12). Because of this capability and considering that the computational cost of calibration is usually not critical when compared with real-time vision computations, we use polynomials of order $L = 12$.

2.3   The Optical Center

The optical center of a lens is defined as the point where the optical axis passing through the lens intersects the image plane of the camera. Alternatively, the optical center is the image point where no distortions appear, radial or tangential. That is to say, where $\hat{r}_{ij} = r_{ij}$ and $\hat{\theta}_{ij} = \theta_{ij}$.

2.4   The Optical Center

The optical center of a lens is defined as the point where the optical axis passing through the lens intersects the image plane of the camera. Alternatively, the optical center is the image point where no distortions appear, radial or tangential. That is to say, where $\hat{r}_{ij} = r_{ij}$ and $\hat{\theta}_{ij} = \theta_{ij}$. In addition, radial distortion is point-symmetric at the optical center and, consequently, the one-dimensional polynomial in r is accurate only when aligned with the optical center. Figure 3 shows plots of $(\hat{r}_{ij}, r_{ij})$ and $(\hat{\theta}_{ij}, \theta_{ij})$ at and away from the optical center, in which the point-scattering effect becomes apparent as the ploynomial fit is gradually decentered from the optical center. This effect is reflected in the values of $\chi_r^2(\mathbf{x}_c, \mathbf{x}_p, \theta_\mathbf{u}, \theta_\mathbf{v})$ and $\chi_\theta^2(\mathbf{x}_c, \mathbf{x}_p)$ functions around the optical center, as illustrated by Figure 4.

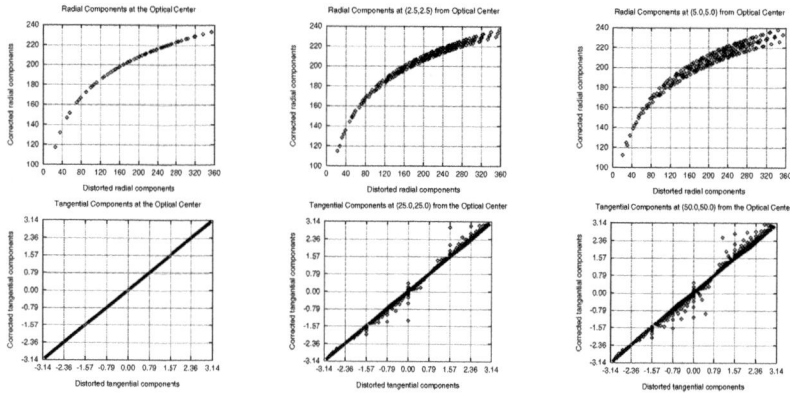

Fig. 3. Plots of $(\hat{r}_{ij}, r_{ij})$ and $(\hat{\theta}_{ij}, \theta_{ij})$. **a) (top, from left to right):** $\hat{r}_{ij}$ and r_{ij} at the optical center, $(2.5, 2.5)$ and $(5.0, 5.0)$ image units away from it. **b) (bottom, from left to right):** $\hat{\theta}_{ij}$ and θ_{ij} at the optical center, $(25.0, 25.0)$ and $(50.0, 50.0)$ image units away from it. The increasing scattering of the plots as the distance from the optical center increases prevents accurate modelling of the lens. The effect is most apparent for the r_{ij}'s, yet it is also observed with the θ_{ij}'s.

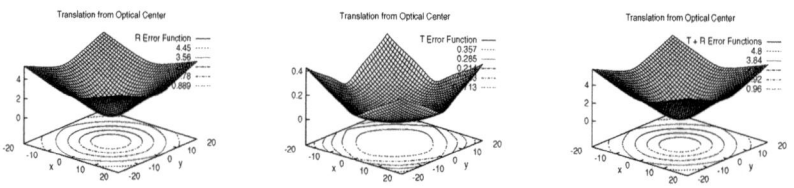

Fig. 4. Effect of translation from the optical center on $\chi_r^2(\mathbf{x}_c, \mathbf{x}_p, \theta_\mathbf{u}, \theta_\mathbf{v})$ and $\chi_\theta^2(\mathbf{x}_c, \mathbf{x}_p)$. **a) (left):** Plot of the $\chi_r^2(\mathbf{x} - \mathbf{x}_c, \mathbf{x}_p, \theta_\mathbf{u}, \theta_\mathbf{v})$ function. **b) (center):** Plot of the $\chi_\theta^2(\mathbf{x} - \mathbf{x}_c, \mathbf{x}_p)$ function. **c) (right):** Plot of the $\chi_r^2(\mathbf{x} - \mathbf{x}_c, \mathbf{x}_p, \theta_\mathbf{u}, \theta_\mathbf{v}) + \chi_\theta^2(\mathbf{x} - \mathbf{x}_c, \mathbf{x}_p)$ function.

2.5   CCD Sensor Array Misalignments

CCD sensor misalignments are due to imperfections at the time of assembly. These imperfections, however minute, introduce additional noise as some types of misalignments influence the value of the $\chi_r^2(\mathbf{x}_c, \mathbf{x}_p, \theta_\mathbf{u}, \theta_\mathbf{v})$ function. We have studied the effect of such misalignments by rotating the image plane of the synthetic camera model about its origin. Figure 5 shows the $\chi_r^2(\mathbf{x}_c, \mathbf{x}_p, \theta_\mathbf{u}, \theta_\mathbf{v})$ and $\chi_\theta^2(\mathbf{x}_c, \mathbf{x}_p)$ functions for rotations $\theta_\mathbf{u}$, $\theta_\mathbf{v}$ and $\theta_\mathbf{n}$ about the $\mathbf{u}$, $\mathbf{v}$ and $\mathbf{n}$ axes of the synthetic camera. The effects have been studied in isolation to one another and, in these experiments, the optical center projected onto the origin of the synthetic camera.

As expected, rotations about the line of sight axis $\mathbf{n}$ have no effect on the $\chi_r^2(\mathbf{x}_c, \mathbf{x}_p, \theta_\mathbf{u}, \theta_\mathbf{v})$ function, as they do not break the point-symmetry of radial distortion. However, rotations about the axes of the image plane $\mathbf{u}$ and $\mathbf{v}$ introduce errors reflected in $\chi_r^2(\mathbf{x}_c, \mathbf{x}_p, \theta_\mathbf{u}, \theta_\mathbf{v})$ (see Figure 5a). As expected, this type of rotation breaks the point-symmetry of radial distortion.

In all three types of rotations, the $\chi_\theta^2(\mathbf{x}_c, \mathbf{x}_p)$ function remains undisturbed, as shown in Figure 5b. Since the position of the optical center is not shifted by the rotations, no violation of the line-symmetry of the tangential distortion is introduced. If such rotations were to be centered away from the image position of the optical center, then errors would be introduced because of the breaking of the line-symmetry. This is also illustrated by Figure 6 where, for the three types of rotation, the plots of $(\hat{\theta}_{ij}, \theta_{ij})$ describe a bijection and do not indroduce approximation errors in the fit, contrary to the plots of $(\hat{r}_{ij}, r_{ij})$ in Figure 3a.

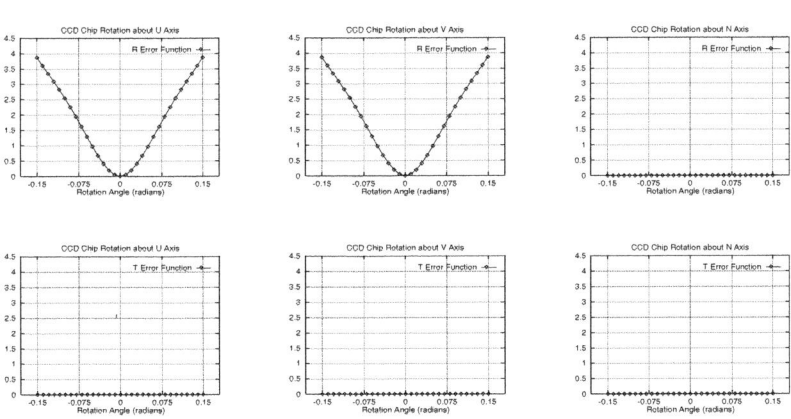

Fig. 5. Effect of CCD array rotation on $\chi_r^2(\mathbf{x}_c, \mathbf{x}_p, \theta_\mathbf{u}, \theta_\mathbf{v})$ and $\chi_\theta^2(\mathbf{x}_c, \mathbf{x}_p)$ functions. **a) (top, from left to right):** The $\chi_r^2(\mathbf{x}_c, \mathbf{x}_p, \theta_\mathbf{u}, \theta_\mathbf{v})$ resudual function against rotations around the $\mathbf{u}$, $\mathbf{v}$ and $\mathbf{n}$ axes. **b) (bottom, from left to right):** The $\chi_\theta^2(\mathbf{x}_c, \mathbf{x}_p)$ residual function against rotations around the $\mathbf{u}$, $\mathbf{v}$ and $\mathbf{n}$ axes.

Another phenomenon affecting the value of the residual is the alignment of the synthetic pinhole calibration dots with the spherical points as imaged by the lens. Given an ideal situation in which the central calibration point is imaged at the image center and that this location coincides with the optical center, then the residual is at a minimum. However, any deviation from this situation substantially increases the value of the residual, and for certain is by no means related to the calibration parameters of the camera. Additionally, we cannot require that the central calibration dot be imaged at the optical center, since it is one of the parameters to be estimated.

In light of this, we also model translation of the camera parallel to the calibration plane as translation of the synthetic pinhole calibration points $\hat{\mathbf{p}}_{ij}$. Consequently, the calibrtation method must minimize the residual with respect to the following parameters:

- $\mathbf{x}_c$: The amount of translation of imaged spherical points $\mathbf{p}_{ij}$, which models translation of the CCD sensor array in the $(\mathbf{u}, \mathbf{v})$ plane. In other words, $\mathbf{x}_c$ is the translation from the image center to the optical center.
- $\mathbf{x}_p$: The amount of translation of the synthetic pinhole calibration points $\hat{\mathbf{p}}_{ij}$, which models the translation of the camera in the $(\mathbf{X},\mathbf{Y})$ plane, parallel to the calibration surface.
- $\theta_{\mathbf{u}}, \theta_{\mathbf{v}}$: The pitch and yaw angles of the CCD sensor array.

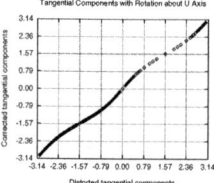 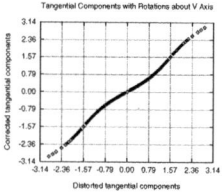 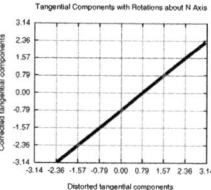

Fig. 6. Plots of $(\hat{\theta}_{ij}, \theta_{ij})$ under rotations of 0.8 radians around **a) (left):** the **u** axis, **b) (center)** the **v** axis and **c) (right):** the **n** axis.

3   Synthetic Camera Model

We calibrate against a standard, synthetic pinhole camera described by linear transformation matrices containing the instrinsic parameters to be calibrated. The first transformation is from the world coordinate system to that of the synthetic camera, expressed by the camera position $\mathbf{r}$ in world coordinates and orthogonal unit vectors $\mathbf{u} = (u_x, u_y, u_z)^T$, $\mathbf{v} = (v_x, v_y, v_z)^T$ and $\mathbf{n} = (n_x, n_y, n_z)^T$. In addition, since the vector joining the image plane at the optical center and the focal point may not be perpendicular to the image plane, we model the focal length in the coordinate system of the camera as a vector $\mathbf{f} = (f_u, f_v, f_n)^T$. The translation from optical center to image center $\mathbf{x}_c = (x_c, y_c)^T$ and the scaling factors s_x and s_y from synthetic camera image to real image also are parameters forming the synthetic camera model. Combining these into a homogeneous linear transformation yields the matrix C:

$$
\begin{pmatrix}
s_x u_x - f_n^{-1} n_x (f_u s_x - x_c) & s_y v_x - f_n^{-1} n_x (f_v s_y - y_c) & n_x & -f_n^{-1} n_x \\
s_x u_y - f_n^{-1} n_y (f_u s_x - x_c) & s_y v_y - f_n^{-1} n_y (f_v s_y - y_c) & n_y & -f_n^{-1} n_y \\
s_x u_z - f_n^{-1} n_z (f_u s_x - x_c) & s_y v_z - f_n^{-1} n_z (f_v s_y - y_c) & n_z & -f_n^{-1} n_z \\
s_x r'_x - f_n^{-1} r'_z (f_u s_x - x_c) + x_c & s_y r'_y - f_n^{-1} r'_y (f_v s_y - y_c) + y_c & r'_z & f_n^{-1} r'_z + 1
\end{pmatrix}
$$

where $r'_x = -\mathbf{r}^T \mathbf{u}$, $r'_y = -\mathbf{r}^T \mathbf{v}$ and $r'_z = -\mathbf{r}^T \mathbf{n}$. Planar points $\mathbf{P}_{ij}$ are projected onto the imaging plane of the pinhole camera as $C^T \mathbf{P}_{ij} = \hat{\mathbf{p}}_{ij}$. To obtain the points $\mathbf{p}_{ij}$ as imaged by a hypothetical spherical lens, we use the fish-eye transform due to Basu and Licardie to distort the $\hat{\mathbf{p}}_{ij}$'s. The fish-eye transformation is given by

$$
\mathbf{p}_{ij} = s \log(1 + \lambda \|\hat{\mathbf{p}}_{ij}\|_2) \boldsymbol{\rho}_{ij} \tag{13}
$$

where $\mathbf{p}_{ij} = (x_{ij}, y_{ij})^T$, $\hat{\mathbf{p}}_{ij} = (\hat{x}_{ij}, \hat{y}_{ij})^T$, $\boldsymbol{\rho}_{ij} = (\cos \xi, \sin \xi)^T$, and $\xi = \tan^{-1} \frac{\hat{y}_{ij}}{\hat{x}_{ij}}$. The symbols s and λ are scaling and radial distortion factors, respectively.

4   Description of Algorithm

As a first step, we generate calibration points using the synthetic pinhole camera. The analytic calibration plane is conveniently located in the (X, Y) plane of the world coordinate system and the line of sight of the pinhole camera coincides with the Z axis.

The synthetic image plane is at 340 mm from the calibration plane and the focal length is set to 100 mm. The pinhole calibration points are then projected onto the image plane of the synthetic camera as $C^T \mathbf{P}_{ij} = \hat{\mathbf{p}}_{ij}$ and kept in polar coordinates as $(\hat{r}_{ij}, \hat{\theta}_{ij})$.

Using the spherical camera, oriented perpendicularly from the real calibration plane, a frame of the calibration points is grabbed. The lens of the spherical camera is at 280 mm from the calibration plane. Figure 7b and c show such frames. We perform point detection on this image by computing the centroids of the calibration points and obtain spherical image points (r_{ij}, θ_{ij}). Both sets of points $(\hat{r}_{ij}, \hat{\theta}_{ij})$ and (r_{ij}, θ_{ij}) are scaled to the canonical space $[(-1, -\frac{\pi}{2}), (1, \frac{\pi}{2})]$ where the minimization procedure is to begin.

We use a gonjugate gradient minimization procedure due to Polak-Ribiere [8] which we apply on the function $\chi^2 = \chi_r^2(\mathbf{x}_c, \mathbf{x}_p, \theta_\mathbf{u}, \theta_\mathbf{v}) + \chi_\theta^2(\mathbf{x}_c, \mathbf{x}_p)$. In order to perform the minimization, the partial derivatives $\frac{\partial \chi^2}{\partial x_c}$, $\frac{\partial \chi^2}{\partial y_c}$, $\frac{\partial \chi^2}{\partial x_p}$, $\frac{\partial \chi^2}{\partial y_p}$, $\frac{\partial \chi^2}{\partial \theta_\mathbf{u}}$ and $\frac{\partial \chi^2}{\partial \theta_\mathbf{v}}$ need to be evaluated for various values of $(\mathbf{x}_c, \mathbf{x}_p, \theta_\mathbf{u}, \theta_\mathbf{v})$.

To evaluate the partial derivatives with respect to $\mathbf{x}_c$, we perform translations of the detected spherical calibration points $\mathbf{p}_{ij} = (r_{ij}, \theta_{ij})$ onto the image plane and perform least-squares fits to obtain the χ^2 values then used for computing 5-point central differences. Evalutation of partial derivatives with respect to CCD array angles is more involved. The first step is to reproject the pinhole calibration points $\hat{\mathbf{p}}_{ij}$ back onto the calibration plane using C^{-1}, the inverse of the pinhole camera transformation. Rotations of these reprojected points in 3D and reprojection onto the image plane of the pinhole camera provide the χ^2

values for computing 5-point central differences. The minimzation is performed with the shifted and rotated calibration points and is guided by the 6D gradient vector $(\frac{\partial\chi^2}{\partial x_c}, \frac{\partial\chi^2}{\partial y_c}, \frac{\partial\chi^2}{\partial x_p}, \frac{\partial\chi^2}{\partial y_p}, \frac{\partial\chi^2}{\partial\theta_u}, \frac{\partial\chi^2}{\partial\theta_v})$. The output of the algorithm is the optical center $\mathbf{x}_c$, represented as the shift from the image center, the camera translation $\mathbf{x}_p$ parallel to the calibration surface with respect to the central calibration point, the CCD sensor array pitch and yaw angles $\theta_\mathbf{u}$ and $\theta_\mathbf{v}$ and the polynomials in r and θ for image transformation from spherical to pinhole. In essence, the procedure is to find the parameter values that best explain the detected calibration points as imaged by the spherical lens.

5   Numerical Results

We study the convergence rate of the calibration procedure, its resistance to input noise and the results obtained with the calibration images of Figure 7b and c, corresponding to spherical cameras A and B, respectively. Figure 7a shows a typical frame taken by a spherical camera, while 7b and c show frames of the calibration plane grabbed with our spherical cameras A and B. The calibration plane has a width and height of 8 feet and the 529 calibration dots are spaced by 4 inches both horizontally and vertically. In order to capture the calibration images, the spherical cameras are mounted on a tripod and approximately aligned with the central calibration dot. The sperical lenses are at a distance of 280 mm from the calibration plane.

The convergence and noise resistance study is performed with a simulated spherical lens. We use equation (13) in order to compute the spherical points $\mathbf{p}_{ij}$ from the synthetic pinhole calibration dots $\hat{\mathbf{p}}_{ij}$. To model CCD sensor array misalignments, we perform 3D rotations of the synthetic pinhole camera and reproject the synthetic calibration points onto the so rotated image plane prior to using (13). In addition, we translate the spherical calibration points $\mathbf{p}_{ij}$ to model the distance of the optical center from the center of the image and also translate the synthetic pinhole calibration points $\hat{\mathbf{p}}_{ij}$ to model the camera translation parallel to the calibration surface.

Input noise is introduced in each synthetic pinhole calibration dot $\mathbf{p}_{ij}$ as Gaussian noise with standard deviations σ_x and σ_y expressed in image units (pixels). This step is performed before using (13) and models only the positional inaccuracy of calibration dots. We proceed to evaluate the performance of the calibration procedure with respect to convergence rates and input noise levels with a simulated spherical lens and present experiments on real spherical camera images (our spherical cameras A and B) for which we have computed their calibration parameters.

5.1   Convergence Analysis

In order to study the convergence rate of the calibration method, we monitored the values of the error function χ^2 with respect to the number of iterations

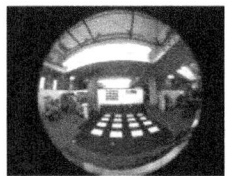

Fig. 7. a) (left): A typical image from a spherical lens camera. **b) (center):** Image of the calibration plane grabbed with spherical camera A. **c) (right):** Image of the calibration plane grabbed with spherical camera B.

performed in the 6D minimization procedure using the Polak-Ribiere conjugate gradient technique. Figure 8 reports three experiments performed with various calibration parameters. The start of the 6D search always begins at $(\mathbf{x}_c, \mathbf{x}_p, \theta_\mathbf{u}, \theta_\mathbf{v}) = \mathbf{0}$ and, as expected, the number of required iterations to converge to the solution is proportional to the distance of the calibration parameters to the initial search values. We used a tolerance of 1×10^{-8} on convergence and we computed the various derivatives of the error function χ^2 with 5-point differences with intervals of 0.2 image units for translation and intervals of 0.0002 radians for rotations.

As figure 8 demonstrates, convergence rates are steep and, in general, 40 iterations are sufficient to obtain adequate calibration parameters. Figure 8a shows the convegence for calibration parameters $(\mathbf{x}_c, \mathbf{x}_p, \theta_\mathbf{u}, \theta_\mathbf{v}) = (5.0, 5.0, -0.1, 0.01)$; Figure 8b) shows the convergence for calibration parameters $(15.0, -5.0, 0.0, 0.2)$ and Figure 8c, for $(15.0, -15.0, -0.1, 0.2)$.

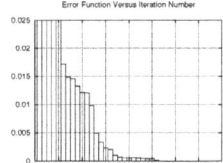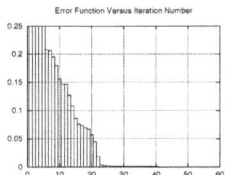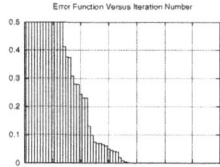

Fig. 8. Convergence analysis of χ^2 for various configurations of calibration parameters $(\mathbf{x}_c, \mathbf{x}_p, \theta_\mathbf{u}, \theta_\mathbf{v})$. **a) (left):** $(5.0, 5.0, -0.1, 0.01)$. **b) (center):** $(15.0, -5.0, 0.0, 0.2)$. **c) (right):** $(15.0, -15.0, -0.1, 0.2)$.

5.2 Noise Robustness Analysis

In order to determine the robustness of the procedure with respect to input noise, we introduced various levels of Gaussian noise into the synthetic pinhole calibration dots. We used zero-mean Gaussian noise levels of $\|(\sigma_x, \sigma_y)\|_2 = 0, 1.4142, 2.8284, 4.2426, 5.6569$ and 7.0711, expressed in image units. The effects of noise onto the calibration parameters $\mathbf{x}_c$, $\mathbf{x}_p$, $\theta_\mathbf{u}$ and $\theta_\mathbf{v}$ and the the values of the residual χ^2 are depicted by the graphs of Figure 9, which show these values for the noise levels we chose. As can be observed, the ground truth calibration parameters $(\mathbf{x}_c, \mathbf{x}_p, \theta_\mathbf{u}, \theta_\mathbf{v}) = \mathbf{0}$ show a linear behavior to input noise whereas the residual shows a quadratic growth with respect to input noise.

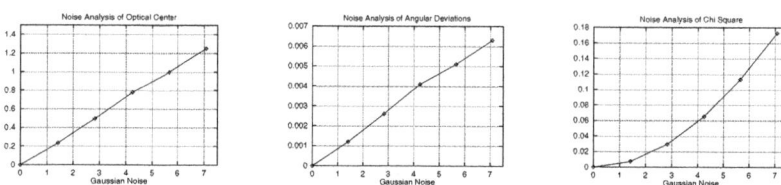

Fig. 9. The effect of input zero-mean Gaussian noise on the calibration parameters and the residual χ^2. **a)** **(left):** The behavior of $\|\mathbf{x}_c\|_2$ with respect to input noise levels $\|(\sigma_x, \sigma_y)\|_2$. **b)** **(center):** The behavior of $\|(\theta_\mathbf{u}, \theta_\mathbf{v})\|_2$ and **c)** **(right):** the behavior of χ^2.

5.3 Calibration of Spherical Images

We have applied our calibration procedure to both of our spherical cameras and determined their calibration parameters. Tables 1 and 2 show the parameters obtained from spherical cameras A and B, respectively. Figure 10 and 11 show the synthetic pinhole calibration points, the spherical points detected from calibration images 7b and c, and the polynomial reconstruction of those detected points with the calibration coefficients a_i and b_i.

As figure 10c demonstrates, our spherical camera A has a serious assembly misalignment. The yaw angle is in excess of 0.16 radians. However, spherical camera B does not show such misalignments and Figure 11c shows a quasi fronto-parallel polynomial reconstruction of the detected spherical calibration points. In the case of camera A, the misalignment of the CCD array is visible by careful visual examination of the device.

5.4 Removing Distortion in Spherical Images

The transformation polynomials $\hat{\theta}_{ij}$ and $\hat{r}_{ij}$ represent a mapping from spherical to perspective image locations. However, to compensate for distortion, the

Table 1. The calibration parameters for spherical camera A.

Calibration Parameters for Spherical Camera A					
Tangential Distortion Coefficients a_i					
a_1	a_2	a_3	a_4	a_5	a_6
-0.0039	3.3274	-0.0216	-0.1836	0.0166	-1.3416
a_7	a_8	a_9	a_{10}	a_{11}	a_{12}
-0.1516	0.6853	0.2253	-0.3347	-0.0879	-0.0092
Radial Distortion Coefficients b_i					
b_1	b_2	b_3	b_4	b_5	b_6
199.6790	-2634.8104	13799.4582	-26999.8134	8895.5168	23348.2599
b_7	b_8	b_9	b_{10}	b_{11}	b_{12}
4858.0468	-17647.3126	-24277.7749	-12166.4282	12108.0938	40070.6891
Singular Values ω_i for χ_θ^2					
ω_1	ω_2	ω_3	ω_4	ω_5	ω_6
23.0001	16.2318	9.6423	5.4287	2.6397	1.3043
ω_7	ω_8	ω_9	ω_{10}	ω_{11}	ω_{12}
0.5012	0.2400	0.0736	0.0325	0.0068	0.0028
Singular Values ω_i for χ_r^2					
ω_1	ω_2	ω_3	ω_4	ω_5	ω_6
525.1062	50.7337	22.1506	7.6035	2.3874	0.6154
ω_7	ω_8	ω_9	ω_{10}	ω_{11}	ω_{12}
0.1383	0.0260	0.0	0.0	0.0	0.0
x_c	y_c	$\theta_\mathbf{u}$	$\theta_\mathbf{v}$	χ^2	
-0.0753	-3.2792	-0.0314	-0.1722	0.0543	

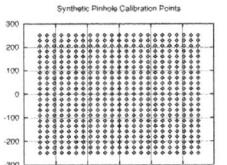 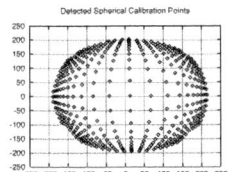 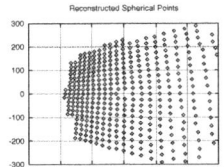

Fig. 10. Calibration experiment with spherical camera A. **a) (left):** The pinhole calibration points, as imaged by the synthetic camera. **b) (center):** The spherical points as detected from image in Figure 7b. **c) (right):** The polynomial reconstruction obtained for this set of calibration points.

Table 2. The calibration parameters for spherical camera B.

Calibration Parameters for Spherical Camera B					
Tangential Distortion Coefficients a_i					
a_1	a_2	a_3	a_4	a_5	a_6
-0.0097	3.1918	-0.0053	-0.2562	0.0658	0.1847
a_7	a_8	a_9	a_{10}	a_{11}	a_{12}
-0.1615	0.4940	0.1577	-0.8093	-0.0553	0.3371
Radial Distortion Coefficients b_i					
b_1	b_2	b_3	b_4	b_5	b_6
-30.4219	458.6032	-1240.1970	1394.3862	1003.5856	-610.6167
b_7	b_8	b_9	b_{10}	b_{11}	b_{12}
-1433.4416	-1063.6945	54.0374	1359.5348	2472.7284	3225.6347
Singular Values ω_i for χ_θ^2					
ω_1	ω_2	ω_3	ω_4	ω_5	ω_6
23.6078	17.0001	9.9003	5.6505	2.7189	1.3567
ω_7	ω_8	ω_9	ω_{10}	ω_{11}	ω_{12}
0.5264	0.2489	0.0770	0.0336	0.0071	0.0030
Singular Values ω_i for χ_r^2					
ω_1	ω_2	ω_3	ω_4	ω_5	ω_6
29.7794	10.8641	3.6978	1.0619	0.2580	0.0536
ω_7	ω_8	ω_9	ω_{10}	ω_{11}	ω_{12}
0.0095	0.0014	0.0	0.0	0.0	0.0
x_c	y_c	θ_u	θ_v	χ^2	
0.0118	-0.8273	0.0091	0.0031	0.1188	

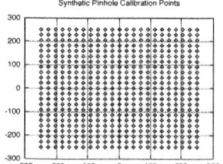 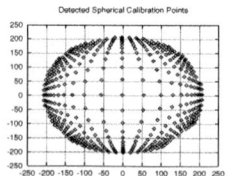 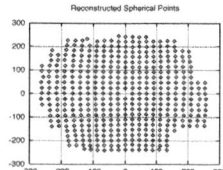

Fig. 11. Calibration experiment with spherical camera B. **a) (left):** The pinhole calibration points, as imaged by the synthetic camera. **b) (center):** The spherical points as detected from image in Figure 7c. **c) (right):** The polynomial reconstruction obtained for this set of calibration points.

inverse transformation is required and, in general, the inverse of a polynomial function cannot be found analytically. In light of this, we use the calibration parameters obtained during the modelling phase to:

1. shift and rotate the planar image points to construct by $\mathbf{x}_p$, $\theta_{\mathbf{u}}$ and $\theta_{\mathbf{v}}$ respectively;
2. shift the detected spherical points by $-\mathbf{x}_c$;

and compute the polynomial coefficients of the inverse transformation as

$$\theta_{ij} = \sum_{k=0}^{L} a_k \hat{\theta}'_{ij} \quad \text{and} \quad r_{ij} = \sum_{k=0}^{L} b_k \hat{r}'_{ij} \tag{14}$$

using a procedure identical to solving (4). The polynomials in (14) are the pseudo-inverses of (4) and are used to remove radial and tangential distortions from spherical images. Figures 12 and 13 show the distortion removal on the calibration images and on a typical stereo pair acquired with the spherical cameras. A lookup table without interpolation (linear or other) was used to implement the transformation.

5.5 Image Processing Issues

Removing distortions from spherical images is not as important as the transformation of image processing results into a perspective space. The advantages of such approaches are many. For instance, the costly transformation of complete image sequences is avoided; image processing algorithms directly applied to spherical images do not suffer from the noise introduced with the distortion removal process, and the results of image processing algorithms are generally more compact with respect to the original signal and hence faster to transform to a perspective space.

6   Conclusion

Spherical cameras are variable-resolution imaging systems that have been recognized as promising devices for autonomous navigation purposes, mainly because of their wide viewing angle which increases the capabilities of vision-based obstacle avoidance schemes. In addition, spherical lenses resemble the primate eye in their projective models and are biologically relevant. We presented a novel method for spherical-lens camera calibration which models the lens radial and tangential distortions and determines the optical center and the angular deviations of the CCD sensor array within a unified numerical procedure. Contrary to other methods, there is no need for special equipment such as low-power laser beams or non-standard numerical procedures for finding the optical center. Numerical experiments and robustness analyses are presented and the results have shown adequate convergence rates and resistance to input noise. The method was successfully applied to our pair of spherical cameras and allowed us to diagnose a severe CCD array misalignment of camera A.

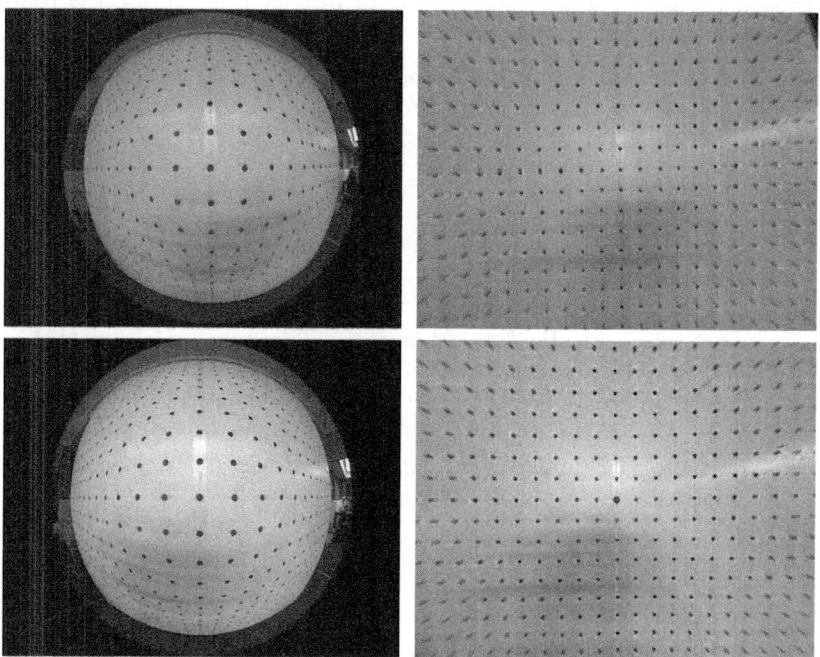

Fig. 12. Disrtortion removal from calibration images. (**left**): Camera A. (**right**): Camera B.

A   Point Detection Algorithm

We use a calibration plane with a grid of $n \times n$ points (where n is odd) for the calibration process. Using a spherical camera perpendicular to the calibration plane, frames of the calibration points are acquired. In this section we describe the algorithm used to detect the calibration points on this spherical image.

The grid points are numbered according to their position in the image plane coordinate system. The central point is $\mathbf{p}_{00}$, the points on the x-axis are defined from left to right by $\{\mathbf{p}_{i0}\}$ where $-m \leq i \leq m$, $m = \frac{n-1}{2}$ and the points of the y-axis from bottom to top by $\{\mathbf{p}_{0j}\}$, $-m \leq j \leq m$. $\mathbf{p}_{ij}$ is the point that lies in the jth row and the ith column of the grid, relative to the origin. The value of $\mathbf{p}_{ij}$ is a 2D vector of its centroid position or **fail** for a point that was not detected.

An iterative algorithm is used to detect the grid points. In the first iteration ($k = 0$) the point at the center of the grid, $\mathbf{p}_{00}$, is detected. In the kth iteration, $1 \leq k \leq 2m$, all the points $\mathbf{p}_{ij}$ such that $|i| + |j| = k$ are found. The first step in detecting any grid point is defining an image pixel from which the search for this point is to begin. The initial pixel is used as an input to the **detect** procedure

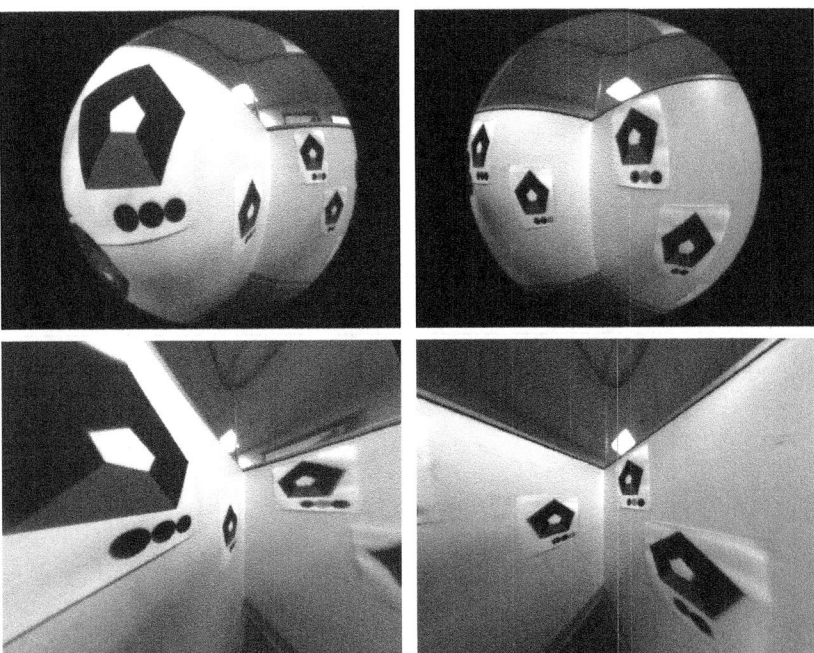

Fig. 13. Disrtortion removal from typical images. (**left**): Camera A. (**right**): Camera B.

which outputs the centroid of the requested grid point, or **fail** if the point is not found.

The initial pixel for searching the central point is the pixel at the center of the image. For any other point, the positions of neighboring grid points that were detected in earlier iterations are used to define the initial pixel. When detecting a grid point $\mathbf{p}_{i0}$ on the x-axis, the initial pixel depends on the location of $\mathbf{p}_{i'0}$ which is the point next to $\mathbf{p}_{i0}$ and closer to the center. The initial pixel in this case is calculated by adding to $\mathbf{p}_{i'0}$ a vector $\mathbf{c}_{i'}$ with magnitude equal to the width of the grid point $\mathbf{p}_{i'0}$ directed from the center towards $\mathbf{p}_{i'0}$. The initial pixel used for detecting points on the y-axis is calculated in a similar way. When detecting the point $\mathbf{p}_{ij}$ in iteration k, the points $\mathbf{p}_{i'j'}$, $\mathbf{p}_{ij'}$ and $\mathbf{p}_{i'j}$ are already detected in iterations $k-1$ and $k-2$. We start the search for $\mathbf{p}_{ij}$ from the pixel defined by $\mathbf{p}_{ij'} + \mathbf{p}_{i'j} - \mathbf{p}_{i'j'}$ (see figure 14).

The **detect** procedure uses a threshold mechanism to separate the pixels that are within the grid points from the background pixels. Since the image contains

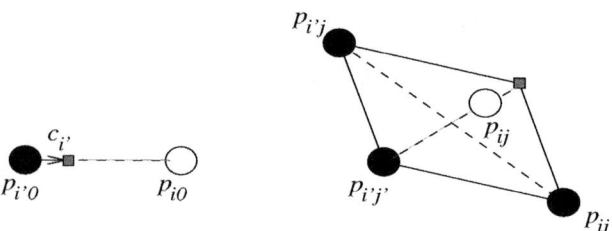

Fig. 14. a) (left): Finding point $\mathbf{p}_{i0}$ based on $\mathbf{p}_{i'0}$. **b) (right):** Finding point $\mathbf{p}_{ij}$ based on $\mathbf{P}_{i'j'}$, $\mathbf{p}_{ij'}$ and $\mathbf{p}_{i'j}$. The gray rectangle marks the initial pixel.

```
p₀₀ ← detect(0, 0)
for k = 1 to 2m
    for each pᵢⱼ such that |i| + |j| = k do
        i' = sign(i) · (|i| − 1)
        j' = sign(j) · (|j| − 1)
        if i = 0 then
            if pᵢ'₀ ≠ fail then
                pᵢ₀ ← detect(pᵢ'₀ + cᵢ')
            else pᵢ₀ ← fail
        else if j = 0 then
            if p₀ⱼ' ≠ fail then
                p₀ⱼ ← detect(p₀ⱼ' + cⱼ')
            else p₀ⱼ ← fail
        else if pᵢⱼ', pᵢ'ⱼ, pᵢ'ⱼ' ≠ fail then
            pᵢⱼ ← detect(pᵢⱼ' + pᵢ'ⱼ − pᵢ'ⱼ')
        else pᵢⱼ ← fail
```

Fig. 15. Algorithm for detecting grid points on a spherical image.

areas with different illumination levels, we use multi-level thresholding to detect the points in all areas of the image.

We define an initial threshold level as the minimum gray level such that at least 4% of the image pixels are below the threshold. The **detect** procedure finds a pixel closest to the input pixel with a gray level that is lower than the defined threshold. It assumes that this pixel is contained within the grid point. If no such pixel is found, the threshold is increased and the search is repeated until such pixel is found or until the threshold gets the maximum gray value (white). In the later case the procedure returns **fail**. If a pixel with a low gray level is found, all the neighboring pixels with gray levels that are lower than the threshold are grouped to form a grid point. The smallest rectangle that bounds the grid point is found. The center of the grid point is the mean of the pixels contained in the bounding rectangle calculated in the following way: let R be the bounding rectangle, where $R = \{(x,y)|x_1 \leq x \leq x_2 \text{ and } y_1 \leq y \leq y_2\}$, then the mean over the pixels in R is:

$$M_x(R) = \frac{\sum_{x=x_1}^{x_2} \sum_{y=y_1}^{y_2} x(C-\mathbf{I}(x,y))}{\sum_{x=x_1}^{x_2} \sum_{y=y_1}^{y_2} C-\mathbf{I}(x,y)} \quad M_y(R) = \frac{\sum_{x=x_1}^{x_2} \sum_{y=y_1}^{y_2} y(C-\mathbf{I}(x,y))}{\sum_{x=x_1}^{x_2} \sum_{y=y_1}^{y_2} C-\mathbf{I}(x,y)} \quad (15)$$

where $\mathbf{I}(x,y)$ is the gray level of the pixel (x,y) and C is the maximum grayvalue. If the bounding rectangle contains more than just the grid point, which might be the case with a high threshold the procedure returns **fail**.

References

[1] R. L. Anderson, N. Alvertos, and E. L. Hall. Omnidirectional real time imaging using digital restoration. *SPIE High Speed Photograph*, 348, 1982.

[2] S. Baker and S. K. Nayar. A theory of catadioptric image formation. In *Proceedings of ICCV*, pages 35–42, Bombay, India, January 1998.

[3] A. Basu and S. Licardie. Alternative models for fish-eye lenses. *Pattern Recognition Letters*, 16(4):433–441, 1995.

[4] Y. Kuniyoshi, N. Kita, and K. Sugimoto. A foveated wide angle lens for active vision. In *IEEE Proceedings Robotics and Automation*, 1995.

[5] K. Myiamoto. Fish eye lens. *J. Lett.*, pages 1060–1061, 1964.

[6] Y. Nomura, M. Sagara, H. Naruse, and A. Ide. Simple calibration algorithm for high-distortion-lens camera. *IEEE PAMI*, 14(11):1095–1099, 1992.

[7] American Society of Photogrammetry. *Manual of Photogrammetry, 4th edition.* 1980.

[8] E. Polak. *Computational Methods in Optimization.* Academic Press, New-York, 1971.

[9] S. Shah and J. K. Aggarwal. Autonomous mobile robot navigation using fish-eye lenses. *Image Analysis Applications and Computer Graphics*, 1024:9–16, 1995.

[10] S. Shah and J. K. Aggarwal. Intrinsic parameter calibration procedure for a (high distortion) fish-eye lens camera with distortion model and accuracy estimation. *Pattern Recognition*, 29(11):1775–1778, 1996.

[11] S. Shah and J. K. Aggarwal. Mobile robot navigation and scene modeling using stereo fish-eye lens system. *Machine Vision and Applications*, 10(4):159–173, 1997.

[12] S. W. Shih, Y. P. Hung, and W. S. Lin. When should we consider lens distortion in camera calibration. *Pattern Recognition*, 28(3):447–461, 1995.

[13] R. Y. Tsai. A versatile camera calibration technique for high-accuracy 3d machine vision metrology using off-the-shelf tv cameras and lenses. *IEEE Journal of Robotics and Automation*, 3(4):323–344, 1987.

[14] J. Weng, P. Cohen, and M. Herniou. Camera calibration with distortion models and accuracy evaluation. *IEEE PAMI*, 14(10):965–980, 1992.

Geometry of Eye Design: Biology and Technology

Cornelia Fermüller and Yiannis Aloimonos

Computer Vision Laboratory, Center for Automation Research
Institute for Advanced Computer Studies, and the Department of Computer Science
University of Maryland, College Park, MD 20742-3275, USA
yiannis@cfar.umd.edu

Abstract. Natural or artificial vision systems process the images that they collect with their eyes or cameras in order to derive information for performing tasks related to navigation and recognition. Since the way images are acquired determines how difficult it is to perform a visual task, and since systems have to cope with limited resources, the eyes used by a specific system should be designed to optimize subsequent image processing as it relates to particular tasks. Different ways of sampling light, i.e., different eyes, may be less or more powerful with respect to particular competences. This seems intuitively evident in view of the variety of eye designs in the biological world. It is shown here that a spherical eye (an eye or system of eyes providing panoramic vision) is superior to a camera-type eye (an eye with restricted field of view) as regards the competence of three-dimensional motion estimation. This result is derived from a statistical analysis of all the possible computational models that can be used for estimating 3D motion from an image sequence. The findings explain biological design in a mathematical manner, by showing that systems that fly and thus need good estimates of 3D motion gain advantages from panoramic vision. Also, insights obtained from this study point to new ways of constructing powerful imaging devices that suit particular tasks in robotics, visualization and virtual reality better than conventional cameras, thus leading to a new camera technology.

When classifying eye designs in biological systems, one can differentiate between the different ways of gathering light at the retina, whether single or multiple lenses are used, the spatial distribution of the photoreceptors, the shapes of the imaging surfaces, and what geometrical and physical properties of light are measured (frequency, polarization). A landscape of eye evolution is provided by Michael Land in [3]. Considering evolution as a mountain, with the lower hills representing earlier steps in the evolutionary ladder, and the highest peaks representing later stages of evolution, the situation is pictured in Fig. 1. At the higher levels of evolution one finds the compound eyes of insects and crustaceans and the camera-type eyes such as the corneal eyes of land vertebrates and fish. These two categories constitute two fundamentally different designs. Fundamental differences also arise from the positions in the head where camera-type eyes are

R. Klette et al. (Eds.): Multi-Image Analysis, LNCS 2032, pp. 22–38, 2001.

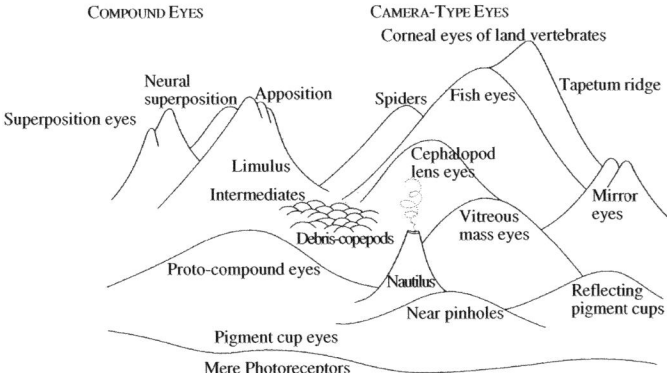

Fig. 1. Michael Land's landscape of eye evolution (from [3])

placed, for example, close to each other as in humans and primates, or on opposite sides of the head as in birds and fish, providing panoramic vision. It appears that the eyes of an organism evolve in a way that best serves that organism in carrying out its tasks. Thus, the success of an eye design should not be judged in an anthropicanic manner, i.e., by how accurately it forms an image of the outside world; rather, it should be judged in a purposive sense. A successful eye design is one that makes the performance of the visual tasks a system is confronted with as easy as possible (fast and robust) [18]. The discovery of principles relating eye design to system behavior will shed light on the problem of evolution in general, and on the structure and function of the brain in particular. At the same time, it will contribute to the development of alternative camera technologies; cameras replace eyes in artificial systems and different camera designs will be more or less appropriate for different tasks. Cameras used in alarm systems, inspection processes, virtual reality systems and human augmentation tasks need not be the same; they should be designed to facilitate the tasks at hand. This paper represents a first effort to introduce structure into the landscape of eyes as it relates to tasks that systems perform.

Although the space of tasks or behaviors performed by vision systems is difficult to formalize, there exist a few tasks that are performed by the whole spectrum of vision systems. All systems with vision move in their environments. As they move, they need to continuously make sense of the moving images they receive on their retinae and they need to solve problems related to navigation; in particular, they need to know how they themselves are moving [1], [4], [20]. Inertial sensors can help in this task, but it is vision that can provide accurate answers. Regardless of the way in which a system moves (walks, crawls, flies, etc.), its eyes move rigidly. This rigid motion can be described by a translation and a rotation; knowing how a system moves amounts to knowing the parameters describing its instantaneous velocity. This is not to say, of course, that a vision system has an explicit representation of the parameters of the rigid motion that its eyes undergo. This knowledge could be implicit in the circuits that perform specific tasks, such as stabilization, landing, pursuit, etc. [9], [14], [26], [28], but successful completion of navigation-related tasks presupposes some knowledge of the egomotion parameters or subsets of them. Thus, a comparison of eyes with regard to egomotion estimation should lead to a better understanding of one of the most basic visual competences.

Two fundamentally different eye designs are compared here, a spherical eye and a planar, camera-type eye (Fig. 2). Spherical eyes model the compound eyes of insects, while planar eyes model the corneal eyes of land vertebrates as well as fish. In addition, the panoramic vision of some organisms, achieved by placing camera-type eyes on opposite sides of the head, is approximated well by a spherical eye. The essential difference between a spherical and a planar eye lies in the field of view, 360 degrees in the spherical case and a restricted field in the planar case. The comparison performed here demonstrates that spherical eyes are superior to planar eyes for 3D motion estimation. "Superior" here means that the ambiguities inherent in deriving 3D motion from planar image sequences are not present in the spherical case. Specifically, a geometrical/statistical analysis is conducted to investigate the functions that can be used to estimate 3D motion, relating 2D image measurements to the 3D scene. These functions are expressed in terms of errors in the 3D motion parameters and they can be understood as multi-dimensional surfaces in those parameters. 3D motion estimation amounts to a minimization problem; thus, our approach is to study the relationships among the parameters of the errors in the estimated 3D motion at the minima of the surfaces, because these locations provide insight into the behaviors of the estimation procedures. It is shown that, at the locations of the minima, the errors in the estimates of both the translation and rotation are non-zero in the planar case, while in the spherical case either the translational or rotational error becomes zero. Intuitively, with a camera-type eye there is an unavoidable confusion between translation and rotation, as well as between translational errors and the actual translation. This confusion does not occur with a spherical eye. The implication is that visual navigation tasks involving 3D motion parameter estimation are easier to solve with spherical eyes than with planar eyes.

The basic geometry of image motion is well understood. As a system moves in its environment, every point of the environment has a velocity vector relative to the system. The projections of these 3D velocity vectors on the retina of the system's eye constitutes the motion field. For an eye moving with translation $\mathbf{t}$ and rotation $\boldsymbol{\omega}$ in a stationary environment, each scene point $\mathbf{R} = (X, Y, Z)$ measured with respect to a coordinate system $OXYZ$ fixed to the nodal point of the eye has velocity $\dot{\mathbf{R}} = -\mathbf{t} - \boldsymbol{\omega} \times \mathbf{R}$. Projecting $\dot{\mathbf{R}}$ onto a retina of a given shape gives the image motion field. If the image is formed on a plane (Fig. 2a) orthogonal to the Z axis at distance f (focal length) from the nodal point, then an image point $\mathbf{r} = (x, y, f)$ and its corresponding scene point $\mathbf{R}$ are related by $\mathbf{r} = \frac{f}{\mathbf{R} \cdot \mathbf{z}_0} \mathbf{R}$, where $\mathbf{z}_0$ is a unit vector in the direction of the Z axis. The motion field becomes

$$\dot{\mathbf{r}} = -\frac{1}{(\mathbf{R} \cdot \mathbf{z}_0)}(\mathbf{z}_0 \times (\mathbf{t} \times \mathbf{r})) + \frac{1}{f}\mathbf{z}_0 \times (\mathbf{r} \times (\boldsymbol{\omega} \times \mathbf{r})) = \frac{1}{Z}\mathbf{u}_{\mathrm{tr}}(\mathbf{t}) + \mathbf{u}_{\mathrm{rot}}(\boldsymbol{\omega}), \quad (1)$$

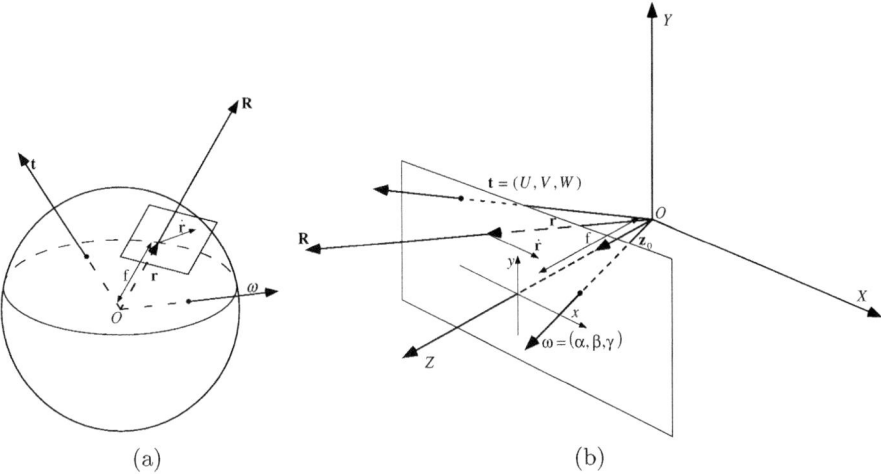

Fig. 2. Image formation on the sphere (a) and on the plane (b). The system moves with a rigid motion with translational velocity **t** and rotational velocity ω. Scene points **R** project onto image points **r** and the 3D velocity $\dot{\mathbf{R}}$ of a scene point is observed in the image as image velocity $\dot{\mathbf{r}}$

with $Z = \mathbf{R} \cdot \mathbf{z}_0$ representing the depth. If the image is formed on a sphere of radius f (Fig. 2b) having the center of projection as its origin, the image **r** of any point **R** is $\mathbf{r} = \frac{\mathbf{R}f}{|\mathbf{R}|}$, with R being the norm of **R** (the range), and the image motion is

$$\dot{\mathbf{r}} = \frac{1}{|\mathbf{R}|f} \left((\mathbf{t} \cdot \mathbf{r})\mathbf{r} - \mathbf{t} \right) - \omega \times \mathbf{r} = \frac{1}{R} \mathbf{u}_{\mathrm{tr}}(\mathbf{t}) + \mathbf{u}_{\mathrm{rot}}(\omega). \qquad (2)$$

The motion field is the sum of two components, one, $\mathbf{u}_{\mathrm{tr}}$, due to translation and the other, $\mathbf{u}_{\mathrm{rot}}$, due to rotation. The depth Z or range R of a scene point is inversely proportional to the translational flow, while the rotational flow is independent of the scene in view. As can be seen from (1) and (2), the effects of translation and scene depth cannot be separated, so only the direction of translation, $\mathbf{t}/|\mathbf{t}|$, can be computed. We can thus choose the length of **t**; throughout the following analysis f is set to 1, and the length of **t** is assumed to be 1 on the sphere and the Z-component of **t** to be 1 on the plane. The problem of egomotion then amounts to finding the scaled vector **t** and the vector ω from a representation of the motion field.

To set up mathematical formulations for 3D motion estimation, the following questions should be answered. The first question to be addressed is, what description containing information about 3D motion does a system use to represent the image sequence? One might envision a sophisticated system that could attempt to estimate the motion field, termed the optic flow field [15]. On the other hand, it is also easy to envision a system that does not have the capacity to estimate the motion field, but only to obtain a partial description of it. An example of a description containing minimal information about image motion is the normal motion field. This amounts to the projection of the motion field onto the direction of the image gradient at each point, and represents the movement of each local edge element in the direction perpendicular to itself. Normal flow can be estimated from local spatiotemporal information in the image [22], [23], [24], [27]. If $\mathbf{n}$ is a unit vector at an image point denoting the orientation of the gradient at that point, the normal flow v_n satisfies

$$v_n = \dot{\mathbf{r}} \cdot \mathbf{n}. \tag{3}$$

Unlike normal flow, the estimation of optic flow is a difficult problem because information from different image neighborhoods must be compared and used in a smoothing scheme to account for discontinuities [10], [12]. Although it is not yet known exactly what kinds of image representations different visual systems recover, it is clear that such descriptions should lie somewhere between normal flow fields and optic flow fields. Thus, when comparing eye designs with regard to 3D motion estimation, one must consider both kinds of flow fields.

The second question to be addressed is, through what geometric laws or constraints is 3D motion coded into image motion? The constraints are easily observed from (1–3). Equations (1) and (2) show how the motions of image points are related to 3D rigid motion and to scene depth. By eliminating depth from these equations, one obtains the well known epipolar constraint [19]; for both planar and spherical eyes it is

$$(\mathbf{t} \times \mathbf{r}) \cdot (\dot{\mathbf{r}} + \boldsymbol{\omega} \times \mathbf{r}) = 0. \tag{4}$$

Equating image motion with optic flow, this constraint allows for the derivation of 3D rigid motion on the basis of optic flow measurements. One is interested in the estimates of translation $\hat{\mathbf{t}}$ and rotation $\hat{\boldsymbol{\omega}}$ which best satisfy the epipolar constraint at every point $\mathbf{r}$ according to some criterion of deviation. The Euclidean norm is usually used, leading to the minimization [11], [21] of the function[1]

$$M_{ep} = \iint_{image} \left[(\hat{\mathbf{t}} \times \mathbf{r}) \cdot (\dot{\mathbf{r}} + \hat{\boldsymbol{\omega}} \times \mathbf{r}) \right]^2 d\mathbf{r}. \tag{5}$$

On the other hand, if normal flow is given, the vector equations (1) and (2) cannot be used directly. The only constraint is scalar equation (3), along with the inequality $Z > 0$ which states that since the surface in view is in front of the eye its depth must be positive. Substituting (1) or (2) into (3) and solving for the estimated depth $\hat{Z}$ or range $\hat{R}$, we obtain for a given estimate $\hat{\mathbf{t}}, \hat{\boldsymbol{\omega}}$ at each point $\mathbf{r}$:

$$\hat{Z}(\text{or } \hat{R}) = \frac{\mathbf{u}_{tr}(\hat{\mathbf{t}}) \cdot \mathbf{n}}{(\dot{\mathbf{r}} - \mathbf{u}_{rot}(\hat{\boldsymbol{\omega}})) \cdot \mathbf{n}}. \tag{6}$$

---

[1] Because $\mathbf{t} \times \mathbf{r}$ introduces the sine of the angle between $\mathbf{t}$ and $\mathbf{r}$, the minimization prefers vectors $\mathbf{t}$ close to the center of gravity of the points $\mathbf{r}$. This bias has been recognized [25] and alternatives have been proposed that reduce this bias, but without eliminating the confusion between rotation and translation.

If the numerator and denominator of (6) have opposite signs, negative depth is computed. Thus, to utilize the positivity constraint one must search for the motion $\hat{\mathbf{t}}, \hat{\omega}$ that produces a minimum number of negative depth estimates. Formally, if $\mathbf{r}$ is an image point, define the indicator function

$$I_{nd}(\mathbf{r}) = \begin{cases} 1 \text{ for } \left(\mathbf{u}_{tr}(\hat{\mathbf{t}}) \cdot \mathbf{n}\right)\left(\dot{\mathbf{r}} - \mathbf{u}_{rot}(\hat{\omega})\right) < 0 \\ 0 \text{ for } \left(\mathbf{u}_{tr}(\hat{\mathbf{t}}) \cdot \mathbf{n}\right)\left(\dot{\mathbf{r}} - \mathbf{u}_{rot}(\hat{\omega})\right) > 0 \end{cases}.$$

Then estimation of 3D motion from normal flow amounts to minimizing [4], [5], [13] the function

$$M_{nd} = \iint\limits_{\text{image}} I_{nd}(\mathbf{r})d\mathbf{r}. \tag{7}$$

Expressing $\dot{\mathbf{r}}$ in terms of the real motion from (1) and (2), functions (5) and (7) can be expressed in terms of the actual and estimated motion parameters $\mathbf{t}$, ω, $\hat{\mathbf{t}}$ and $\hat{\omega}$ (or, equivalently, the actual motion parameters $\mathbf{t}, \omega$ and the errors $\mathbf{t}_\epsilon = \mathbf{t} - \hat{\mathbf{t}}$, $\omega_\epsilon = \omega - \hat{\omega}$) and the depth Z (or range R) of the viewed scene. To conduct any analysis, a model for the scene is needed. We are interested in the statistically expected values of the motion estimates resulting from all possible scenes. Thus, as our probabilistic model we assume that the depth values of the scene are uniformly distributed between two arbitrary values $Z_{\min}$(or $R_{\min}$) and $Z_{\max}$(or $R_{\max}$) $(0 < Z_{\min} < Z_{\max})$. For the minimization of negative depth values, we further assume that the directions in which flow measurements are made are uniformly distributed in every direction for every depth. Parameterizing $\mathbf{n}$ by ψ, the angle between $\mathbf{n}$ and the x axis, we thus obtain the following two functions:

$$E_{ep} = \int_{Z=Z_{\min}}^{Z_{\max}} M_{ep}dZ, \qquad (8) \qquad E_{nd} = \int_{\psi=0}^{\pi}\int_{Z=Z_{\min}}^{Z_{\max}} M_{nd}dZ \, d\psi, \qquad (9)$$

measuring deviation from the epipolar constraint and the amount of negative depth, respectively. Functions (8) and (9) are five-dimensional surfaces in $\mathbf{t}_\epsilon, \omega_\epsilon$, the errors in the motion parameters.

We are interested in the topographic structure of these surfaces, in particular, in the relationships among the errors and the relationships of the errors to the actual motion parameters at the minima of the functions. The idea behind this is that in practical situations any estimation procedure is hampered by errors and usually local minima of the functions to be minimized are found as solutions.

Independent of the particular algorithm, procedures for estimating 3D motion can be classified into those estimating either the translation or rotation as a first step and the remaining component (that is, the rotation or translation) as a second step, and those estimating all components simultaneously. Procedures of the former kind result when systems utilize inertial sensors which provide them with estimates of one of the components, or when two-step motion estimation algorithms are used.

Thus, three cases need to be studied: the case were no prior information about 3D motion is available and the cases where an estimate of translation or rotation is available with some error. Imagine that somehow the rotation has been estimated, with an error $\boldsymbol{\omega}_\epsilon$. Then our functions become two-dimensional in the variables $\mathbf{t}_\epsilon$ and represent the space of translational error parameters corresponding to a fixed rotational error. Similarly, given a translational error $\mathbf{t}_\epsilon$, the functions become three-dimensional in the variables $\boldsymbol{\omega}_\epsilon$ and represent the space of rotational errors corresponding to a fixed translational error. To study the general case, one needs to consider the lowest valleys of the functions in 2D subspaces which pass through 0. In the image processing literature, such local minima are often referred to as ravine lines or courses.[2] Each of the three cases is studied for four optimizations: epipolar minimization for the sphere and the plane and minimization of negative depth for the sphere and the plane. Thus, there are twelve (four times three) cases, but since the effects of rotation on the image are independent of depth, it makes no sense to perform minimization of negative depth assuming an estimate of translation is available. Thus, we are left with ten different cases which are studied below. These ten cases represent all the possible, meaningful motion estimation procedures on the plane and sphere.

Epipolar Minimization on the Plane. Denote estimated quantities by letters with hat signs, actual quantities by unmarked letters, and the differences between actual and estimated quantities (the errors) by the subscript "ϵ." Furthermore, let $\mathbf{t} = (x_0, y_0, 1)$ and $\boldsymbol{\omega} = (\alpha, \beta, \gamma)$. Since the field of view is small, the quadratic terms in the image coordinates are very small relative to the linear and constant terms, and are therefore ignored.

Considering a circular aperture of radius e, setting the focal length $f = 1$, $W = 1$ and $\hat{W} = 1$, the function in (8) becomes

$$
E_{ep} = \int_{Z=Z_{\min}}^{Z_{\max}} \int_{r=0}^{e} \int_{\phi=0}^{2\pi} \left\{ r \left(\left(\frac{x - x_0}{Z} - \beta_\epsilon + \gamma_\epsilon y + x \right) (y - \hat{y}_0) \right. \right.
$$

$$
\left. \left. - \left(\frac{y - y_0}{Z} + \alpha_\epsilon - \gamma_\epsilon x + y \right) (x - \hat{x}_0) \right)^2 \right\} dr \, d\phi \, dZ
$$

where (r, ϕ) are polar coordinates ($x = r\cos\phi, y = r\sin\phi$). Performing the integration, one obtains

$$
E_{ep} = \pi e^2 \left((Z_{\max} - Z_{\min}) \left(\frac{1}{3}\gamma_\epsilon^2 e^4 + \frac{1}{4} \left(\gamma_\epsilon^2 \left(\hat{x}_0^2 + \hat{y}_0^2 \right) + 6\gamma_\epsilon \left(\hat{x}_0 \alpha_\epsilon + \hat{y}_0 \beta_\epsilon \right) + \alpha_\epsilon^2 \right. \right.
$$

---

[2] One may wish to study the problem in the presence of noise in the flow measurements and derive instead the expected values of the local and global minima. It has been shown, however, that noise which is of no particular bias does not alter the local minima, and the global minima fall within the valleys of the function without noise. In particular, we considered in [7] noise N of the form $N = \epsilon \frac{1}{Z} + \delta$, with ϵ, δ 2D, independent, stochastic error vectors. As such noise does not alter the function's overall structure, it won't be considered here; the interested reader is referred to [7].

$$+ \beta_\epsilon^2 \Big) e^2 + (\hat{x}_0 \alpha_\epsilon + \hat{y}_0 \beta_\epsilon)^2 \Big) + (\ln(Z_{\max}) - \ln(Z_{\min})) \left(\frac{1}{2} (3\gamma_\epsilon (x_{0_\epsilon} y_0 \right.$$

$$- y_{0_\epsilon} x_0) + x_{0_\epsilon} \beta_\epsilon - y_{0_\epsilon} \alpha_\epsilon) e^2 + 2 (x_{0_\epsilon} y_0 - y_{0_\epsilon} x_0) (\hat{x}_0 \alpha_\epsilon + \hat{y}_0 \beta_\epsilon) \Big)$$

$$+ \left(\frac{1}{Z_{\min}} - \frac{1}{Z_{\max}} \right) \left(\frac{1}{4} (y_{0_\epsilon}^2 + x_{0_\epsilon}^2) e^2 + (x_{0_\epsilon} y_0 - y_{0_\epsilon} x_0)^2 \right) \Big) \tag{10}$$

(a) Assume that the translation has been estimated with a certain error $\mathbf{t}_\epsilon = (x_{0_\epsilon}, y_{0_\epsilon}, 0)$. Then the relationship among the errors in 3D motion at the minima of (10) is obtained from the first-order conditions $\frac{\partial E_{ep}}{\partial \alpha_\epsilon} = \frac{\partial E_{ep}}{\partial \beta_\epsilon} = \frac{\partial E_{ep}}{\partial \gamma_\epsilon} = 0$, which yield

$$\alpha_\epsilon = \frac{y_{0_\epsilon} (\ln(Z_{\max}) - \ln(Z_{\min}))}{Z_{\max} - Z_{\min}}; \quad \beta_\epsilon = \frac{-x_{0_\epsilon} (\ln(Z_{\max}) - \ln(Z_{\min}))}{Z_{\max} - Z_{\min}}; \quad \gamma_\epsilon = 0 \tag{11}$$

It follows that $\alpha_\epsilon / \beta_\epsilon = -x_{0_\epsilon}/y_{0_\epsilon}, \gamma_\epsilon = 0$, which means that there is no error in γ and the projection of the translational error on the image is perpendicular to the projection of the rotational error. This constraint is called the "orthogonality constraint."

(b) Assuming that rotation has been estimated with an error $(\alpha_\epsilon, \beta_\epsilon, \gamma_\epsilon)$, the relationship among the errors is obtained from $\frac{\partial E_{ep}}{\partial x_{0_\epsilon}} = \frac{\partial E_{ep}}{\partial y_{0_\epsilon}} = 0$. In this case, the relationship is very elaborate and the translational error depends on all the other parameters—that is, the rotational error, the actual translation, the image size and the depth interval.

(c) In the general case, we need to study the subspaces in which E_{ep} changes least at its absolute minimum; that is, we are interested in the direction of the smallest second derivative at 0, the point where the motion errors are zero. To find this direction, we compute the Hessian at 0, that is the matrix of the second derivatives of E_{ep} with respect to the five motion error parameters, and compute the eigenvector corresponding to the smallest eigenvalue. The scaled components of this vector amount to

$$x_{0_\epsilon} = x_0 \qquad y_{0_\epsilon} = y_0 \qquad \beta_\epsilon = -\alpha_\epsilon \frac{x_0}{y_0} \qquad \gamma_\epsilon = 0$$

$$\alpha_\epsilon = 2 y_0 Z_{\min} Z_{\max} (\ln(Z_{\max}) - \ln(Z_{\min})) \Big/$$

$$\left((Z_{\max} - Z_{\min}) (Z_{\max} Z_{\min} - 1) + \left((Z_{\max} - Z_{\min})^2 (Z_{\max} Z_{\min} - 1)^2 \right. \right.$$

$$\left. \left. + 4 Z_{\max}^2 Z_{\min}^2 (\ln(Z_{\max}) - \ln(Z_{\min}))^2 \right)^{1/2} \right)$$

As can be seen, for points defined by this direction, the translational and rotational errors are characterized by the orthogonality constraint $\alpha_\epsilon / \beta_\epsilon = -x_{0_\epsilon}/y_{0_\epsilon}$ and by the constraint $x_0/y_0 = \hat{x}_0/\hat{y}_0$; that is, the projection of the actual translation and the projection of the estimated translation lie on a line passing through the image center. We refer to this second constraint as the "line constraint." These results are in accordance with previous studies [2], [21], which found that the translational components along the x and y axes are confused with rotation around the y and x axes, respectively, and the "line constraint" under a set of restrictive assumptions.

Epipolar Minimization on the Sphere. The function representing deviation from the epipolar constraint on the sphere takes the simple form

$$
E_{ep} = \int_{R_{\min}}^{R_{\max}} \int\int_{\text{sphere}} \left\{ \left(\frac{\mathbf{r} \times (\mathbf{r} \times \mathbf{t})}{R} - (\boldsymbol{\omega}_\epsilon \times \mathbf{r}) \right) \cdot (\hat{\mathbf{t}} \times \mathbf{r}) \right\}^2 dA\, dR
$$

where A refers to a surface element. Due to the sphere's symmetry, for each point $\mathbf{r}$ on the sphere, there exists a point with coordinates $-\mathbf{r}$. Since $\mathbf{u}_{tr}(\mathbf{r}) = \mathbf{u}_{tr}(-\mathbf{r})$ and $\mathbf{u}_{rot}(\mathbf{r}) = -\mathbf{u}_{rot}(-\mathbf{r})$, when the integrand is expanded the product terms integrated over the sphere vanish. Thus

$$
E_{ep} = \int_{R_{\min}}^{R_{\max}} \int\int_{\text{sphere}} \left\{ \frac{\left((\mathbf{t} \times \hat{\mathbf{t}}) \cdot \mathbf{r} \right)^2}{R^2} + \left((\boldsymbol{\omega}_\epsilon \times \mathbf{r}) \cdot (\hat{\mathbf{t}} \times \mathbf{r}) \right)^2 \right\} dA\, dR
$$

(a) Assuming that translation $\hat{\mathbf{t}}$ has been estimated, the $\boldsymbol{\omega}_\epsilon$ that minimizes E_{ep} is $\boldsymbol{\omega}_\epsilon = 0$, since the resulting function is non-negative quadratic in $\boldsymbol{\omega}_\epsilon$ (minimum at zero). The difference between sphere and plane is already clear. In the spherical case, as shown here, if an error in the translation is made we do not need to compensate for it by making an error in the rotation ($\boldsymbol{\omega}_\epsilon = 0$), while in the planar case we need to compensate to ensure that the orthogonality constraint is satisfied!

(b) Assuming that rotation has been estimated with an error $\boldsymbol{\omega}_\epsilon$, what is the translation $\hat{\mathbf{t}}$ that minimizes E_{ep}? Since R is uniformly distributed, integrating over R does not alter the form of the error in the optimization. Thus, E_{ep} consists of the sum of two terms:

$$
K = K_1 \int\int_{\text{sphere}} \left((\mathbf{t} \times \hat{\mathbf{t}}) \cdot \mathbf{r} \right)^2 dA \quad \text{and} \quad L = L_1 \int\int_{\text{sphere}} \left((\boldsymbol{\omega}_\epsilon \times \mathbf{r}) \cdot (\hat{\mathbf{t}} \times \mathbf{r}) \right)^2 dA,
$$

where K_1, L_1 are multiplicative factors depending only on $R_{\min}$ and $R_{\max}$. For angles between $\mathbf{t}, \hat{\mathbf{t}}$ and $\hat{\mathbf{t}}, \boldsymbol{\omega}_\epsilon$ in the range of 0 to $\pi/2$, K and L are monotonic functions. K attains its minimum when $\mathbf{t} = \hat{\mathbf{t}}$ and L when $\hat{\mathbf{t}} \perp \boldsymbol{\omega}_\epsilon$. Consider a certain distance between $\mathbf{t}$ and $\hat{\mathbf{t}}$ leading to a certain value K, and change the position of $\hat{\mathbf{t}}$. L takes its minimum when $(\mathbf{t} \times \hat{\mathbf{t}}) \cdot \boldsymbol{\omega}_\epsilon = 0$, as follows from the cosine theorem. Thus E_{ep} achieves its minimum when $\hat{\mathbf{t}}$ lies on the great circle passing through $\mathbf{t}$ and $\boldsymbol{\omega}_\epsilon$, with the exact position depending on $|\boldsymbol{\omega}_\epsilon|$ and the scene in view.

(c) For the general case where no information about rotation or translation is available, we study the subspaces where E_{ep} changes the least at its absolute minimum, i.e., we are again interested in the direction of the smallest second derivative at 0. For points defined by this direction we calculate $\mathbf{t} = \hat{\mathbf{t}}$ and $\boldsymbol{\omega}_\epsilon \perp \mathbf{t}$.

To study the negative depth values described by function (9) a more geometric interpretation is needed. Substituting into (6) the value of $\dot{\mathbf{r}}$ from (1) or (2) gives

$$\hat{Z}(\text{or } \hat{R}) = \frac{\mathbf{u}_{\text{tr}}(\hat{\mathbf{t}}) \cdot \mathbf{n}}{\left(\frac{\mathbf{u}_{\text{tr}}(\mathbf{t})}{Z(\text{or } R)} - \mathbf{u}_{\text{rot}}(\boldsymbol{\omega}_\epsilon)\right) \cdot \mathbf{n}}$$

This equation shows that for every $\mathbf{n}$ and $\mathbf{r}$ a range of values for Z (or R) is obtained which result in negative estimates of $\hat{Z}$ (or $\hat{R}$). Thus for each direction $\mathbf{n}$, considering all image points $\mathbf{r}$, we obtain a volume in space corresponding to negative depth estimates. The sum of all these volumes for all directions is termed the "negative depth" volume, and calculating 3D motion in this case amounts to minimizing this volume. Minimization of this volume provides conditions for the errors in the motion parameters.

Minimizing Negative Depth Volume on the Plane. This analysis is given in [6]. The findings are summarized here:

(a) Assume that rotation has been estimated with an error $(\alpha_\epsilon, \beta_\epsilon, \gamma_\epsilon)$. Then the error $(x_{0_\epsilon}, y_{0_\epsilon})$ that minimizes the negative depth volume satisfies the orthogonality constraint $x_{0_\epsilon}/y_{0_\epsilon} = -\beta_\epsilon/\alpha_\epsilon$.
(b) In the absence of any prior information about the 3D motion, the solution obtained by minimizing the negative depth volume has errors that satisfy the orthogonality constraint $x_{0_\epsilon}/y_{0_\epsilon} = -\beta_\epsilon/\alpha_\epsilon$, the line constraint $x_0/y_0 = \hat{x}_0/\hat{y}_0$ and $\gamma_\epsilon = 0$

Minimizing Negative Depth Volume on the Sphere

(a) Assuming that the rotation has been estimated with an error $\boldsymbol{\omega}_\epsilon$, what is the optimal translation $\hat{\mathbf{t}}$ that minimizes the negative depth volume?
Since the motion field along different orientations $\mathbf{n}$ is considered, a parameterization is needed to express all possible orientations on the sphere. This is achieved by selecting an arbitrary vector $\mathbf{s}$; then, at each point $\mathbf{r}$ of the sphere, $\frac{\mathbf{s} \times \mathbf{r}}{\|\mathbf{s} \times \mathbf{r}\|}$ defines a direction in the tangent plane. As $\mathbf{s}$ moves along half a circle, $\frac{\mathbf{s} \times \mathbf{r}}{\|\mathbf{s} \times \mathbf{r}\|}$ takes on every possible orientation (with the exception of the points $\mathbf{r}$ lying on the great circle of $\mathbf{s}$). Let us pick $\boldsymbol{\omega}_\epsilon$ perpendicular to $\mathbf{s}$ ($\mathbf{s} \cdot \boldsymbol{\omega}_\epsilon = 0$).
We are interested in the points in space with estimated negative range values $\hat{R}$. Since $\mathbf{n} = \frac{\mathbf{s} \times \mathbf{r}}{\|\mathbf{s} \times \mathbf{r}\|}$, $\mathbf{s} \cdot \boldsymbol{\omega}_\epsilon = 0$, the estimated range $\hat{R}$ amounts to $\hat{R} = R\frac{(\hat{\mathbf{t}} \times \mathbf{s}) \cdot \mathbf{r}}{(\mathbf{t} \times \mathbf{s}) \cdot \mathbf{r} - R(\boldsymbol{\omega}_\epsilon \cdot \mathbf{r})(\mathbf{s} \cdot \mathbf{r})}$. $\hat{R} < 0$ if $\text{sgn}[(\hat{\mathbf{t}} \times \mathbf{s}) \cdot \mathbf{r}] = -\text{sgn}[(\mathbf{t} \times \mathbf{s}) \cdot \mathbf{r} - R(\boldsymbol{\omega}_\epsilon \cdot \mathbf{r})(\mathbf{s} \cdot \mathbf{r})]$, where $\text{sgn}(x)$ provides the sign of x. This constraint divides the surface of the

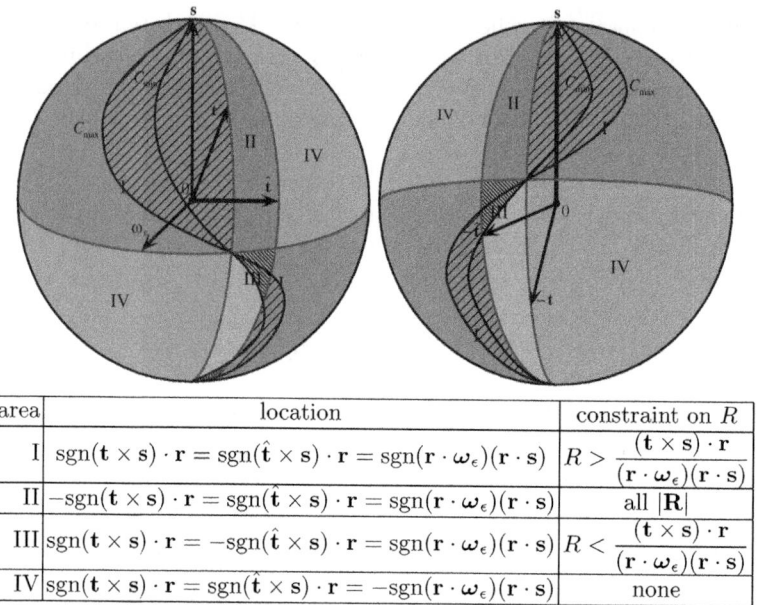

area	location	constraint on R
I	$\mathrm{sgn}(\mathbf{t} \times \mathbf{s}) \cdot \mathbf{r} = \mathrm{sgn}(\hat{\mathbf{t}} \times \mathbf{s}) \cdot \mathbf{r} = \mathrm{sgn}(\mathbf{r} \cdot \boldsymbol{\omega}_\epsilon)(\mathbf{r} \cdot \mathbf{s})$	$R > \dfrac{(\mathbf{t} \times \mathbf{s}) \cdot \mathbf{r}}{(\mathbf{r} \cdot \boldsymbol{\omega}_\epsilon)(\mathbf{r} \cdot \mathbf{s})}$
II	$-\mathrm{sgn}(\mathbf{t} \times \mathbf{s}) \cdot \mathbf{r} = \mathrm{sgn}(\hat{\mathbf{t}} \times \mathbf{s}) \cdot \mathbf{r} = \mathrm{sgn}(\mathbf{r} \cdot \boldsymbol{\omega}_\epsilon)(\mathbf{r} \cdot \mathbf{s})$	all $|\mathbf{R}|$
III	$\mathrm{sgn}(\mathbf{t} \times \mathbf{s}) \cdot \mathbf{r} = -\mathrm{sgn}(\hat{\mathbf{t}} \times \mathbf{s}) \cdot \mathbf{r} = \mathrm{sgn}(\mathbf{r} \cdot \boldsymbol{\omega}_\epsilon)(\mathbf{r} \cdot \mathbf{s})$	$R < \dfrac{(\mathbf{t} \times \mathbf{s}) \cdot \mathbf{r}}{(\mathbf{r} \cdot \boldsymbol{\omega}_\epsilon)(\mathbf{r} \cdot \mathbf{s})}$
IV	$\mathrm{sgn}(\mathbf{t} \times \mathbf{s}) \cdot \mathbf{r} = \mathrm{sgn}(\hat{\mathbf{t}} \times \mathbf{s}) \cdot \mathbf{r} = -\mathrm{sgn}(\mathbf{r} \cdot \boldsymbol{\omega}_\epsilon)(\mathbf{r} \cdot \mathbf{s})$	none

Fig. 3. Classification of image points according to constraints on R. The four areas are marked by different colors. The textured parts (parallel lines) in areas I and III denote the image points for which negative depth values exist if the scene is bounded. The two hemispheres correspond to the front of the sphere and the back of the sphere, both as seen from the front of the sphere

sphere into four areas, I to IV, whose locations are defined by the signs of the functions $(\hat{\mathbf{t}} \times \mathbf{s}) \cdot \mathbf{r}$, $(\mathbf{t} \times \mathbf{s}) \cdot \mathbf{r}$ and $(\boldsymbol{\omega}_\epsilon \cdot \mathbf{r})(\mathbf{s} \cdot \mathbf{r})$, as shown in Fig. 3.

For any direction $\mathbf{n}$ a volume of negative range values is obtained consisting of the volumes above areas I, II and III. Areas II and III cover the same amount of area between the great circles $(\mathbf{t} \times \mathbf{s}) \cdot \mathbf{r} = 0$ and $(\hat{\mathbf{t}} \times \mathbf{s}) \cdot \mathbf{r} = 0$, and area I covers a hemisphere minus the area between $(\mathbf{t} \times \mathbf{s}) \cdot \mathbf{r} = 0$ and $(\hat{\mathbf{t}} \times \mathbf{s}) \cdot \mathbf{r} = 0$. If the scene in view is unbounded, that is, $R \in [0, +\infty]$, there is for every $\mathbf{r}$ a range of values above areas I and III which result in negative depth estimates; in area I the volume at each point $\mathbf{r}$ is bounded from below by $R = \frac{(\mathbf{t} \times \mathbf{s}) \cdot \mathbf{r}}{(\boldsymbol{\omega}_\epsilon \cdot \mathbf{r})(\mathbf{s} \cdot \mathbf{r})}$, and in area III it is bounded from above by $R = \frac{(\mathbf{t} \times \mathbf{s}) \cdot \mathbf{r}}{(\boldsymbol{\omega}_\epsilon \cdot \mathbf{r})(\mathbf{s} \cdot \mathbf{r})}$. If there exist lower and upper bounds $R_{\min}$ and $R_{\max}$ in the scene, we obtain two additional curves $C_{\min}$ and $C_{\max}$ with $C_{\min} = (\mathbf{t} \times \mathbf{s}) \cdot \mathbf{r} - R_{\min}(\boldsymbol{\omega}_\epsilon \cdot \mathbf{r})(\mathbf{s} \cdot \mathbf{r}) = 0$ and $C_{\max} = (\mathbf{t} \times \mathbf{s}) \cdot \mathbf{r} - R_{\max}(\boldsymbol{\omega}_\epsilon \cdot \mathbf{r})(\mathbf{s} \cdot \mathbf{r}) = 0$, and we obtain negative depth values in area I only between $C_{\max}$ and $(\mathbf{t} \times \mathbf{s}) \cdot \mathbf{r} = 0$ and in area III only between $C_{\min}$ and $(\boldsymbol{\omega}_\epsilon \times \mathbf{r})(\mathbf{s} \times \mathbf{r}) = 0$. We are given $\boldsymbol{\omega}_\epsilon$ and $\mathbf{t}$, and we are interested in the $\hat{\mathbf{t}}$ which minimizes the negative range volume. For any $\mathbf{s}$ the corresponding negative range volume becomes smallest if $\hat{\mathbf{t}}$ is on the great circle through $\mathbf{t}$ and $\mathbf{s}$, that is, $(\mathbf{t} \times \mathbf{s}) \cdot \hat{\mathbf{t}} = 0$, as will be shown next.

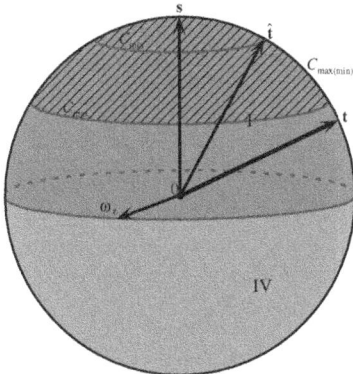

Fig. 4. Configuration for $\mathbf{t}$ and $\hat{\mathbf{t}}$ on the great circle of $\mathbf{s}$ and $\boldsymbol{\omega}_\epsilon$ perpendicular to $\mathbf{s}$. The textured part of area I denotes image points for which negative depth values exist if the scene is bounded

Let us consider a $\hat{\mathbf{t}}$ such that $(\mathbf{t} \times \mathbf{s}) \cdot \hat{\mathbf{t}} \neq 0$ and let us change $\hat{\mathbf{t}}$ so that $(\mathbf{t} \times \mathbf{s}) \cdot \hat{\mathbf{t}} = 0$. As $\hat{\mathbf{t}}$ changes, the area of type II becomes an area of type IV and the area of type III becomes an area of type I. The negative depth volume is changed as follows: It is decreased by the spaces above area II and area III, and it is increased by the space above area I (which changed from type III to type I). Clearly, the decrease is larger than the increase, which implies that the smallest volume is obtained for $\mathbf{s}, \mathbf{t}, \hat{\mathbf{t}}$ lying on a great circle. Since this is true for any $\mathbf{s}$, the minimum negative depth volume is attained for $\mathbf{t} = \hat{\mathbf{t}}$.[3]

(b) Next, assume that no prior knowledge about the 3D motion is available. We want to know for which configurations of $\hat{\mathbf{t}}$ and $\boldsymbol{\omega}_\epsilon$ the negative depth values change the least in the neighborhood of the absolute minimum, that is, at $\mathbf{t}_\epsilon = \boldsymbol{\omega}_\epsilon = 0$. From the analysis above, it is known that for any $\boldsymbol{\omega}_\epsilon \neq 0$, $\mathbf{t} = \hat{\mathbf{t}}$. Next, we show that $\boldsymbol{\omega}_\epsilon$ is indeed different from zero: Take $\mathbf{t} \neq \hat{\mathbf{t}}$ on the great circle of $\mathbf{s}$ and let $\boldsymbol{\omega}_\epsilon$, as before, be perpendicular to $\mathbf{s}$.

Since $(\mathbf{t} \times \mathbf{s}) \times \boldsymbol{\omega}_\epsilon = 0$, the curves $C_{\max}$ and $C_{\min}$ can be expressed as $C_{\max(\min)} = (\boldsymbol{\omega}_\epsilon \cdot \mathbf{r})(\frac{\sin \angle(\mathbf{t},\mathbf{s})}{|\boldsymbol{\omega}_\epsilon| R_{\max(\min)}} - (\mathbf{s} \cdot \mathbf{r})) = 0$, where $\sin \angle(\mathbf{t}, \mathbf{s})$ denotes the angle between vectors $\mathbf{t}$ and $\mathbf{s}$. These curves consist of the great circle $\boldsymbol{\omega}_\epsilon \cdot \mathbf{r} = 0$ and the circle $\frac{\sin \angle(\mathbf{t},\mathbf{s})}{|\boldsymbol{\omega}_\epsilon| R_{\max(\min)}} - (\mathbf{s} \cdot \mathbf{r}) = 0$ parallel to the great circle $(\mathbf{s} \cdot \mathbf{r}) = 0$ (see Fig. 4). If $\frac{\sin \angle(\mathbf{t},\mathbf{s})}{|\boldsymbol{\omega}_\epsilon| R_{\max(\min)}} > 1$, this circle disappears.

Consider next two flow directions defined by vectors $\mathbf{s}_1$ and $\mathbf{s}_2$ with $(\mathbf{s}_1 \times \mathbf{t}) = -(\mathbf{s}_2 \times \mathbf{t})$ and $\mathbf{s}_1$ between $\mathbf{t}$ and $\hat{\mathbf{t}}$.

---

[3] A word of caution about the parameterization used for directions $\mathbf{n} = \frac{\mathbf{s} \cdot \mathbf{r}}{\|\mathbf{s} \times \mathbf{r}\|}$ is needed. It does not treat all orientations equally (as $\mathbf{s}$ varies along a great circle with constant speed, $\mathbf{s} \times \mathbf{r}$ accelerates and decelerates). Thus to obtain a uniform distribution, normalization is necessary. The normalization factors, however, do not affect the previous proof, due to symmetry.

For every point $\mathbf{r}_1$ in area III defined by $\mathbf{s}_1$ there exists a point $\mathbf{r}_2$ in area I defined by $\mathbf{s}_2$ such that the negative estimated ranges above $\mathbf{r}_1$ and $\mathbf{r}_2$ add up to $R_{\max} - R_{\min}$. Thus the volume of negative range obtained from $\mathbf{s}_1$ and $\mathbf{s}_2$ amounts to the area of the sphere times $(R_{\max} - R_{\min})$ (area II of $\mathbf{s}_1$ contributes a hemisphere; area III of $\mathbf{s}_1$ and area I of $\mathbf{s}_2$ together contribute a hemisphere). The total negative range volume can be decomposed into three components: a component V_1 originating from the set of $\mathbf{s}$ between $\mathbf{t}$ and $\hat{\mathbf{t}}$, a component V_2 originating from the set of $\mathbf{s}$ symmetric in $\mathbf{t}$ to the set in V_1, and a component V_3 corresponding to the remaining $\mathbf{s}$, which consists of range values above areas of type I only. If for all $\mathbf{s}$ in V_3, $\frac{\sin \angle(\mathbf{t},\mathbf{s})}{R_{\max}|\boldsymbol{\omega}_\epsilon|} \geq 1$, V_3 becomes zero. Thus for all $|\boldsymbol{\omega}_\epsilon|$ with $|\boldsymbol{\omega}_\epsilon| \leq \frac{\sin \angle(\mathbf{t},\hat{\mathbf{t}})}{R_{\max}}$, the negative range volume is equally large and amounts to the area on the sphere times $(R_{\max} - R_{\min})$ times $\angle(\mathbf{t},\hat{\mathbf{t}})$. Unless $R_{\max} = \infty$, $|\boldsymbol{\omega}_\epsilon|$ takes on values different from zero.

This shows that for any $\mathbf{t}_\epsilon \neq 0$, there exist vectors $\boldsymbol{\omega}_\epsilon \neq 0$ which give rise to the same negative depth volume as $\boldsymbol{\omega}_\epsilon = 0$. However, for any such $\boldsymbol{\omega}_\epsilon \neq 0$ this volume is larger than the volume obtained by setting $\mathbf{t}_\epsilon = 0$. It follows that $\mathbf{t} = \hat{\mathbf{t}}$. From Fig. 3, it can furthermore be deduced that for a given $\boldsymbol{\omega}_\epsilon$ the negative depth volume, which for $\mathbf{t} = \hat{\mathbf{t}}$ only lies above areas of type I, decreases as $\mathbf{t}$ moves along a great circle away from $\boldsymbol{\omega}_\epsilon$, as the areas between $C_{\min}$ and $C_{\max}$ and between $C_{\min}$ and $(\mathbf{t} \times \mathbf{s}) \cdot \mathbf{r} = 0$ decrease. This proves that in addition to $\mathbf{t} = \hat{\mathbf{t}}$, $\mathbf{t} \perp \boldsymbol{\omega}_\epsilon$.

The preceding results demonstrate the advantages of spherical eyes for the process of 3D motion estimation. Table 1 lists the eight out of ten cases which lead to clearly defined error configurations. It shows that 3D motion can be estimated more accurately with spherical eyes. Depending on the estimation procedure used—and systems might use different procedures for different tasks—either the translation or the rotation can be estimated very accurately. For planar eyes, this is not the case, as for all possible procedures there exists confusion between the translation and rotation. The error configurations also allow systems with inertial sensors to use more efficient estimation procedures. If a system utilizes a gyrosensor which provides an approximate estimate of its rotation, it can employ a simple algorithm based on the negative depth constraint for only translational motion fields to derive its translation and obtain a very accurate estimate. Such algorithms are much easier to implement than algorithms designed for completely unknown rigid motions, as they amount to searches in 2D as opposed to 5D spaces [4]. Similarly, there exist computational advantages for systems with translational inertial sensors in estimating the remaining unknown rotation.

In nature, systems that walk and perform sophisticated manipulation have camera-type eyes, and systems that fly usually have panoramic vision, either through compound eyes or a combination of camera-type eyes. The obvious explanation for this difference is the need for a larger field of view in flying species, and the need for very accurate segmentation and shape estimation, and thus high resolution in a limited field of view, for land-walking species. As shown in this paper, the geometry of the sphere also provides a computational advantage; it allows for more efficient and accurate egomotion estimation (even at the expense

Table 1. Summary of results

	I Spherical Eye	II Camera-type Eye
Epipolar mini- mization, given optic flow	(a) Given a translational er- ror $\mathbf{t}_\epsilon$, the rotational error $\boldsymbol{\omega}_\epsilon = 0$ (b) Without any prior informa- tion, $\mathbf{t}_\epsilon = 0$ and $\boldsymbol{\omega}_\epsilon \perp \mathbf{t}$	(a) For a fixed translational er- ror $(x_{0_\epsilon}, y_{0_\epsilon})$, the rotational error $(\alpha_\epsilon, \beta_\epsilon, \gamma_\epsilon)$ is of the form $\gamma_\epsilon = 0$, $\alpha_\epsilon/\beta_\epsilon = -x_{0_\epsilon}/y_{0_\epsilon}$ (b) Without any a priori infor- mation about the motion, the errors satisfy $\gamma_\epsilon = 0$, $\alpha_\epsilon/\beta_\epsilon = -x_{0_\epsilon}/y_{0_\epsilon}$, $x_0/y_0 = x_{0_\epsilon}/y_{0_\epsilon}$
Minimization of negative depth volume, given normal flow	(a) Given a rotational error $\boldsymbol{\omega}_\epsilon$, the translational error $\mathbf{t}_\epsilon = 0$ (b) Without any prior informa- tion, $\mathbf{t}_\epsilon = 0$ and $\boldsymbol{\omega}_\epsilon \perp \mathbf{t}$	(a) Given a rotational error, the translational error is of the form $-x_{0_\epsilon}/y_{0_\epsilon} = \alpha_\epsilon/\beta_\epsilon$ (b) Without any error infor- mation, the errors satisfy $\gamma_\epsilon = 0$, $\alpha_\epsilon/\beta_\epsilon = -x_{0_\epsilon}/y_{0_\epsilon}$, $x_0/y_0 = x_{0_\epsilon}/y_{0_\epsilon}$

of trading off resolution in some systems, for example, in insects), and this is much more necessary for systems flying and thus moving with all six degrees of freedom than for systems moving with usually limited rigid motion on surfaces.

The above results also point to ways of constructing new, powerful eyes by taking advantage of both the panoramic vision of flying systems and the high-resolution vision of primates. An eye like the one in Fig. 5, assembled from a few video cameras arranged on the surface of a sphere,[4] can easily estimate 3D motion since, while it is moving, it is sampling a spherical motion field! Even more important for today's applications is the reconstruction of the shape of an object or scene in a very accurate manner. Accurate shape models are needed in many applications dealing with visualization, as in video editing/manipulation or in virtual reality settings [16], [17]. To obtain accurate shape reconstruction, both the 3D transformation relating two views and the 2D transformation relating two images are needed with good precision. Given accurate 3D motion $(\mathbf{t}, \boldsymbol{\omega})$ and image motion $(\dot{\mathbf{r}})$, (1–3) can be used in a straightforward manner to estimate depth (Z) or range (R) and thus object shape. An eye like the one in Fig. 5 not only has panoramic properties, eliminating the rotation/translation

---

[4] Like a compound eye with video cameras replacing ommatidia.

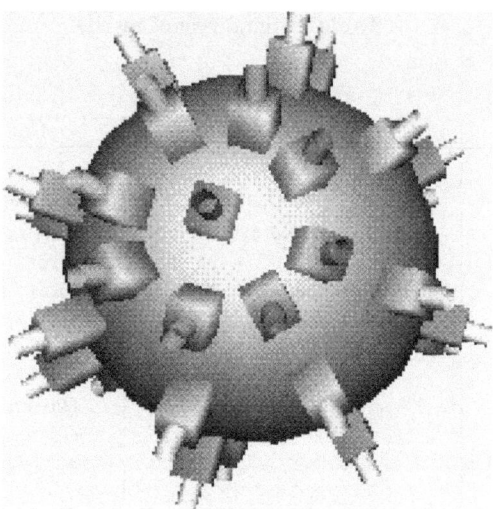

Fig. 5. A compound-like eye composed of conventional video cameras, arranged on a sphere and looking outward

confusion, but it has the unexpected benefit of making it easy to estimate image motion with high accuracy. Any two cameras with overlapping fields of view also provide high-resolution stereo vision, and this collection of stereo systems makes it possible to locate a large number of depth discontinuities. Given scene discontinuities, image motion can be estimated very accurately [8]. As a consequence, the eye in Fig. 5 is very well suited to developing accurate models of the world, and many experiments have confirmed this finding. However, such an eye, although appropriate for a moving robotic system, may be impractical to use in a laboratory. Fortuitously from a mathematical viewpoint, it makes no difference whether the cameras are looking inward or outward!

Consider, then, a "negative" spherical eye like the one in Fig. 6, where video cameras are arranged on the surface of a sphere pointing toward its center. Imaging a moving rigid object at the center of the sphere creates image motion fields at the center of each camera which are the same as the ones that would be created if the whole spherical dome were moving with the opposite rigid motion! Thus, utilizing information from all the cameras, the 3D motion of the object inside the sphere can be accurately estimated, and at the same time accurate shape models can be obtained from the motion field of each camera. The negative spherical eye also allows for accurate recovery of models of action, such as human movement, because putting together motion and shape, sequences of 3D motion fields representing the motion inside the dome can be estimated. Such action models will find many applications in telereality, graphics and recognition. The above described configurations are examples of alternative sensors, and they also demonstrate that multiple-view vision has great potential. Different arrangements best suited for other problems can be imagined. This was

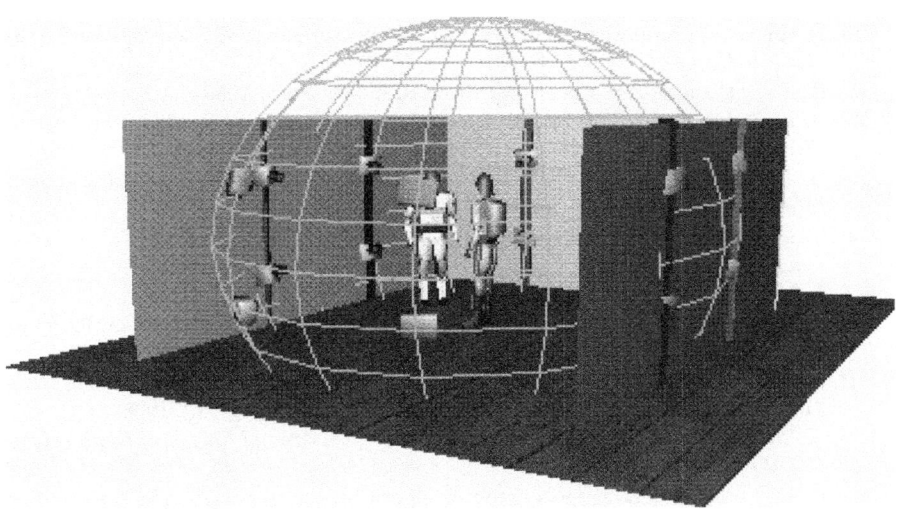

Fig. 6. A "negative" spherical eye, consisting of conventional video cameras arranged on a sphere and pointing inward

perhaps foreseen in ancient Greek mythology, which has Argus, the hundred-eyed guardian of Hera, the goddess of Olympus, defeating a whole army of Cyclopes, one-eyed giants!

References

[1] Y. Aloimonos and A. Rosenfeld. Computer vision. *Science*, 253:1249–1254, 1991.
[2] K. Daniilidis and M. E. Spetsakis. Understanding noise sensitivity in structure from motion. In Y. Aloimonos, editor, *Visual Navigation: From Biological Systems to Unmanned Ground Vehicles*, Advances in Computer Vision, chapter 4. Lawrence Erlbaum Associates, Mahwah, NJ, 1997.
[3] R. Dawkins. *Climbing Mount Improbable*. Norton, New York, 1996.
[4] C. Fermüller and Y. Aloimonos. Direct perception of three-dimensional motion from patterns of visual motion. *Science*, 270:1973–1976, 1995.
[5] C. Fermüller and Y. Aloimonos. Qualitative egomotion. *International Journal of Computer Vision*, 15:7–29, 1995.
[6] C. Fermüller and Y. Aloimonos. Ambiguity in structure from motion: Sphere versus plane. *International Journal of Computer Vision*, 28:137–154, 1998.
[7] C. Fermüller and Y. Aloimonos. What is computed by structure from motion algorithms? In *Proc. European Conference on Computer Vision*, pages 359–375, Freiburg, Germany, 1998.
[8] C. Fermüller, F. Defoort, and Y. Aloimonos. Motion segmentation for a binocular observer. Technical Report CAR-TR-884, Center for Automation Research, University of Maryland, April 1998.
[9] T. Hamada. Vision, action, and navigation in animals. In Y. Aloimonos, editor, *Visual Navigation: From Biological Systems to Unmanned Ground Vehicles*, chapter 2. Lawrence Erlbaum Associates, Mahwah, NJ, 1997.

[10] E. Hildreth. Computations underlying the measurement of visual motion. *Artificial Intelligence*, 23:309–354, 1984.

[11] B. K. P. Horn. *Robot Vision*. McGraw Hill, New York, 1986.

[12] B. K. P. Horn and B. Schunck. Determining optical flow. *Artificial Intelligence*, 17:185–203, 1981.

[13] B. K. P. Horn and E. J. Weldon, Jr. Direct methods for recovering motion. *International Journal of Computer Vision*, 2:51–76, 1988.

[14] G. A. Horridge. What can engineers learn from insect vision? *Proc. Royal Society, London B*, August 1992.

[15] J. J. Koenderink. Optic flow. *Vision Research*, 26:161–180, 1986.

[16] K. N. Kutulakos and S. M. Seitz. What do *N* photographs tell us about 3D shape? Computer Science Technical Report 692, University of Rochester, 1998.

[17] K. N. Kutulakos and J. R. Vallino. Calibration-free augmented reality. *IEEE Transactions on Visualization and Computer Graphics*, 4:1–20, 1998.

[18] M. Land and R. D. Fernald. The evolution of eyes. *Annual Review of Neuroscience*, 15:1–29, 1992.

[19] H. C. Longuet-Higgins. A computer algorithm for reconstructing a scene from two projections. *Nature*, 293:133–135, 1981.

[20] H. C. Longuet-Higgins and K. Prazdny. The interpretation of a moving retinal image. *Proc. Royal Society, London B*, 208:385–397, 1980.

[21] S. J. Maybank. *Theory of Reconstruction from Image Motion*. Springer, Berlin, 1993.

[22] T. Poggio and W. Reichardt. Considerations on models of movement detection. *Kybernetik*, 13:223–227, 1973.

[23] W. Reichardt. Autocorrelation, a principle for evaluation of sensory information by the central nervous system. In W. A. Rosenblith, editor, *Sensory Communication: Contributions to the Symposium on Principles of Sensory Communication*, pages 303–317. John Wiley and Sons, New York, 1961.

[24] W. Reichardt. Evaluation of optical motion information by movement detectors. *Journal of Comparative Physiology*, 161:533–547, 1987.

[25] M. E. Spetsakis and J. Aloimonos. Optimal motion estimation. In *Proc. IEEE Workshop on Visual Motion*, pages 229–237, 1989.

[26] M. V. Srinivasan, S. W. Zhang, and K. C. Shekara. Evidence for two distinct movement detecting mechanisms in insect vision. *Naturwissenschaften*, 80:38–41, 1993.

[27] J. P. H. van Santen and G. Sperling. Temporal covariance model of human motion perception. *Journal of the Optical Society of America A*, 1:451–473, 1984.

[28] S. M. Zeki. *A Vision of the Brain*. Blackwell Scientific Publications, 1993.

Epipolar Geometry in Polycentric Panoramas

Fay Huang, Shou Kang Wei, and Reinhard Klette

CITR, Computer Science Department, The University of Auckland,
Tamaki Campus, Auckland, New Zealand
{fay,shoukang,reinhard}@citr.auckland.ac.nz

Abstract. This paper proposes a new and general model of panoramic images, namely *polycentric panoramas*, which formalizes the essential characteristics of panoramic image acquisition geometry. This new model is able to describe a wide range of panoramic images including those which have been previously introduced such as single-center, multi-perspective, or concentric panoramas [1, 5,11,14] and that are potentially of interest in further research. This paper presents a study of epipolar geometry for pairs of polycentric panoramas. The first and unique epipolar curve equation derived provides a unified approach for computing epipolar curves in more specific types of panoramic images. Examples of epipolar curves in different types of panoramic images are also discussed in the paper.

1 Introduction

A panoramic image can be acquired by rotating a (slit) camera with respect to a fixed rotation axis and taking images consecutively at equidistant angles. This paper only discusses panoramic images in cylindrical representation. The panoramic image acquisition model has been formally discussed in [16]. There are three essential parameters in this image acquisition model: f, r, and ω, where f is the camera effective focal length, r is the distance between the camera's focal point and the rotation axis, and ω specifies the orientation of the camera (see more details in the next section). *Polycentric panoramas* are a collection of panoramic images acquired with respect to different rotation axes, where the associated parameters for each image may differ. Note that r can be either greater than or equal to zero.

Multi-perspective panoramic images have recently received increasing attentions for applications of 3D scene visualizations and reconstructions, for instance, [5,11,12,13, 14,15]. Polycentric panoramas are able to describe a wide range of multi-perspective panoramic images such as concentric and single-center panoramas. A collection of (multi-perspective) panoramic images all acquired with respect to the same rotation axis is referred to as a set of *concentric panoramic images*. H-Y. Shum and R. Szeliski [15] have shown that epipolar geometry consists of horizontal lines if two concentric panoramic images are *symmetric* with respect to the camera viewing direction, which is when the associated angular parameters of these two panoramic images are ω and $-\omega$ respectively. A panoramic image acquired with a single focal point, i.e. $r = 0$, is referred to as a *single-center panoramic image* [1,9,10]. A study about epipolar curves in a pair

R. Klette et al. (Eds.): Multi-Image Analysis, LNCS 2032, pp. 39–50, 2001.
© Springer-Verlag Berlin Heidelberg 2001

of single-center panoramic images can be found in [9]. Some examples of stereo reconstructions and 3D scene visualizations based on a given set of single-center panoramic
images applications can be found in [1,7].

Geometric studies such as epipolar geometry or 3D reconstruction, are well established for pairs of planar images [2,4,6,8,17]. Compared to that, the computer vision
literature still lacks work on pairs of panoramic images. Due to differences in image geometry between planar and a panoramic image models, geometric properties for planar
images may not necessarily be true for panoramic images. In this paper, we focus on the
derivation of an epipolar curve equation for a pair of polycentric panoramic images. The
epipolar curve equation derived provides a unified approach for the epipolar geometry
study in any of the more specific classes of panoramic images above-mentioned.

The paper is organized as follows. The acquisition model of polycentric panoramic
images is given in Section 2. The derivation of the epipolar curve equation through
various geometric transformations is elaborated in Section 3. In Section 4, the epipolar
curves in some special cases of panoramic images are presented mathematically and
graphically. Concluding remarks and comments on future work are in Section 5.

2   Image Acquisition Model

Polycentric panoramic images can be acquired by different imaging methods. One of
the possible ways is using a slit camera. A slit camera is characterized geometrically
by a single focal point and a 1D linear image slit[1]. Ideally, the focal point lies on the
bisector of an image slit. The focal point of a slit camera is denoted as C, the effective
focal length is denoted as f, and the slit image captured is denoted as $\mathcal{I}$.

To acquire a panoramic image, a slit camera rotates with respect to a fixed 3D axis
(e.g. the rotation axis of a turntable) and captures one slit image for every subsequent
angular interval of constant size. We assume that the distance between the slit camera's
focal point and the rotation axis, r, remains constant during such a panoramic image
acquisition process. We further assume that these focal points are in a single plane
(exactly) orthogonal to the rotation axis, i.e. they lie on the circle $\mathfrak{C}$ of radius r. We call
this circle the *base circle*. It follows that the optical axis of a slit camera is always in the
plane of this base circle. We call this plane the *base plane* and denote it as $\mathfrak{D}$.

Each slit image contributes to one column of a panoramic image. A panoramic
image, denoted as $\mathcal{P}$, can be considered as being a planar $h \times \ell$ rectangular array, where
h specifies the resolution of the slit camera and ℓ specifies the number of slit images
acquired for one panoramic image.

Besides of parameters f and r, our acquisition model allows a slit camera to have one
more degree of freedom: a horizontal rotation parallel to the plane of the base circle. It
is specified by an angle, ω, between the normal vector of the base circle at the associated
focal point and the optical axis of the slit camera. Altogether, these three parameters,
f, r, and ω, are the essential parameters characterizing a single *panoramic image*. They
remain constant throughout one acquisition process for such a panoramic image.

---

[1] An image slit is defined by a line segment and the receptors (i.e. photon-sensing elements)
positioned on this line segment.

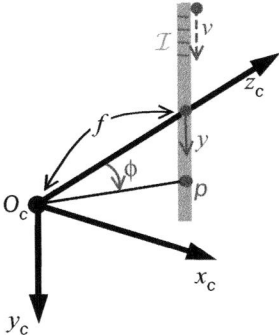

Fig. 1. Slit-image and slit-camera coordinate systems. An image point p on the image slit can be represented either by an angular coordinate ϕ or the coordinates $(0, y, f)$, where f is the effective focal length of the slit camera. See text for further details.

3   Derivation of an Epipolar Curve Equation

In this section, we elaborate the derivation of a general epipolar curve equation for a pair of polycentric panoramas. Various coordinate systems are defined beforehand to help clarifying the geometrical transformation calculation in the derivation process.

3.1   Coordinate Systems

We define a 1D discrete image coordinate system for each slit image with the coordinate denoted by v. The unit of this coordinate system is defined in terms of an image pixel. We define another 1D real-number image-slit coordinate system with the coordinate denoted by y. The origins of the image and the image-slit coordinate systems are at the top and the center of the image slit respectively. Let v_c be the principle point[2] in discrete image space. The conversion between these two coordinates v and y is $y = d(v - v_c)$, where d is the size of an image pixel in units of y. The image coordinate systems are shown in Fig. 1.

We define a 2D discrete image coordinate system for each polycentric panoramic image. The coordinates are denoted as (u, v), which is an image pixel at column u and row v. Each column itself is a slit image, thus the coordinate v here is identical to the coordinate v in the slit image coordinate system. We define another 2D real-number image-surface coordinate system for each polycentric panoramic image with the coordinates (x, y). The origin of this coordinate system is defined at the center of the initial image slit. The conversion between these two coordinates (u, v) and (x, y) is $x = du$ and $y = d(v - v_c)$, where d is the size of an image pixel in units of y.

---

[2] The center pixel of the slit image where the optical axis of the slit camera passes through the image.

A 3D slit-camera coordinate system, shown in Fig. 1, is defined as follows. The origin coincides with the focal point of a slit camera, denoted as O_c. The z-axis is perpendicular to the image slit and passes through the center of the image slit. The y-axis is parallel to the image slit towards the direction of the positive y value in the image-slit coordinate system. An image point p on the image slit can be represented by the coordinates $(0, y, f)$, where f is the effective focal length of the slit camera. Another way of representing an image point p is by an angular coordinate ϕ, which is the angle between the z-axis and the line passing through both the focal point and the image point. The conversion between the coordinates $(0, y, f)$ and ϕ is $\phi = \tan^{-1}(y/f)$.

Each column of a polycentric panoramic image associates with a slit camera coordinate system. All the origins of the slit camera coordinate systems lie on the circle $\mathfrak{C}$. A 3D turning-rig[3] coordinate system is defined for each polycentric panoramic image. The origin, denoted as O_o, coincides with the center of the circle $\mathfrak{C}$. The z-axis passes through the center of the initial column of the panoramic image. The y-axis is parallel to all the slit images and towards the same direction as the y-axis of the slit camera coordinate system. We define an angle θ to be the angle between the z-axis of the turning-rig coordinate system and the segment $\overline{O_o C}$. The orientation and the location of a slit camera coordinate system with respect to the turning-rig coordinate system can be described by a 3 × 3 rotation matrix R_{oc},

$$R_{oc} = \begin{bmatrix} \cos(\theta+\omega) & 0 & -\sin(\theta+\omega) \\ 0 & 1 & 0 \\ \sin(\theta+\omega) & 0 & \cos(\theta+\omega) \end{bmatrix},$$

where ω is the angle between the normal vector of the circle $\mathfrak{C}$ at O_c and the optical axis of the slit camera, and a 3 × 1 translation vector

$$T_{oc} = \begin{pmatrix} r\sin\theta \\ 0 \\ r\cos\theta \end{pmatrix},$$

where r is the radius of the circle $\mathfrak{C}$. Figure 2 depicts the relationship between the slit camera coordinate systems and the turning-rig coordinate system. The conversion between the coordinate u and the angle θ is $\theta = (2\pi u)/\ell$, where ℓ denotes the length (in pixel) of the panoramic image.

A 3D world coordinate system is defined for the conversion between any pair of turning-rig coordinate systems for two polycentric panoramic images. The origin is denoted as O_w. The relationship between the world coordinate system and a turning-rig coordinate system associated to a panoramic image can be described by a 3 × 3 rotation matrix R_{wo} and a 3D translation vector T_{wo}.

3.2   Derivation

Given is an image point of a polycentric panoramic image $\mathcal{P}$ (the source image), the task is to calculate the epipolar curve in another panoramic image $\mathcal{P}'$ (the destination image).

---
[3] For example, a turntable or a turning head on a tripod.

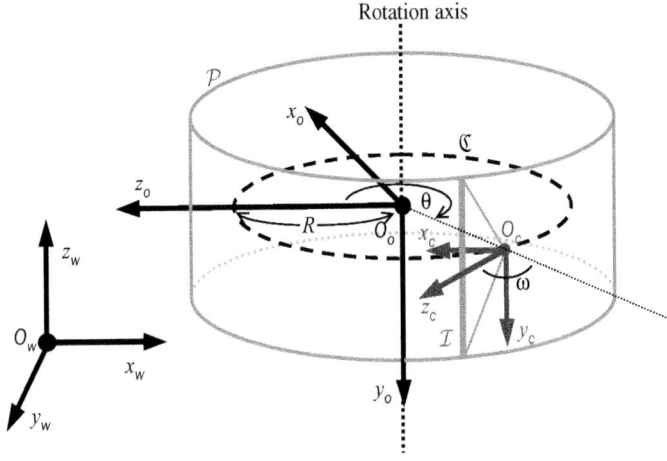

Fig. 2. The geometrical relationship among a slit camera coordinate system (with origin at O_c), an associated turning-rig coordinate system (with origin at O_o), and the world coordinate system (with origin at O_w). See text for further details.

Every symbol associated with the destination panoramic image is added with a $(')$ besides it to make a distinction from the corresponding symbol of the source panoramic image.

If an image point p of $\mathcal{P}$ is given, then a 3D projection ray, denoted as $\mathfrak{L}_c$, emitting from a focal point C through the point p is defined. The projection ray $\mathfrak{L}_c$ with respect to the slit camera coordinate system can be described by $P + \lambda D$, where P is a zero 3-vector, $\lambda \in \Re$ is any scalar, and D is a unit directional vector:

$$D = \left(0, \frac{y}{\sqrt{y^2 + f^2}}, \frac{f}{\sqrt{y^2 + f^2}}\right)^{\mathrm{T}}$$
$$= (0, \sin\phi, \cos\phi)^{\mathrm{T}}.$$

The projection ray $\mathfrak{L}_c$ is first transformed to the turning-rig coordinate system of the panoramic image $\mathcal{P}$. The resulting ray is denoted as $\mathfrak{L}_o$. The transformation formula is as follows:

$$\mathfrak{L}_o = R_{oc}^{-1}P + T_{oc} + \lambda R_{oc}^{-1}D$$
$$= T_{oc} + \lambda R_{oc}^{-1}D.$$

The projection ray $\mathfrak{L}_o$ is then transformed to the turning-rig coordinate system of the destination panoramic image $\mathcal{P}'$ through the world coordinate system. The resulting ray is denoted as $\mathfrak{L}_{o'}$. The transformation formula is as follows:

$$\mathfrak{L}_{o'} = R_{wo'}(R_{wo}^{-1}T_{oc} + T_{wo} - T_{wo'}) + \lambda R_{wo'}R_{wo}^{-1}R_{oc}^{-1}D$$
$$= R_{wo'}\left[R_{wo}^{-1}\begin{bmatrix} r\sin\theta \\ 0 \\ r\cos\theta \end{bmatrix} + T_{wo} - T_{wo'}\right] + \lambda R_{wo'}R_{wo}^{-1}\begin{bmatrix} \sin(\theta+\omega)\cos\phi \\ \sin\phi \\ \cos(\theta+\omega)\cos\phi \end{bmatrix}. \quad (1)$$

The epipolar curve equation is an equation in terms of x' and y' which are the image-surface coordinates of the destination panoramic image $\mathcal{P}'$. Every point (x', y') is the projection of some 3D point on the ray $\mathcal{L}_{o'}$. In other words, every (x', y') is possibly the corresponding point of the given image point (u, v) of $\mathcal{P}$. Let $\mathcal{I}'$ denote the slit image contributed to the column x' of $\mathcal{P}'$ and let C' denote the associated slit camera's focal point. For each column x', the corresponding y' value can be found by the following two steps. First calculate the intersection point, denoted as Q', of the ray $\mathcal{L}_{o'}$ and the plane $\mathfrak{P}_{o'}$ passing through C' and $\mathcal{I}'$. Second, project point Q' to the slit image $\mathcal{I}'$ to obtain the value of y'.

The associated angle θ' is $(2\pi x')/(\ell')$, where ℓ' is the length of the destination panoramic image. The position of the focal point C' with respect to the turning-rig coordinate system of $\mathcal{P}'$ can be described by $(r' \sin \theta', 0, r' \cos \theta')$, where r' is the radius of the circle $\mathcal{C}'$. A unit vector perpendicular to the plane $\mathfrak{P}_{o'}$ is $(-\cos(\theta' + \omega'), 0, \sin(\theta' + \omega'))$, where ω' is the angle between the normal vector of $\mathcal{C}'$ at C' and plane $\mathfrak{P}_{o'}$. Therefore, the equation of plane $\mathfrak{P}_{o'}$ is

$$- \cos(\theta' + \omega')x + \sin(\theta' + \omega')z = r' \sin \omega', \tag{2}$$

where the variables x and z are with respect to the turning-rig coordinate system of the destination panoramic image $\mathcal{P}'$.

We substitute the x- and z- components of the projection ray $\mathcal{L}_{o'}$ in Equ. 1 into the plane equation Equ. 2, and solve the value of λ. The intersection point Q' can then be calculated from Equ. 1. We denote the obtained coordinates of Q' as $(x_{o'}, y_{o'}, z_{o'})$. We have

$$\begin{bmatrix} x_{c'} \\ y_{c'} \\ z_{c'} \end{bmatrix} = \begin{bmatrix} x_{o'} \cos(\theta' + \omega') - z_{o'} \sin(\theta' + \omega') + r' \sin \omega' \\ y_{o'} \\ x_{o'} \sin(\theta' + \omega') + z_{o'} \cos(\theta' + \omega') - r' \cos \omega' \end{bmatrix},$$

which transforms the point Q' to the slit camera coordinate system associated to the slit image $\mathcal{I}'$ and denote it as $(x_{c'}, y_{c'}, z_{c'})$.

A 3D point is allowed to project onto the slit image if and only if the x-component of the coordinates with respect to the slit camera coordinate system is equal to zero. Therefore, the projection of a 3D point $(0, y_{c'}, z_{c'})$ on the slit image $\mathcal{I}'$ is

$$\begin{bmatrix} 0 \\ \frac{f' y_{o'}}{x_{o'} \sin(\theta' + \omega') + z_{o'} \cos(\theta' + \omega') - r' \cos \omega'} \\ f' \end{bmatrix},$$

where f' is the effective focal length of the slit camera acquiring p'. Convert the projection of a 3D point in the slit image $\mathcal{I}'$ back to the image-surface coordinate system of the panoramic image $\mathcal{P}'$. Given x', the value of y' is

$$y' = \frac{f' y_{o'}}{x_{o'} \sin(\frac{2\pi x'}{\ell'} + \omega') + z_{o'} \cos(\frac{2\pi x'}{\ell'} + \omega') - r' \cos \omega'}.$$

To draw an epipolar curve in a discrete image, the coordinates (x', y') are converted to the discrete image coordinate system (u', v') by $u' = x'/d'$ and $v' = v_c + y'/d'$, where d' is the size of an image pixel in units of y'.

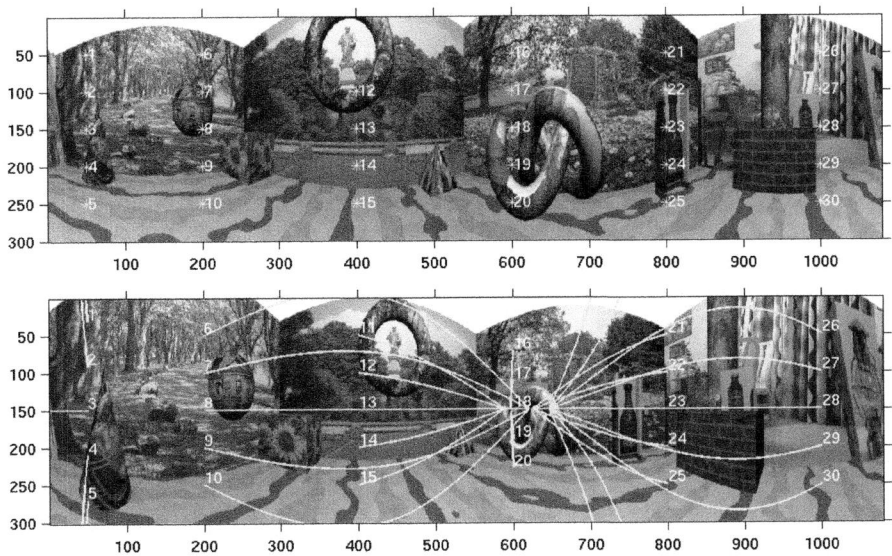

Fig. 3. An example of epipolar curves in a pair of horizontally-aligned polycentric panoramic images.

4   Epipolar Curves in Special Cases

We discuss the general equation in the context of a few special cases of panoramic images.

4.1   Epipolar Curve in Horizontally-Aligned Polycentric Panoramas

Consider two polycentric panoramic images, $\mathcal{P}$ and $\mathcal{P}'$. The orientations and positions of their turning-rig coordinate systems with respect to the world coordinate system are: $R_{wo} = R_{wo'} = I_{3\times 3}$ and $T_{wo} = (0,0,0)^{\mathrm{T}}$ and $T_{wo'} = (t_x, 0, t_z)^{\mathrm{T}}$ respectively. These two panoramic images are called *horizontally-aligned polycentric panoramas*. Given is an image point (x, y) on $\mathcal{P}$, the equation of the epipolar curve on $\mathcal{P}'$ is

$$y' = y\left(\frac{f'}{f}\right) \cdot \left(\frac{r' \sin \omega' - r \sin\left(\frac{2\pi x'}{\ell'} - \frac{2\pi x}{\ell} + \omega'\right) - t_x \cos\left(\frac{2\pi x'}{\ell'} + \omega'\right) + t_z \sin\left(\frac{2\pi x'}{\ell'} + \omega'\right)}{-r \sin \omega - r' \sin\left(\frac{2\pi x'}{\ell'} - \frac{2\pi x}{\ell} - \omega\right) - t_x \cos\left(\frac{2\pi x}{\ell} + \omega\right) + t_z \sin\left(\frac{2\pi x}{\ell} + \omega\right)}\right).$$

Figure 3 shows an example of a pair of horizontally-aligned polycentric panoramas in a 3D synthetic scene: a squared room containing different objects such as a sphere, a box, a knot etc. with mapped real-images. The upper image shows the source panoramic image, $\mathcal{P}$, with 30 test points in labeled '$*$' and enumerated positions. The lower image shows the destination panoramic image, $\mathcal{P}'$, with the corresponding epipolar curves. The turning-rig coordinate systems associated to the top panoramic image is set to the world

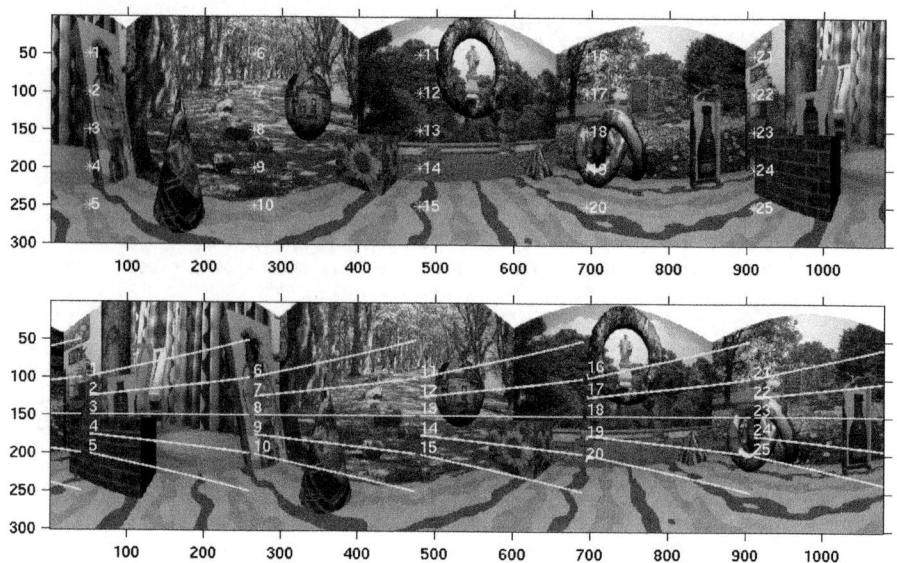

Fig. 4. An example of epipolar curve in a pair of concentric panoramic images.

coordinate system. The lower panoramic image $\mathcal{P}'$ was acquired at the same height[4], with $2m$ to the east and $1m$ to the north of the upper panoramic image $\mathcal{P}$. The orientations of these two panoramic images are set to be identical. The effective focal lengths of the slit cameras used for acquiring these two panoramic images are both equal to 35.704 mm. The radiuses of the circles, where slit camera's focal points lie on, are both equal to 40 mm. The orientations of the slit cameras with respect to each rotation axes are both equal to $45°$. Each slit camera takes 1080 slit images for one panoramic image. Both image pixel's width and height are equal to $1/6$ mm.

4.2 Epipolar Curve in Concentric Panoramas

A set of polycentric panoramic images is called *concentric panoramic panoramas* [3] if the associated turning-rig coordinate systems are all coincident. Consider two concentric panoramic images, $\mathcal{P}$ and $\mathcal{P}'$. Given an image point (x, y) on $\mathcal{P}$, the equation of the epipolar curve on $\mathcal{P}'$ is

$$y' = y \cdot \left(\frac{f'}{f}\right) \cdot \left(\frac{r' \sin \omega' - r \sin\left(\frac{2\pi x'}{\ell'} - \frac{2\pi x}{\ell} + \omega'\right)}{-r \sin \omega - r' \sin\left(\frac{2\pi x'}{\ell'} - \frac{2\pi x}{\ell} - \omega\right)}\right). \tag{3}$$

Figure 4 shows an example of the epipolar curve in a pair of concentric panoramas. The effective focal lengths of slit cameras are both equal to 35.704 mm. The radiuses of the

---

[4] It follows that the y-components of the world coordinates of the associated rotation centers are equal.

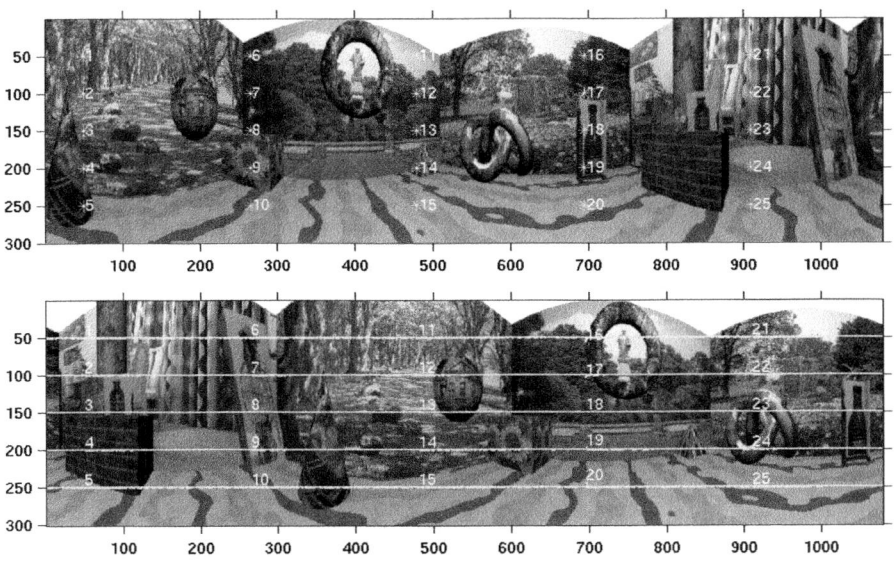

Fig. 5. An example of the epipolar curves in a symmetric pair of concentric panoramas.

circles are both equal to 40 mm. The orientation of the slit camera with respect to the rotation axis of the upper panoramic image is equal to $10°$ and of the lower image is equal to $300°$.

In particular $\omega' = (2\pi - \omega)$, the two concentric panoramic images are called *symmetric pair* [15,14]. An important property about the symmetric panoramic image pair is that the epipolar curves become straight lines and coincide with image rows. The property can be shown from equation Equ. 3 by setting $f = f'$, $r = r'$, $\ell = \ell'$, and most critically $\omega' = (2\pi - \omega)$, we have

$$y' = y \cdot 1 \cdot \left(\frac{r\sin(2\pi - \omega) - r\sin(\frac{2\pi x'}{\ell'} - \frac{2\pi x}{\ell} + 2\pi - \omega)}{-r\sin\omega - r\sin(\frac{2\pi x'}{\ell'} - \frac{2\pi x}{\ell} - \omega)} \right)$$

$$= y \cdot \left(\frac{-\sin\omega - \sin(\frac{2\pi x'}{\ell'} - \frac{2\pi x}{\ell} - \omega)}{-\sin\omega - \sin(\frac{2\pi x'}{\ell'} - \frac{2\pi x}{\ell} - \omega)} \right)$$

$$= y.$$

The value of y' is equal to y. Figure 5 shows an example of the epipolar lines in a symmetric pair of concentric panoramas. The parameters are the same as the previous settings. Only the orientations of the slit cameras are different. One is equal to $10°$ and the other is equal to $300°$. Note that all the epipolar curves become straight lines and coincide with image rows.

4.3   Epipolar Curve in Single-Center Panoramas

A set of polycentric panoramic images acquired with all the slit camera's focal points coincided at a single point is called *single-center panoramas*. Consider two single-center panoramic images, $\mathcal{P}$ and $\mathcal{P}'$. The orientations and positions of their turning-rig coordinate systems with respect to the world coordinate system are: $R_{wo} = R_{wo'} = I_{3\times3}$ and $T_{wo} = (0,0,0)^{\mathrm{T}}$ and $T_{wo'} = (t_x, 0, t_z)^{\mathrm{T}}$ respectively. Each associated circle $\mathfrak{C}$ becomes a single points and angle $\omega = 0$, we have $r = r' = 0$ and $\omega = \omega' = 0$. Given an image point (x,y) on $\mathcal{P}$, the equation of the epipolar curve in $\mathcal{P}'$ is

$$y' = y \cdot \left(\frac{f'}{f}\right) \cdot \left(\frac{-t_x \cos(\frac{2\pi x'}{\ell'}) + t_z \sin(\frac{2\pi x'}{\ell'})}{-t_x \cos(\frac{2\pi x}{\ell}) + t_z \sin(\frac{2\pi x}{\ell})}\right)$$

$$= y \cdot k \cdot \left(t_z \sin\left(\frac{2\pi x'}{\ell'}\right) - t_x \cos\left(\frac{2\pi x'}{\ell'}\right)\right),$$

where

$$k = \left(\frac{f'}{f\left(t_z \sin(\frac{2\pi x}{\ell}) - t_x \cos(\frac{2\pi x}{\ell})\right)}\right)$$

is a scalar. Figure 6 shows an example of the epipolar curves in a pair of single-center panoramas. The parameters of these two panoramic image acquisitions are identical to those of the polycentric panoramic pair except the orientations of the slit cameras are both equal to $0°$ and the radiuses of the circles are both equal to 0 mm.

5   Conclusion and Further Work

This paper proposes polycentric panoramas as a new model of panoramic images. We have shown that this model is able to describe a wide range of existing panoramic images. Hence, the epipolar curve equation derived is applicable in those more specific types of panoramic images. So far, only the epipolar curve equation itself is derived, no mathematical analysis has been done. Since there are many parameters involved in the equation, it is interesting to see how each of them affects the behavior of the epipolar curve. How to classify the epipolar curves based on properties of the curves? How many equivalent classes can be found? Given a set of uncalibrated panoramic images of one particular class, how many corresponding points are necessary to calibrate the desired parameters? In this paper, the panoramic image surface is chosen to be a perfect cylinder. However, there are other geometric forms such as an ellipse etc exist for use in some applications. It is interesting to derive a more general epipolar curve equation for those panoramic images.

References

[1] S. E. Chen: QuickTimeVR - an image-based approach to virtual environment navigation. *Proc. SIGGRAPH'95*, Los Angeles, California, USA (August 1995) pp. 29–38.

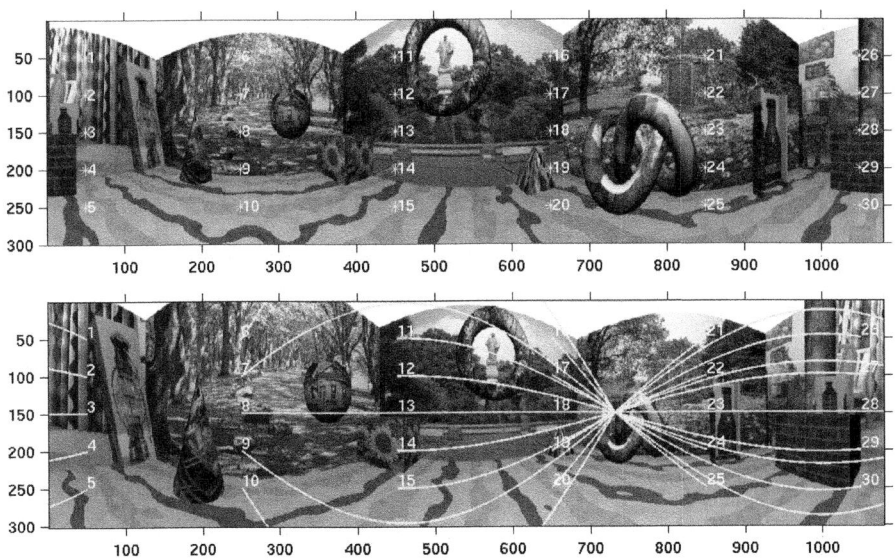

Fig. 6. An example of the epipolar curves in a pair of single-center panoramas.

[2] O. Faugeras: *Three-Dimensional Computer Vision: A Geometric Viewpoint.* The MIT Press, London, England (1993).

[3] F. Huang, T. Pajdla: Epipolar geometry in concentric panoramas. Research Report CTU–CMP–2000–07, Center for Machine Perception, Czech Technical University, Prague, Czech Republic (March 2000).

[4] R. Hartley, A. Zisserman: *Multiple View Geometry in Computer Vision.* Cambridge Uni. Press, United Kingdom (2000).

[5] H. Ishiguro, M. Yamamoto, S. Tsuji: Omni-directional stereo. *PAMI* **14**(2) (February 1992) pp. 257–262.

[6] K. Kanatani: *Geometric Computation for Machine Vision.* Oxford Uni. Press, New York (1993).

[7] S.-B. Kang, R. Szeliski: 3-d scene data recovery using omnidirectional multibaseline stereo. *IJCV* **25**(2) (November 1997) pp. 167–183.

[8] R. Klette, K. Schlüns, A. Koschan: *Computer Vision - Three-Dimensional Data from Images.* Springer, Singapore (1998).

[9] L. McMillan, G. Bishop: Plenoptic modeling: an image-based rendering system. *Proc. SIG-GRAPH'95,* Los Angeles, California, USA (August 1995) pp. 39–46.

[10] T. Matsuyama, T. Wada: Cooperative distributed vision - dynamic integration of visual perception, action, and communication. *Proc. CDV-WS98,* Kyoto, Japan (November 1998) pp. 1–40.

[11] S. Peleg, M. Ben-Ezra: Stereo panorama with a single camera. *Proc. CVPR99,* Fort Collins, Colorado, USA (June 1999) pp. 395–401.

[12] S. Peleg, Y. Pritch, M. Ben-Ezra: Cameras for stereo panoramic imaging. *Proc. CVPR00,* Hilton Head Island (June 2000) pp. 208-214.

[13] H.-Y. Shum, L.-W. He: Rendering with concentric mosaics. *Proc. SIGGRAPH'99,* Los Angeles, California, USA (August 1999) pp. 299–306.

[14] H. Shum, A. Kalai, S. Seitz: Omnivergent stereo. *Proc. ICCV99*, Korfu, Greece (September 1999) pp. 22–29.

[15] H.-Y. Shum, R. Szeliski: Stereo reconstruction from multiperspective panoramas. *Proc. ICCV99*, Korfu, Greece (September 1999) pp. 14-21.

[16] S.-K. Wei, F. Huang, R. Klette: Classification and characterization of image acquisition for 3d scene visualization and reconstruction applications. Technical Report, CITR-TR-59, Centre for Image Technology and Robotics, The University of Auckland, New Zealand (June 2000).

[17] G. Xu, Z. Zhang: *Epipolar Geometry in Stereo, Motion and Object Recognition - A Unified Approach*. Kluwer Academic Publishers, Netherlands (1996).

Image-Based Rendering from Uncalibrated Lightfields with Scalable Geometry

Reinhard Koch[1*], Benno Heigl[2], and Marc Pollefeys[3]

[1] Institut für Informatik, Christian-Albrechts-Universität Kiel, Germany
[2] Lehrstuhl für Mustererkennung, Universität Erlangen-Nürnberg, Germany
[3] Laboratory for Processing of Speech and Images, PSI-ESAT, K.U. Leuven, Belgium
rk@is.informatik.uni-kiel.de

Abstract. We combine uncalibrated Structure-from-Motion, lightfield rendering and view-dependent texture mapping to model and render scenes from a set of images that are acquired from an uncalibrated hand-held video camera. The camera is simply moved by hand around the 3D scene of interest. The intrinsic camera parameters like focal length and the camera positions are automatically calibrated with a Structure-From-Motion approach. Dense and accurate depth maps for each camera viewpoint are computed with multi-viewpoint stereoscopic matching. The set of images, their calibration parameters and the depth maps are then utilized for depth-compensated image-based rendering. The rendering utilizes a scalable geometric approximation that is tailored to the needs of the rendering hardware.

1 Introduction

This contribution discusses realistic scene reconstruction and visualization from real image streams that are recorded by an uncalibrated, freely moving hand-held camera. This approach allows to easily acquire 3D scene models from real-world scenes with high fidelity and minimum effort on equipment and calibration.

Recently, quite some approaches to this problem have been investigated. Plenoptic modeling [11], lightfield rendering [10] and the lumigraph [5] have received a lot of attention, since they can capture the appearance of a 3D scene from images only, without the explicit use of 3D geometry. Thus one may be able to capture objects with very complex geometry that can not be modeled otherwise. Basically one caches views from many different directions all around the scene and interpolate new views from this large image collection. For realistic rendering, however, very many views are needed to avoid interpolation errors for in-between views.

Structure from motion (SFM) approaches like [13] on the other hand try to model the 3D scene and the camera motion geometrically and capture scene details on polygonal (triangular) surface meshes. A limited set of camera views of the scene are sufficient to reconstruct the 3D scene. Texture mapping adds

---

* Work was performed during stay at the Laboratory for Processing of Speech and Images, PSI-ESAT, K.U. Leuven, Belgium

the necessary fidelity for photo-realistic rendering of the object surface. Dense and accurate 3D depth estimates are needed for realistic image rendering from the textured 3D surface model. Deviation from the true 3D surface will distort the rendered images.

The problem common to both approaches is the need to calibrate the image sequence. Recently it was proposed to combine a structure from motion approach with plenoptic modeling to generate lightfields from uncalibrated hand-held camera sequences [8]. When generating lightfields from a hand-held camera sequence, one typically generates images with a specific distribution of the camera viewpoints. Since we want to capture the appearance of the object from all sides, we will sample the viewing sphere, thus generating a *mesh of view points*. To fully exploit hand-held sequences, we will therefore have to deviate from the regular lightfield data structure and adopt a more flexible rendering data structure based on the viewpoint mesh. Another important point in combining SFM and lightfield rendering is the use of scene geometry for image interpolation. The geometric reconstruction yields a geometric approximation of the real scene structure that might be insufficient when static texture mapping is used. However, view-dependent texture mapping as in [2] will adapt the texture dynamically to a static, approximate 3D geometry.

In this contribution we will discuss the combination of Structure-from-Motion, lightfield rendering, and dynamic surface texturing. SFM delivers camera calibration and dense depth maps that approximate the scene geometry. Rendering is then performed by depth-compensated image interpolation from a mesh of camera viewpoints as generated by SFM. The novel image-based rendering method takes advantage of the irregular viewpoint mesh generated from hand-held image acquisition. We will first give a brief overview of the calibration and reconstruction techniques by SFM. We will then focus on the depth-compensated image interpolation and show that only a coarse geometric approximation is necessary to guide the rendering process. Experiments on calibration, geometric approximation and image-based rendering verify the approach.

2   Calibration and 3D-Reconstruction

Uncalibrated *Structure From Motion* (SFM) is used to recover camera calibration and scene geometry from images of the scene alone without the need for further scene or camera information. Faugeras and Hartley first demonstrated how to obtain uncalibrated projective reconstructions from image point matches alone [4,6]. Beardsley et al. [1] proposed a scheme to obtain projective calibration and 3D structure by robustly tracking salient feature points throughout an image sequence. This sparse object representation outlines the object shape, but does not give sufficient surface detail for visual reconstruction. Highly realistic 3D surface models need a dense depth reconstruction and can not rely on few feature points alone.

In [13] the method of Beardsley was extended in two directions. On the one hand the projective reconstruction was updated to metric even for varying internal camera parameters, on the other hand a dense stereo matching technique [3] was applied between two selected images of the sequence to obtain a dense depth map for a single viewpoint. From this depth map a triangular surface wire-frame was constructed and texture mapping from one image was applied to obtain realistic surface models. In [7] the approach was further extended to multi-viewpoint depth analysis. The approach can be summarized in 3 steps:

- Camera self-calibration and metric structure is obtained by robust tracking of salient feature points over the image sequence,
- dense correspondence maps are computed between adjacent image pairs of the sequence,
- all correspondence maps are linked together by multiple view point linking to fuse depth measurements over the sequence.

2.1 Calibration of a Mesh of Viewpoints

When very long image sequences have to be processed with the above described approach, there is a risk of calibration failure due to several factors. For one, the calibration as described above is built sequentially by adding one view at a time. This may result in accumulation errors that introduce a bias to the calibration. Secondly, if a single image in the sequence is not matched, the complete calibration fails. Finally, sequential calibration does not exploit the specific image acquisition structure used in this approach to sample the viewing sphere.

In [8] a multi-viewpoint calibration algorithm has been described that allows to actually weave the viewpoint sequence into a connected viewpoint mesh. This approach is summarized in the following section.

Image pair matching. The basic tool for viewpoint calibration is the two-view matcher. Corresponding image features m_i, m_k have to be matched between the two images of the camera viewpoints P_i, P_k. The image features are projections of a 3D feature point M into the Images I_i, I_k in homogeneous coordinates:

$$m_i = \rho_i P_i M \quad , \quad m_k = \rho_k P_k M \quad , \quad P = K\left[R^T | - R^T c\right] \tag{1}$$

with ρ a non-zero scaling factor, K = camera calibration matrix, R = orientation and c = position of the camera. To solve for P from m_i, m_k we employ a robust computation of the Fundamental matrix F_{ik} with the RANSAC (RANdom SAMpling Consensus) method [14]. Between all image correspondences the fundamental image relation (the epipolar constraint) holds

$$m_i^T F_{i,k} m_k = 0 \tag{2}$$

$F_{i,k(3x3)}$ is a linear rank-2 matrix. A minimum set of 7 feature correspondences is picked from a large list of potential image matches to compute a specific F. For this particular F the support is computed from the other potential matches. This procedure is repeated randomly to obtain the most likely F_{ik} with best support in feature correspondence. From F we can compute the

3×4 camera projection matrices P_i and P_k. The fundamental matrix alone does not suffice to fully compute the projection matrices. In a bootstrap step for the first two images we follow the approach by Beardsley e.a. [1]. Since the camera calibration matrix K is unknown a priori we assume an approximate $\tilde{K}$ to start with. The first camera is then set to $P_0 = \tilde{K}[I|0]$ to coincide with the world coordinate system, and the second camera P_1 can be derived from the epipole e (projection of camera center into the other image) and F as

$$P_1 = \tilde{K} \left[[e]_x F + ea^T | \rho e \right] \ , \ [e]_x = \begin{bmatrix} 0 & -e_3 & e_2 \\ e_3 & 0 & -e_1 \\ -e_2 & e_1 & 0 \end{bmatrix} \tag{3}$$

P_1 is defined up to global scale ρ and the unknown plane $\pi_{\inf}$, encoded in a^T (see also [12]). Thus we can only obtain a projective reconstruction. The vector a^T should be chosen such that the left 3×3 matrix of P_i best approximates an orthonormal rotation matrix. The scale ρ is set such that the baseline length between the first two cameras is unity. K and a^T will be determined during camera self-calibration.

Once we have obtained the projection matrices we can triangulate the corresponding image features m_i, m_k with P_i, P_k to obtain the corresponding 3D object features M. The object points are determined such that their reprojection error in the images is minimized. In addition we compute the point uncertainty covariance to keep track of measurement uncertainties. The 3D object points serve as the *memory* for consistent camera tracking, and it is desirable to track the projection of the 3D points through as many images as possible. This process is repeated by adding new viewpoints and correspondences throughout the sequence. Finally constraints are applied to the cameras to obtain a metric reconstruction. A detailed account of this approach can be found in [12,13].

Estimating the viewpoint topology. Since we are collecting a large amount of images from all possible viewpoints distributed over the viewing sphere, it is no longer reasonable to consider a sequential processing along the sequence frame index alone. Instead we would like to evaluate the image collection in order to robustly establish image relationships between all nearby images. We need to define a distance measure that allows to estimate the proximity of two viewpoints from image matches alone. We are interested in finding those camera viewpoints that are near to the current viewpoint and that support calibration. Obvious candidates for these are the preceding and following frames in a sequence, but normally those viewpoints are taken more or less on a linear path due to camera motion. This near-linear motion may lead to degeneracies and problems in the calibration. We are therefore also interested in additional viewpoints that are perpendicular to the current direction of the camera motion. If the camera sweeps back and forth over the viewpoint surface we will likely approach the current viewpoint in previous and future frames. Our goal is now to determine which of all viewpoints are nearest and most evenly distributed around our current view. So far we do not know the position of the cameras, but we can compute the F-Matrix from corresponding image points. For each potential neighbor image I_i

we compute $F_{c,i}$ w.r.t. the current image I_c. To measure *proximity* and *direction* of the matched viewpoint w.r.t. the current one, we can exploit the image epipole as well as the distribution of the correspondence vectors.

Direction: The epipole determines the angular direction α_e of the neighboring camera position w.r.t. the current image coordinates, since it represents the projection of the camera center into the current image. Those viewpoints whose epipoles are most evenly distributed over all image quadrants should be selected for calibration.

Proximity: The distribution of the corresponding matches determines the distance between two viewpoints. Consider a non-planar scene and general motion between both cameras. If both camera viewpoints coincide we can cancel out the camera orientation change between the views with a projective mapping (rectification) and the corresponding points will coincide since no depth parallax is involved. For a general position of the second camera viewpoint, the depth parallax will cause a residual correspondence error e_r after rectification that is proportional to the baseline distance between the viewpoints. We can approximate the projective rectification by a linear affine mapping that is estimated from the image correspondences. We therefore define the residual correspondence error e_r after rectification as proximity measure for nearby viewpoints. The viewpoints with smallest e_r are closest to the current viewpoint.

Weaving the viewpoint mesh. With the distance measure at hand we can build a topological network of viewpoints. We start with an arbitrary image of the sequence and compute α_e and e_r for subsequent images. If we choose the starting image as first image of the sequence, we can proceed along the frame index and find the nearest adjacent viewpoints in all directions. From this seed views we proceed recursively, building the viewpoint mesh topology over all views. The mesh builds along the shortest camera distances very much like a wave propagating over the viewpoint surface.

2.2   3D Geometry Estimation

Once we have retrieved the metric calibration of the cameras we can use image correspondence techniques to estimate scene depth. We rely on stereo matching techniques that were developed for dense and reliable matching between adjacent views. The small baseline paradigm suffices here since we use a rather dense sampling of viewpoints.

For dense correspondence matching an area-based disparity estimator is employed. The matcher searches at each pixel in one image for maximum normalized cross correlation in the other image by shifting a small measurement window (kernel size 7x7) along the corresponding epipolar line. Dynamic programming is used to evaluate extended image neighborhood relationships and a pyramidal estimation scheme allows to reliably deal with very large disparity ranges [3].

The geometry of the viewpoint mesh is especially suited for further improvement with a multi viewpoint refinement [7]. Each viewpoint is matched with all adjacent viewpoints and all corresponding matches are linked together to form a reliable depth estimate. Since the different views are rather similar we will observe every object point in many nearby images. This redundancy is exploited to improve the depth estimation for each object point, and to refine the depth values to high accuracy.

2.3   Experimental Results for Surface Mesh Calibration

To evaluate our approach, we recorded a test sequence with known ground truth from a calibrated robot arm. The camera is mounted on the arm of a robot of type SCORBOT-ER VII. The position of its gripper arm is known from the angles of the 5 axes and the dimensions of the arm. The robot sampled a 8×8 spherical viewing grid with a radius of 230 mm. The viewing positions enclosed a maximum angle of 45 degrees which gives an extension of the spherical viewpoint surface patch of 180×180 mm^2. The scene (with size of about $150 \times 150 \times 100$ mm^3) consists of a cactus and some metallic parts on a piece of rough white wallpaper.

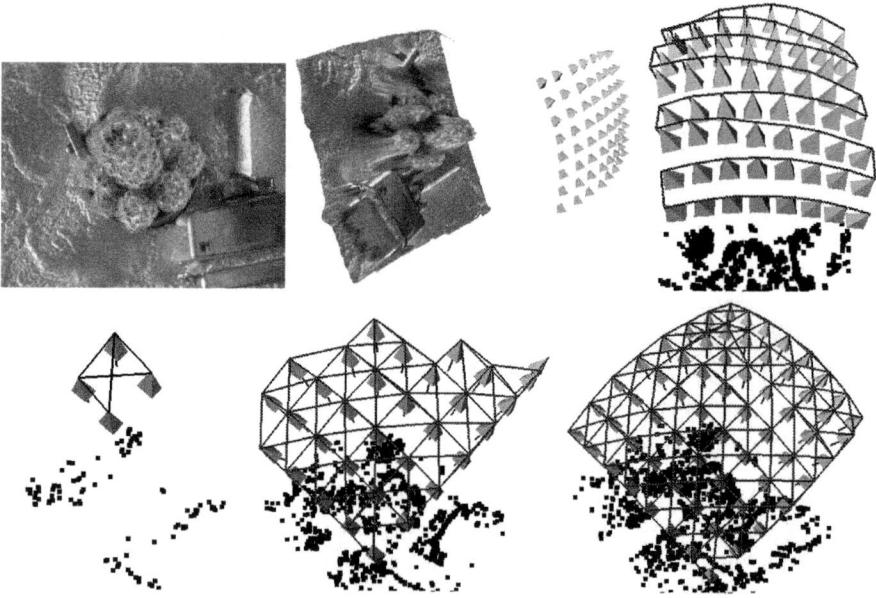

Fig. 1. Top left: one image of the robot sequence. Top middle: The distribution of the camera viewpoints over the 3D scene. Top right: sequential camera path as obtained from tracking along the camera path. Bottom: Intermediate steps of the mesh building after 4, 32, and 64 images. The camera viewpoints are indicated by pyramids that are connected by the viewpoint mesh. The black points in the background are tracked 3D feature points. One can see how the 2D mesh topology is building over the viewpoint surface.

Table 1. Ground truth comparison of 3D camera positional error between the 64 estimated and the known robot positions [in % of the mean object distance of 250 mm].

Camera position	projective		similarity	
Tracking Error [%]	mean	s.dev	mean	s.dev
sequential	1.08	0.69	2.31	1.08
2D viewpoints	0.57	0.37	1.41	0.61

One of the original images is shown in fig. 1(top left) together with the distribution of the camera viewpoints of the robot arm (top middle). Each camera position is visualized as little pyramid. In fig. 1(bottom) calibration using a viewpoint mesh results are shown. The mesh buildup is indicated by the estimated camera viewpoints (pyramids) and their topological relation (mesh connecting the cameras). Each connection indicates that the fundamental matrix between the image pair has been computed.

A quantitative evaluation of the tracking was performed by comparing the estimated metric camera pose with the known Euclidean robot positions. We anticipate two types of errors: 1) a stochastic measurement noise on the camera position, and 2) a systematic error due to a remaining projective skew from imperfect self-calibration. We also compared the simple sequential calibration that estimates $F_{i,k}$ along adjacent images of the recording path only (fig 1, top right), with the novel 2D mesh calibration method (see fig 1, bottom).

For comparison we transform the measured metric camera positions into the Euclidean robot coordinate frame. With a projective transformation we can eliminate the skew and estimate the measurement error. We estimated the projective transform from the 64 corresponding camera positions and computed the residual distance error. The distance error was normalized to relative depth by the mean surface distance of 250 mm. The mean residual error dropped from 1.1% for sequential tracking to 0.58% for viewpoint weaving (see table 1). The position repeatability error of the robot itself is 0.08%.

If we assume that no projective skew is present then a similarity transform will suffice to map the coordinate sets onto each other. A systematic skew however will increase the residual error. To test for skew we estimated the similarity transform from the corresponding data sets and evaluated the residual error. Here the mean error increased to 1.4% for mesh tracking which is still good for pose and structure estimation from fully uncalibrated sequences.

3   Plenoptic Modeling and Rendering

After determining the pose and projection properties of the moving camera we want to use the calibrated cameras to create a scene model for visualization.

One possible method is *lightfield rendering*[10]. To create a lighfield model for real scenes, a large number of views from many different angles are taken. Each view can be considered as bundle of light rays passing through the optical center of the camera. The set of all views contains a discrete sampling of light rays with according color values and hence we get discrete samples of the plenoptic function. The light rays which are not represented have to be interpolated.

The original 4–D lightfield data structure uses a two–plane parameterization. Each light ray passes through two parallel planes with plane coordinates (s, t) and (u, v). Thus the ray is uniquely described by the 4–tuple (u, v, s, t). The (s, t)–plane is the *viewpoint plane* in which all camera focal points are placed on regular grid points. The projection parameters of each camera are constructed such, that the (u, v)–plane is their common image plane and that their optical axes are perpendicular to it.

Often, real objects are supposed to be *Lambertian*, meaning that one surface point has the same radiance value viewed from all possible directions. This implies that two viewing rays have the same color value if they intersect the surface at the same point. If specular effects occur, this is not true any more. The radiance value will change with changing viewing direction, but for a small change of the viewing angle, the color value also will change just a little. Consequently, two viewing rays have similar color values, if their direction is similar and if their point of intersection is near the surface of the scene.

To render a new view we suppose to have a virtual camera pointing to the scene. For each pixel we can determine the position of the corresponding virtual viewing ray. The nearer a recorded ray is to this virtual ray the greater is its support to its color value. So the general task of rendering views from a collection of images will be to determine those viewing rays which are *nearest* to the virtual one and to interpolate between them depending on their proximity.

Linear interpolation between the viewpoints in (s, t) and (u, v) introduces a blurred image with ghosting artifacts. In reality we will always have to choose between high density of stored viewing rays with high data volume and high fidelity, or low density with poor image quality. If we know an approximation of the scene geometry (see fig. 2, left), the rendering result can be improved by an appropriate depth-dependent warping of the nearest viewing rays as described in [5].

Having a sequence of images taken with a hand–held camera, in general the camera positions are not placed at the grid points of the viewpoint plane. In [5] a method is shown for resampling this regular two–plane parameterization from real images recorded from arbitrary positions (*re-binning*). The required regular structure is re-sampled and gaps are filled by applying a multi–resolution approach, considering depth corrections. The disadvantage of this re-binning step is that the interpolated regular structure already contains inconsistencies and ghosting artifacts due to errors in the scantily approximated geometry. To render views, a depth corrected look–up is performed. During this step, the effect of ghosting artifacts is repeated, so duplicate ghosting effects occur.

3.1 Representation with Recorded Images

Our goal is to overcome the problems as described in the last section by relaxing the restrictions imposed by the regular lightfield structure and to render views directly from the calibrated sequence of recorded images using local depth maps. Without loosing performance we directly map the original images onto a surface viewed by a virtual camera.

2–D Mapping: In this paragraph, a formalism for mapping image coordinates onto a plane A is described. The following approaches will use this formalism to map images onto planes and vice versa. We define a local coordinate system on A giving one point $\mathbf{a_0}$ on the plane and two vectors $\mathbf{a_1}$ and $\mathbf{a_2}$ spanning the plane. So each point $\mathbf{p}$ of the plane can be described by the coordinates x_A, y_A: $\mathbf{p} = (\mathbf{a_1}, \mathbf{a_2}, \mathbf{a_0}) (x_\mathbf{A}, y_\mathbf{A}, 1)^T$. The point $\mathbf{p}$ is perspectively projected into a camera which is represented by the 3×3 matrix $\mathbf{Q} = \mathbf{K R^T}$ and the projection center $\mathbf{c}$ (same notations as above). Matrix $\mathbf{R}$ is the orthonormal rotation matrix and $\mathbf{K}$ is an upper triangular calibration matrix. The resulting image coordinates x, y are determined by $\rho(x, y, 1)^T = \mathbf{Qp} - \mathbf{Qc}$. Inserting above equation for $\mathbf{p}$ results in

$$\rho \begin{pmatrix} x \\ y \\ 1 \end{pmatrix} = \mathbf{Q}(\mathbf{a_1}, \mathbf{a_2}, \mathbf{a_0} - \mathbf{c}) \begin{pmatrix} x_A \\ y_A \\ 1 \end{pmatrix} . \tag{4}$$

The value ρ is an unknown scale factor. Each mapping between a local plane coordinate system and a camera can be described by a single 3×3 matrix $\mathbf{B} = \mathbf{Q}(\mathbf{a_1}, \mathbf{a_2}, \mathbf{a_0} - \mathbf{c})$.

We can extend our mapping procedure to re–project the image of one camera (with center $\mathbf{c_i}$) onto the plane followed by a projection into the other camera (with center $\mathbf{c_V}$). Then the whole mapping is performed by

$$(x_V, y_V, 1)^T = \mathbf{B_V B_i^{-1}} (\mathbf{x_i}, \mathbf{y_i}, 1)^\mathbf{T} . \tag{5}$$

The 3×3–matrix $\mathbf{B_V B_i^{-1}}$ describes the projective mapping from one camera to another via a given plane. Figure 2(right) shows this situation for two camera positions $\mathbf{c_V}$ and $\mathbf{c_i}$.

Mapping via global plane: We apply the previously described method of mapping an image via a given plane to create a virtual scene view directly from real ones. In a first approach, we approximate the scene geometry by a single plane A. This step seems to be really erroneous but as mentioned before, the lightfield–approach exactly supposes this approximation. In the most simple approach, we follow this method, although at regions, where the scene surface differs much from the plane A, a blurring effect will be visible. But in the next section we will improve our approach for refined geometric scene descriptions.

Following the lightfield approach, we have to interpolate between neighboring views to construct a specific virtual view. Considering the fact mentioned above

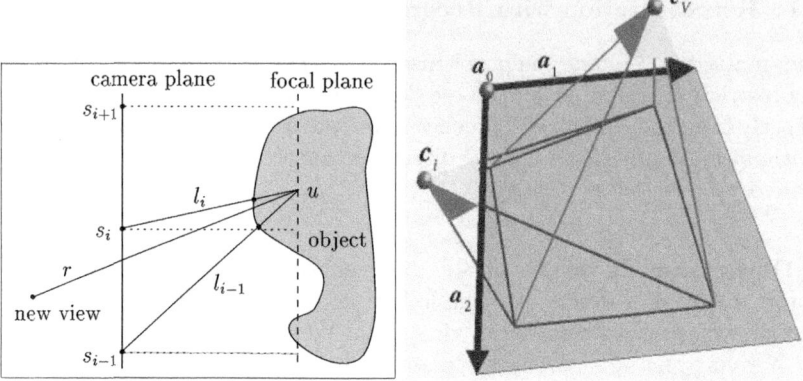

Fig. 2. Left: depth-dependent interpolation errors in the two-plane lightfield approach. The new viewing ray r is interpolated by the weighted sum of l_i and l_{i+1} from the adjacent cameras s_i and s_{i+1}. Since the real surface geometry deviates from the planar intersection point u at the focal plane, ghosting artifacts occur. Right: Projective mapping from one camera into another via a plane.

that the *nearest* rays give the best support to the color value of a given ray, we conclude that those views give the most support to the color value of a particular pixel whose projection center is closest to the viewing ray of this pixel. This is equivalent to the fact that those real views give the most support to a specified pixel of the virtual view whose projected camera centers are close to its image coordinate. We restrict the support to the nearest three cameras (see figure 3). To determine these three neighbors we project all camera centers into the virtual image and perform a 2–D triangulation. Then the neighboring cameras of a pixel are determined by the corners of the triangle which this pixel belongs to. The texture of such a triangle — and consequently a part of the reconstructed image — is drawn as a weighted sum of three textured triangles.

These textures are extracted from the original views by directly mapping the coordinates x_i, y_i of image i into the virtual camera coordinates x_V, y_V by applying equation 5.

To overlay these three textures, we calculate a weighted sum of the color values. Each triangle is weighted with factor 1 at the corner belonging to the projection center of the corresponding real view and with weight 0 at both others. In between, the weights are interpolated linearly similar to Gouraud–Shading, where the weights describe a plane ramp in barycentroic coordinates. Within the triangle, the sum of the three weights is 1 at each point. The total image is built as a mosaic of these triangles. Although this technique assumes a very sparse approximation of geometry, the rendering results show only few ghosting artifacts (see section 4) at those regions where the scene geometry differs much from the approximating plane.

Mapping via local planes: The results can be further improved by considering local depth maps. Spending more time for each view, we can calculate the approximating plane of geometry for each triangle in dependence on the actual view. As the approximation is not done for the whole scene but just for that part of the image which is seen through the actual triangle, we don't need a consistent 3-D model but we can use the — normally erroneous — local depth maps. The depth values are given as functions z_i of the coordinates in the recorded images $z_i((x_i, y_i, 1)^T)$. They describe the distance of a point perpendicular to the image plane. Using this depth function, we calculate the 3-D coordinates of those scene points which have the same 2-D image coordinates in the virtual view as the projected camera centers of the real views. The 3-D point $\mathbf{p_i}$ which corresponds to the real camera i can be calculated as

$$\mathbf{p_i} = \mathbf{z_i}(\mathbf{Q_i}\mathbf{d_i})\mathbf{d_i} + \mathbf{c_i}   , \tag{6}$$

where $\mathbf{d_i} = n(\mathbf{c_i} - \mathbf{c_V})$. The function n scales the given 3-D vector such, that its third component equals one. We can interpret the points $\mathbf{p_i}$ as the intersection of the line $\overline{\mathbf{c_V}\mathbf{c_i}}$ with the scene geometry (see figure 3). The 3-D coordinates of triangle corners define a plane which we can use to apply the same rendering technique as described above for one global plane.

Refinement: Finally, if the triangles exceed a given size, they can be subdivided into four sub-triangles by splitting the three sides into two parts, each. We determine the 3-D points corresponding to the midpoint of each side by applying

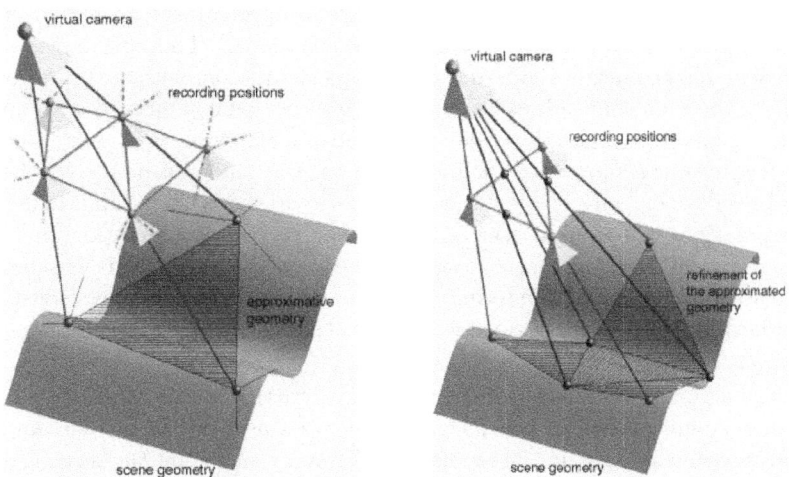

Fig. 3. Left: Drawing triangles of neighboring projected camera centers and approximating scene geometry by one plane for the whole scene or for one camera triple. Right: Refinement of triangulation by inserting new 3-D points corresponding to the midpoints of the triangle sides.

the same look–up method as used for radiance values to find the corresponding depth value. After that, we reconstruct the 3–D point using equation 6 and project it into the virtual camera resulting in a point near the side of the triangle. It is just in the neighborhood of the side, but this doesn't matter really. Merely, the triangulation structure will be changed slightly. One has to take care of avoiding inconsistencies caused by this look-up. For a given pair of neighboring views, the look-up always has to be done in the same depth map. A simple method is to do this look-up not for each triangle causing several look-ups for the same triangle side, but to determine the 3-D points for each pair of neighboring views in a preprocessing step. This also improves efficiency.

For each of these so created sub–triangles, a separate approximative plane is calculated in the above manner. Of course, further subdivision can be done in the same way to improve accuracy. Especially, if just few triangles contribute to a single virtual view, this subdivision is really necessary. This hierarchical refinement of the geometry can be performed adaptively depending on the required accuracy and available computational resources, hence allowing easy scalability towards scene complexity.

3.2   Scalable Geometry for Interpolation

The approach as discussed above can be used directly for scalable geometric scene approximation. The SFM reconstruction delivers local depth maps that contain the 3D scene geometry for a particular view point. However, sometimes the depth maps are sparse due to a lack of features. In that case, no dense geometric reconstruction is possible, but one can construct an approximate geometry (a mean global plane or a very coarse triangulated scene model). This coarse model is not sufficient for geometric rendering but allows depth compensated interpolation. In fact, the viewpoint-adaptive light field interpolation combined with approximative geometry combines to viewpoint-dependent texture mapping. Since only the nearby images are used for interpolation, the rendered image will be quite good even when only a very coarse geometry is used. The standard lightfield interpolation for example uses only a planar scene approximation that is not even adjusted to the mean scene geometry. Hence our approach is less distorting than standard lightfield rendering. The rendering will also be more realistic than standard texture mapping since we capture the reflectance characteristics of the scene.

The adaptive refinement of the geometry (starting with a mean global planar geometry and adapting to surface detail) can be used to control the amount of geometry that we need for interpolation. For every viewpoint the scene is divided into local planes until a given image quality (measured by image distortion) has been reached. On the other hand, one can select a fixed level of geometric subdivision based on the available rendering power of the texture mapping hardware. For a given performance one can therefore guarantee that rendering is done in constant time.

This geometric scalability is very useful in realtime environments where a fixed frame rate is required, or in high realism rendering where imaging quality is premium.

4   Experimental Results

We tested our approach also with an uncalibrated hand-held sequence. A digital consumer video camera (Sony DCR-TRV900 with progressive scan) was swept

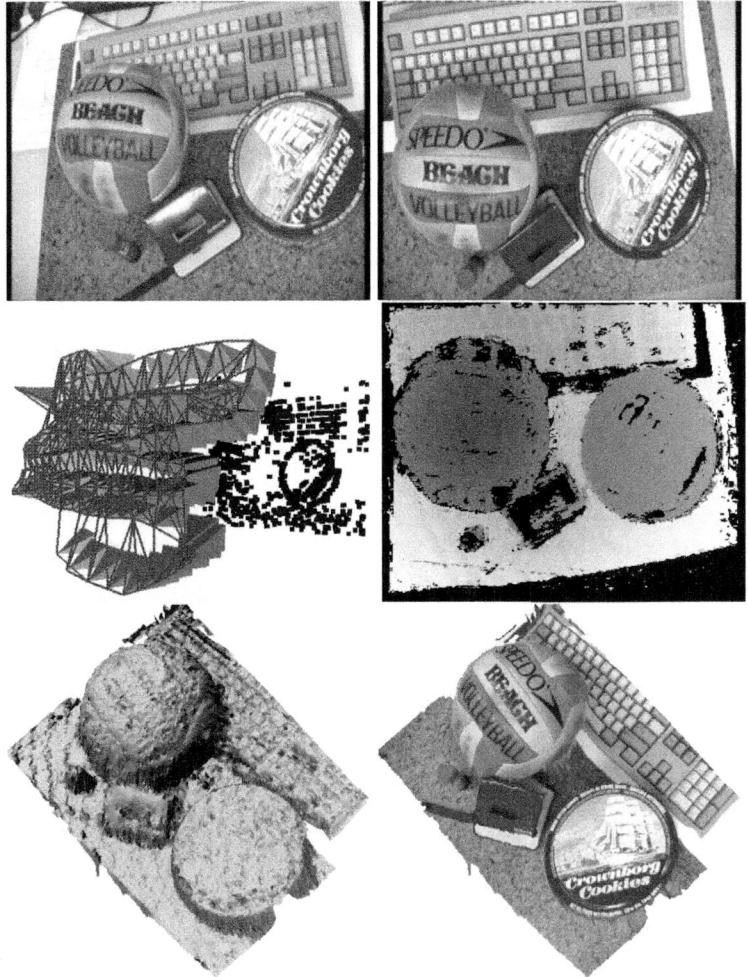

Fig. 4. Top: Two images from hand-held office sequence. Please note the changing surface reflections in the scene. Middle: Camera tracking with viewpoint mesh(left) and depth map from a specific viewpoint (right). Bottom: 3D surface model of scene rendered with shading (left) and texture (right).

freely over a cluttered scene on a desk, covering a viewing surface of about $1\ m^2$. The resulting video stream was then digitized on an SGI O2 by simply grabbing 187 frames at more or less constant intervals. No care was taken to manually stabilize the camera sweep.

Fig. 4 (top) shows two images of the sequence. Fig. 4 (middle, left) illustrates the zigzag route of the hand movement as the camera scanned the scene. The viewpoint mesh is irregular due to the arbitrary hand movements. The black dots represent the reconstructed 3D scene points. From the calibrated sequence we can compute any geometric or image based scene representation. As an example we show in fig. 4 (bottom) a geometric surface model of the scene with local scene geometry that was generated from the depth map (see fig. 4 middle, right).

Fig. 5 shows different refinement levels of the same geometry as viewed from a particular camera viewpoint. Even with this very rough approximation, very realistic view interpolation can be achieved.

Fig. 6 shows rendering of the same scene without depth compensation (left) and with depth compensation using geometric refinement (mesh 1x subdivided, middle). Even without geometry the rendering looks good, but due to the missing depth compensation some ghosting artifacts occur. This is the result achievable with the standard lightfield approach, but already exploiting the general viewpoint mesh calibration. With geometry compensation the rendering is improved substantially and the ghosting artifacts disappear. Note that we utilized a very coarse geometrical approximation only as displayed in fig 5 (top right) but still achieve high rendering quality.

The main advantage of lightfield rendering is that the rendering is *local*, meaning that all depth and color information for a pixel is taken from the three nearest camera images only. This allows changes in surface reflectivity when viewing the scene from different angles. Some rendering results with surface

Fig. 5. Viewpoint geometry for depth-compensated interpolation with with different levels of adaptive refinement (level of mesh subdivision: 0,1,2, 4 (top left to bottom right).

Fig. 6. Top: Novel views rendered from the viewpoint mesh without (left) and with (middle) depth-compensation. Only a coarse geometrical approximation is used (see upper right image of fig. 5). Right: Two views of the scene rendered from different viewpoints with changing reflections. The rendering quality is very high due to the natural appearance of the reflections.

reflections are shown in fig. 6 (right). The same part of the scene is rendered from different viewpoints, demonstrating that the reflections are preserved and the images appear very natural.

5   Conclusions

We have presented a system for calibration, reconstruction, and plenoptic rendering of scenes from an uncalibrated hand-held video camera. The calibration exploits the proximity of viewpoints by building a viewpoint mesh that spans the viewing sphere around a scene. Once calibrated, the viewpoint mesh can be used for image-based rendering or 3D geometric modeling of the scene. The image-based rendering approach was discussed in detail and a new rendering approach was presented that renders directly from the calibrated viewpoint using depth-compensated image interpolation. The level of geometric approximation is scalable, which allows to adapt the rendering to the given rendering hardware. For the rendering only standard planar projective mapping and Gouraud-weighting is employed which is available in most rendering hardware.

Acknowledgments. We acknowledge support from the German Research Foundation (DFG) under the grant number SFB 603. Thanks to Luc Van Gool for his support.

References

[1] P. Beardsley, P. Torr and A. Zisserman: 3D Model Acquisition from Extended Image Sequences. *ECCV 96*, LNCS 1064, vol.2, pp.683-695.Springer 1996.

[2] P. Debevec, Y. Yu, G. Borshukov: Efficient View-Dependent Image-Based Rendering with Projective Texture Mapping. Proceedings SIGGRAPH '98, ACM Press, New York, 1998.

[3] L.Falkenhagen: Hierarchical Block-Based Disparity Estimation Considering Neighborhood Constraints. Intern. Workshop on SNHC and 3D Imaging, Rhodes, Greece, Sept. 1997.

[4] O. Faugeras: What can be seen in three dimensions with an uncalibrated stereo rig. *Proc. ECCV'92*, pp.563-578.

[5] S. Gortler, R. Grzeszczuk, R. Szeliski, M. F. Cohen: The Lumigraph. Proceedings SIGGRAPH '96, pp 43–54, ACM Press, New York, 1996.

[6] R. Hartley: Estimation of relative camera positions for uncalibrated cameras. *ECCV'92*, pp.579-587.

[7] R. Koch, M. Pollefeys, and L. Van Gool: Multi Viewpoint Stereo from Uncalibrated Video Sequences. *Proc. ECCV'98*, Freiburg, June 1998.

[8] R. Koch, M. Pollefeys, B. Heigl, L. Van Gool, H. Niemann: Calibration of Handheld Camera Sequences for Plenoptic Modeling. Proc. of ICCV'99, Korfu, Greece, Sept. 1999.

[9] R. Koch, M. Pollefeys and L. Van Gool: Robust Calibration and 3D Geometric Modeling from Large Collections of Uncalibrated Images. Proceedings DAGM'99, Bonn, Sept. 1999.

[10] M. Levoy, P. Hanrahan: Lightfield Rendering. Proceedings SIGGRAPH '96, pp 31–42, ACM Press, New York, 1996.

[11] L. McMillan and G. Bishop, "Plenoptic modeling: An image-based rendering system", *Proc. SIGGRAPH'95*, pp. 39-46, 1995.

[12] M. Pollefeys, R. Koch, M. Vergauwen and L. Van Gool: Metric 3D Surface Reconstruction from Uncalibrated Image Sequences. In: 3D Structure from Multiple Images of Large Scale Environments. LNCS Series Vol. 1506, pp. 139-154. Springer-Verlag, 1998.

[13] M. Pollefeys, R. Koch and L. Van Gool: Self-Calibration and Metric Reconstruction Inspite of Varying and Unknown Intrinsic Camera Parameters. Int. Journal of Computer Vision 32(1), 7-27 (1999), Kluver 1999.

[14] P.H.S. Torr: Motion Segmentation and Outlier Detection. PhD thesis, University of Oxford, UK, 1995.

Recent Progress in Digital Photogrammetric Stereo Cameras and Data Evaluation

Ralf Reulke

German Aerospace Centre (DLR)
Institute for Space Sensor Technology and Planetary Exploration, Berlin, Germany
Ralf.Reulke@dlr.de

Abstract. At the moment, fundamental changes in sensors, platforms, and applications are taking place. Commercial digital camera systems on airborne- and spaceborne platforms are becoming available. This paper describes current activities in sensor development and data processing. The German Aerospace Centre (DLR) has been involved in digital camera experiments for the last 15 years. An example is the satellite sensor MOMS-02, which was successfully flown on the space shuttle D2 mission and later on PRIRODA, a module of the Russian space station MIR. In the last two years the DLR Institute for Space Sensor Technology and Planetary Exploration has been involved in a commercial camera development of the LH-Systems digital three line stereo sensor ADS40. The institute also delivers digital image data from flight campaigns with the digital camera HRSC-A for stereo processing together with the French company ISTAR.

1   Introduction

Today a lot of government agencies, private companies and science institutions make use of airborne and satellite remote sensing products for mapping resources, land use/land cover and for monitoring changing phenomena. Remote sensing, combined with geographic information system technologies, can produce information about current and future resource potentials.

For mapping up to now film-based aerial cameras with traditional techniques have normally been used. The digital workflow starts after film development with the scanning of the film and image processing including stereo visualisation. By using different types of films these cameras can also be used for remote sensing to some extent.

Extensive research and industrial developments within the last 10 years in CCD technology, increasing computer performance and data storage capacity offer the opportunity to replace the film-based aerial camera for many applications and also to improve the quality of the photogrammetric and remote sensing products.

Digital systems are cost saving when used over a longer time period (no film, no photo lab and better automation possibility), the product derivation is time saving (no film development, no scanning and possible automation of the digital

R. Klette et al. (Eds.): Multi-Image Analysis, LNCS 2032, pp. 67–80, 2001.

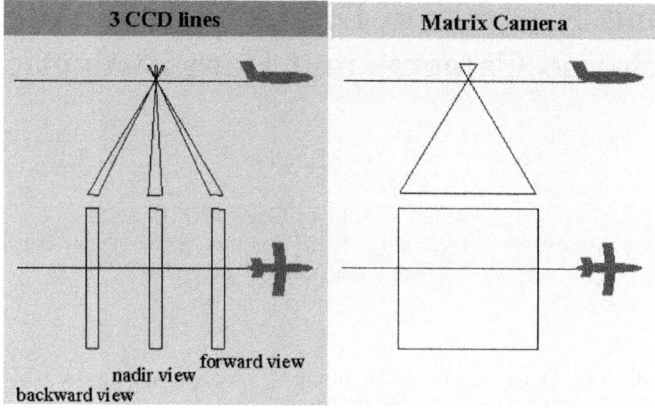

Fig. 1. CCD-line and matrix imaging principle

workflow), and the images can be of higher quality (higher radiometric resolution and accuracy, reproducible colour and in-flight image control).

Digital systems make new applications possible, because of new kinds of information (e.g. multispectral measurements), new products (multispectral information together with digital elevation models) and digital image processing for multimedia applications.

2   Imaging Principles for Airborne Digital Sensors

An airborne digital sensor must provide a large field of view and swath width, high radiometric and geometric resolution and accuracy, multispectral imagery and stereo. This can be realised with area and line CCD-arrays. The different imaging principles are shown in figure 1.

Benefits of the matrix camera are a defined rigid geometry of the image, central perspective image geometry and a simple interfacing to an existing softcopy system. The main disadvantages are that available models have 4k · 7k pixels or less, matrices are extremely expensive, a shutter for matrix readout is necessary and the realisation of true colour needs additional cameras.

The three-line (stereo) concept achieves in views forward from the aircraft, vertically down and looking backward. The imagery from each scan line provides information about the objects on the ground from different viewing angles assembled into strips (figure 2). Attitude disturbances of the airborne platform results in image distortions. With exact knowledge of the flight path an image and also stereo reconstruction of the surface is possible.

The main advantage of the CCD-line camera is the best achievable relation between pixel number in the image and prize, a simple realisation of colour (RGB and NIR) is possible and no shutter is needed. The continuous data stream allows

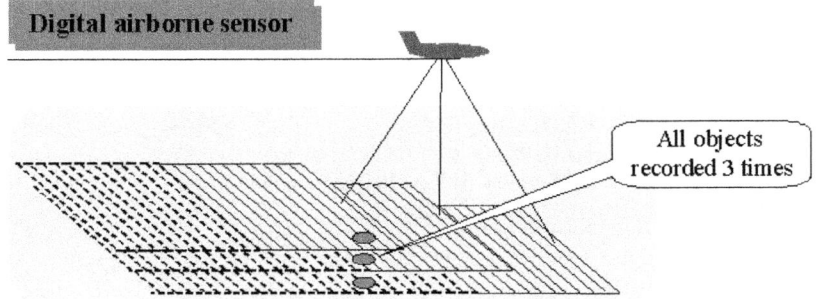

Fig. 2. CCD-line and matrix imaging principle

simple (on-line) correction of defects and PRNU of the CCD as well as a simple data compression. The disadvantages are that accurate exterior orientation is necessary for each measured line and some products are only available after complete stereo processing.

3   Detectors for Digital Mapping Sensors

In the last few month new detectors entered the market and are available now. Table 1 lists available CCD-matrices and Table 2 the CCD-lines.

Both large format CCDs from Philips and Fairchild are only available as experimental examples. They are extremely expensive and not available in larger numbers. Most of the digital imaging systems are based on 4k · 4k and 4k · 7k matrixes.

Large format CCD-matrices have smaller numbers of pixel along one image dimension in comparison to CCD-lines. To fit the resolution/swath width requirements for airborne digital cameras, multiple camera head solutions must be used.

Table 1. Large format CCD-matrices

Manufacturer	Model	Photopixel	Pixelsize $[\mu m^2]$
Kodak	KAF 16800	4096 · 4096	9 · 9
FAIRCHILD		4096 · 4096	15 · 15
Philips	FTF7040	7000 · 4000	12 · 12
Philips		9216 · 7168	12 · 12
FAIRCHILD		9216 · 9216	8.75 · 8.75

Table 2. CCD-lines for high resolution scanner

Manufacturer	Model	Photopixel	Pixelsize $[\mu m^2]$
THOMSON	TH7834	12,000	$6.5 \cdot 6.5$
THOMSON	customise	$2 \cdot 12,000$ (staggered)	$6.5 \cdot 6.5$
EEV	CCD21-40	12.288	$8 \cdot 8$
KODAK	KLI-10203	$3 \cdot 10,200$ (true color)	$7 \cdot 7$
KODAK	KLI-14403	$3 \cdot 14,204$ (true color)	$5 \cdot 5$
FAIRCHILD	CCD194	12,000	$10 \cdot 8.5$
SONY	ILX734K	$3 \cdot 10,500$ (true color)	$8 \cdot 8$

4 High Resolution Airborne Sensors

In this chapter examples of airborne matrix- and line-cameras will be presented.

4.1 Airborne Matrix-Camera

The following system are examples or test systems

IGN-Sensor [1]

IGN (Institut GÈographique National, Paris - France) has been testing its system for several years. The panchromatic system is based on the 4k·4k Kodak matrix CCD. To improve the signal-to-noise ratio the system can be run in a TDI (time delay and integration) mode.

Z/I DMC [2]

DMC (Digital Modular Camera) is the first commercial system, which is based on a matrix detector. The Z/I Imaging Corporation is a joint venture of Intergraph and Carl Zeiss. This system was first announced at the Photogrammetric Week, September 1999. A prototype was exhibited at the ISPRS 2000 conference. Camera description and data workflow can be found in [2].

To reach the resolution/swath width criterion, a four camera head solution was established (figure 3). Four additional cameras at the same platform makes true colour and NIR images possible. The system is based on the Philips 4k · 7k matrix. The ground coverage of this camera is shown in figure 3.

The Z/I approach needs additional calibration procedures and processing to form one image from the four parts with an image size of about 13k · 8k. The camera can also use TDI to improve radiometric image quality. Additional attitude disturbances (roll, pitch and yaw) can influence the geometric image quality in the TDI-mode. Figure 4 shows an example image. The Siemens star-image gives an impression of image quality.

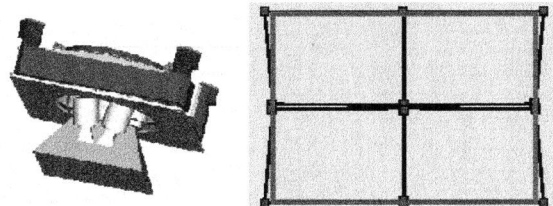

Fig. 3. DMC camera head (left) and ground coverage of the 4 camera-head system (right)

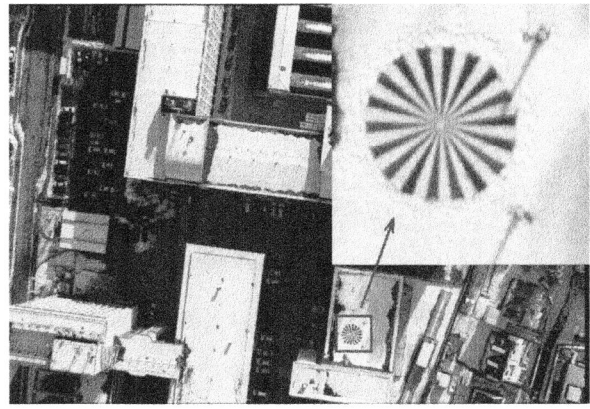

Fig. 4. First example image of the DMC, flight height was 300m and GSD 5 cm

4.2 Airborne Line Scanner

Since the end of the 80's various CCD-line stereo scanner have been flown on airborne platforms. All known systems are summarised with their main parameters in Table 3.

The MEOSS, WAOSS and HRSC systems are mainly designed for operation on spacecraft and only used for system/data testing and evaluation. WAAC and HRSC-A are derived from spacecraft systems (WAOSS, HRSC) for airborne applications. TLC is the only non German system. Most of the systems (except TLC and DPA) were designed and build from or together with DLR. The typical stereo angle is between 20° and 25°. To overcome occlusion effects, e.g. in cities in HRSC and ADC/ADS smaller stereo angles are implemented. In the DPA and ADS40 panchromatic stereo lines consist of two lines. DPA is a solution with two optics, a three line focal plate with 6k CCD lines in each camera, and the ADS stereo line are staggered arrays. In the following WAAC, HRSC and ADS40 will explained more in detail.

Table 3. Large format CCD-matrices

System	Focal-length	Pixels	FOV	Stereo-angle	Bit's	GSD/Swath/Height
MEOSS	61.6 mm	3236	30°	23.5°	8 bit	2m/6.4km/11km
WAOSS	21.7 mm	5184	80°	25°	11 bit	1m/5km/3km
DPA	80 mm	2·6,000	74°	25°	8 bit	25cm/3km/2km
WAAC	21.7 mm	5185	80°	25°	11 bit	1m/5km/3km
TLS	38.4 mm	7500	83°	21.5°	10 bit	10cm/750m/500m
HRSC-A	175 mm	5184	12°	18.9°, 12.8°	8 bit	12cm/620m/3km
ADC-EM	80 mm	12,000	52°	17°, 25°	12 bit	25cm/3km/3km
ADS40	62.5 mm	2·12,000	64°	17°, 25°	12 bit	12.5cm/3km/3km

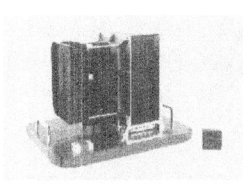 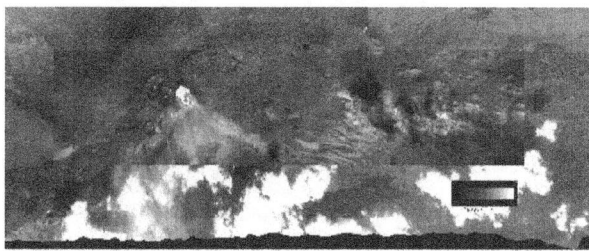

Fig. 5. WAAC (left), Multisensor example (right): WAAC and DAIS (infrared channel)

WAOSS / WAAC [3]

WAOSS (Wide Angle Optoelectronic Stereo Scanner) was a part of the imaging payload for the Mars 96 mission [Alberts, 1996], which failed in November 1996. This camera was mainly designed for medium and large scale observation. Therefore the camera's field of view is 80°. WAAC (Wide Angle Airborne Scanner) is a modified airborne instrument. The camera has some outstanding features:

- Before the on-line compression all necessary correction of PRNU (pixel response non-uniformity) and shading effects are corrected.
- WAOSS/WAAC is the first imaging system, which provides more than 8 bit.
- It is the smallest and most lightweight system in comparison to all other scanners (about 4.5 kg for WAAC).

Swath width and GSD are appropriate for multisensor applications. As an example, a joint flight together with the hyperspectral imaging spectrometer DAIS is shown in figure 5.

Background image are orthorectified WAAC data merged with the thermal infrared channel of the DAIS. This example is a flight over the volcano Aetna, Italy.

Fig. 6. HRSC (left), HRSC image from the Reichstag, Berlin (right)

HRSC [4]

HRSC (High Resolution Stereo Scanner) has five stereo lines. In addition to the nadir line, two pairs of forward/backward lines with different stereo angles and four additional multispectral lines are assembled on the focal plate. Like WAOSS, HRSC was a part of the imaging payload of the Mars96 mission and was first flown on an airborne platform in 1997.

HRSC is the first system which worked operationally. Together with the French ISTAR company city models were derived from digital airborne data.

The LH-System ADS40 [5]

The ADS40 is the first commercially available digital airborne stereo scanner and is a joint development between LH Systems and the German Aerospace Centre, DLR. This system is a real alternative to the familiar aerial film-based camera for a spatial resolution range (Ground Sample Distance) between 10 cm and 1 m.

The camera has three panchromatic CCD lines of 2·12,000 pixels each, staggered by 3.25 mm and four multispectral CCD lines of 12,000 pixels each. Panchromatic image strips can therefore have more than 20,000 pixels in line direction and are comparable to the performance of aerial film-based camera for this application range. Imaging principles and resolution investigations for this staggered line approach can be found in [6].

The colour design of the camera was focused on multispectral applications. True colour must be derived from the measurements of multispectral lines. Contrary to all other CCD-line scanners the RGB colour lines are optically superimposed during the flight using a special dichroic beamsplitter. True colour images can be derived directly from the measured data. The near infrared channels are slightly offset with respect to the panchromatic nadir CCD lines. The following table shows the parameters of ADS40 more in detail.

Table 4. Large format CCD-matrices

	Photogrammetric Lines	Spectral Lines
Focal Length, f	62.5 mm	62.5 mm
FOV (Across the Track)	64°	64°
Number of CCD- Lines	3	4
Elements per CCD- Line	2 · 12,000	12,000
Stereo Angle		
Forward-Nadir	26°	
Backward-Nadir	16°	
Forward-Backward	42°	
Dynamic Range	12 bit	12 bit
Radiometric Resolution	8 bit	8 bit
Flight Height	3000 m	
Ground Sample Distance	16 cm	32 cm
Swath Width 3000 m		
Data Compression Factor	2...5	2...5
Data Compression Method	JPEG, Loss Less	JPEG, Loss Less
Output Data Rate	12...60 MWord/s	6...30MWord/s
Mass Memory for one hour	≤ 200 Gbyte	≤ 100 Gbyte

The main features of the ADS40 are the staggered lines for the panchromatic stereo lines to achieve both requirements: Small ground sample distance and large swath width. The effect of staggering is shown in figure 7. The left image shows the image with a 12k linear sensor which corresponds to 6.5 mm and a ground sampling distance of about 20 cm (resampled to 10 cm). Because of the optics-limited frequency of about 150 lp/mm, aliasing effects are visible. The right image shows the result of the processed 12k staggered sensor, resampled to 10 cm. The data rate is fourfold. In this image no aliasing effects are visible and the image has a visually better resolution. The Siemens star image does not change significantly, because this test chart measures the MTF of the imaging system.

The following images shows the effect of radiometric zoom. The left image shows a balanced radiometry as a reference. In contradiction to the left image the right image is overdriving. In the shadowed part of the quadrangle structures can be differentiate, which are not visible in the left. This is a new possibility of the CCD cameras, which have a much better radiometry than film-based systems.

Line scanner cameras are sensitive to attitude disturbances of the platform. The waveform of the building corner is a result of the aircraft movement. The exact measurement of the aircraft's attitude allows a correction of this effect. This effect and the correction is shown in figure 9.

Fig. 7. ADS40 (left), testchart unsteggered and staggered (right)

 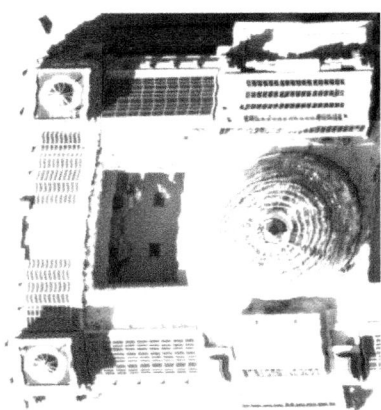

Fig. 8. Effect of radiometric zoom (Reichstag, Berlin)

5   High Resolution Imaging Sensors on Satellite Platforms

These sensors are line sensors. Because of the extreme speed of the spacecraft (ca. 7 km/s) the cycle time of the camera's panchromatic channel must be between 0.1 ms and 0.2 ms. To overcome radiometric problems (especially for multispectral channels) TDI-lines are used. Time delay and integrating sensors (TDI) for linear imaging are area sensors. The vertical CCD registers are clocked to ensure that the charge packets are transferred at the same rate and in the same direction as the image. This ensures that the signal charge building up in the CCD remains aligned under the same part of the image. In this way, the image signal can be integrated for much longer and this enhances the signal-to-noise ratio. The following table shows typical technical parameters of high resolution satellite sensors:

Fig. 9. Attitude correction of line scanner airborne imagery

Table 5. Typical technical parameters of high resolution satellite snsors

Ground Sample Distance	1 m
Focal Length	up to 10 m
Stereo Mode	in-track and/or across-track
Swath Width	6 to 36 km
Altitude	460 to 680 kilometers
Orbit time	ca. 100 minutes
Orbit type	sun-synchronous
Repetition Rate	1 to 4 days

The first commercial system for earth resource mapping was SPOT. The SPOT satellite Earth Observation System was designed by the CNES (Centre National d'Etudes Spatiales), France, and was developed with the participation of Sweden and Belgium. The SPOT system has been operational for more than ten years. SPOT 1 was launched on 22 February 1986 and was withdrawn from active service on 31 December 1990. SPOT 2 was launched on 22 January 1990 and is still operational. SPOT 3 was launched on 26 September 1993. An accident on 14 November, 1996 disabled SPOT 3. Last satellite was SPOT 4, which was launched 1998. SPOT 5 is to be launched in late 2002. Ground sample distance of SPOT 1-4 is 10 m. With SPOT 5 a GSD of about 2.5 m will be reached. Apart from this simple nadir mapping stereo views are also possible. Oblique viewing of the SPOT system makes it possible to produce stereo pairs by combining two images of the same area acquired on different dates and at different angles (across-track stereo). Figure 10 shows this approach.

The main disadvantage of this approach is that the investigated region is viewed under different illumination and weather conditions.

Another possibility is the three line principle, which was described for airborne sensors (in-track stereo). Because of the long focal length a single focal

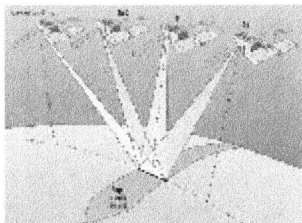

Fig. 10. Stereoscopy with oblique viewing

plane is impossible. Therefore three cameras are necessary and makes the system large and expensive. An example of this approach is MOMS-02 (Modularer Optoelektronischer Multispektraler Stereoscanner), which was flown on the D2 shuttle mission 1993 and the MIR space station (since 1996).

The third possibility is a sensor-tilt in and across track direction. The system first scans the patch in the forward view and after obtaining this measurement the mirror tilts to another view to measure the same patch under a different view angle.

Since 1999 a new era of spaceborne imaging systems with commercial systems, which have a GSD of better than 1 m have started to be used. The first successful system was IKONOS [7]. Table 6 summarises these satellites. An interesting point is that the Indian IRS 1C/D system, which has been operational since 1995, was the imaging system with the highest resolution up to the launch of IKONOS.

Table 6. High resolution satellite sensors

System	Launch	Company	Stereo	GSD/Swath/Height	Comment
IRS-1C/D	1995	India (Gov)	Across	5m/70km/817km	In operation
EarlyBird	1997	Earthwatch	In-/across	3m/3km/600km	Failed
Ikonos	1998	Space Imaging	In-/across	1m/11km/681km	Failed
Ikonos	1999	Space Imaging	In-/across	1m/11km/681km	In operation
QuickBird	2000	Earthwatch	In-/across	1m/22km/600km	Not launched
OrbView	2000	Orbimage	In-/across	1m/8km/470km	Not launched

The first real 1m satellite is IKONOS. Therefore this system should be explained more in detail. The digital camera system was designed and built by Eastman Kodak Company, Rochester, NY. Each camera can see objects less than one meter square on the ground. This capability from an orbital altitude of 680 km represents a significant increase in image resolution over any other commercial remote sensing satellite system. Figure 11 displays a part of the first image of IKONOS of the Washington memorial.

Fig. 11. First image of IKONOS, the Washington memorial

The camera system of the IKONOS satellite is able to collect simultaneously panchromatic (grey-scale) imagery with one-meter resolution and multispectral data (red, green, blue, and near infrared) with four-meter resolution, across an 11 km swath of the Earth's surface. The panchromatic imagery will provide highly accurate Earth imagery, enabling geographic information system (GIS) users to generate precision maps. The multispectral data will have a variety of scientific applications, including environmental and agricultural monitoring.

Airborne and spaceborne sensors complement each other. Spaceborne imagery can not replace airborne imagery, because of limitations in ground resolution and flexibility in the "orbit" choice. Certainly with spaceborne sensors it is possible to map regions which are not accessible by aeroplane.

6 Multispectral Channels of Airborne and Spaceborne Scanners

Multispectral channels, in addition to the stereo channels, are incorporated in the panchromatic and stereo channels. Multispectral imagery with high spatial resolution opens new remote sensing capabilities. Data fusion between the channels and other sensors together with additional digital elevation models derived from panchromatic stereo data create new scientific opportunities. Besides multispectral applications, true colour images become more important for photogrammetric applications and are to be derived from colour processed multispectral images.

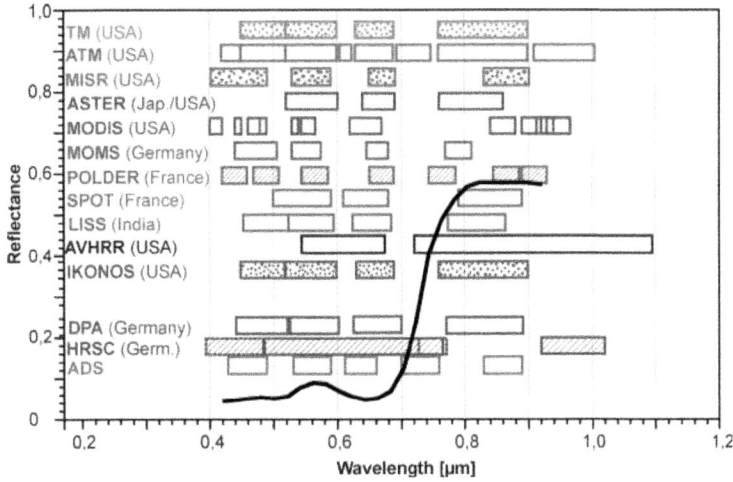

Fig. 12. Spectral channels of selected airborne and spaceborne instruments

When choosing multispectral bands narrow band filters on interesting spectral features are necessary. Therefore true colour images have to be derived from the multispectral channels. Figure 12 shows the spectral channels of selected airborne and spaceborne instruments. For comparison a vegetation reflection curve is visualise. TM (Thematic Mapper) is the prototype for all multispectral systems. The upper block (from TM to IKONOS) are spaceborne systems. Except IKONOS all systems are only multispectral systems. DPA, HRSC and ADS are airborne systems.

7   Photogrammetric and Cartographic Data Processing

The photogrammetric processing includes:

- digital image matching
- digital surface model (DSM) and orthoimage generation
- mosaicing and merging of multispectral data

For geo-referencing, a combined INS and differential GPS based data processing routine is necessary. The main problem for processing stereo line scanner images is that all image processing tasks (e.g. matching, etc.) are possible only in attitude corrected images. On the other hand, internal calibration and external orientation information is connected with the original disturbed dataset. Therefore each pixel needs a relation between the corrected and the disturbed image. Another problem is the matching in a non-epipolar geometry in the attitude corrected images where disparities in both image directions occur.

The first step is a combination of a hierarchical based feature and area based matching. The digital surface model (DSM) is derived from multiple ray intersections. Based on the DSM information, various cartographic products can be generated. The results are

- 3 dimensional images and maps
- True colour and multispectral images
- Relief maps of the target area
- Video animation of virtual flights over the target area

A completely automatic photogrammetric and cartographic processing is possible with existing stereo workstations. Adaptations for different scanner models are possible.

8   Conclusions

The article gives an overview about the existing high resolution imaging systems on spaceborne and airborne platforms. Beside test and research systems like MOMS, commercial systems are also in operation. Since August 1999 image data of the high resolution spaceborne system IKONOS has been available. At the ISPRS2000 conference in July 2000 in Amsterdam, the airborne scanner ADS40 was introduced. The change into the digital domain from image generation over image processing to data evaluation (GIS) is completed. Additional colour channels allow true colour images and multispectral data evaluation.

References

[1] Ch. Thom, J-P. Souchon; The IGN Digital Camera System; Proceedings of the OEEPE-Workshop 1999; pp. 91

[2] A. Hinz, C. D-rstel, H. Heier; Digital Modular Camera: System Concept and Data Processing Workflow; International Archives of Photogrammetry and Remote Sensing. Vol. XXXIII, Part B2. Amsterdam 2000; pp. 164

[3] R. Sandau, A. Eckardt; The Stereo Camera Family WAOSS/WAAC for Spaceborne / Airborne Applications; International Archives of Photogrammetry and Remote Sensing, Vol. XXXI, part B1, Vienna 1996, pp. 170

[4] J. Albertz, H. Ebner, G. Neukum; Camera Experiment on the Mars96 Mission - A Photogrammetric and Cartographic View of the Project, Int. Archives of Photogrammetry, Vol. XXXI, Part B4, Vienna 1996, pp. 58

[5] R. Sandau, B. Braunecker, H. Driescher, A. Eckardt, S. Hilbert, J. Hutton, W. Kirchofer, E. Lithopoulos, R. Reulke, S. Wicki; Design Principles of the LH SYSTEMS ADS40 Airborne Digital Sensor; International Archives of Photogrammetry and Remote Sensing. Vol. XXXIII, Part B1. Amsterdam 2000; pp.258ff

[6] H. Jahn, R. Reulke; Staggered Line Arrays in Pushbroom Cameras: Theory and Application, International Archives of Photogrammetry and Remote Sensing. Vol. XXXIII, Part B1. Amsterdam 2000; pp.164-172

[7] F. Gerlach; Characteristics of Space Imaging's One-Meter Resolution Satellite Imagery Products; International Archives of Photogrammetry and Remote Sensing. Vol. XXXIII, Part B1. Amsterdam 2000; pp. 128

Classification and Characterization of Image Acquisition for 3D Scene Visualization and Reconstruction Applications

Shou Kang Wei, Fay Huang, and Reinhard Klette

CITR, Computer Science Department, The University of Auckland,
Tamaki Campus, Auckland, New Zealand
{shoukang,fay,reinhard}@citr.auckland.ac.nz

Abstract. This paper discusses the techniques of image acquisition for 3D scene visualization and reconstruction applications (3DSVR). The existing image acquisition approaches in 3DSVR applications are briefly reviewed. There are still lacks of studies about what principles are essential in the design and how we can characterize the limitations of an image acquisition model in a formal way. This paper addresses some of the main characteristics of existing image acquisition approaches, summarized through a classification scheme and illustrated with many examples. The results of the classification lead to general characterizations in establishing the notions (basic components) for design, analysis and assessment of image acquisition models. The notions introduced include: focal set, receptor set, reflector set etc. The formal definitions of the notions and the exploration of relationships among the components are given. Various examples are provided for demonstrating the flexibility and compactness in characterizing different types of image acquisition models such as concentric, polycentric, cataoptrical panoramas etc. The observations, important issues, and future directions from this study are also elaborated.

1 Introduction

Image acquisition is a process for obtaining data from real 3D scenes. The role of the image acquisition process has critical impacts on subsequent processes in 3D scene visualization and reconstruction (3DSVR) applications. The applications using panoramic images include, for instance, stereoscopic visualization [8,24, 36], stereo reconstruction [12,14,21,33,37], image-based rendering [4,13,19,26], localization, route planning or obstacle detection in robot-navigation [12,38].

An *image acquisition model* defines image-acquiring components and their usages in the image acquisition process for a particular application. The specifications of image acquisition models typically differ between different applications except of some basic characterizations which will be discussed later. A scenario for developing an image acquisition model may go through the following steps:

R. Klette et al. (Eds.): Multi-Image Analysis, LNCS 2032, pp. 81–92, 2001.

(1) list the requirements and specifications of the application under investigation; (2) sketch the problem(s) and possible solution(s) or approaches; (3) design an image acquisition model, involving pose planning, sensor design, illumination conditioning etc., which may lead to solutions and satisfaction of practical constraints; (4) implement and test the image acquisition model.

Conceptually, the closer the relation between the data acquired and the outcome expected in a 3DSVR application, the simpler the processes involved as well as the better the performance. QuicktimeVR [4] serves as a good example. However in reality physical constraints (such as temporal and spatial factors) and practical issues (e.g. cost, availability) that complicate the design and the realization of an image acquisition model for a 3DSVR application. Therefore it is important to study the constraints and issues as well as how they influence the design of image acquisition models.

Since different image acquisition models result into different subsequent processes providing different characteristics in respect to both geometrical and photometrical analysis, it is very risky developing 3DSVR applications without serious considerations of the suitability of the image data acquired for use in the intended application. Failures to assess the data may not only cause an unnecessary complexity to the subsequent processes but even lead to an inability to fulfill the requirements of the application.

Some researchers see a need for designing new image acquisition system(s) especially for 3DSVR applications. The point of view is that the traditional image acquisition models may/should not be able to serve all kinds of tasks in 3DSVR applications. Researchers in the image-based rendering community have also noticed this need/inadequacy. They reconfigured some components from the traditional image acquisition models (e.g. a pinhole projection model with a pre-defined camera motion) and received some interesting results (i.e. novel view generations without 3D reconstructions) [5,18,26,31,35]. However there are still lacks of studies about what principles are essential in the design and how we can characterize the limitations of an image acquisition model in a formal way.

For being able to design, analyze and assess an image acquisition model, we need to establish the building-blocks (basic components) which construct the architecture of image acquisition models. In the next section, the classification of recent image acquisition approaches for 3DSVR applications is presented. The results of the classification characterize the existing image acquisition approaches and lead to general characterizations in Section 3 where we introduce some basic/general components/notions for design, analysis and assessment of image acquisition models. The observations, important issues, and future directions from this study are addressed in the conclusion.

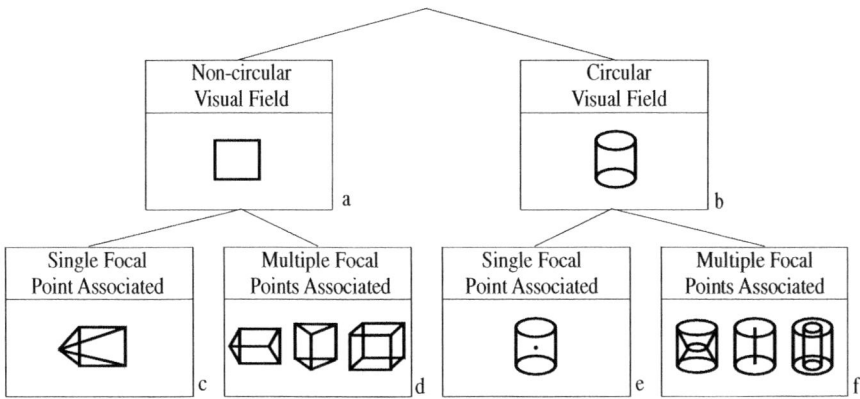

Fig. 1. The examples of the first two classification rules: visual field and focal points associated with each image. See text for details.

2   Classification

For simplicity, this paper mainly focuses on passive imaging[1] and leaves the factors introduced by active imaging to be incorporated later. To avoid the problems where the resulting classification becomes untraceable or lost in excessive detail, four binary classification rules are used. They are defined as follows:

Visual field: Circular/Non-circular
Focal point(s) associated with each image: Single/Multiple
Acquiring time: Different/Same
Acquiring pose: Different/Same

In Fig.1 the examples of the intermediate classes from the first two classification rules are depicted. A planar image and a cylindrical image (Fig.1 a and b) are examples for the non-circular and the circular visual field classes. A pinhole projection model (Fig.1 c) is the example for the class of a planar image associated with a single focal point. For the class of a planar image associated with multiple focal points the three examples (Fig.1 d) are: each image column associates with a focal point (left); each image row associates with a focal point (middle); and each image pixel associates with a focal point (i.e. orthographic projection) (right). A central-projection panorama (Fig.1 e) is the example for the class of a cylindrical image associated with a single focal point. For the class of a cylindrical image associated with multiple focal points the three examples (Fig.1 f) are: each image column associates with a focal point (left); each image

---

[1] The terms, *active imaging* and *passive imaging*, are frequently used to distinguish whether or not equipment (such as lighting device or laser) is acting on the physical scene while carrying out image acquisition [16].

row associates with a focal point (middle); and each image pixel associates with a focal point (right).

Note that the temporal classification rule may be used in a flexible way, that is, the acquiring time can be conceptually rather than physically the same. For example, a binocular stereo pair, used in stereo matching, acquired in a static scene under an almost constant illumination condition can be regarded conceptually as having the same acquiring time. For the acquiring pose classification rule, two other characteristics, translation and rotation, may be used to further specify the possible classes.

Now let us look at some examples of the existing image acquisition approaches in the different classes. The conditions of each class are specified in Tab.1 A typical example for class 1 is a video camera acquiring a video sequence. A video surveillance system is an example for class 2 because it fixes the image acquisition system at a particular place. In class 3, the binocular stereo pair acquisition is a typical example. More recently approaches such as in light field [18] and Lumigraph [5] also fall into class 3, where both approaches arrange the poses of a pinhole camera to a planar grid layout and assume a constant acquiring time for their applications. Re-sampling the acquired image data, which are parameterized into a 4D function, generates a novel view for use in their visualization applications. Other examples in class 3 are [2,15,17,20,28,30]. In class 4, single still image capturing, currently the most common image acquisition model, serves as an example.

In class 5, the image acquisition model used in three light-sources photometric stereo method [16] for 3D reconstruction is one of the examples, where the orthographic projection (non-circular visual field and multiple focal centers); with only one of light sources on for each image capturing (different acquiring time); and multiple views (different acquiring poses) for a full 3D reconstruction are used. Another example in class 5 is reported in [26]. Considering 2.5D reconstruction of a 3D scene from a single viewing pose, a well-known passive approach, depth from de/focusing, is usually adopted. An example of such an approach which falls into class 6 is the multi-focus camera with a coded aperture proposed in [9].

For class 7, an example is a three-line scanner system (pushbroom camera [6] on an airplane) used in the terrain reconstruction or heat-spot sensing [27, 29]. This setup is characterized by (1) non-circular visual field; (2) each image column associates with a focal point, (3) acquiring time is conceptually the same as performing the stereo matching; and (4) the poses of each line-scanner are inherently different.

Now we look at some examples of the approaches with circular visual field. In class 9, there are quite a few systems already developed in research institutes or commercialized in industry [39]. One of the applications for this so-called *dynamic-panorama-video* system is to allow the user to visualize a real scene by virtually walking along a path (where data is acquired) and looking around

Table 1. The 16 proposed classes of image acquisitions for 3D scene visualization and reconstruction applications with their conditions and the selected examples. Note that '[-]' indicates that the authors have not been aware of existing examples; whereas '[*]' means that the class is very common and there are too many examples to be cited here.

Class	Visual Field		Focal Pt. Assoc.		Acq. Time		Acq. Pose		Example
	Non-circ	Circular	Single	Multiple	Diff.	Same	Diff.	Same	
1	√		√		√		√		[*]
2	√		√		√			√	[*]
3	√		√			√	√		[2,5,15,17,18, 20,28,30]
4	√		√			√		√	[*]
5	√			√	√		√		[16,26]
6	√			√	√			√	[9]
7	√			√		√	√		[6,27,29]
8	√			√		√		√	[*]
9		√	√		√		√		[39]
10		√	√		√			√	[40]
11		√	√			√	√		[3,7,8,14,19,22, 23,34]
12		√	√			√		√	[4]
13		√		√	√		√		[-]
14		√		√	√			√	[-]
15		√		√		√	√		[12,10,11,24, 25,31,32,33,36]
16		√		√		√		√	[-]

360° from any point in the path[2]. For instance, to visualize the interior of a building (i.e. walking through corridor, lobby, rooms, etc), the path is planed and a robot (on which a dynamic-panorama-video system is installed) implements the image acquisition. An interactive explorer[3] needs to be developed, providing an interface for the user to explore the interior of a building. Some image-based rendering techniques can be used to interpolate the missing data (i.e. gaps/holes in synthesized image) or extrapolate the acquired data to some extent such that the viewing space can be expanded to a certain degree.

The applications (e.g. environmental study; surveillance, etc) requiring a panoramic-video system to be fixed at one position for a long period of time are members of class 10 (i.e. *static-panorama-video* system). For example, a system was deployed on the bank of a lake (West-lake, China) for monitoring environmental change and acquiring 360° panorama continuously for the whole year in 1998. Some examples of the surveillance application can be found in [40].

---

[2] The density of view points on a path depends on the frame rate of the video camera and the speed of the movement during the image acquisition.

[3] A software that synthesizes a view (image) via resampling the acquired data according to current user's viewing condition.

A well-known example for a single-focal-point panorama is QuickTimeVR [4] from Apple Inc., which falls into class 12. Using multiple single-focal-point panoramas to reconstruct a 3D scene, class 11, S.B. Kang and R. Szeliski reported their results in [14]. Other similar examples are [8,19,22]. The families of cataoptrical panorama used for 3D scene reconstruction [3,7,23,34] mostly belong to class 11, except for the configuration: pinhole projection model with a spherical mirror in which case it goes to class 15.

H. Ishiguro et al. first proposed an image acquisition model that is able to produce multiple panoramas by a single swiveling of a pinhole-projection camera, where each panorama is associated with multiple focal points. It is of class 15. The model was created for the 3D reconstruction of an indoor environment. Their approach reported in 1992 in [12] already details essential features of the image acquisition model. The modifications and extensions of their model have been discussed by other works such as [10,24,31,32,33]. Other examples of this class are [25,36].

3   Characterization

In this section we introduce some notions in an abstract level for characterizing the essential components of image acquisition models used in 3DSVR applications. The notions include *focal set* $\mathcal{F}$, *receptor set* $\mathcal{S}$, *projection-ray set* $\mathcal{U}$, *reflector set* $\mathcal{R}$, *reflected-ray set* $\mathcal{V}$, plus temporal and spatial factors. The formal definitions are given followed by the exploration of relationships among the components. Various examples are provided for demonstrating the flexibility and compactness in characterizing different types of image acquisition models.

Definition 1. A *focal set* $\mathcal{F}$ is a non-empty (finite) set of focal points in 3D space. A focal point, an element of $\mathcal{F}$, can be represented as a 3-vector in $\mathbb{R}^3$.

Definition 2. A *receptor set* $\mathcal{S}$ is a non-empty infinite or finite set of receptors (photon-sensing elements) in 3D space. A receptor, an element of $\mathcal{S}$, can be characterized geometrically as 3-vectors in $\mathbb{R}^3$.

In practice, a focal set $\mathcal{F}$ contains a finite number of focal points, but a receptor set $\mathcal{S}$ may either have an infinite or finite number of receptors depending on the type of photon-sensing device used. For instance, the radiational film (negative) is regarded as containing infinite many photon-sensing elements; and the CCD chip in a digital camera contains only a finite number of photon-sensing elements.

It is convenient to express a collection of points by a supporting geometric primitive such as a straight line, curve, plane, quadratic surface etc. where all of the points lie on. For examples, the pinhole projection model consists of a single focal point (i.e. the cardinality of the focal set is equal to 1 or formally $\#(\mathcal{F}) = 1$) and a set of coplanar receptors. The orthographic projection model consists of a set of coplanar focal points and a set of coplanar receptors. The single-center panoramic image model (e.g. QuickTimeVR) consists of a single focal point and a set of receptors lie on a cylindrical or spherical surface. The multi-perspective panoramic image model consists of a set of focal points on various geometrical forms (such as a vertical straight line, a 2D circular path, a disk, or a cylinder etc.) and a set of receptors lie on a cylinder.

Space is filled with a dense volume of light rays of various intensities. A single light ray with respect to a point in 3D space at one moment of time can be described by seven parameters, that is, three parameters describing the point's location, two parameters describing the ray's emitting angle, one parameter describing the wavelength of the light in the visible spectrum, and one parameter describing the time. A function taking these seven parameters as inputs and outputting a measure of the intensity is called *plenoptical function* [1]. All possible light rays in a specified 3D space and time interval form a *light field*, denoted as $\mathcal{L}$.

The association between focal points in $\mathcal{F}$ and receptors in $\mathcal{S}$ determines a particular proper subset of the light field. For instance, a complete bipartite set of focal and receptor sets is defined as

$$\mathcal{B}_{\mathcal{F} \times \mathcal{S}} = \{(p, q) : p \in \mathcal{F} \text{ and } q \in \mathcal{S}\},$$

where each element (p, q) specifies a light ray passing through the point p and striking on point q. Note that a complete bipartite set of focal and receptor sets is a proper subset of the light field (i.e. $\mathcal{B}_{\mathcal{F} \times \mathcal{S}} \subset \mathcal{L}$).

Definition 3. A *focal-to-receptor association rule* defines an association between a focal point and a receptor, where a receptor is said to be associated with a focal point if and only if any light ray which is incident with the receptor passes through the focal point.

Each image acquisition model has it's own association rule for the focal and receptor sets. Sometimes, a single rule is not enough to specify complicate associating conditions between the two sets, thus a list of association rules is required. A pair of elements satisfies a list of association rules if and only if the pair satisfies each individual association rule.

Definition 4. A *projection-ray set* $\mathcal{U}$ is a non-empty subset of the complete bipartite set of focal and receptor sets (i.e. $\mathcal{U} \subseteq \mathcal{B}_{\mathcal{F} \times \mathcal{S}} \subset \mathcal{L}$), which satisfies the following conditions:

1. It holds $(p, q) \in \mathcal{U}$ if and only if (p, q) satisfies a (list of) pre-defined association rule(s);
2. For every $p \in \mathcal{F}$, there is at least a $q \in \mathcal{S}$ such that $(p, q) \in \mathcal{U}$;
3. For every $q \in \mathcal{S}$, there is at least a $p \in \mathcal{F}$ such that $(p, q) \in \mathcal{U}$.

For example, the projection-ray set $\mathcal{U}$ of the traditional pinhole projection model is the complete bipartite set of focal and receptor sets, because there is only a single focal point and every receptor defines a unique projection-ray through the focal point. Moreover, the projection-ray set in this case is a proper subset of the *pencil*[4] of rays at that focal point.

The projection-ray set $\mathcal{U}$ of a multi-perspective panoramic image acquisition model [11,24,32] is a subset of the complete bipartite set of focal and receptor sets and can be characterized formally as follows. The focal points in $\mathcal{F}$ are an ordered finite sequence, $p_1, p_2, \ldots, p_n$, which all lie on a 1D circular path in 3D space. The set of receptors form a uniform (orthogonal) 2D grid and lie on a 2D cylindrical surface that is co-axial to the circular path of the focal points. The number of columns of the grid is equal to n. The association rules determining whether (p, q) belongs to the projection-ray set $\mathcal{U}$ are as follows:

1. All $q \in \mathcal{S}$ which belong to the same column must be assigned to an unique $p_i \in \mathcal{F}$.
2. There is an ordered one-to-one mapping between the focal points $p_i \in \mathcal{F}$ and the columns of the grid. In other words, the columns of the grid, either counterclockwise or clockwise, may be indexed as $c_1, c_2, \ldots, c_n$ such that every $q \in c_i$ is mapped to $p_i, i \in [1..n]$.

Definition 5. A *reflector set* $\mathcal{R}$ is a set of reflectors' surface equations, usually a set of first or second order continuous and differentiable surfaces in 3D space.

A reflector set, e.g. mirror(s), is used to characterize how light rays can be captured indirectly by the receptors. For instance, a hyperbolic mirror is used in conjunction with the pinhole projection model for acquiring a wide visual field of a scene (e.g. 360° panorama). Similarly, with the orthographic projection model, the parabolic mirror is adopted. Such type of image acquisition model allows that all the reflected projection rays intersect at the focus of the hyperboloid [3,34], which possess a simple computational model which supports possible 3DSVR applications.

Let $\mathcal{P}(\mathcal{R})$ denote the power set of the reflector set. Define a geometrical transformation T as follows:

$$T : \mathcal{U} \times \mathcal{P}(\mathcal{R}) \to \mathcal{A},$$
$$((p, q), s) \mapsto (p', q'),$$

where $\mathcal{A}$ is a non-empty subset of the light felid. The element of $\mathcal{A}$, a light ray, is represented by a pair of points, denoted as (p', q'), specifying its location and the orientation. The transformation T is a function which transforms a projection ray with respect to an element of $\mathcal{P}(\mathcal{R})$ to a reflected ray.

Definition 6. A *reflected-ray set* $\mathcal{V}$ is a non-empty set of light rays, which is a subset of the light field. Formally,

$$\mathcal{V} = \{T((p, q), s) : (p, q) \in \mathcal{U}\},$$

where s is one particular element of the power set of a reflector set (i.e. $s \in \mathcal{P}(\mathcal{R})$).

---

[4] The set of all rays passing through one point in space is called a *pencil*.

Note that, when a transformation of a projection-ray set takes place, only one element of $\mathcal{P}(\mathcal{R})$ is used. In particular, as $\emptyset \in \mathcal{P}(\mathcal{R})$ is chosen, the resulting reflected-ray set is identical to the original projection-ray set. When the number of elements of the chosen s is more than one, the transformation behaves like ray-tracing.

A single projection-ray set (or a reflected-ray set - we omit to repeat this in the following) is referred to as a set of light rays defined by an image acquisition model at a moment of time and a specific location. Two factors are added to characterize multiple projection-ray sets. The temporal factor describes the acquisition time, and the spatial factor describes the pose of the model. A collection of (or multiple) projection-ray sets is denoted as $\{\mathcal{U}_{t,\rho}\}$, where t and ρ indicating time and pose, respectively. Multiple images, i.e. a collection of projection-ray sets acquired at different times or poses $\{\mathcal{U}_{t,\rho}\}$, are a subset of the light field.

Some 3DSVR applications use only a single projection-ray set to approximate a complete light field in a restricted viewing zone [4,31] and some require multiple images in order to perform special tasks such as depth from stereo. Regardless of the time factor, to acquire a complete light field of a medium-to-large scale space is already known to be very difficult, or say, almost impossible to achieve based on the technology available to date. Usually, a few sampled projection-ray sets are acquired for approximating a complete light field. Due to the nature of scene complexity, the selection of a set of optimal projection-ray samples become an important factor to determine the quality of the approximation of a complete light field of a 3D scene.

4   Conclusions

This paper discusses image acquisition approaches for 3D scene visualization and reconstruction applications. The importance of the role of image acquisition and the impacts to the subsequent processes in developing a 3DSVR application are addressed. It may be risky and inappropriate both in research and developments of 3DSVR applications if we do not consider the possibility that other/better image acquisition models might exist.

We designed and applied a classification scheme for the existing image acquisition approaches for 3DSVR applications. Some existing image acquisition approaches in 3DSVR applications are briefly reviewed. The results of the classification lead to general characterizations in establishing notions (basic components) for design, analysis and assessment of image acquisition models.

In future we will look further into the relationship between applications and image acquisition models. Given some conditions with respect to a particular 3DSVR application: (1) what is the capability and limitation of an image acquisition model; and (2) what criteria should be used to evaluate the developed image acquisition model in respect to its application?

An extension of this study could develop into an approach that automatically generates (optimal) solution(s) of image acquisition models satisfying the image acquisition requirements from a 3DSVR application. The success of the model has direct practical benefits for 3DSVR applications. With respect to a theoretical aspect[5] it helps us to understand what image acquisition can support a 3DSVR application (capability analysis) as well as how far the support may go (limitation analysis).

References

[1] E.H. Adelson, J.R. Bergen: The plenoptic function and the elements of early vision. *Computational Models of Visual Proceeding*, Cambridge, Massachusetts, USA (March 1991) pp. 3–20.

[2] S. Avidan, A. Shashua: Novel view synthesis in tensor space. *Proc. CVPR97*, San Juan, Puerto Rico (June 1997) pp. 1034–1040.

[3] S. Baker, S.K. Nayar: A theory of single-viewpoint catadioptric image formation. *IJCV* **35**(2) (November 1999) pp. 1–22.

[4] S. E. Chen: QuickTimeVR - an image-based approach to virtual environment navigation. *Proc. SIGGRAPH'95*, Los Angeles, California, USA (August 1995) pp. 29–38.

[5] S.J. Gortler, R. Grzeszczuk, R. Szeliski, M.F. Cohen: The lumigraph. *Proc. SIGGRAPH'96*, New Orleans, Louisiana, USA (August 1996) pp. 43–54.

[6] R. Gupta, R.I. Hartley: Linear pushbroom cameras. *PAMI* **19**(9) (September 1997) pp. 963–975.

[7] J. Gluckman, S.K. Nayar, K.J. Thorek: Real-time panoramic stereo. *Proc. DARPA98*, Monterey, California, USA (November 1998) pp. 299–303.

[8] H.-C. Huang, Y.-P. Hung: Panoramic stereo imaging system with automatic disparity warping and seaming. *GMIP* **60**(3) (May 1998) pp. 196–208.

[9] S. Hiura, T. Matsuyama: Multi-focus camera with coded aperture: real-time depth measurement and its applications. *Proc. CDV-WS98*, Kyoto, Japan (November 1998) pp. 101–118.

[10] F. Huang, T. Pajdla: Epipolar geometry in concentric panoramas. Research Report CTU–CMP–2000–07, Center for Machine Perception, Czech Technical University, Prague, Czech Republic March 2000.

[11] F. Huang, S.-K. Wei, R. Klette: Generalized epipolar curve equation for a polycentric panorama pair. *Proc. IVCNZ'00*, Hamilton, New Zealand (November 2000) pp. 280–285.

[12] H. Ishiguro, M. Yamamoto, S. Tsuji: Omni-directional stereo. *PAMI* **14**(2) (February 1992) pp. 257–262.

[13] S.-B. Kang, P.K. Desikan: Virtual navigation of complex scenes using clusters of cylindrical panoramic images. Technical Report CRL 97/5, Digital Equipment Corporation, Cambridge Research Lab, USA, September 1997.

[14] S.-B. Kang, R. Szeliski: 3-d scene data recovery using omnidirectional multibaseline stereo. *IJCV* **25**(2) (November 1997) pp. 167–183.

[15] K.N. Kutulakos, S. Seitz: A theory of shape by space carving. *Proc. ICCV99*, Corfu, Greece (September 1999) pp. 307–314.

[16] R. Klette, K. Schlüns, A. Koschan: *Computer Vision - Three-Dimensional Data from Images*. Springer, Singapore (1998)

---

[5] The study of image acquisition should be carried out beyond the current technology for the theoretical merit.

[17] S. Laveau, O. Faugeras: 3-d scene representation as a collection of images. *Proc. ICPR94*, Seattle, Washington, USA (June 1994) pp. 689–691.

[18] M. Levoy, P. Hanrahan: Light field rendering. *Proc. SIGGRAPH'96*, New Orleans, Louisiana, USA (August 1996) pp. 31–42.

[19] L. McMillan, G. Bishop: Plenoptic modeling: an image-based rendering system. *Proc. SIGGRAPH'95*, Los Angeles, California, USA (August 1995) pp. 39–46.

[20] W.R. Mark, L. McMillan, G. Bishop: Post-rendering 3d warping. *Proceedings of 1997 Symposium on Interactive 3D Graphics*, Providence, Rhode Island, USA (April 1997) pp. 7–16.

[21] D.W. Murray: Recovering range using virtual multicamera stereo. *CVIU* **61**(2) (March 1995) pp. 285–291.

[22] T. Matsuyama, T. Wada: Cooperative distributed vision - dynamic integration of visual perception, action, and communication. *Proc. CDV-WS98*, Kyoto, Japan (November 1998) pp. 1–40.

[23] M. Ollis, H. Herman, S. Singh: *Analysis and Design of Panoramic Stereo Vision Using Equi-Angular Pixel Cameras*. Technical Report CMU-RI-TR-99-04, The Robotics Institute, Carnegie Mellon University, Pittsburgh, USA 1999

[24] S. Peleg, M. Ben-Ezra: Stereo panorama with a single camera. *Proc. CVPR99*, Fort Collins, Colorado, USA (June 1999) pp. 395–401.

[25] S. Peleg, Y. Pritch, M. Ben-Ezra: Cameras for stereo panoramic imaging. *Proc. CVPR00*, Hilton Head Island (June 2000) pp. 208-214.

[26] P. Rademacher, G. Bishop: Multiple-center-of-projection images. *Proc. SIGGRAPH'98*, Los Angeles, California, USA (August 1998) pp. 199–206.

[27] R. Reulke, M. Scheel: CCD-line digital imager for photogrammetry in architecture. *Int. Archives of Photogrammetry and Remote Sensing* **XXXII**(5C1B), (1997) pp. 195–201.

[28] S. Seitz, C. Dyer: Photorealistic scene reconstruction by space coloring. *Proc. CVPR97*, San Juan, Puerto Rico, USA (June 1997) pp. 1067-1073.

[29] R. Sandau, A. Eckardt: The stereo camera family WAOSS/WAAC for space-borne/airborne applications. *Int.Archives of Photogrammetry and Remote Sensing* **XXXI**(B1), (1996) pp. 170–175.

[30] J.W. Shade, S.J. Gortler, L.-W. He, R. Szeliski: Layered depth images. *Proc. SIGGRAPH'98*, Los Angeles, California, USA (August 1998) pp. 231–242.

[31] H.-Y. Shum, L.-W. He: Rendering with concentric mosaics. *Proc. SIGGRAPH'99*, Los Angeles, California, USA (August 1999) pp. 299–306.

[32] H. Shum, A. Kalai, S. Seitz: Omnivergent stereo. *Proc. ICCV99*, Korfu, Greece (September 1999) pp. 22–29.

[33] H.-Y. Shum, R. Szeliski: Stereo reconstruction from multiperspective panoramas. *Proc. ICCV99*, Korfu, Greece (September 1999) pp. 14-21.

[34] T. Svoboda: *Central Panoramic Cameras Design, Geometry, Egomotion*. PhD Thesis, Czech Technical University, Prague, Czech Republic (1999)

[35] D.N. Wood, A. Finkelstein, J.F. Hughes, C.E. Thayer, D.H. Salesin: Multiperspective panoramas for CEL animation. *Proc. SIGGRAPH'97*, Los Angeles, California, USA (August 1997) pp. 243–250.

[36] S.-K. Wei, F. Huang, R. Klette: Three dimensional view synthesis from multiple images. Technical Report, CITR-TR-42, Centre for Image Technology and Robotics, The University of Auckland, New Zealand March 1999.

[37] S.-K. Wei, F. Huang, R. Klette: Three-dimensional scene navigation through anaglyphic panorama visualization. *Proc. CAIP99*, Ljubljana, Slovenia (September 1999) pp. 542–549.

[38] J.-Y. Zheng, S. Tsuji: Panoramic representation for route recognition by a mobile robot. *IJCV* **9**(1) (October 1992) pp. 55–76.

[39] http://www.cis.upenn.edu/~kostas/omni.html.

[40] http://www.eecs.lehigh.edu/~tboult/vsam/.

Structure Multivector for Local Analysis of Images[*]

Michael Felsberg and Gerald Sommer

Christian-Albrechts-University of Kiel
Institute of Computer Science and Applied Mathematics
Cognitive Systems
Preußerstraße 1-9, 24105 Kiel, Germany
`mfe@ks.informatik.uni-kiel.de`

Abstract. The structure multivector is a new approach for analyzing the local properties of a two-dimensional signal (e.g. image). It combines the classical concepts of the structure tensor and the analytic signal in a new way. This has been made possible using a representation in the algebra of quaternions. The resulting method is linear and of low complexity. The filter-response includes local phase, local amplitude and local orientation of intrinsically one-dimensional neighborhoods in the signal. As for the structure tensor, the structure multivector field can be used to apply special filters to it for detecting features in images.

1 Introduction

In image and image sequence processing, different paradigms of interpreting the signals exist. Regardless of they are following a constructive or an appearance based strategy, they all need a capable low-level preprocessing scheme. The analysis of the underlying structure of a signal is an often discussed topic. Several capable approaches can be found in the literature, among these the quadrature filters derived from the 2D analytic signal [7], the structure tensor [6,8], and steerable filters [5].

Since the preprocessing is only the first link in a long chain of operations, it is useful to have a linear approach, because otherwise it would be nearly impossible to design the higher-level processing steps in a systematic way. On the other hand, we need a rich representation if we want to treat as much as possible in the preprocessing. Furthermore, the representation of the signal during the different operations should be complete, in order to prevent a loss of information. These constraints enforce us to use the framework of geometric algebra which is also advantageous if we combine image processing with neural computing and robotics (see [9]).

---

[*] This work has been supported by German National Merit Foundation and by DFG Graduiertenkolleg No. 357 (M. Felsberg) and by DFG Grant So-320-2-2 (G. Sommer).

R. Klette et al. (Eds.): Multi-Image Analysis, LNCS 2032, pp. 93–104, 2001.

In the one-dimensional case, quadrature filters are a frequently used approach for processing data. They are derived from the analytic signal by bandpass filtering. The classical extension to two dimensions is done by introducing a preference direction of the Hilbert transform [7] and therefore, the filter is not very satisfying because the orientation has to be sampled.

The alternative approach is to design a steerable quadrature filter pair [5], which needs an additional preprocessing step for estimating the orientation. As a matter of course, this kind of orientation adaptive filtering is not linear.

The structure tensor (see e.g. [8]) is a capable approach for detecting the existence and orientation of local, intrinsic one-dimensional neighborhoods. From the tensor field the orientation vector field can be extracted and by a normalized or differential convolution special symmetries can be detected [6]. The structure tensor can be computed with quadrature filters but the tensor itself does not possess the typical properties of a quadrature filter. Especially the linearity and the split of the identity is lost, because the phase is neglected.

In this paper, we introduce a new approach for the 2D analytic signal which enables us to substitute the structure tensor by an entity which is linear, preserves the split of the identity and has a geometrically meaningful representation: the structure multivector.

2   A New Approach for the 2D Analytic Signal

2.1   Fundamentals

Since we work on images, which can be treated as sampled intervals of $\mathbb{R}^2$, we use the geometric algebra $\mathbb{R}_{0,2}$ which is isomorphic to the algebra of quaternions $\mathbb{H}$. The whole complex signal theory naturally embeds in the algebra of quaternions, i.e. complex numbers are considered as a subspace of quaternions here. The basis of the quaternions reads $\{1, i, j, k\}$ while the basis of the complex numbers reads $\{1, i\}$. Normally, the basis vector 1 is omitted.

Throughout this paper, we use the following notations:

- vectors are bold face, e.g. $\boldsymbol{x} = x_1 \boldsymbol{i} + x_2 \boldsymbol{j}$
- the Fourier transform is denoted[1] $f(\boldsymbol{x}) \circ\!\!-\!\bullet F(\boldsymbol{u}) = \int f(\boldsymbol{x}) \exp(i2\pi\boldsymbol{u}\cdot\boldsymbol{x})\,d\boldsymbol{x}$
- the real part, the $\boldsymbol{i}$-part, the $\boldsymbol{j}$-part, and the $\boldsymbol{k}$-part of a quaternion q is obtained by $\mathcal{R}\{q\}, \mathcal{I}\{q\}, \mathcal{J}\{q\}$, and $\mathcal{K}\{q\}$, respectively

The 1D analytic signal is defined as follows. The signal which is obtained from $f(\boldsymbol{x})$ by a phase shift of $\pi/2$ is called the Hilbert transform $f_H(\boldsymbol{x})$ of $f(\boldsymbol{x})$. Since $f_H(\boldsymbol{x})$ is constrained to be real-valued, the spectrum must have an odd symmetry. Therefore, the transfer function has the form[2] $H(\boldsymbol{u}) = i\,\text{sign}(\boldsymbol{u})$. If we combine a signal and its Hilbert transform corresponding to

---

[1] Note that the dot product of two vectors is the negative scalar product $(\boldsymbol{x}\cdot\boldsymbol{u} = -\langle\boldsymbol{x},\boldsymbol{u}\rangle)$.

[2] Since we use vector notation for 1D functions, we have to redefine some real-valued functions according to $\text{sign}(\boldsymbol{u}) = \text{sign}(u)$, where $\boldsymbol{u} = u\boldsymbol{i}$.

$$f_A(\boldsymbol{x}) = f(\boldsymbol{x}) - f_H(\boldsymbol{x})i \ , \tag{1}$$

we get a complex-valued signal, which is called the analytic signal of $f(\boldsymbol{x})$.

According to the transfer function of the Hilbert transform, the Fourier transform of the analytic signal $f_A(\boldsymbol{x})$ is located in the right half-space of the frequency domain, i.e. $f_A(\boldsymbol{x}) \circ\!\!-\!\!\bullet\, 2F(\boldsymbol{u})\delta_{-1}(\boldsymbol{u})$ (δ_{-1}: Heaviside function).

2.2 The 2D Phase Concept

We want to develop a new 2D analytic signal for intrinsically 1D signals (in contrast to the 2D analytic signal in [2] which is designed for intrinsically 2D signals), which shall contain three properties: local amplitude, local phase and local orientation. Compared to the 1D analytic signal we need one additional angle. We cannot choose this angle without constraints: if the signal is rotated by π, we obtain the same analytic signal, but conjugated. Therefore, we have the following relationship: negation of the local phase is identical to a rotation of π.

Note the difference between *direction* and *orientation* in this context; the direction is a value in $[0; 2\pi)$ and the orientation is a value in $[0; \pi)$.

Any value of the 2D analytic signal can be understood as a 3D vector. The amplitude fixes the sphere on which the value is located. The local phase corresponds to rotations on a great circle on this sphere. To be consistent, a rotation of the signal must then correspond to a rotation on a small circle (local orientation).

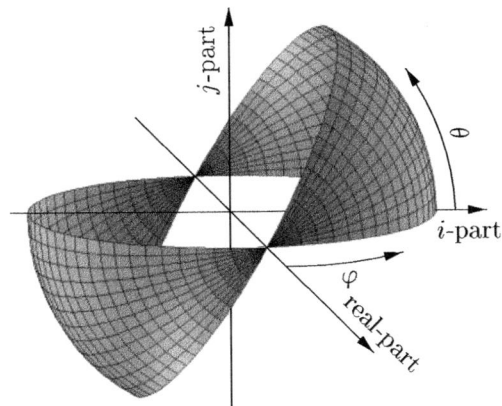

Fig. 1. Coordinate system of the 2D phase approach

The coordinate system defined in this way is displayed in figure 1. It is the same as in [6], but Granlund and Knutsson use the 2D phase in the context of orientation adaptive filtering.

The angles φ and θ are obtained by $\theta = \frac{1}{2} \arg((\mathcal{I}\{q\} + \mathcal{J}\{q\}i)^2)$ (*local orientation*) and $\varphi = \arg(\mathcal{R}\{q\} - (\mathcal{J}\{q\} - \mathcal{I}\{q\}i)e^{-i\theta})$ (*local phase*), where $q \in \mathbb{H}$ with $\mathcal{K}\{q\} = 0$ and $\arg(z) \in [0; 2\pi)$.

Note that this definition of the quaternionic phase is different from that of the quaternionic Fourier transform (see e.g. [2]). The reason for this will be explained in section 2.3.

2.3 The Monogenic Signal

Now, having a phase concept which is rich enough to code all local properties of intrinsically 1D signals, we construct a generalized Hilbert transform and an analytic signal for the 2D case, which make use of the new embedding.

The following definition of the Riesz transform[3] is motivated by theorem 1, which establishes a correspondence between the Hilbert transform and the Riesz transform. The transfer function of the *Riesz transform* reads

$$H(\boldsymbol{u}) = \frac{\boldsymbol{u}}{|\boldsymbol{u}|} \quad , \tag{2}$$

and $F_H(\boldsymbol{u}) = H(\boldsymbol{u})F(\boldsymbol{u}) \bullet\!\!-\!\!\circ f_H(\boldsymbol{x})$.

Example: the Riesz transform of $f(\boldsymbol{x}) = \cos(2\pi\boldsymbol{u}_0 \cdot \boldsymbol{x})$ is
$$f_H(\boldsymbol{x}) = -\exp(\boldsymbol{k}\theta_0)\sin(2\pi\boldsymbol{u}_0 \cdot \boldsymbol{x}) \text{ where } \theta_0 = \arg(\boldsymbol{u}_0).$$

Obviously, the Riesz transform yields a function which is identical to the 1D Hilbert transforms of the cosine function, except for an additional rotation in the $\boldsymbol{i} - \boldsymbol{j}$ plane (the exponential function).

Up to now, we have only considered a special example, but what about general signals? What kind of signals can be treated with this approach? The answer can be found easily: the orientation phase must be independent of the frequency coordinate. This sounds impossible, but in fact, the orientation phase is constant, if the spectrum is located on a line through the origin.

Signals which have a spectrum of this form are intrinsically 1D (i.e. they are constant in one direction). This is exactly the class of functions the structure tensor has been designed for and we have the following theorem:

Theorem 1 *Let $f(t)$ be a one-dimensional function with the Hilbert transform $f_H(t)$. Then, the Riesz transform of the two-dimensional function $f'(\boldsymbol{x}) = f((\boldsymbol{x} \cdot \boldsymbol{n})i)$ reads $f'_H(\boldsymbol{x}) = -\boldsymbol{n}i\, f_H((\boldsymbol{x} \cdot \boldsymbol{n})i)$, where $\boldsymbol{n} = \cos(\theta)\boldsymbol{i} + \sin(\theta)\boldsymbol{j}$ is an arbitrary unit vector.*

Now we simply adapt (1) for the 2D case and obtain the *monogenic signal* of a 2D signal. Using this definition, we obtain for our example: $f_A = \exp(\frac{\boldsymbol{u}_0}{|\boldsymbol{u}_0|} 2\pi\boldsymbol{u}_0 \cdot \boldsymbol{x})$.

---

[3] Originally, we used the term spherical Hilbert transform in [4]. We want to thank T. Bülow for alluding to the existence of the Riesz transform and for giving us the reference [10] which enabled us to identify the following definition with it.

Hence, the monogenic signal uses the phase concept, which has been defined in section 2.2. According to theorem 1, the monogenic signal of an intrinsically one-dimensional signal $f'(\boldsymbol{x}) = f((\boldsymbol{x} \cdot \boldsymbol{n})\boldsymbol{i})$ reads

$$f'_A(\boldsymbol{x}) = f((\boldsymbol{x} \cdot \boldsymbol{n})\boldsymbol{i}) - \boldsymbol{n} f_H((\boldsymbol{x} \cdot \boldsymbol{n})\boldsymbol{i}) \ . \tag{3}$$

Of course, the monogenic signal can be computed for *all* functions which are Fourier transformable. However, for signals which do not have an intrinsic dimension of one[4], the correspondence to the 1D analytic signal is lost.

Independently of the intrinsic dimensionality of the signal, the analytic signal can also be calculated in a different way. The 1D analytic signal is obtained in the Fourier domain by the transfer function $1 + \operatorname{sign}(\boldsymbol{u})$. For the monogenic signal we have the same result if we modify the Fourier transform according to $\tilde{f}(\boldsymbol{x}) = \int_{\mathbb{R}^2} \exp(\boldsymbol{k}\theta/2) F(\boldsymbol{u}) \exp(\boldsymbol{i}2\pi\boldsymbol{u} \cdot \boldsymbol{x}) \exp(-\boldsymbol{k}\theta/2) \, d\boldsymbol{u}$, the *inverse spherical Fourier transform*. Then, we have $f_A(\boldsymbol{x}) = \tilde{f}(\boldsymbol{x})$ (see [4]).

Since the integrand of $\tilde{f}(\boldsymbol{x})$ is symmetric, we can also integrate over the half domain and multiply the integral by two. Therefore, we can use any transfer function of the form $1 + \operatorname{sign}(\boldsymbol{u} \cdot \boldsymbol{n})$ without changing the integral. By simply omitting half of the data, the redundancy in the representation is removed.

In order to calculate the energy of the monogenic signal, we need the transfer function, which changes $F(\boldsymbol{u})$ to $F_A(\boldsymbol{u})$: it is obtained from (2) and (1) and reads $1 - \frac{\boldsymbol{u}}{|\boldsymbol{u}|}\boldsymbol{i} = 1 + \cos(\theta) + \sin(\theta)\boldsymbol{k}$. The energy of the monogenic signal is

$$\int_{\mathbb{R}^2} |(1 + \cos(\theta) + \sin(\theta)\boldsymbol{k})F(\boldsymbol{u})|^2 \, d\boldsymbol{u} = 2 \int_{\mathbb{R}^2} |F(\boldsymbol{u})|^2 \, d\boldsymbol{u} \ , \tag{4}$$

i.e. it is two times the energy of the original signal[5].

From the group of similarity transformations (i.e. shifts, rotations and dilations) only the rotation really affects the monogenic signal; the orientation phase is changed according to the rotation. If we interpret the monogenic signal as a vector field in 3D (see also section 3.2), the group of 2D similarity transforms[6] even commutes with the operator that yields the monogenic signal.

The reader might ask, why do we use a quaternion-valued spectral approach which differs from the one of the QFT (see e.g. [2]). The reason is not obvious. The QFT covers more symmetry concepts than the complex Fourier transform. The classical transform maps a reflection through the origin onto the conjugation operator. The QFT maps a reflection in one of the axes onto one of the algebra automorphisms. We can use $\mathbb{C} \otimes \mathbb{C}$ instead of $\mathbb{H}$ to calculate the QFT. Moreover,

---

[4] The case of intrinsic dimension zero (i.e. a constant signal) is irrelevant, because the Hilbert transform is zero in both cases.

[5] This is only valid for DC free signals. The energy of the DC component is not doubled as in the case of the 1D analytic signal.

[6] Note that in the context of a 3D embedding, the group of 2D similarity transforms is the subgroup of the 3D transforms restricted to shifts in $\boldsymbol{i}$ or $\boldsymbol{j}$ direction, rotations around the real axis and a dilation of the $\boldsymbol{i}$ and $\boldsymbol{j}$ axes.

we have $\mathbb{C} \otimes \mathbb{C} \cong \mathbb{C}^2$ (see e.g. [3]) and consequently, we can calculate the QFT of a real signal by two complex transformations using the formula

$$F_q(\boldsymbol{u}) = F(\boldsymbol{u})\frac{1-k}{2} + F(u_1 i - u_2 j)\frac{1+k}{2} \qquad (5)$$

and the symmetry wrt. the axes is obvious.

In this paper, we want to present an isotropic approach which means that symmetry wrt. the axes is not sufficient. Therefore, we had to design the new transform. The design of isotropic discrete filters is a quite old topic, see e.g. [1].

3   Properties of the Monogenic Signal

3.1   The Spatial Representation

The definition of the Riesz transform in the frequency domain can be transformed into a spatial representation. The transfer function (2) can be split into two functions: $\frac{u_1}{|u|}$ and $\frac{u_2}{|u|}$. The only thing left is to calculate the inverse Fourier transform of these functions. In [10] the transform pairs can be found: $\frac{x_1}{2\pi|x|^3} \circ\!\!-\!\!\bullet -i\frac{u_1}{|u|}$ and $\frac{x_2}{2\pi|x|^3} \circ\!\!-\!\!\bullet -i\frac{u_2}{|u|}$.

The functions $\frac{x_1}{2\pi|x|^3}$ and $\frac{x_2}{2\pi|x|^3}$ are the kernels of the 2D Riesz transform in vector notation. From a mathematician's point of view, the Riesz transform is the multidimensional generalization of the Hilbert transform. Consequently, the monogenic signal is directly obtained by the convolution

$$f_A(\boldsymbol{x}) = \int_{\mathbb{R}^2}\left(\delta_0(t) + \frac{t}{2\pi|t|^3}\right)f(\boldsymbol{x}-t)\,dt \ .$$

The graph in figure 2 sums up all ways to calculate the monogenic signal from the preceding sections. The inverse spherical Fourier transform is denoted $\mathcal{F}_s^{-1}$.

3.2   The Structure Multivector

Normally, images are intrinsically two-dimensional, so the concepts described in section 2.3 cannot be applied globally. On the other hand, large areas of images are intrinsically one-dimensional, at least on a certain scale. Therefore, a local processing would take advance of the new approach.

The classical approach of the analytic signal has its local counterpart in the quadrature filters. A pair of quadrature filters (or a complex quadrature filter) is characterized by the fact that the impulse response is an analytic signal. On the other hand, both impulse responses are band-limited and of finite spatial extent, so that the problem of the unlimited impulse response of the Hilbert filter is circumvented.

An example of the output of a 1D quadrature filter can be found in figure 3.

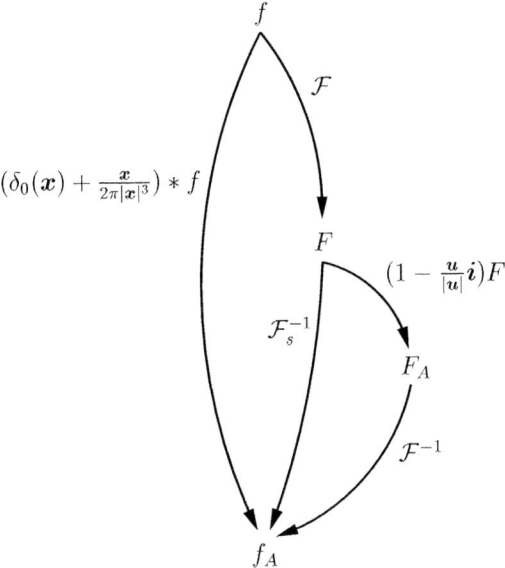

Fig. 2. Three ways to calculate the monogenic signal

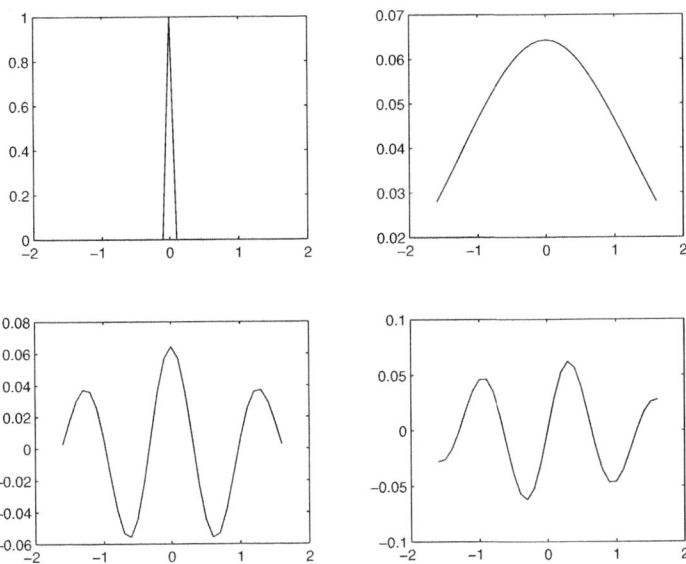

Fig. 3. Upper left: impulse, upper right: magnitude of filter output, lower left: real part of filter output, lower right: imaginary part of filter output

While the representation in figure 3 is very common, we will introduce now a different representation. One-dimensional signals can be interpreted as surfaces in 2D space. If we assign the real axis to the signal values and the imaginary axis to the abscissa, we obtain a representation in the complex plane. The analytic signal can be embedded in the same plane – it corresponds to a vector field which is only non-zero on the imaginary axis (see figure 4).

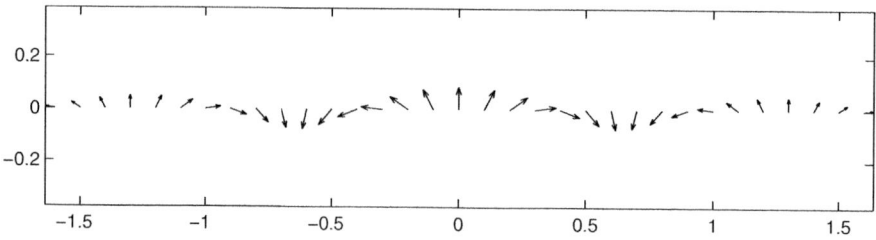

Fig. 4. Representation of the 1D analytic signal as a vector field

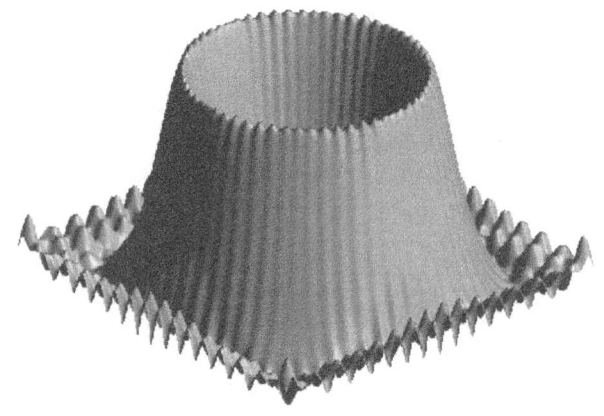

Fig. 5. Siemens-star convolved with a spherical quadrature filter (magnitude)

Based on the monogenic signal, we introduce the *spherical quadrature filters*. They are defined according to the 1D case as a hypercomplex filter whose impulse response is a monogenic signal.

It is remarkable that the spherical quadrature filters have isotropic energy and exactly choose the frequency bands they are designed for. In figure 5 it can be seen that the energy is isotropic and that it is maximal for the radius 77.8, which corresponds to a frequency of $\frac{16.3}{256}$. The used bandpass has a center frequency of $\frac{1}{16}$.

Fig. 6. From left to right: impulse-line; filter output: amplitude, real part, combined imaginary parts

In figure 6 the output of a spherical quadrature filter applied to an impulse-line is displayed. The lower right image shows the combined imaginary parts which means that instead of the imaginary unit i the unit vector n is used.

Same as for 1D signals, 2D signals can be embedded as a surface in 3D space. The signal values are assigned to the real axis and the spatial coordinates to the i- and the j-axis. The monogenic signal can be represented in the same embedding. It corresponds to a vector field, which is only non-zero in the plane spanned by i and j (see figure 7).

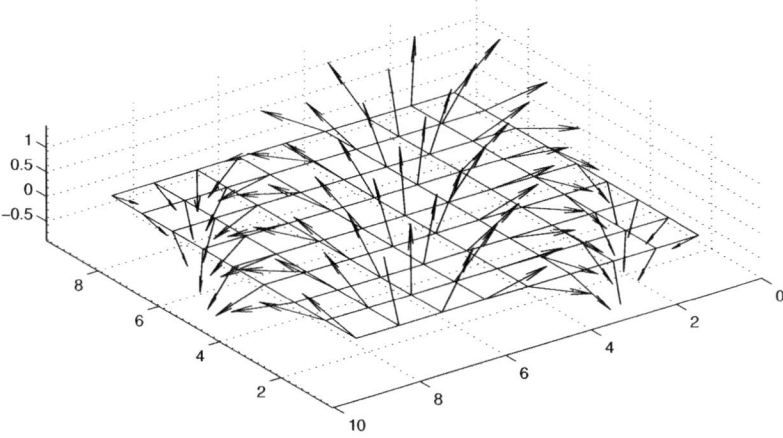

Fig. 7. Representation of the monogenic signal as a vector field

The result of filtering a signal with a spherical quadrature filter is a quaternion-valued field. Though the k-component (*bivector*) of the field is always zero, we denote this field as a multivector field or the *structure multivector* of the signal. As already the name induces, the structure multivector is closely related to the structure tensor. The structure tensor as defined in [6] mainly includes the following information: the amplitude as a measurement for the existence of local structure and the orientation of the local structure.

Jähne [8] extracts an additional information: the coherence. The coherence is the relationship between the oriented gradients and all gradients, so it is a measurement for the degree of orientation in a structure and it is closely related to the variance of the orientation. The variance is a second order property. It includes a product of the arguments and therefore, it is not linear. Consequently, the coherence cannot be measured by a linear approach like the structure multivector. Two structures with different orientations simply yield the vector sum of both multivector fields.

The structure multivector consists of three independent components (local phase, local orientation and local amplitude) and it codes three properties. Consequently, there is no additional information possible. The structure tensor possesses three degrees of freedom (it is a symmetric tensor). Therefore, apart from the amplitude and the orientation one can extract a third information, the coherence.

4   Experiments and Discussion

4.1   Experiments

For the computation of the structure multivector we use a multi-scale approach, i.e. we couple the shift of the Gaussian bandpass with the variance as for the Gabor wavelets.

For the experiments, we chose some synthetic examples with letters as gray level or textured images.

(a)   (b)

Fig. 8. (a) Structure multivector of an image without texture. Upper left: original, upper right: amplitude, lower left: φ-phase, lower right: θ-phase.
(b) Structure multivector of an image with one texture. Upper left: original, upper right: amplitude, lower left: φ-phase, lower right: θ-phase

In figure 8(a) it can be seen that the structure multivector responds only at the edges. Therefore, the amplitude is a measure for the presence of structure.

The φ-phase is linear, which can only be guessed in this representation. But it can be seen that the φ-phase is monotonic modulo a maximal interval (which is in fact 2π). The θ-phase represents the orientation of the edge. Note that the highest and the lowest gray level (standing for π and zero, respectively) represent the same orientation.

In figure 8(b) it can be seen that the structure multivector responds also inside the object. The amplitude is nearly constant, which corresponds to a texture with constant energy. Of course, this property is lost if the wrong scale is considered. The φ-phase is linear, see notes above. The θ-phase represents the orientation of the texture. A constant gray level corresponds to a constant estimated orientation. The small spikes in the figure are produced by the extraction of the local orientation angle. The underlying quaternion-valued field does not show these artifacts.

Fig. 9. (a) Structure multivector of an image with two superposed textures. Upper left: original, upper right: amplitude, lower left: φ-phase, lower right: θ-phase.
(b) Structure multivector of an image with two superposed textures and textured background. Upper left: original, upper right: amplitude, lower left: φ-phase, lower right: θ-phase

In figure 9(a) it can be seen that the structure multivector responds only with respect to the dominant texture (the one with higher frequency). The magnitude of the response is modulated with that component of the weaker texture that is normal to the dominant texture. This effect is even more obvious in figure 9(b). The φ-phase is always directed parallel to the dominant texture. The θ-phase represents the orientation of the dominant texture in each case.

4.2   Conclusion

We have presented a new approach to the 2D analytic signal: the monogenic signal. It has an isotropic energy distribution and deploys the same local phase approach as the 1D analytic signal. There is no impact of the orientation on the local phase which is one of the most important drawbacks of the classical 2D analytic signal.

Additionally, the monogenic signal includes information about the local orientation and therefore, it is related to the structure tensor. On the other hand, there are two differences compared to the latter approach: the structure multivector does not include coherence information and it is linear.

The local counterpart to the monogenic signal is the structure multivector. The latter is the response of the spherical quadrature filters which are a generalization of the 1D quadrature filters. From the structure multivector one obtains a stable orientation estimation (as stable as the orientation vector field of the structure tensor). In contrast to the classical quadrature filters, the spherical quadrature filters do not have a preference direction. Therefore, the orientation need not be sampled or steered.

We introduced an interpretation technique for the analytic and the monogenic signal in form of vector fields. Furthermore, we tried to explain the impact of simple structures and textures on the structure multivector. Applications can easily be designed, e.g. texture segmentation (see also [2]).

References

[1] Brady, J. M., and Horn, B. M. P. Rotationally symmetric operators for surface interpolation. *Computer Vision, Graphics, and Image Processing 22*, 1 (April 1983), 70–94.

[2] Bülow, T. *Hypercomplex Spectral Signal Representations for the Processing and Analysis of Images*. PhD thesis, Christian-Albrechts-University of Kiel, 1999.

[3] Felsberg, M., Bülow, T., and Sommer, G. Commutative Hypercomplex Fourier Transforms of Multidimensional Signals. In *Geometric Computing with Clifford Algebra*, G. Sommer, Ed. Springer, Heidelberg, 2001.

[4] Felsberg, M., and Sommer, G. Structure multivector for local analysis of images. Tech. Rep. 2001, Institute of Computer Science and Applied Mathematics, Christian-Albrechts-University of Kiel, Germany, February 2000. http://www.ks.informatik.uni-kiel.de/~mfe/Techn_Report.ps.gz.

[5] Freeman, W. T., and Adelson, E. H. The design and use of steerable filters. *IEEE Transactions on Pattern Analysis and Machine Intelligence 13*, 9 (September 1991), 891–906.

[6] Granlund, G. H., and Knutsson, H. *Signal Processing for Computer Vision*. Kluwer Academic Publishers, Dordrecht, 1995.

[7] Hahn, S. L. *Hilbert Transforms in Signal Processing*. Artech House, Boston, London, 1996.

[8] Jähne, B. *Digitale Bildverarbeitung*. Springer, Berlin, 1997.

[9] Sommer, G. The global algebraic frame of the perception-action cycle. In *Handbook of Computer Vision and Applications* (1999), B. Jähne, H. Haußecker, and P. Geissler, Eds., vol. 3, Academic Press, San Diego, pp. 221–264.

[10] Stein, E., and Weiss, G. *Introduction to Fourier Analysis on Euclidean Spaces*. Princeton University Press, New Jersey, 1971.

Matching Multiple Views by the Least Square Correlation

Georgy Gimel'farb and Jian Zhong

Centre for Image Technology and Robotics, and Department of Computer Science
Tamaki Campus, University of Auckland
Private Bag 92019, Auckland 1, New Zealand
g.gimelfarb@auckland.ac.nz

Abstract. We consider the potentialities of matching multiple views of a 3D scene by the least square correlation provided that relative projective geometric distortions of the images are affinely approximated. The affine transformation yielding the (sub)optimal match is obtained by combining an exhaustive and directed search in the parameter space. The directed search is performed by a proposed modification of the Hooke–Jeeves unconstrained optimization. Experiments with the RADIUS multiple-view images of a model board show a feasibility of this approach.

1 Introduction

Generally, the uncalibrated multiple-view 3D scene reconstruction involves a set of images with significant relative geometric distortions (because of different exterior and interior parameters of cameras ised for image acquisition). This complicates the search for initial stereo correspondences for starting an iterative process of simultaneous cameras calibration and 3D surface recovery [5,7,8]. If the images form a sequence such that each neighbouring pair has rather small geometric deviations, then the search for correspondences is usually reduced to detection of identical points-of-interest (POI) such as corners [5,8]. But generally due to significant geometric and photometric image distortions, the identical POIs may not be simultaneously detected in different images. Therefore it is more reliable to directly match large image areas by taking account of possible relative distortions.

We restrict our consideration to the simplified case when image distortions can be closely approximated by affine transformations [6,10]. Then the least square correlation [2,3,4] can be used for finding a transformation that yields the largest cross-correlation of the images.

The least square correlation is widely used in computational binocular stereo if relative geometric distortions in a stereo pair are comparatively small [3,4]. In this case, although the correlation function is generally multimodal, the gradient (steepest ascent) search is used to find the maximum correlation [2]. Such a search is based on normal equations obtained by linear approximation of the cross-correlation function in the vicinity of a starting point in the space of affine parameters.

R. Klette et al. (Eds.): Multi-Image Analysis, LNCS 2032, pp. 105–114, 2001.

The straightforward gradient search is not workable in the multiple–view case because of larger relative distortions of the images. The globally optimum match can be, in principle, found by exhausting all the values of affine parameters in a given range of possible distortions. But this is not computationally feasible.

In this paper we consider more practical (but only suboptimum) approach combining an exhaustion of some affine parameters over a sparse grid of their values with a directed search for all the parameters starting from every grid position. The directed search is based on a modified Hooke–Jeeves unconstrained optimization [1]. The proposed modification is intended to take account of the multi-modality of cross-correlation. Feasibility of the proposed approach is illustrated by experiments with the RADIUS multiple–view images of a 3D model board scene [9].

2   Basic Notation

Let $\mathbf{R}_j$ be a finite arithmetic lattice supporting a greyscale image $g_j : \mathbf{R}_j \rightarrow \mathbf{G}$ where $\mathbf{G}$ is a finite set of grey values. Let $(x, y) \in \mathbf{R}_j$ denote a pixel with the column coordinate x and row coordinate y. For simplicity, the origin $(0,0)$ of the (x, y)-coordinates is assumed to coincide with the lattice centre.

Let g_1 be a rectangular prototype matched in the image g_2 to a quadrangular area specified by an affine transformation $\mathbf{a} = [a_1, \ldots, a_6]$. The transformation relates each pixel (x, y) in the prototype g_1 to the point $(x_\mathbf{a}, y_\mathbf{a})$ in the image g_2:

$$
\begin{aligned}
x_{\bar{\mathbf{a}}} &= a_1 x + a_2 y + a_3; \\
y_{\bar{\mathbf{a}}} &= a_4 x + a_5 y + a_6.
\end{aligned}
\tag{1}
$$

The affine parameters (a_1, a_5), (a_2, a_4), and (a_3, a_6) describe, respectively, the x- and y-scaling, shearing, and shifting of g_2 with respect to g_1.

Grey levels $g_2(x_\mathbf{a}, y_\mathbf{a})$ in the points with non-integer coordinates $(x_\mathbf{a}, y_\mathbf{a})$ are found by interpolating grey values in the neighbouring pixels of the lattice $\mathbf{R}_2$. If the transformed point $(x_\mathbf{a}, y_\mathbf{a})$ falls outside of the lattice, then the original pixel $(x, y) \in \mathbf{R}_1$ is assumed to be excluded from matching.

The least square cross-correlation

$$
C(\mathbf{a}^*) = \max_{\mathbf{a}}\{C(\mathbf{a})\}
\tag{2}
$$

maximizes by the affine parameters $\mathbf{a}$ the conventional cross-correlation

$$
C(\mathbf{a}) = \sum_{(x,y)\in\mathbf{R}_{1,\mathbf{a}}} \frac{g_1(x, y) - m_1}{s_1} \cdot \frac{g_2(x_\mathbf{a}, y_\mathbf{a}) - m_{2,\mathbf{a}}}{s_{2,\mathbf{a}}}
\tag{3}
$$

between the prototype g_1 and affinely transformed image g_2. Here, m and s are the mean values and standard deviations, respectively:

$$
\begin{aligned}
m_1 &= \frac{1}{|\mathbf{R}_{1,\mathbf{a}}|} \sum_{(x,y)\in\mathbf{R}_{1,\mathbf{a}}} g_1(x, y); & s_1^2 &= \frac{1}{|\mathbf{R}_{1,\mathbf{a}}|} \sum_{(x,y)\in\mathbf{R}_{1,\mathbf{a}}} (g_1(x, y) - m_1)^2; \\
m_{2,\mathbf{a}} &= \frac{1}{|\mathbf{R}_{1,\mathbf{a}}|} \sum_{(x,y)\in\mathbf{R}_{1,\mathbf{a}}} g_2(x_\mathbf{a}, y_\mathbf{a}); & s_{2,\mathbf{a}}^2 &= \frac{1}{|\mathbf{R}_{1,\mathbf{a}}|} \sum_{(x,y)\in\mathbf{R}_{1,\mathbf{a}}} (g_2(x_\mathbf{a}, y_\mathbf{a}) - m_{2,\mathbf{a}})^2
\end{aligned}
$$

and $\mathbf{R}_{1,a} = \{(x,y) : ((x,y) \in \mathbf{R}_1) \wedge ((x_\mathbf{a}, y_\mathbf{a}) \in \mathbf{R}_2)\}$ denotes the sublattice which actually takes part in matching the prototype g_1 and the affinely transformed image g_2.

3   Combined Search for Suboptimal Affine Parameters

To approach the least square correlation in Eq. (2), we use the following combined exhaustive and directed search in the affine parameter space. For each given prototype g_1, a sparse grid of the relative shifts $a_3^{[0]}$ and $a_6^{[0]}$ of the matching area in the image g_2 is exhausted. Starting from each grid position, the modified Hooke–Jeeves directed optimization [1] is used to maximize the cross-correlation $C(\mathbf{a})$ by all six affine parameters. The largest correlation over the grid provides the desired affine parameters $\mathbf{a}^*$ of the (sub)optimal match.

The modified Hooke–Jeeves optimization consists of the following two successive stages which are repeated iteratively while the correlation value $C(\mathbf{a})$ continues to increase. Each parameter a_i, $i = 1, \ldots, 6$, varies in a given range $[a_{i,\min}, a_{i,\max}]$, and the search starts with the initial parameter values $\mathbf{a}^{[0]} = [1, 0, a_3^{[0]}, 0, 1, a_6^{[0]}]$.

1. *Exploration stage.* At each step $t = 1, 2, \ldots, T$, the locally best parameter, $j^{[t]}$, is chosen by changing each parameter $i \in \{1, \ldots, 6\}$ under the fixed values, $[a_k^{[t-1]} : k \neq i; k \in \{1, \ldots, 6\}]$, of other parameters. The choice yields the largest increase of the correlation $C(\mathbf{a}^{[t]})$ with respect to $C(\mathbf{a}^{[t-1]})$ providing the parameters $\mathbf{a}^{[t]}$ and $\mathbf{a}^{[t-1]}$ differ by only the value of the locally best parameter $j^{[t]}$. The exploration steps are repeated while the cross-correlation $C(\mathbf{a}^{[t]})$ increases further.
2. *Search stage.* The affine parameters $\mathbf{a}_\lambda = \mathbf{a}_T + \lambda\mathbf{d}$ are changed in the conjectured direction $\mathbf{d} = \mathbf{a}^{[T]} - \mathbf{a}^{[0]}$ of the steepest increase while the cross-correlation $C(\mathbf{a}_\lambda)$ increases further.

Each exploration step exhausts a given number L of the equispaced parameter values in their range to approach the local correlation maximum along a parameter axis, given the fixed previous values of all other parameters. In the experiments below L = 3,...,15. The quadratic approximation of these L correlations provides another possible position of the local maximum. The maximum of the $L + 1$ values found is then locally refined using small increments $\pm\delta_i$ of the parameter.

The exploration steps converge to a final local maximum value $C(\mathbf{a}^{[T]})$, and the parameters $\mathbf{a}^{[T]}$ allow for inferring the possible steepest ascent direction in the parameter space. The search along that direction refines further the obtained least square correlation.

The proposed algorithm replaces the coordinate-wise local search for the closest correlation maximum of the original Hooke–Jeeves exploration stage with the combined exhaustive and directed search. This allows to roughly take into account the multimodal character of the cross-correlation function in the parameter space and escape some non-characteristic minor modes. Figure 1 shows

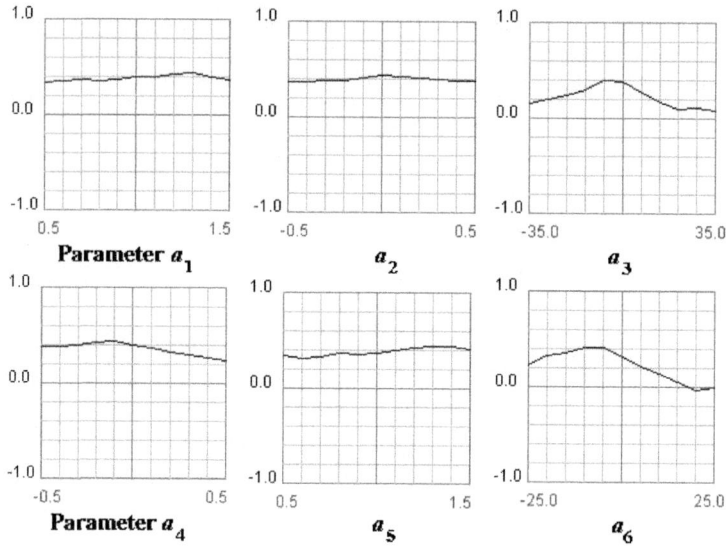

Fig. 1. Typical cross-correlations at the exploration steps.

the typical multi-modal dependence of the cross-correlation from a single affine parameter, given the fixed values of other affine parameters.

Comparing to the conventional least square matching [2], our algorithm does not linearize the correlation function in the parameter space and hence does not build and use the normal equation matrix. This latter is usually ill-conditioned because it depends on the image derivatives with respect to affine parameters.

4   Experiments with the RADIUS Images

Image pairs M15–M28, M24–M25, and M29–M30 selected for experiments from the RADIUS-M set [9] are shown in Figure 2. The images of size 122×96 and 244×192 represent, respectively, the top and the next–to–top levels of image pyramids. Each pyramid is built by reducing the original image 1350×1035 to 976×768 at the first level and then by the twofold demagnification at each next level of the pyramid.

Some results of matching the top–level image pairs in Figure 2 using the rectangular prototype windows of size 49×81 are shown in Table 1 and Figure 3. The prototype g_1 is placed to the central position $(61, 48)$ in the initial image. In these experiments, the search grid 5×5 of step 5 in both directions is centered to the same position $(61, 48)$ in the other image (that is, the shift parameters for the central grid point are $a_3^{[0]} = 0$ and $a_6^{[0]} = 0$), and the parameter $L = 11$.

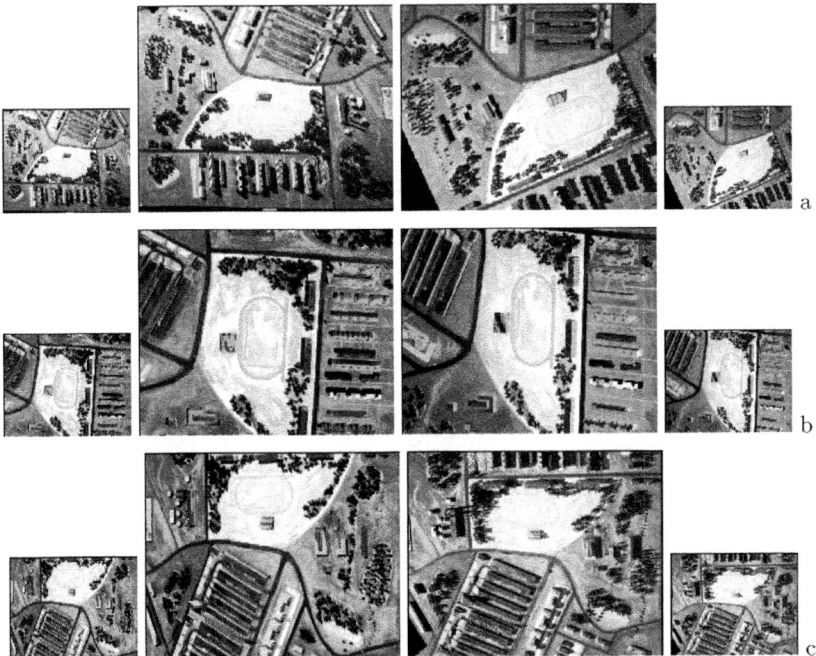

Fig. 2. RADIUS images M15–M28 (a), M24–M25 (b), and M29–M30 (c) at the top and next–to–top pyramid level.

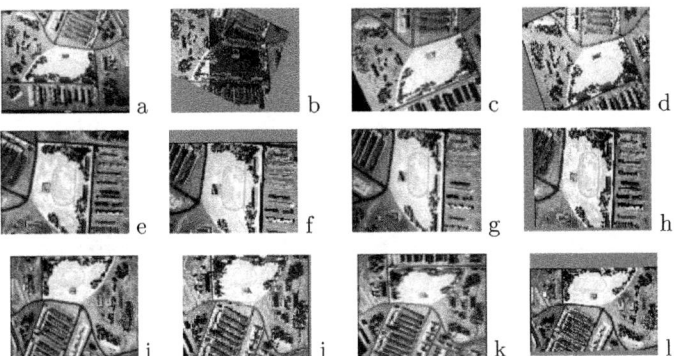

Fig. 3. Initial top–level RADIUS images M15 (a), M28 (c), M24 (e), M25 (g), M29 (i), M30 (k) and the affinely transformed images M28 (b), M15 (d), M25 (f), M24 (h), M30 (j), M29 (l) adjusted to M15, M28, M24, M25, M29, M30, respectively, with the parameters presented in Table 1.

Table 1. The least square correlation values and the corresponding affine parameters obtained by matching the top–level RADIUS images M15–M28, M24–M25, and M29–M30 in Figure 3.

Transformation	$C(\mathbf{a})$	Affine parameters $\mathbf{a}^*$					
		a_1^*	a_2^*	a_3^*	a_4^*	a_5^*	a_6^*
M28 to M15	0.62	1.03	0.35	18.4	-0.50	1.05	5.6
M15 to M28	0.52	0.90	-0.30	-11.0	0.30	0.70	-7.0
M25 to M24	0.66	0.90	0.00	2.0	0.00	1.00	-10.8
M24 to M25	0.79	1.12	-0.02	-3.2	-0.02	0.90	7.5
M30 to M29	0.69	1.00	0.00	2.0	-0.01	0.77	3.0
M29 to M30	0.64	0.97	0.00	-2.0	0.00	1.23	-5.0

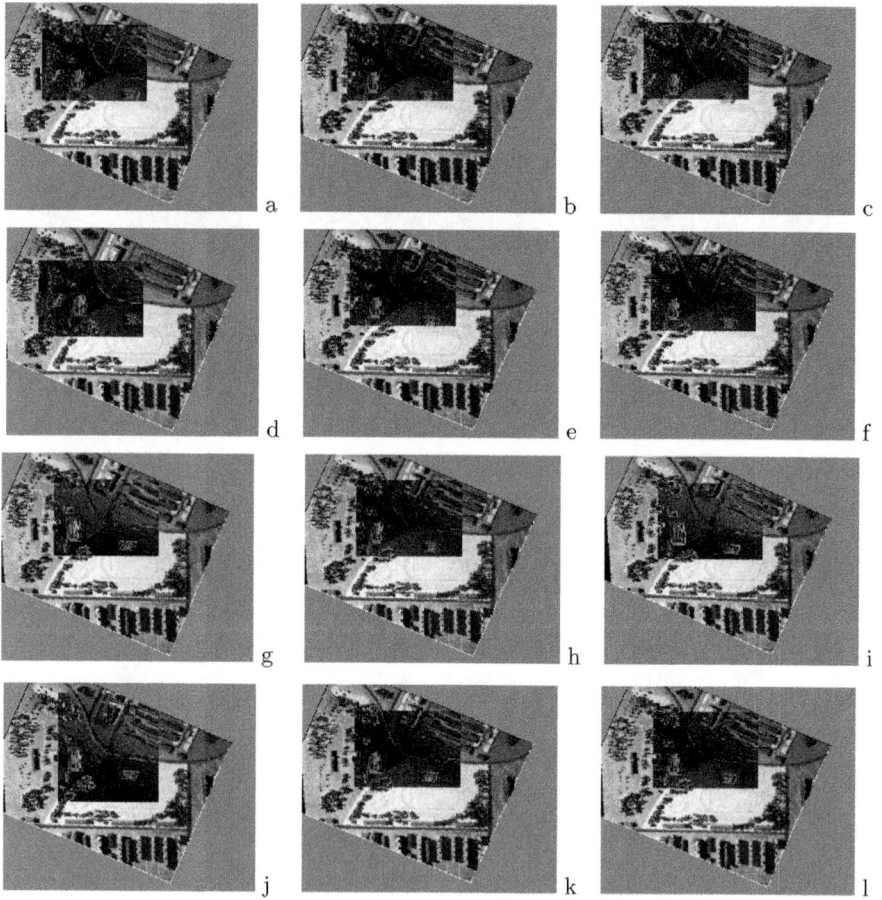

Fig. 4. Next–to–top image M28 affinely adjusted to M15 using the affine parameters in Table 2. The dark rectangles show positions of the prototype windows and the grey-coded values of the residual pixel-wise errors for the least square correlation matching.

Table 2. Characteristics of the prototype windows to be matched, the least square correlation values, and the affine parameters found by matching.

Fig. 4	Window size	Position in g_1	in g_2	Search grid size	step	L	$C(\mathbf{a}^*)$	a_1^*	a_2^*	a_3^*	a_4^*	a_5^*	a_6^*
a	50×35	85,55	90,50	5×5	10	3	0.67	1.11	0.50	11.0	-0.50	1.23	14.0
b	50×35	94,53	97,57	5×5	10	3	0.69	1.10	0.50	10.0	-0.50	1.24	9.0
c	50×35	90,50	95,55	5×5	10	3	0.69	1.09	0.50	8.3	-0.50	1.24	10.0
d	50×35	80,65	100,65	5×5	10	3	0.69	1.09	0.50	15.2	-0.50	1.20	19.0
e	50×35	94,53	105,65	5×5	10	3	0.70	1.09	0.50	10.0	-0.50	1.24	8.9
f	50×35	97,56	109,69	5×5	10	3	0.71	1.08	0.50	11.8	-0.50	1.25	8.0
g	50×35	100,59	110,70	5×5	10	15	0.72	1.10	0.50	14.0	-0.50	1.21	8.0
h	50×35	99,58	111,71	5×5	10	3	0.72	1.10	0.50	13.0	-0.50	1.23	7.8
i	50×35	100,59	110,70	3×3	10	7	0.73	1.13	0.50	14.0	-0.54	1.28	7.7
j	50×50	100,59	110,70	1×1	10	11	0.73	1.10	0.50	14.0	-0.50	1.24	7.0
k	50×35	100,59	110,70	5×5	10	3	0.73	1.10	0.50	14.0	-0.50	1.26	7.4
l	50×35	99,58	110,70	5×5	10	3	0.73	1.11	0.50	13.4	-0.50	1.22	7.9

Table 3. Characteristics of the prototypes to be matched, the least square correlation values, and the affine parameters found by matching.

Fig. 4	Window size	Position in g_1	in g_2	Search grid size	step	L	$C(\mathbf{a}^*)$	a_1^*	a_2^*	a_3^*	a_4^*	a_5^*	a_6^*
a	50×35	100,60	100,60	5×5	15	5	0.49	0.54	0.06	31.0	0.21	0.86	-2.5
b	50×50	110,70	100,60	5×5	10	3	0.52	0.75	-0.28	-12.0	0.12	1.00	-4.0
c	50×50	100,65	100,65	5×5	10	15	0.53	0.83	-0.29	-7.0	0.14	0.97	-6.3
d	75×50	100,65	100,65	5×5	10	15	0.53	0.83	-0.29	-7.0	0.14	0.97	-6.3
e	50×35	100,60	100,60	5×5	10	15	0.68	0.75	-0.36	-10.0	0.32	0.66	-10.0
f	50×50	100,60	100,60	5×5	10	15	0.69	0.74	-0.32	-9.0	0.29	0.68	-10.0
g	50×50	110,70	100,60	5×5	10	11	0.71	0.77	-0.30	-14.0	0.30	0.70	-10.0
h	50×50	110,70	100,60	5×5	10	5	0.71	0.75	-0.30	-14.0	0.31	0.69	-10.0
i	50×35	100,65	100,65	5×5	10	15	0.71	0.75	-0.29	-10.0	0.32	0.64	-11.0
j	50×50	100,59	110,70	1×1	10	11	0.72	0.76	-0.28	-14.0	0.33	0.67	-10.3
k	50×35	110,70	110,70	5×5	10	3	0.72	0.77	-0.31	-14.0	0.32	0.68	-10.0
l	50×35	110,70	100,60	5×5	15	5	0.72	0.76	-0.31	-14.0	0.32	0.68	-10.0

In all our experiments the ranges of the affine parameters a_1, a_4 and a_2, a_3 are $[0.5, 1.5]$ and $[-0.5, 0.5]$, respectively. The ranges of the parameters a_3 and a_6 are given by the width and height of the chosen prototype window.

In these cases, the least square correlation matching allows, at least as a first approximation, to relatively orient all the three image pairs. For comparison, Table 4 presents results of matching the top–level images M15 and M28 using the two larger prototype windows of size 71×51 and 81×61 placed to the central position $(60, 50)$ in M15. Here, the search grid 5×5 of step 10 is sequentially centered to the nine neighbouring positions $(60 \pm 1, 50 \pm 1)$ in M28. Although the photometric distortions of the images are non-uniform, the median values

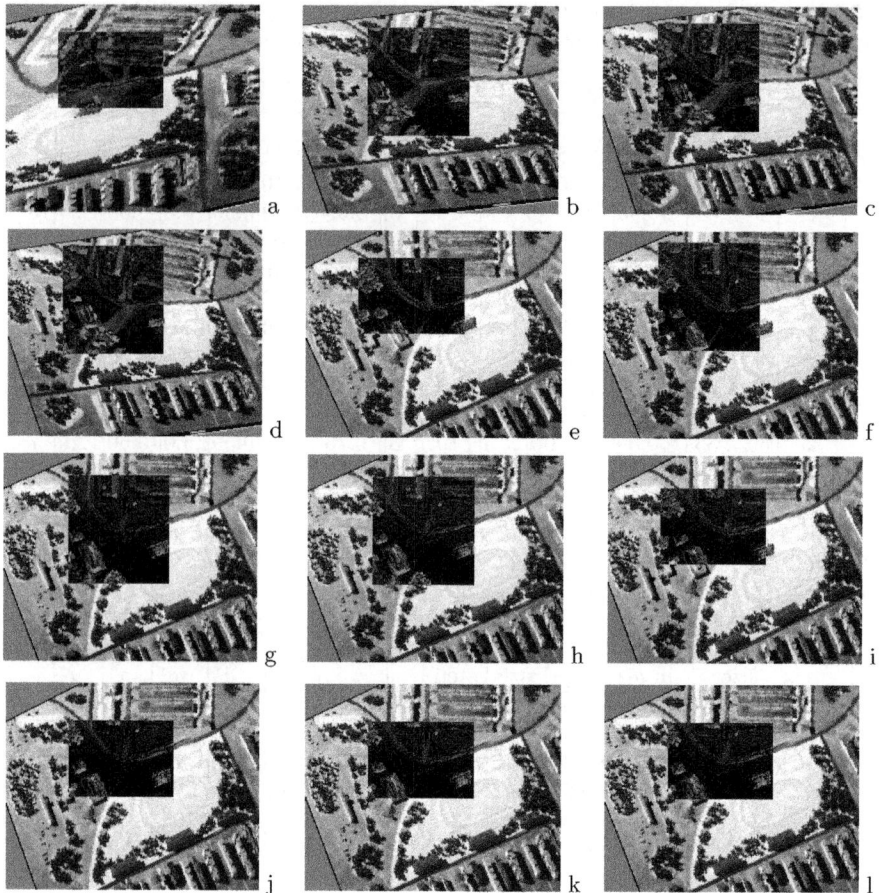

Fig. 5. Next–to–top image M15 affinely adjusted to M28 using the affine parameters in Table 2. The dark rectangles show positions of the prototypes and the grey-coded values of the residual pixel-wise errors for the least square correlation matching.

of the obtained affine parameters $[a_1^*, \ldots, a_6^*]$ for the confident matches with $C(\mathbf{a}^*) \geq 0.55$ are quite similar to the like parameters in Table 1.

Tables 2 – 3 and Figures 4 – 5 show results of matching the images M15 and M28 on the next–to–top level of the pyramids. Here, different prototype windows and various search grids and approximation orders are compared. The position of the prototype window with respect to the image is shown by a dark rectangle giving the grey–coded residual pixel–wise errors of matching (the darker the pixel, the smaller the error).

The matching results are mostly similar although in the general case they depend on the search characteristics, in particular, on the chosen search grid and the parameter L (e.g., Figures 5,a,b,e,g, and the corresponding data in

Table 4. Central positions of the search grid in M28, the least square correlation values, and the affine parameters found by matching M28 to M15.

Window size	Position in M28	$C(\mathbf{a}^*)$	Affine parameters $\mathbf{a}^*$					
			a_1^*	a_2^*	a_3^*	a_4^*	a_5^*	a_6^*
71×51	59,49	0.66	1.10	0.50	18.0	-0.50	1.21	3.0
	60,49	0.59	1.10	0.40	18.0	-0.50	1.10	5.0
	61,49	0.59	1.10	0.40	18.0	-0.50	1.10	5.0
	59,50	0.67	1.09	0.48	18.0	-0.50	1.20	3.0
	60,50	0.67	1.09	0.48	18.0	-0.50	1.20	3.0
	61,50	0.67	1.09	0.48	18.0	-0.50	1.20	3.0
	59,51	0.54	1.10	0.30	19.0	-0.50	1.00	7.0
	60,51	0.52	1.00	0.30	20.0	-0.56	1.00	7.0
	61,51	0.53	1.00	0.40	20.0	-0.56	1.28	4.0
Median parameter values for the confident matches			1.09	0.48	18.0	-0.50	1.20	4.0
81×61	59,49	0.55	1.02	0.50	16.0	-0.40	1.10	6.0
	60,49	0.58	1.10	0.44	18.0	-0.50	1.36	5.0
	61,49	0.65	1.10	0.44	18.0	-0.50	1.20	3.0
	59,50	0.55	1.02	0.50	16.0	-0.40	1.10	6.0
	60,50	0.58	1.10	0.44	18.0	-0.50	1.36	5.0
	61,50	0.65	1.10	0.44	18.0	-0.50	1.20	3.0
	59,51	0.55	1.02	0.50	16.0	-0.40	1.10	6.0
	60,51	0.57	1.00	0.50	15.4	-0.50	1.20	4.0
	61,51	0.60	1.05	0.50	16.0	-0.50	1.20	4.0
Median parameter values for the confident matches			1.10	0.50	16.0	-0.50	1.20	5.0

Table 3). Also, the larger prototype windows may affect the precision of the affine approximation of actually projective image distortions (Figures 5,c,d,i).

The median values of the obtained affine parameters $[a_1^*, \ldots, a_6^*]$ for the seven best matches are as follows:

$g_1 - g_2$	a_1^*	a_2^*	a_3^*	a_4^*	a_5^*	a_6^*
M15–M28:	1.10	0.50	14.0	-0.50	1.24	7.9
M28–M15:	0.75	-0.30	-14.0	0.32	0.68	-10.0

These values are close to the parameters found by matching the top–level images so that the fast top–level matching can provide a first approximation of the relative geometric distortions of these images to be refined at the next levels of the image pyramids. Similar results are also obtained for the image pairs M24–M25 and M29–M30 as well as for other RADIUS images (e.g., M24–M10, M10–M11, M11–M19, M19–M20, M8–M9, M9–M23, M23–M29, M30–M36, etc).

5   Concluding Remarks

These and other experiments show that the proposed modified Hooke–Jeeves optimisation algorithm permits us to successfully match large-size areas in the multiple-view images of a 3D scene by the least square correlation, provided the relative image distortions can be affinely approximated. This approach has a moderate computational complexity, hence in principle it can be used at the initial stage of the uncalibrated multiple-view terrain reconstruction.

The approach exploits almost no prior information about a 3D scene, except for the ranges of the affine parameters for matching. Also, the final cross-correlation value provides a confidence measure for the obtained results: if the correlation is less than or equal to $0.5 - 0.55$, one may conclude that the matching fails, otherwise the larger the correlation, the higher the confidence and, in the most cases, the better the affine approximation of the relative image distortions.

References

[1] Dennis J.E., Schnabel R.B.: *Numerical Methods for Unconstrained Optimization and Nonlinear Equations.* Prentice-Hall, Englewood Cliffs (1983)
[2] Förstner, W.: Image matching. In Haralick, R.M., Shapiro, L.G.: *Computer and Robot Vision*, vol.2, ch.16, p.p.289–378. Addison-Wesley (1993).
[3] Hannah, M. J.: Digital stereo image matching techniques. *International Archives on Photogrammetry and Remote Sensing*, 27 (1988) 280–293.
[4] Helava, U. V.: Object space least square correlation. *Photogrammetric Engineering and Remote Sensing*, 54 (1988) 711–714.
[5] Koch, R. and van Gool, L., eds.: *3D Structure from Multiple Images of Large-Scale Environments (European Workshop, SMILE'98, Freiburg, Germany, June 6-7, 1998, Proc.)*, Lecture Notes in Computer Science 1506. Springer (1998).
[6] Koenderink, J., van Doorn, A.: Affine structure from motion. *Journal of the Optical Society of America*, 8:2 (1991) 377–382.
[7] Maybank, S.J., Faugeras, O.: A theory of self-calibration of a moving camera. *International Journal of Computer Vision*, 8 (1992) 123–152.
[8] Pollefeys, M., Koch, R., van Gool, L.: Self-calibration and metric reconstruction in spite of varying and unknown internal camera parameters. *Int. Journal of Computer Vision*, 32:1 (1999) 7–25.
[9] *RADIUS model board imagery and ground truth* (CD-ROM). Intelligent Machines Lab., University of Washington. Seattle (1996).
[10] Shapiro, L.S.: *Affine Analysis of Image Sequences.* Cambridge University Press (1995).

Gabor Wavelet Networks for Object Representation

Volker Krüger and Gerald Sommer

Christian-Albrechts-University of Kiel
Institute of Computer Science and Applied Mathematics, Cognitive Systems
Preußerstraße 1-9, 24105 Kiel, Germany
vok@ks.informatik.uni-kiel.de

Abstract. In this article we want to introduce first the Gabor wavelet network as a model based approach for an effective and efficient object representation. The Gabor wavelet network has several advantages such as invariance to some degree with respect to translation, rotation and dilation. Furthermore, the use of Gabor filters ensured that geometrical and textural object features are encoded. The feasibility of the Gabor filters as a model for local object features ensures a considerable data reduction while at the same time allowing *any* desired precision of the object representation ranging from a sparse to a photo-realistic representation. In the second part of the paper we will present an approach for the estimation of a head pose that is based on the Gabor wavelet networks.

1 Introduction

Recently, model-based approaches for the recognition and the interpretation of images of variable objects, like the bunch graph approach, PCA, eigenfaces and active appearance models, have received considerable interest [31; 22; 5; 10]. These approaches achieve good results because solutions are constrained to be valid instances of a model. In these approaches, the term "model-based" is understood in the sense that a set of training objects is given in the form of gray value pixel images while the model "learns" the variances of the gray values (PCA, eigenfaces) or, respectively, the Gabor filter responses (bunch graph). With this, model knowledge is given by the variances of pixel gray values, which means that the actual knowledge representation is given on a pixel basis, that is independent from the objects themselves.

In this work we want to introduce a novel approach for object representation that is based on Gabor Wavelet Networks. Gabor Wavelet Networks (GWN) are combining the advantages of RBF networks with the advantages of Gabor wavelets: GWNs represent an object as a linear combination of Gabor wavelets where the parameters of each of the Gabor functions (such as orientation and position and scale) are optimized to reflect the particular local image structure. Gabor wavelet networks have several advantages:

R. Klette et al. (Eds.): Multi-Image Analysis, LNCS 2032, pp. 115–128, 2001.

1. By their very nature, Gabor wavelet networks are invariant to some degree to affine deformations and homogeneous illumination changes,
2. Gabor filters are good feature detectors [20; 21] and the optimized parameters of each of the Gabor wavelets are directly related to the underlying image structure,
3. the weights of each of the Gabor wavelet are directly related to their filter responses and with that they are also directly related to the underlying local image structure,
4. the precision of the representation can be varied to *any* desired degree ranging from a coarse representation to an almost photo-realistic one by simply varying the number of used wavelets.

We will discuss each single point in section 2.

The use of Gabor filters implies a model for the actual representation of the object information. In fact, as we will see, the GWN represents object information as a set of local image features, which leads to a higher level of abstraction and to a considerable data reduction. Both, textural and geometrical information is encoded at the same time, but can be split to some degree.

The variability in precision and the data reduction are the most important advantage in this context, that has several consequences:

1. Because the parameters of the Gabor wavelets and the weights of the network are directly related to the structure of the training image and the Gabor filter responses, a GWN can be seen as a task oriented optimal filter bank: given the number of filters, a GWN defines *that* set of filters that extracts the maximal possible image information.
2. For real-time applications one wants to keep the number of filtrations low to save computational resources and it makes sense in this context to relate the number of filtrations to the amount of image information really needed for a specific task: In this sense, it is possible to relate the representation precision to the specific task and to increment the number of filters if more information is needed. This, we call *progressive attention*.
3. The training speed of neural networks, that correlates with the dimensionality of the input vector.

The *progressive attention* is related to the *incremental focus of attention (IFA)* for tracking [27] or the attentive processing strategy (GAZE) for face feature detection [13]. Both works are inspired by [28] and relate features to scales by using a coarse-to-fine image resolution strategy. In contrary, the *progressive attention* should not relate features to scale but to the object itself that is described by these features. In this sense, the object is considered as a collection of image features and the more information about the object is needed to fulfill a task the more features are extracted from the image.

In the following section we will give a short introduction to GWNs. Also, we will discuss each single point mentioned above, including the invariance properties, the abstraction properties and specificity of the wavelet parameters for the object representation and a task oriented image filtration.

In section 3 we will present the results of our pose estimation experiment where we exploited the optimality of the filter bank and the *progressive attention* property to speed up the response time of the system and to optimize the training of the neural network.

In the last section we will conclude with some final remarks.

2   Introduction to Gabor Wavelet Networks

The basic idea of the wavelet networks is first stated by [34], and the use of Gabor functions is inspired by the fact that they are recognized to be good feature detectors [20; 21].

To define a GWN, we start out, generally speaking, by taking a family of N odd Gabor wavelet functions $\Psi = \{\psi_{\mathbf{n}_1}, \dots, \psi_{\mathbf{n}_N}\}$ of the form

$$
\begin{aligned}
\psi_{\mathbf{n}}(x,y) = \exp\Bigg(&-\frac{1}{2}\Big[s_x\left((x-c_x)\cos\theta - (y-c_y)\sin\theta\right)\Big]^2 \\
&+ \Big[s_y\left((x-c_x)\sin\theta + (y-c_y)\cos\theta\right)\Big]^2\Bigg) \\
&\times \sin\Big(s_x\left((x-c_x)\cos\theta - (y-c_y)\sin\theta\right)\Big) ,
\end{aligned} \tag{1}
$$

with $\mathbf{n} = (c_x, c_y, \theta, s_x, s_y)^T$. Here, c_x, c_y denote the translation of the Gabor wavelet, s_x, s_y denote the dilation and θ denotes the orientation. The choice of N is arbitrary and is related to the maximal representation precision of the network. The parameter vector $\mathbf{n}$ (translation, orientation and dilation) of the wavelets may be chosen arbitrarily at this point. In order to find the GWN for image I, the energy functional

$$
E = \min_{\mathbf{n}_i, w_i \text{ for all } i} \left\| I - \sum_i w_i \psi_{\mathbf{n}_i} \right\|_2^2 \tag{2}
$$

is minimized with respect to the weights w_i and the wavelet parameter vector $\mathbf{n}_i$. Equation (2) says that the w_i and $\mathbf{n}_i$ are optimized (i.e. translation, dilation and orientation of each wavelet are chosen) such that the image I is optimally approximated by the weighted sum of Gabor wavelets $\psi_{\mathbf{n}_i}$. We therefore define a Gabor wavelet network as follows:

Definition: Let $\psi_{\mathbf{n}_i}$, $i = 1, \dots, N$ be a set of Gabor wavelets, I a DC-free image and w_i and $\mathbf{n}_i$ chosen according to the energy functional (2). The two vectors

$$
\Psi = (\psi_{\mathbf{n}_1}, \dots, \psi_{\mathbf{n}_N})^T \text{ and } \mathbf{w} = (w_1, \dots, w_N)^T
$$

define then the *Gabor wavelet network* $(\Psi, \mathbf{w})$ for image f.

It should be mentioned that it was proposed before [8; 9; 17] to use an energy functional (2) in order to find the optimal set of weights w_i for a *fixed set*

Fig. 1. The very right image shows the original face image I, the other images show the image I, represented with 16, 52, 116 and 216 Gabor wavelets (left to right).

Fig. 2. The images show a Gabor wavelet network with $N = 16$ wavelets after optimization (left) and the indicated positions of each single wavelet(right).

of non-orthogonal wavelets $\psi_{\mathbf{n}_i}$. We enhance this approach by finding also the optimal parameter vectors $\mathbf{n}_i$ for each wavelet $\psi_{\mathbf{n}_i}$. The parameter vectors $\mathbf{n}_i$ are chosen from *continuous* phase space $\mathbb{R}^5$ [8] and the Gabor wavelets are positioned with sub-pixel accuracy. This is precisely the main advantage over the discrete approach [8; 17]. While in case of a discrete phase space local image structure has to be approximated by a combination of wavelets, a *single* wavelet can be chosen selectively in the continuous case to reflect *precisely* the local image structure. This assures that a maximum of the image information is encoded.

Using the optimal wavelets Ψ and weights $\mathbf{w}$ of the Gabor wavelet network of an image f, I can be (closely) reconstructed by a linear combination of the weighted wavelets:

$$\hat{I} = \sum_{i=1}^{N} w_i \psi_{\mathbf{n}_i} = \Psi^T \mathbf{w} \ .$$

Of course, the quality of the image representation and of the reconstruction depends on the number N of wavelets used and can be varied to reach almost any desired precision. In section 2.2 we will discuss the relation between I and $\hat{I}$ in more detail. An example reconstruction can be seen in fig. 1: A family of 216 wavelets has been distributed over the inner face region of the very right image I by the minimization formula (2). Different reconstructions $\hat{I}$ with formula (3) with various N are shown in the first four images.

A further example can be seen in fig. 2: The left image shows a reconstruction with 16 wavelets and the right image indicates the corresponding wavelet positions. It should be pointed out that at each indicated wavelet position, just *one* single wavelet is located.

2.1 Feature Representation with Gabor Wavelets

It was mentioned in the introduction that the Gabor wavelets are recognized to be good feature [20; 21] detectors, that are directly related to the local image features by the optimization function in eq. 2. This means that an optimized

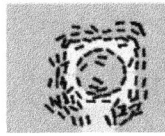 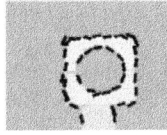

Fig. 3. The figure shows images of a wooden toy block on which a GWN was trained. The black line segments sketch the positions, sizes and orientations of all the wavelets of the GWN (left), and of some automatically selected wavelets (right).

wavelet has e.g. ideally the exact position and orientation of a local image feature. An example can be seen in fig. 3. The figure shows the image of a little wooden toy block, on which a Gabor wavelet network was trained. The left image shows the positions, scales and orientations of the wavelets as little black line segments. By thresholding the weights, the more "important" wavelets may be selected, which leads to the right image. Ideally, each Gabor wavelet should be positioned *exactly* on the image line after optimization. Furthermore, since large weights indicate that the corresponding wavelets represents an edge segment (see sec. 2.2), these wavelets encode local geometrical object information. In reality, however, interactions with other wavelets of the network have to be considered so that most wavelet parameters reflect the position, scale, and orientation of the image line closely, but not precisely. This fact is clearly visible in fig. 3. As it can be seen in fig. 1 an object can be represented almost perfectly with a relatively small set of wavelets. The considerable data reduction is achieved by the introduction of the model for local image primitives, i.e. the introduction of Gabor wavelets.

The use of Gabor filters as a model for local object primitives leads to a higher level of abstraction where object knowledge is represented by a set of local image primitives. The Gabor wavelets in a network that represent edge segments can be easily identified. How to identify wavelets, however, that encode specific textures is not really clear, yet, and subject to future investigation.

Other models for local image primitives have been tested such as Gaussian and their derivatives, which are often used as radial basis functions in RBF networks [1]. It is interesting, however, that all other models have proven to be much less capable.

2.2   Direct Calculation of Weights and Distances

As mentioned earlier, the weights w_i of a GWN are directly related to the filter responses of the Gabor filters $\psi_{\mathbf{n}_i}$ on the training image.

Gabor wavelet functions are not orthogonal. For a given family Ψ of Gabor wavelets it is therefore not possible to calculate a weight w_i directly by a simple projection of the Gabor wavelet $\psi_{\mathbf{n}_i}$ onto the image. Instead one has to consider the family of dual wavelets $\tilde{\Psi} = \{\tilde{\psi}_{\mathbf{n}_1} \ldots \tilde{\psi}_{\mathbf{n}_N}\}$. The wavelet $\tilde{\psi}_{\mathbf{n}_j}$ is the dual wavelet to the wavelet $\psi_{\mathbf{n}_i}$ iff $\langle \psi_{\mathbf{n}_i}, \tilde{\psi}_{\mathbf{n}_j} \rangle = \delta_{i,j}$. With $\tilde{\Psi} = (\tilde{\psi}_{\mathbf{n}_1}, \ldots, \tilde{\psi}_{\mathbf{n}_N})^T$, we can write $\left[\langle \Psi, \tilde{\Psi} \rangle \right] = \mathbb{1}$. In other words: $w_i = \langle I, \tilde{\psi}_{\mathbf{n}_i} \rangle$. We find $\tilde{\psi}_{\mathbf{n}_i}$ to be $\tilde{\psi}_{\mathbf{n}_i} = \sum_j \left(\Psi^{-1} \right)_{i,j} \psi_{\mathbf{n}_j}$, where $\Psi_{i,j} = \langle \psi_{\mathbf{n}_i}, \psi_{\mathbf{n}_j} \rangle$.

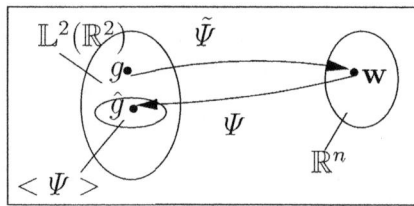

Fig. 4. An image I from the image space $\mathcal{I}$ is mapped by the linear mapping $\tilde{\Psi}$ on the vector $\mathbf{w}$ of the vector space $\mathbb{R}^N$. $<\Psi>$ over the basis functions Ψ. The mapping of $\mathbf{w}$ into $<\Psi> \subset I$ is achieved with the linear mapping Ψ. $\tilde{\Psi}$ can be identified with the pseudo inverse of Ψ and the mapping of I onto $\mathbf{w} \in \mathbb{R}^N$, $I\tilde{\Psi} = \mathbf{w}$, is an orthogonal projection.

The equation $w_i = \langle I, \tilde{\psi}_{\mathbf{n}_i} \rangle$ allows us to define the operator

$$\mathcal{T}_{\Psi} : \mathbb{L}^2(\mathbb{R}^2) \longmapsto <(\psi_{\mathbf{n}_1}, \dots, \psi_{\mathbf{n}_N})> \tag{3}$$

as follows: Given a set Ψ of optimal wavelets of a GWN, the operator $\mathcal{T}_{\Psi}$ realizes an orthogonal projection of a function J onto the closed linear span of Ψ (see eq. (3) and fig. 4), i.e.

$$\hat{J} = \mathcal{T}_{\Psi}(J) = J\tilde{\Psi}\Psi = \sum_{i=1}^{N} w_i \psi_{\mathbf{n}_i} \text{ , with } \mathbf{w} = J\tilde{\Psi} . \tag{4}$$

The direct calculation of the distance between two families of Gabor wavelets, Ψ and Φ, can also be established by applying the above to each of the wavelets $\phi_i \in \Phi$:

$$\mathcal{T}_{\Psi}(\phi_j) = \sum_i \left[\langle \phi_j, \tilde{\psi}_i \rangle \right] \psi_i , \tag{5}$$

which can be interpreted as the representation of each wavelet ϕ_j as a superposition of the wavelets ψ_i. With this, the distance between Ψ and Φ can be given directly by

$$\sqrt{\left[\sum_j \frac{\|\phi_i - \mathcal{T}_{\Psi}(\phi_i)\|}{\|\phi_i\|} \right]^2 + \left[\sum_j \frac{\|\psi_i - \mathcal{T}_{\Phi}(\psi_i)\|}{\|\psi_i\|} \right]^2} , \tag{6}$$

where $\|\cdot\|$ is the euclidian norm. With this distance measurement, the distance between two object representations can be calculated very efficiently.

2.3   Reparameterization of Gabor Wavelet Networks

The task of finding the position, the scale and the orientation of a GWN in a new image is most important because otherwise the filter responses are without any sense. Here, PCA, bunch graphs and GWN have similar properties: In case of the PCA and bunch graph it is important to ensure that corresponding pixels are aligned into a common coordinate system, in case of the GWN, local image primitives have to be aligned. For example, consider an image J that shows the person of fig. 1, left, possibly distorted affinely. Given a corresponding GWN we are interested in finding the correct position, orientation and scaling of the GWN so that the wavelets are positioned on the same facial features as in the original image, or, in other words, how should the GWN be deformed (warped) so that it is aligned with the coordinate system of the new object. An example for a successful warping can be seen in fig. 2, where in the right image the wavelet positions of the *original* wavelet network are marked and in fig. 5, where in new images the wavelet positions of the *reparameterized* Gabor wavelet network are marked. Parameterization of a GWN is established by using a *superwavelet* [26]:

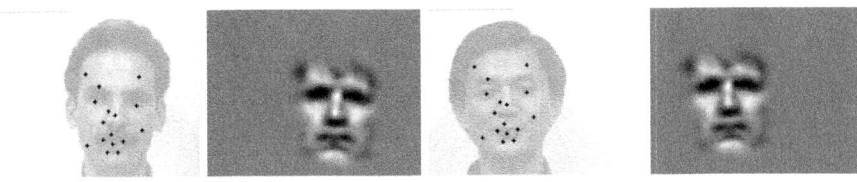

Fig. 5. The images show the positions of each of the 16 wavelets after reparameterizing the wavelet net and the corresponding reconstruction. The reconstructed faces show the same orientation, position and size as the ones they were reparameterized on.

Definition: Let $(\Psi, \mathbf{w})$ be a Gabor wavelet network with $\Psi = (\psi_{\mathbf{n}_1}, \dots, \psi_{\mathbf{n}_N})^T$, $\mathbf{w} = (w_1, \dots, w_N)^T$. A *superwavelet* $\Psi_\mathbf{n}$ is defined to be a linear combination of the wavelets $\psi_{\mathbf{n}_i}$ such that

$$\Psi_\mathbf{n}(\mathbf{x}) = \sum_i w_i \psi_{\mathbf{n}_i}(\mathbf{SR}(\mathbf{x} - \mathbf{c})) , \tag{7}$$

where the parameters of vector $\mathbf{n}$ of superwavelet Ψ define the dilation matrix $\mathbf{S} = \mathrm{diag}(s_x, s_y)$, the rotation matrix $\mathbf{R}$, and the translation vector $\mathbf{c} = (c_x, c_y)^T$.

A superwavelet $\Psi_\mathbf{n}$ is again a wavelet (because of the linearity of the sum) and in particular a continuous function that has the wavelet parameters dilation, translation and rotation. Therefore, we can handle it in the same way as we handled each single wavelet in the previous section. For a new image J we may arbitrarily deform the superwavelet by optimizing its parameters $\mathbf{n}$ with respect to the energy functional E:

$$E = \min_\mathbf{n} \| J - \Psi_\mathbf{n} \|_2^2 \tag{8}$$

Equation (8) defines the operator

$$\mathcal{P}_\Psi : \mathbb{L}^2(\mathbb{R}^2) \longmapsto \mathbb{R}^5 \tag{9}$$
$$g \longrightarrow \mathbf{n} = (c_x, c_y, \theta, s_x, s_y) ,$$

where **n** minimizes the energy functional E of eq. (8). In eq. (9) Ψ is defined to be a superwavelet. For optimization of the superwavelet parameters, the same optimization procedure as for eq. 2 may be used. An example of an optimization process can be seen in fig. 6: Shown are the initial values of **n**, the values after 2 and 4 optimization cycles of the gradient decent method and the final values after 8 cycles, each marked with the white square. The square marks the inner face region and its center position marks the center position of the corresponding superwavelet. The superwavelet used in fig. 6 is the one of fig. 2, i.e. it is derived from the person in fig. 1.

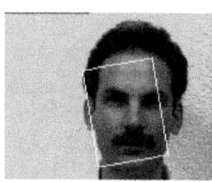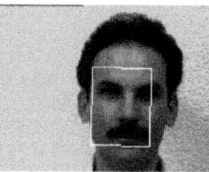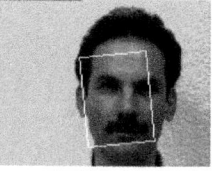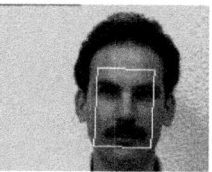

Fig. 6. The images show the 1st, the 2th, the 4th and the 8th (final) step of the gradient descent method optimizing the parameters of a superwavelet. The top left image shows the initial values with 10 px. off from the true position, rotated by 10 and scaled by 20%. The bottom right image shows the final result. As superwavelet, the GWN of figure 1 was used.

The image distortions of a planar object that is viewed under orthographic projection is described by six parameters: translation c_x, c_y, rotation θ, and dilation s_x, s_y and s_{xy}. The degrees of freedom of a wavelet only allow translation, dilation and rotation. However, it is straight forward to include also shearing and thus allow any affine deformation of $\Psi_\mathbf{n}$. For this, we enhance the parameter vector **n** to a six dimensional vector $\mathbf{n} = (c_x, c_y, \theta, s_x, s_y, s_{xy})^T$. By rewriting the scaling matrix **S**,

$$\mathbf{S} = \begin{pmatrix} s_x & s_{xy} \\ 0 & s_y \end{pmatrix} \quad ,$$

we are now able to deform the superwavelet $\Psi_\mathbf{n}$ affinely.

The reparameterization (warping) works quite robust: Using the superwavelet of fig. 1 we have found in several experiments on the various subjects with ≈ 60 pixels in width that the initialization of $\mathbf{n}_0$ may vary from the correct parameters by approx. ± 10 px. in x and y direction, by approx. 20% in scale and by approx. $\pm 10°$ in rotation (see fig. 6). Compared to the AAM, these findings indicate a much better robustness [5]. Furthermore, we found that the warping algorithm converged in 100% of the cases to the correct values when applied on the *same* individual, independently of pose and gesture. The tests were done on the images of the Yale face database [33] and on our own images. The poses were varied within the range of $\approx \pm 20°$ in pan and tilt where all face features were still visible. The various gestures included *normal, happy, sad, surprised, sleepy, glasses, wink*. The warping on other faces depended certainly on the similarity between the training person and the test person and on the number of used wavelets. We found that the warping algorithm always converged correctly on $\approx 80\%$ of the test persons (including the training person) of the Yale face database. The warping algorithm has also been successfully applied for a wavelet based affine real-time face tracking application [16].

2.4   Related Work

There are other models for image interpretation and object representation. Most of them are based on PCA [14], such as the eigenface approach [29]. The eigenface approach has shown its advantages expecially in the context of face recognition. Its major drawbacks are its sensitivity to perspective deformations and to illumination changes. PCA encodes textural information only, while geometrical information is discarded. Furthermore, the alignment of face images into a common coordinate system is still a problem.

Another PCA based approach is the active appearance model (AAM)[5]. This approach enhances the eigenface approach considerably by including geometrical information. This allows an alignment of image data into a common coordinate system while the formulation of the alignment technique can be elegantly done with techniques of the AAM framework. Also, recognition and tracking applications are presented within this framework [10]. An advantage of this approach was demonstrated in [5]: they showed the ability of the AAM to model, in a photo-realistic way, almost any face gesture and gender. However, this is undoubly an expensive task and one might ask for which task such a precision is really needed. In fact, a variation to different precision levels in order to spare computational resources and to restrict considerations to the data actually needed for a certain application seems not easily possible.

The bunch graph approach [31] is based, on the other hand, on the discrete wavelet transform. A set of Gabor wavelets are applied at a set of hand selected prominent object points, so that each point is represented by a set of filter responses, called *jet*. An object is then represented by a set of jets, that encode each a single local texture patch of the object. The jet topology, the so-called *image graph*, encodes geometrical object information. A precise positioning of the image graph onto the test image is important for good matching results and the positioning is quite a slow process. The feature detection capabilities of the Gabor filters are not exploited since their parameters are fixed and a variation to different precision levels has not been considered so far.

The bunch graph approach is inspired by the discrete wavelet transform, where, in contrary to the continuous wavelet transform, the phase space is *discrete*. The problem of how to sample the phase space is a major problem in this context and is widely studied [7; 8; 9; 12; 17; 18; 19]. In general, the discretization scheme depends on the selected wavelet function. It was studied by Lee in [17] how dense the phase space has to be sampled in order to achieve a lossless wavelet representation of an image when a Gabor function (which is non-orthonormal) is used as a wavelet. He found out that for each discrete pixel position one needs eight equidistant orientation samples and five equidistant

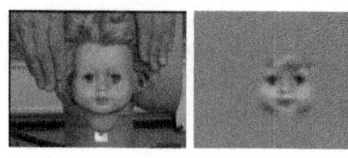

Fig. 7. The left image shows the original doll face image I, the right image shows its reconstruction $\hat{I}_{4,6}$ using formula (3) with an optimal wavelet net Ψ of just $N = 52$ odd Gabor wavelets, distributed over the inner face region. For optimization, the scheme that was introduced in section 2 was applied.

scale samples. One sees that this justifies the choice of 40 Gabor filters as given in [31]. However, one also sees that a image representation with 40 wavelets per pixel is a highly redundant representation and only applicable if reduced to a small set of feature points in the image, as done in [31]. With this, a usual bunch graph representation contains about 20 jets for each object with altogether 800 complex coefficients. The reason for this highly redundant representation [17] is that the set of filters is static, and not dynamic, as in the GWN. Alternatively, one may model the local image structure directly by explicitly selecting the correct Gabor wavelet parameters of the *continuous* phase space. This is the underlying idea of the Gabor wavelet networks. With this, as shown above, as less as 52 Gabor wavelets are sufficient for a good representation of a facial image while already 216 Gabor wavelets reach almost perfect quality.

3   Pose Estimation with GWN

In this section we will present the approach for the estimation of the pose of a head. There exist many different approaches for pose estimation, including pose estimation with color blobs [4; 6; 25], pose estimation applying a geometrical approach [11], stereo information [32] or neural networks [2], to cite just a few. While in some approaches, such as in [6; 25], only an approximate pose is estimated, other approaches have the goal to be very precise so that they could even be used as a basis for gaze detection such as in [30]. The precision of the geometrical approach [11] was extensively tested and verified in [23]. The minimal mean pan/tilt error that was reached was $> 1.6°$. In comparison to this, the neural network approach in [2] reached a minimal pan/tilt error of $> 0.64°$.

The good result in [2] was reached by first detecting the head using a color tracking approach. Within the detected color blob region, 4×4 sets of 4 complex Gabor filters with the different orientations of 0, $\frac{\pi}{4}$, $\frac{\pi}{2}$ and $\frac{3}{4}\pi$ were evenly distributed. The 128 coefficients of these 64 complex projections of the Gabor filters were then fed into a neural LLM network.

At this point, it is reasonable to assume that a precise positioning of the Gabor filters would result into an even lower mean pan/tilt error. In our experiments we therefore trained a GWN on an image I showing a doll's head. For the training of the GWN we used again the optimization scheme introduced in section 2 with $N = 52$ Gabor wavelets (see fig. 7). In order to be comparable with the approach in [2] we used in our experiments *exactly* the same neural network and the same number of training examples as described in [2]. A subspace variant of the Local Linear Map (LLM) [24] was used for learning input

- output mappings [3]. The LLM rests on a locally linear (first order) approximation of the unknown function $f : \mathbb{R}^n \mapsto \mathbb{R}^k$ and computes its output as (winner-take-all-variant) $y(x) = A_{bmu}(x - c_{bmu}) + o_{bmu}$. Here, $o_{bmu} \in \mathbb{R}^k$ is an output vector attached to the best matching unit (zero order approximation) and $A_{bmu} \in \mathbb{R}^{k \times n}$ is a local estimate of the Jacobian matrix (first oder term). Centers are distributed by a clustering algorithm. Due to the first oder term, the method is very sensitive to noise in the input. With a noisy version $x' = x + \eta$ the output differs by $A_{bmu}\eta$, and the LLM largely benefits from projecting to the local subspace, canceling the noise component of η orthogonal to the input manifold M. As basis functions normalized Gaussians were used.

The doll's head was connected to a robot arm, so that the pan/tilt ground truth was known. During the training and testing, the doll's head was first tracked using our wavelet based face tracker [16]. For each frame we proceeded in two steps:

1. optimal reparameterization of the GWN by using the positioning operator $\mathcal{P}$
2. calculating the optimal weights for the optimally repositioned GWN by using the projection operator $\mathcal{T}$.

See fig. 8 for example images. The weight vector that was calculated with the

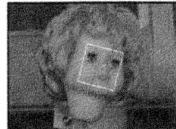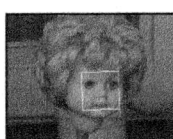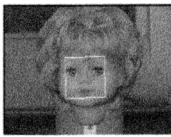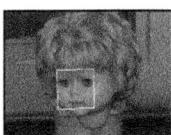

Fig. 8. The images show different orientations of the doll's head. The head is connected to a robot arm so that the ground truth is known. The white square indicates the detected position, scale and orientation of the GWN.

operator $\mathcal{T}$ was then fed into the same neural network that was used in [2]. The training was done exactly as it was described in [2]: We used 400 training images, evenly distributed within the range of $\pm 20°$ in pan and tilt direction (this is the range where all face features appeared to be visible). With this, we reached a minimal mean pan/tilt error of $0.19°$ for a GWN with 52 wavelets and a minimal mean pan/tilt error of $0.29°$ for a GWN with 16 wavelets. The maximal errors were $0.46°$ for 52 wavelets and $0.81°$ for 16 wavelets, respectively. The experiments were carried out on an experimental setup, that has not yet been integrated into a complete, single system. A complete system should reach a speed on a 450 MHz Linux Pentium of $> \approx 5$ fps for the 52 wavelet network and $> \approx 10$ fps for the 16 wavelet network [1].

In comparison, for the *gaze* detection in [30], 625 training images were used, with a 14-D input vector, to train an LLM-network. The user was advised to

---

[1] This is a conservative estimation, various optimizations should allow higher frame rates.

fixate a 5×5 grid on the computer screen. The minimal errors after training for pan and tilt were $1.5°$ and $2.5°$, respectively, while the system speed was 1 Hz on a SGI (Indigo, High Impact). A direct comparison to geometrical approaches is difficult, because, by their very nature, the cited ones are less precise, less robust but much faster.

4   Conclusions

The contribution of this article is twofold:

1. We introduced the concepts of the *Gabor wavelet network* and the *Gabor superwavelet* that allow a data reduction and the use of the *progressive attention* approach:
   - The representation of an object with variable degree of precision, from a coarse representation to an almost photo-realistic one,
   - the definition of an optimal set of filters for a selective filtering
   - the representation of object information on a basis of local image primitives and
   - the possibility for affine deformations to cope with perspective deformations.

   In the second section we discussed these various properties in detail. In [15; 16], GWNs have already been used successfully for wavelet based affine real time face tracking and pose invariant face recognition. It is future work, to fully exploit the advantages of the data reduction by reducing considerations to the vector space over the set of Gabor wavelet networks.
2. We exploited all these advantages of the GWN for the estimation of the head pose. The experimental results show quite impressively that it is sensible for an object representation to reflect the specific individual properties of the object rather than being independent of the individual properties such as general representations are. This can especially be seen when comparing the presented approach with the one in [2]: While having used the same experimental setup and the same type of neural network, the precision of the presented approach is twice as good with only 16 coefficients (vs. 128), and three times as good with only about half the coefficients. Furthermore, the experiment shows, how the precision in pose estimation and the system speed change with an increasing number of filters. A controllable variability of precision and speed has a major advantage: The system is able to decide how precise the estimation should be in order to minimize the probability that the given task is not fulfilled satisfactorily. It is future work to incorporate the experimental setup into a complete system. An enhancement for the evaluation of the positions of the irises for a precise estimation of gaze is about to be tested.

Acknowledgment. The images used are derived from the Yale Face Database.

References

[1]   C.M. Bishop. *Neural Networks for Pattern Recognition*. Clarendon Press, Oxford, 1995.

[2]   J. Bruske, E. Abraham-Mumm, J. Pauli, and G. Sommer. Head-pose estimation from facial images with subspace neural networks. In *Proc. of Int. Neural Network and Brain Conference*, pages 528–531, Beijing, China, 1998.

[3]   J. Bruske and G. Sommer. Intrinsic dimensionality extimation with optimally topology preserving maps. *IEEE Trans. Pattern Analysis and Machine Intelligence*, 20(5):572–575, 1998.

[4]   Q. Chen, H. Wu, T. Fukumoto, and M. Yachida. 3d head pose estimation without feature tracking. In *Proc. Int. Conf. on Automatic Face- and Gesture-Recognition*, pages 88–93, Nara, Japan, April 14-16, 1998.

[5]   T.F. Cootes, G.J. Edwards, and C.J. Taylor. Active appearance models. In *Proc. Fifth European Conference on Computer Vision*, volume 2, pages 484–498, Freiburg, Germany, June 1-5, 1998.

[6]   T. Darrell, B. Moghaddam, and A. Pentland. Active face tracking and pose estimation in an interactive room. In *IEEE Conf. Computer Vision and Pattern Recognition, CVPR*, pages 67–72, Seattle, WA, June 21-23, 1996.

[7]   I. Daubechies. Orthonormal bases of compactly supported wavelets. *Commun. Pure Appl. Math*, 41:909–996, 1988.

[8]   I. Daubechies. The wavelet transform, time-frequency localization and signal analysis. *IEEE Trans. Informat. Theory*, 36, 1990.

[9]   J. Daugman. Complete discrete 2D Gabor transform by neural networks for image analysis and compression. *IEEE Trans. Acoustics, Speech, and Signal Processing*, 36(7):1169–1179, 1988.

[10] G.J. Edwards, T.F. Cootes, and C.J. Taylor. Face recognition using active appearance models. In *Proc. Fifth European Conference on Computer Vision*, volume 2, pages 581–595, Freiburg, Germany, June 1-5, 1998.

[11] A. Gee and R. Cipolla. Determining the gaze of faces in images. *Image and Vision Computing*, 12(10):639–647, 1994.

[12] A. Grossmann and J. Morlet. Decomposition of hardy functions into square integrable wavlets of constant shape. *SIAM J. Math Anal.*, 15:723–736, 1984.

[13] R. Herpers, H. Kattner, H. Rodax, and G. Sommer. Gaze: An attentive processing strategy to detect and analyze t he prominent facial regions. In *Proc. Int. Workshop on Automatic Face- and Gesture-Recognition*, pages 214–220, Zurich, Switzerland, June 26-28, 1995.

[14] I. Jolliffe. *Principal Component Analysis*. Springer Verlag, New York, 1986.

[15] V Krüger, Sven Bruns, and G. Sommer. Efficient head pose estimation with gabor wavelet networks. In *Proc. British Machine Vision Conference*, Bristol, UK, Sept. 12-14, 2000.

[16] V Krüger and G. Sommer. Affine real-time face tracking using gabor wavelet networks. In *Proc. Int. Conf. on Pattern Recognition*, Barcelona, Spain, Sept. 3-8, 2000.

[17] T. S. Lee. Image representation using 2D Gabor wavelets. *IEEE Trans. Pattern Analysis and Machine Intelligence*, 18(10):959–971, 1996.

[18] S. Mallat. Multifrequency channel decompositions of images and wavelet models. *IEEE Trans. on Acoustic, Speech, and Signal Processing*, 37(12):2091–2110, Dec. 1989.

[19] S. Mallat. A theory for multiresolution signal decomposition: The wavelet representation. *IEEE Trans. Pattern Analysis and Machine Intelligence*, 11(7):674–693, 1989.

[20] B.S. Manjunath and R. Chellappa. A unified approach to boundary perception: edges, textures, and illusory contours. *IEEE Trans. Neural Networks*, 4(1):96–107, 1993.

[21] R. Mehrotra, K.R. Namuduri, and R. Ranganathan. Gabor filter-based edge detection. *Pattern Recognition*, 52(12):1479–1494, 1992.

[22] B. Moghaddam and A. Pentland. Probabilistic visual learning for object detection. *IEEE Trans. Pattern Analysis and Machine Intelligence*, 17(7):696–710, Juli 1997.

[23] Eleni Petraki. Analyse der blickrichtung des menschen und er kopforientierung im raum mittels passiver bildanalyse. Master's thesis, Technical University of Hamburg-Harburg, 1996.

[24] H. Ritter, T. Martinez, and K. Schulten. *Neuronale Netze*. Addison-Wesley, 1991.

[25] B. Schiele and A. Waibel. Gaze tracking based on face-color. In *Proc. Int. Workshop on Automatic Face- and Gesture-Recognition*, pages 344–349, Zurich, Switzerland, June 26-28, 1995.

[26] H. Szu, B. Telfer, and S. Kadambe. Neural network adaptive wavelets for signal representation and classification. *Optical Engineering*, 31(9):1907–1961, 1992.

[27] K. Toyama and G. Hager. Incremental focus of attention for robust visual tracking. In *IEEE Conf. Computer Vision and Pattern Recognition, CVPR*, pages 189–195, 1996.

[28] J.K. Tsotsos. Analyzing vision at the complexity level. *Behavioral and Brain Sci.*, 13:423–469, 1990.

[29] M. Turk and A. Pentland. Eigenfaces for recognition. *Int. Journal of Cognitive Neuroscience*, 3(1):71–89, 1991.

[30] A.C. Varchmin, R. Rae, and H. Ritter. Image based recognition of gaze direction using adaptive methods. In I. Wachsmuth, editor, *Proceedings of the International Gesture Workshop*, lncs, pages 245–257. Springer, 1997.

[31] L. Wiskott, J. M. Fellous, N. Krüger, and C. v. d. Malsburg. Face recognition by elastic bunch graph matching. *IEEE Trans. Pattern Analysis and Machine Intelligence*, 19(7):775–779, July 1997.

[32] M. Xu and T. Akatsuka. Detecting head pose from stereo image sequences for active face recognition. In *Proc. Int. Conf. on Automatic Face- and Gesture-Recognition*, pages 82–87, Nara, Japan, April 14-16, 1998.

[33] Yale Face Database. Yale university. http://cvc.yale.edu/projects/yalefaces/yalefaces.html.

[34] Q. Zhang and A. Benveniste. Wavelet networks. *IEEE Trans. Neural Networks*, 3(6):889–898, Nov. 1992.

Multi-valued Images and Their Separation[*]

Yoav Y. Schechner[1], Nahum Kiryati[2], and Joseph Shamir[3]

[1] Columbia University, New York NY 10027, USA,
yoav@cs.columbia.edu
[2] Tel-Aviv University, Ramat Aviv 69978, Israel,
nk@eng.tau.ac.il
[3] Technion - Israel Institute of Technology, Haifa 32000, Israel,
jsh@ee.technion.ac.il

Abstract. Consider scenes deteriorated by reflections off a semi-reflecting medium (e.g., a glass window) that lies between the observer and an object. We present two approaches to recover the superimposed scenes. The first one is based on a focus cue, and can be generalized to volumetric imaging with multiple layers. The second method, based on a polarization cue, can automatically label the reconstructed scenes as reflected/transmitted. It is also demonstrated how to blindly determine the imaging PSF or the orientation of the invisible (semi-reflecting) surface in space in such situations.

1 Introduction

This work deals with the situation in which the projection of the scene on the image plane is multi-valued due to the superposition of several contributions. This situation is encountered while looking through a window, where we see both the outside world (termed *real object* [12,13]), and a semi-reflection of the objects inside, termed *virtual objects*. It is also encountered in microscopy and tomography, where viewing a transparent object slice is disturbed by the superposition of adjacent defocused slices. Our goal is to clear the the disturbing crosstalk of the superimposing contributions, and gain information on the scene structure.

Previous treatment of this situation has been based mainly on motion [3,7,9, 13,23,26], and stereo [4,22]. Polarization cues have been used for such scenarios in Refs. [8,12]. Thorough polarization analysis, that enabled the labeling of the layers was done in [17,18,19,21]. This paper refers to these methods, and deals also with the use of depth of field (DOF) to analyze images. DOF has been utilized for analysis of transparent layers mainly in microscopy [1,5,6,11], but mainly in cases of opaque (and occluding) layers, as in [2,10].

---

[*] © IEEE, Kluwer Academic Publishers, and the Optical Society of America. Parts of this paper were reproduced, with permission, from the Proc. Int. Conf. on Computer Vision, Vol. II, p. 814-819 (Kerkyra, 20/Sep/1999); Proc. Conf. on Computer Vision and Pattern Recognition, Vol. I, p. 38-43 (Hilton Head Island, 12/Jun/2000); Int. J. on Computer Vision; and J. Optical Society America A, Vol. 17 p. 276-284 (2000).

Following [14] we show that the methods that rely on motion and stereo are closely related to approaches based on DOF. Then, we show how to recover the transparent layers using a focus cue. In the case of semireflections, we follow Refs. [15,16,20] to show that two raw images are adequate to recover the layers. The recovery is done in conjunction to a simple way to estimate the transfer function between the images, based on the raw images, yielding the optimal layer separation. We then show how to label each layer as reflected or transmitted using a polarization cue, which also indicates the orientation of the invisible semi-reflecting window in space. Following [17,18,19,21], our use of the polarization cue is effective also away from the Brewster angle.

2   Distance Cues

2.1   Defocus vs. Stereo or Motion

Depth cues are usually very important for the separation of transparent layers. In microscopy, each superimposing layer is at a different distance from the objective. Hence when one layer is focused (at a certain *image slice*) the others are defocus blurred, and this serves as the handle for removal of the inter-layer crosstalk. In case of semi-reflected scenes, the real object is unrelated to the virtual object. So, it is reasonable that also in this case the distance of each layer from the imaging system is different. Therefore, if the scene is viewed by a stereo system, each layer will have a different disparity; if the camera is moved, each layer will have different motion parameters; and again, if one layer is focused, the other is defocused.

Note that depth from defocus blur or focus are *realizations of triangulation* just as depth from stereo or motion are realizations of this principle [14]. Consider Fig. 1, where a stereo (or depth from motion) system is viewing the same scene as a monocular wide aperture camera of the *same physical dimensions*: the stereo baseline D is the the same as the lens aperture, the distance from the lens to the sensor, v, is the same, and the stereo system is fixated on a point at the same distance at which the wide-aperture system is focused. Then, the disparity is equal to the defocus blur diameter, under the geometric optics approximation [14].

Therefore, algorithms developed based on defocus blur can be applied to approaches based on stereo or motion, and vice-versa. Besides, these approaches will have similar fundamental limitations. Particularly for the scenarios treated in this work, seeking a separation of two transparent layers out of two raw images, in each of which the focus is different, is equivalent to separating the layers using two raw images in which the disparities are different. Blind estimation of the defocus blur kernels (or the transfer functions of the imaging system) is equivalent to seeking the motion parameters between the two stereo raw images.

In this section we treat the transparent-layers problem using methods that rely on defocus blur. However, due to the close relationship of defocus to stereo and motion, the reader may generally interchange the "defocus parameters" with "motion parameters" and extend the conclusions to classical triangulation approaches.

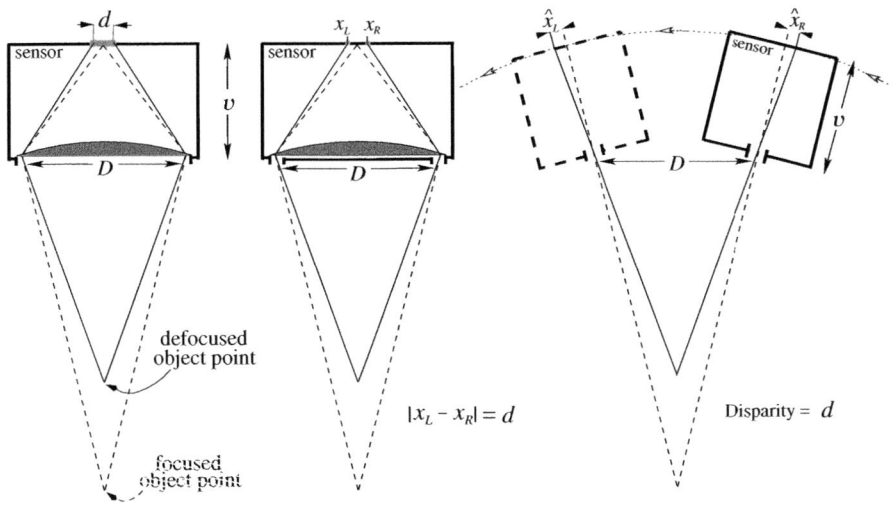

Fig. 1. [Left] The image of a defocused object point at a certain distance is a blur circle of diameter d. [Middle] Its image becomes two points separated by d, if the lens is blocked except for two pinholes at opposite sides on the lens perimeter. [Right] The disparity equals the same d in a stereo/motion system having the same physical dimensions and fixating on the point at the same distance as the point focused by the system on the left.

2.2 Recovery from Known Transfer Functions

Consider a two-layered scene. We acquire two images, such that in each image one of the layers is in focus. Assume for the moment that we also have an estimate of the blur kernel operating on each layer, when the camera is focused on the other one. Let layer f_1 be superimposed on layer f_2. We consider only the slices g_a and g_b, in which either layer f_1 or layer f_2, respectively, is in focus. The other layer is blurred. Modeling the blur as convolution with blur kernels,

$$g_a = f_1 + f_2 * h_{2a} \qquad g_b = f_2 + f_1 * h_{1b} \ . \tag{1}$$

In the frequency domain Eqs. (1) take the form

$$G_a = F_1 + H_{2a}F_2 \qquad G_b = F_2 + H_{1b}F_1 \ . \tag{2}$$

The naive inverse filtering solution of the problem is

$$\widehat{F}_1 = B(G_a - G_b H_{2a}) \qquad \widehat{F}_2 = B(G_b - G_a H_{1b}) \ , \tag{3}$$

where

$$B = (1 - H_{1b}H_{2a})^{-1} \ . \tag{4}$$

As the frequency decreases, $H_{2a}H_{1b} \to 1$, and then $B \to \infty$, hence the solution is unstable. Moreover, due to energy conservation, the average gray level (DC) is not affected by defocusing ($H_{2a}H_{1b} = 1$), hence its recovery is ill posed. However, the problem is well posed and stable at the high frequencies. This behavior also exists in separation methods that rely on motion [15,16], as expected from the discussion in section 2.1. Note that this is quite opposite to typical reconstruction problems, in which instability and noise amplification appear in the high frequencies.

If $H_{2a}H_{1b} \neq 1$ (that is, except at the DC), B can be approximated by the series

$$\widehat{B}(m) = \sum_{k=1}^{m} (H_{1b}H_{2a})^{k-1} \ . \tag{5}$$

The approximate solutions $\widehat{F}_1(m), \widehat{F}_2(m)$ are thus parameterized by m which controls how close the filter $\widehat{B}(m)$ is to the inverse filter, and is analogous to regularization parameters in typical inversion methods. We define the *basic solution* as the result of using $m = 1$.

Another approach to layer separation is based on using as input a pinhole image and a focused slice, rather than two focused slices. Acquiring one image via a very small aperture ("pinhole camera") leads to a simpler algorithm, since just a single slice with one of the layers in focus is needed. The advantage is that the two images are taken without changing the axial positions of the system components, hence no geometric distortions arise. The "pinhole" image is described by

$$g_0 = (f_1 + f_2)/a \ , \tag{6}$$

where $1/a$ is the attenuation of the intensity due to contraction of the aperture. This image is used in conjunction with one of the focused slices of Eq. (1), for example g_a. The inverse filtering solution is

$$\widehat{F}_1 = S(G_a - aG_0H_{2a}) \qquad \widehat{F}_2 = S(aG_0 - G_a) \ , \tag{7}$$

where

$$S = (1 - H_{2a})^{-1} \ . \tag{8}$$

Also in this method the filter S can be approximated by

$$\widehat{S}(m) = \sum_{k=1}^{m} H_{2a}^{k-1}. \tag{9}$$

2.3   Blind Estimation of the Transfer Functions

The imaging PSFs (and thus their corresponding transfer functions) may be different than the ones we estimate and use in the reconstruction algorithm. As shown in [16,20] an error in the PSF leads to contamination of the recovered layer by its complementary. The larger $\widehat{B}$ is, the stronger is the amplification of this disturbance. Note that $\widehat{B}(m)$ monotonically increases with m, within the support of the blur transfer function if $H_{1b}H_{2a} > 0$, as is the case when the recovery PSFs are Gaussians. Thus, we may expect that the best sense of separation will be achieved in the basic solution, even though the low frequencies are less attenuated and better balanced with the high frequencies at higher m's.

We wish to achieve self-calibration, i.e., to estimate the kernels out of the images themselves. This enables blind separation and restoration of the layers. Thus, we need a criterion for layer separation. It is reasonable to assume that the statistical dependence of the real and virtual layers is small since they usually originate from unrelated scenes. Mutual information measures how far the images are from statistical independence [16]. We thus assume that if the layers are correctly separated, each of their estimates contains *minimum information* about the other. Mutual information was suggested and used as a criterion for alignment in [24,25], where its maximum was sought. We use this measure to look for the highest discrepancy between images, thus minimizing it. To decrease the dependence of the estimated mutual information on the dynamic range and brightness of the individual layers, it was normalized by the mean entropy of the estimated layers, when treated as individual images. This measure, denoted $\mathcal{I}_n$, indicates the ratio of mutual information to the self information of a layer. Additional details are given in [16,20].

The recovered layers depend on the kernels used. Therefore, seeking the kernels can be stated as a minimization problem:

$$[\tilde{h}_{1b}, \tilde{h}_{2a}] = \arg \min_{h_{1b}, h_{2a}} \mathcal{I}_n(\hat{f}_1, \hat{f}_2) \ . \qquad (10)$$

As noted above, errors in the kernels lead to crosstalk (contamination) of the estimated layers, which is expected to increase their mutual information. To simplify the problem, the kernels can be assumed to be Gaussians. Then, the kernels are parameterized only by their standard deviations (proportional to the blur radii). The blurring along the sensor raster rows may be different than the blurring along the columns. So, generally we assigned a different blur "radius" to each axis. If two slices are used, there are two kernels, and the optimization is done over a total of four parameters. When a single focused slice is used in conjunction with a "pinhole" image, the problem is much simpler. We need to determine the parameters of only one kernel, and the factor a. a can be indicated from the ratio of the *f-numbers* of the camera in the two states, or from the ratio of the average values of the images.

2.4   Recovery Experiments

A print of the "Portrait of Doctor Gachet" (by van-Gogh) was positioned closely behind a glass window. The window partly reflected a more distant picture, a part of a print of the "Parasol" (by Goya). The cross correlation between the raw (focused) images is 0.98. The normalized mutual information is $\mathcal{I}_n \approx 0.5$ indicating that significant separation is achieved by the focusing process, but that substantial crosstalk remains. The basic solution ($m = 1$) based on the optimal parameters is shown at the middle row of Fig. 2. It has $\mathcal{I}_n \approx 0.006$ (two orders of magnitude better than the raw images). Using $m = 5$ yields better a balance between the low and high frequency components, but $\mathcal{I}_n$ increased to about 0.02. As noted above, the theory [16,20] indicates that an error in the PSF

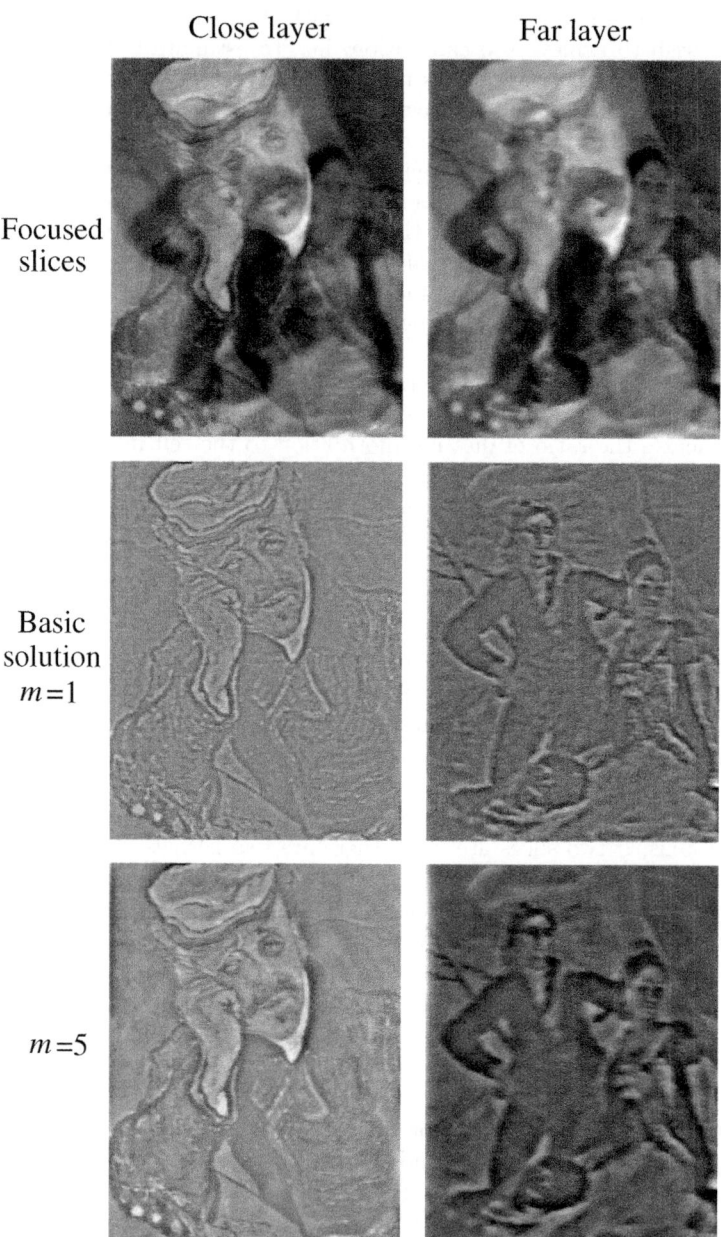

Fig. 2. [Top]: The slices in which either of the transparent layers is focused. [Middle row]: The basic solution ($m = 1$). [Bottom row]: Recovery with $m = 5$.

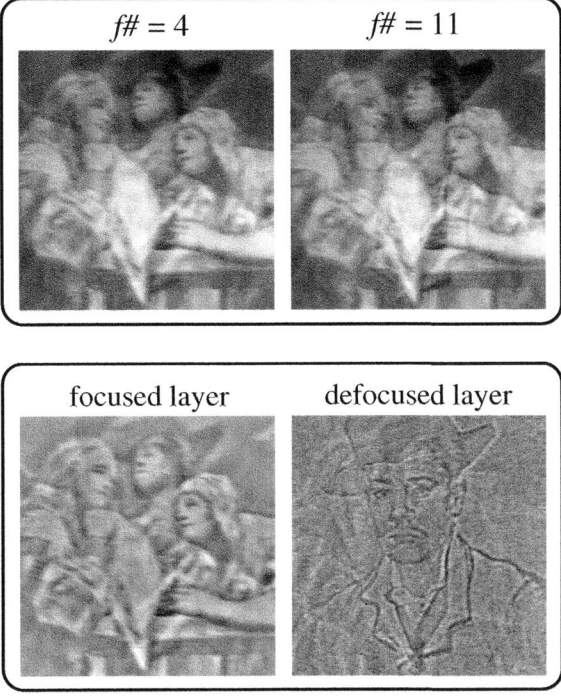

Fig. 3. [Top]: Raw images: the far layer is focused when viewed with a wide aperture, and with a "pinhole" setup. [Bottom]: The basic recovery.

model, yields a stronger crosstalk for larger m. Hence this increase in $\mathcal{I}_n$ may originate from the inaccuracy of our assumption of a Gaussian model.

In another example, the scene consisted of a print of the "Portrait of Armand Roulin" as the close layer and a print of a part of the "Miracle of San Antonio" as the far layer. Here we used a fixed focus setting, and changed the aperture between image acquisitions. The slice in which the far layer is focused (using the wide aperture) is at the top-left of Fig. 3, and the "pinhole" image is to its right. The basic solution based on the optimal parameters is shown on the bottom of Fig. 3. The "Portrait" is revealed.

3   Labeling by a Polarization Cue

3.1   Recovery from a Known Inclination Angle

Distance cues do not indicate which of the layers is the reflected (virtual) one, and which is the transmitted (real) one. However, polarization cues give us a simple way to achieve both the layer separation and their labeling as real/virtual. At the semi-reflecting medium (e.g, a glass window) the reflection coefficients are different for each of the light polarization components, and are denoted by $\tilde{R}_\perp$ and $\tilde{R}_\parallel$ for the polarization components perpendicular and parallel to the plane of incidence, respectively. They can be analytically derived as functions of the surface inclination (angle of incidence, φ) from the Fresnel equations [17,21], taking into account the effect of internal reflections [17,19] in the medium. The transmission coefficient of each component is given by

$$\tilde{T} = 1 - \tilde{R} \ . \qquad (11)$$

We denote the image due to the real layer (with no window) by I_T and the image due to the virtual layer (assuming a perfect mirror replacing the window) by I_R. The light coming from the real object is superimposed with the light coming from the virtual object. Let the scene be imaged through a linear polarizer, by which we can select to sense the perpendicular or the parallel components ($g_\perp$ and $g_\parallel$, respectively) of the observed light coming from the scene. Thus, the two raw images are:

$$g_\perp = I_R \tilde{R}_\perp / 2 + I_T \tilde{T}_\perp / 2 \qquad g_\parallel = I_R \tilde{R}_\parallel / 2 + I_T \tilde{T}_\parallel / 2 \ , \qquad (12)$$

for initially unpolarized natural light. Solving these equations for the two images we obtain the estimated intensities of the layers as a function of an assumed angle of incidence, φ:

$$\hat{I}_T(\varphi) = \left[\frac{2\tilde{R}_\perp(\varphi)}{\tilde{R}_\perp(\varphi) - \tilde{R}_\parallel(\varphi)} \right] g_\parallel - \left[\frac{2\tilde{R}_\parallel(\varphi)}{\tilde{R}_\perp(\varphi) - \tilde{R}_\parallel(\varphi)} \right] g_\perp \qquad (13)$$

$$\hat{I}_R(\varphi) = \left[\frac{2 - 2\tilde{R}_\parallel(\varphi)}{\tilde{R}_\perp(\varphi) - \tilde{R}_\parallel(\varphi)} \right] g_\perp - \left[\frac{2 - 2\tilde{R}_\perp(\varphi)}{\tilde{R}_\perp(\varphi) - \tilde{R}_\parallel(\varphi)} \right] g_\parallel \ . \qquad (14)$$

Therefore, the layers are recovered by simple weighted subtractions of the raw images. Moreover, the equation for $\hat{I}_T$ is distinct from the equation for $\hat{I}_R$, so the separate layers are automatically *labeled* as reflected/transmitted (i.e., virtual/real). Note, however, that the weights in these subtractions are functions of the angle at which the invisible (but semireflecting) medium is inclined with respect to the viewer.

3.2   The Inclination of the Invisible Surface

In case the angle of incidence used in the reconstruction process is not the true inclination angle of the surface φ_{true}, each recovered layer will contain traces of the complimentary layer (crosstalk). In an experiment we performed [19,21], a scene composed of several objects was imaged through an upright glass window. The window semi-reflected another scene (virtual object). A linear polarizer was rotated in front of the camera between consecutive image acquisitions. The reflected layer is attenuated in $g_\parallel$ (Fig. 4) but its disturbance is still significant, since $\varphi_{\text{true}} = 27.5^o \pm 3^o$, was far from the Brewster angle 56° (at which the reflection disappears in $g_\parallel$). Having assumed that the true angle of incidence is

Fig. 4. The raw images. [Left]: $g_\perp$. [Right]: Although the reflected component is smaller in $g_\parallel$, the image is still unclear.

unknown, φ was guessed. As seen in Fig. 5, when the angle was underestimated negative traces appeared in the reconstruction (bright areas in $\hat{I}_R$ are darker than their surroundings in $\hat{I}_T$). When the angle was overestimated, the traces are positive (bright areas in $\hat{I}_R$ are brighter than their surroundings in $\hat{I}_T$). When the correct angle is used, the crosstalk is removed, and the labeled layers are well separated.

An automatic way to detect this angle is by seeking the reconstruction that minimizes the mutual information between the estimated layers, in a similar manner to the procedure of section 2.3:

$$\hat{\varphi} = \arg \min_{\varphi} \mathcal{I}_n[\hat{I}_T(\varphi), \hat{I}_R(\varphi)] \ . \tag{15}$$

In this experiment $\mathcal{I}_n$ is minimized at $\varphi = 25.5^o$. The angle at which the esti-mated layers are decorrelated is $\varphi = 27^o$ (Fig. 5). Both these values are within the experimental error of the physical measurement of φ_{true}. Note that the cor-relation sign is consistent with the "positive/negative" traces when the assumed angle is wrong.

The reconstruction of the real layer ($\hat{I}_T$) in the experiment is more sensitive to an error in the angle of incidence, than the reconstruction of the virtual layer ($\hat{I}_R$). In Fig. 5 the contamination in the estimated $\hat{I}_R$ by I_T is hardly visible, if at all. On the other hand, the contamination in the estimated $\hat{I}_T$ by I_R is more apparent. This result is consistent with a theoretical prediction published in Ref. [21]. In that work, the relative contamination of each recovered layer by its complimentary was derived. It was normalized by the "signal to noise ratio" of the layers when no polarizer is used. We outline here just the final result of the first-order derivation from Ref. [21]. Fig. 6 plots (solid line) the first order of c_T, which is the theoretical relative contamination of the transmitted layer by the virtual layer. It is much larger than the relative contamination c_R of the recovered reflected layer by the real layer (dashed line).

According to Fig. 6, at $\varphi_{\text{true}} = 27^o$, $\hat{I}_T$ will be $\approx 8\%$ contaminated by I_R per 1° error in φ. Thus for the 10° error of Fig. 5 we get $\approx 80\%$ contamination (if the first order approximation still holds), when the reflected contribution is as bright as the transmitted one. If the reflection is weaker, the contamination will

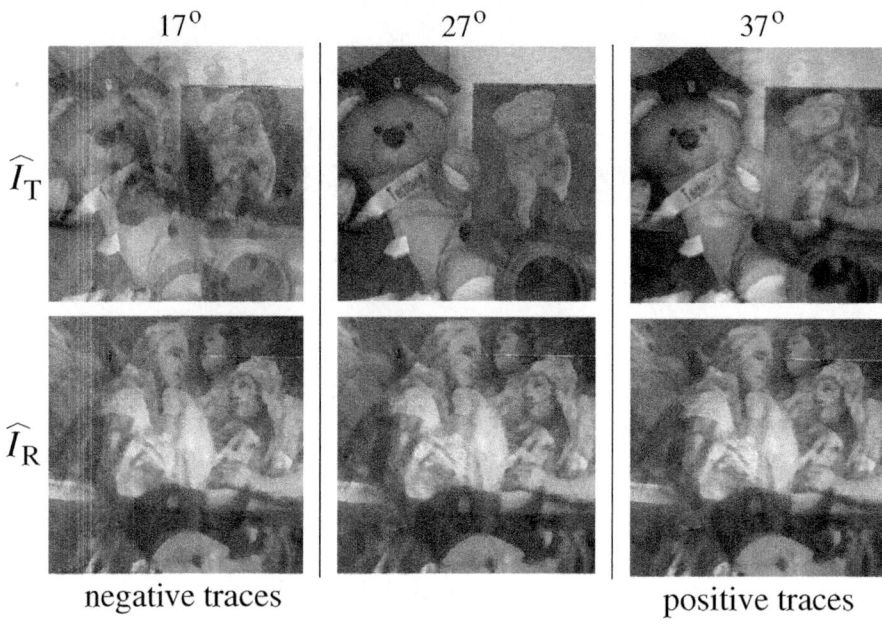

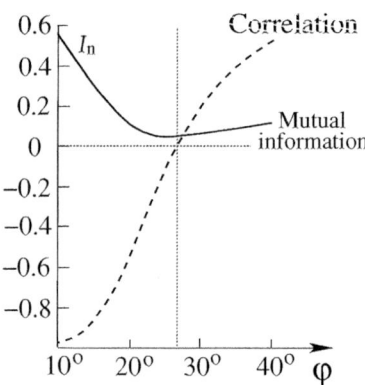

Fig. 5. Experimental results. When the assumed angle of incidence is correct ($\varphi = \varphi_{\text{true}} = 27°$), the separation is good. In cases of under-estimation or over-estimation of the angle, negative or positive traces of the complementary layer appear, respectively. This is also seen in the increase of mutual information and in the correlation of the estimated layers. The traces are stronger in $\hat{I}_T$ than in $\hat{I}_R$, in consistency with Fig. 6.

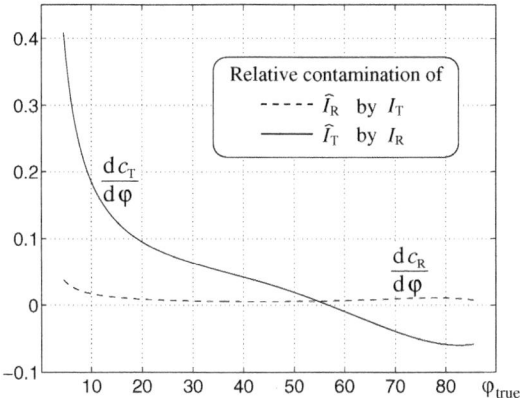

Fig. 6. The relative contamination of the each layer, per 1° of error in the angle of incidence, if the reflected contribution is as bright as the transmitted one (after the incidence on a glass window).

be proportionally smaller. On the other hand, $\hat{I}_R$ will be just $\approx 3\%$ contaminated by I_T at 10° error from φ_{true}, when the reflected contribution is as bright as the transmitted one. This is the reason why in this experiment $\hat{I}_R$ appears to be much more robust to the angle error than $\hat{I}_T$.

4   Discussion

This paper concentrated on the analysis of multi-valued images that occur when looking through a semi-reflecting surface, such as a glass window. We have shown that two raw images suffice to separate the two contributing layers. Polarization cues enable the labeling of each of the layers as real or virtual. They also enable the extraction of information on the clear semi-reflecting surface itself (its inclination in space). However, it seems to be very difficult to use this approach if the problem is scaled to more than two contributing layers. Another shortcoming of this approach is that it is not applicable if the transparent layers do not involve reflections (as occur in volumetric specimens).

The distance cue can easily be scaled for cases where there are more than two layers. Actually, it is used in volumetric specimens (which may have a continuum of layers), based on the focus cue. Our demonstration is definitely not limited to the focus/defocus cue, since defocus blur, motion blur, and stereo disparity have similar origins [14] and differ mainly in the scale and shape of the kernels. Therefore, the success of the methods that are based on defocus blur is an encouraging step towards understanding and demonstrating the estimation of the motion PSFs or stereo disparities in transparent scenes from as few as 2 images, and recovering the layers from them. However, if a small baseline suffices to separate the layers, then a method based on defocus blur may be preferable since depth from defocus is more stable with respect to perturbations and occlusions than methods that rely on stereo or motion, for the same physical dimensions of the setup [14]. On the other hand, methods that rely on distance cues seem to have an inherent ill-conditioning at the low frequency components, and a labeling ambiguity in cases of semi-reflections.

In microscopy and in tomography, the suggested method for self calibration of the PSF can improve the removal of crosstalk between adjacent slices. However, in these cases significant correlation exists between adjacent layers, so the correlation criterion may not be adequate. This is therefore a possible direction for future research.

Since methods relying of distance cues somewhat complement methods that rely of polarization cues, fusion of these cues for separating semi-reflections is a promising research direction. The ability to separate transparent layers can be utilized to generate special effects. For example, in Ref. [2,10] images were rendered with each of the occluding (opaque) layers defocused, moved and enhanced independently. The same effects, and possibly other interesting ones can now be generated in scenes containing semireflections.

Acknowledgment. We thank Ronen Basri for his helpful advice, and Alex Bekker for helping to set up the experiments.

References

[1] Agard, D. A., Sedat, J. W.: Three-dimensional structure of a polytene nucleus. Nature **302** (1983) 676–681.

[2] Aizawa, K., Kodama, K., Kubota, A.: Producing object-based special effects by fusing multiple differently focused images. IEEE Trans. on Circuits and Systems for Video Technology **10** (2000) 323–330.

[3] Bergen, J. R., Burt, P. J., Hingorani, R., Peleg, S.: A three-frame algorithm for estimating two-component image motion. IEEE Trans. Pattern. Anal. Mach. Intell. **14** (1992) 886–895.

[4] Borga, M., Knutsson, H.: Estimating multiple depths in semi-transparent stereo images. Proc. Scandinavian Conf. on Image Analysis Vol. I (1999) 127–133. Kangerlussuaq, Greenland. Published by the Pattern Recognition Society of Denmark, Lyngby, Denmark.

[5] Castleman, K. R.: Digital image processing (1979) 357–360. Prentice-Hall, New Jersey.

[6] Conchello, J. A., Hansen E. W.: Enhanced 3-D reconstruction from confocal scanning microscope images. I: Deterministic and maximum likelihood reconstructions. Applied Optics bf 29 (1990) 3795–3804.

[7] Darrell, T., Simoncelli, E.: 'Nulling' filters and the separation of transparent motions. Proc. IEEE Computer Society Conference on Computer Vision and Pattern Recognition (1993) 738–739,

[8] Farid H., Adelson, E. H.: Separating reflections from images by use of independent components analysis. J. Opt. Soc. Am. A **16** (1999) 2136–2145.

[9] Irani, M., Rousso, B., Peleg, S.: Computing occluding and transparent motions. Int. J. Comp. Vis. **12** (1994) 5–16.

[10] Kubota, A., Aizawa, K.: Inverse filters for generation of arbitrarily focused images. Proc. SPIE **4067** Visual Communications and Image Processing (2000) 1633–1641.

[11] Marcias-Garza, F., Bovik, A. C., Diller, K. R., Aggarwal, S. J., Aggarwal, J. K.: The missing cone problem and low-pass distortion in optical serial sectioning microscopy. Proc. IEEE International Conference on Acoustics, Speech, and Signal Processing, Vol-II (1988) 890–893.

[12] Ohnishi, N. Kumaki, K., Yamamura T., Tanaka, T.: Separating real and virtual objects from their overlapping images. Proc. European Conf. on Computer Vision Vol. II, Lecture notes in Computer Science **1065** (1996) 636-646.

[13] Oren M., Nayar, S. K.: A theory of specular surface geometry. Proc. IEEE International Conf. on Computer Vision (1995) 740–747

[14] Schechner, Y. Y., Kiryati, N.: Depth from defocus vs. Stereo: How different really are they? Int. J. Computer Vision **39** (2000) 141–162.

[15] Schechner, Y. Y., Kiryati N., Basri, R.: Separation of transparent layers using focus. Proc. IEEE International Conf. on Computer Vision 1061–1066 (1998) Mumbai, India.

[16] Schechner, Y. Y., Kiryati N., Basri, R.: Separation of transparent layers using focus. International J. on Computer Vision, **39** (2000) 25–39.

[17] Schechner, Y. Y., Kiryati N., Shamir, J.: Separation of transparent layers by polarization analysis. Proc. Scandinavian Conf. on Image Analysis, Vol. I (1999) 235–242. Published by the Pattern Recognition Society of Denmark, Lyngby, Denmark.

[18] Schechner, Y. Y., Shamir, J., Kiryati, N.: Vision through semireflecting media: Polarization analysis. Optics Letters **24** (1999) 1088-1090.

[19] Schechner, Y. Y., Shamir, J., Kiryati, N.: Polarization-based decorrelation of transparent layers: The inclination angle of of an invisible surface. Proc. IEEE International Conf. on Computer Vision, Vol. II (1999) 814–819.

[20] Schechner, Y. Y., Kiryati, N., Shamir, J.: Blind recovery of transparent and semireflected scenes. Proc. IEEE Computer Society Conference on Computer Vision and Pattern Recognition, Vol. I (2000) 38–43,

[21] Schechner, Y. Y., Shamir, J., Kiryati, N.: Polarization and statistical analysis of scenes containing a semireflector. J. Opt. Soc. Am. A **17** (2000) 276–284.

[22] Shizawa, M.: On visual ambiguities due to transparency in motion and stereo. Proc. European Conf. on Computer Vision. Lecture notes in Computer Science **588** (1992) 411–419.

[23] Shizawa, M., Mase, K.: Simultaneous multiple optical flow estimation. Proc. International Conference on Pattern Recognition, Vol. 1 (1990) 274–278.

[24] Thevenaz, P., Unser, M.: An efficient mutual information optimizer for multiresolution image registration. Proc. IEEE Computer Society International Conference on Image Processing, Vol. I (1998) 833–837.

[25] Viola, P., Wells, W. M. III: Alignment by maximization of mutual information. Int. J. of Computer Vision **24** (1997) 137-154.

[26] Wang, J. Y. A., Adelson, E. H.: Layered representation for motion analysis. Proc. IEEE Computer Society Conference on Computer Vision and Pattern Recognition (1993) 361–365.

Towards Segmentation from Multiple Cues: Symmetry and Color

Roy Shor and Nahum Kiryati

Dept. of Electrical Engineering–Systems, Tel Aviv University
Tel Aviv 69978, Israel
nk@eng.tau.ac.il

Abstract. Towards segmentation from multiple cues, this paper demonstrates the combined use of color and symmetry for detecting regions of interest (ROI), using the detection of man-made wooden objects and the detection of faces as working examples. A functional that unifies color compatibility and color-symmetry within elliptic supports is defined. Using this functional, the ROI detection problem becomes a five-dimensional global optimization problem. Exhaustive-search is inapplicable due its prohibitive computational cost. Genetic search converges rapidly and provides good results. The added value obtained by combining color and symmetry is demonstrated.

1 Introduction

Most segmentation methods associate a scalar measurement or a vector of measurements with each pixel, characterizing its grey level, color or the texture to which it belongs. Once the measurement space has been defined, segmentation can be viewed as an optimization problem: regions should be uniform internally, different from adjacent ones and "reasonable" in their number and shapes. Formalizing these vague concepts in the form of an objective function and devising an efficient way to perform the search are both difficult problems.

The gestalt school suggested grouping principles that guide human perceptual organization. They include similarity, proximity, continuation, symmetry, simplicity and closure. Incorporating the gestalt principles in machine vision is an attractive idea [25]. In particular, the gestalt principles relate to *global* shape properties and represent *a-priori* visual preferences, issues that a successful segmentation method should address. Note, however, that studies in human perceptual organization are often limited to binary images, commonly to dot patterns. In computer vision, using binarized images requires successful edge detection, which is largely equivalent to segmentation, thus relying on the unknown. Application of the gestalt principles to image segmentation is thus desirable, but not straightforward.

Symmetry is one of the gestalt grouping principles. It appears in man made objects and is also common in nature [17,29]. The omnipresence of symmetry

R. Klette et al. (Eds.): Multi-Image Analysis, LNCS 2032, pp. 142–152, 2001.
© Springer-Verlag Berlin Heidelberg 2001

has motivated many studies on symmetry in images, see e.g., [21,22,26,32]. The possibility of rapidly finding symmetric areas in raw gray level images, as shown in [22], encourages the use of symmetry as a cue for segmentation. However, symmetry is not always maximal where expected. One example in [22] shows greater symmetry between a tree and its shadow than the symmetry of the tree itself. This indicates that symmetry alone is insufficient and that additional cues should be used. Our long term goal is to develop a unified low-level vision module, in which several basic visual tasks, each difficult when carried out separately, assist one another towards accomplishing their missions. This will simplify vision system design, require less top-down feedback and lead to more stable and robust performance.

This paper is a step towards computationally efficient symmetry aided segmentation. The idea of carrying out segmentation in conjunction with symmetry detection is not new in itself [18,21,22,28,31], but the concept is still in its infancy and much remains to be studied. Our approach is quite general, but is presented here in the context of two specific vision tasks: the detection of man-made wooden objects, and the well-studied frontal-view face detection task [2,8, 12]. Starting from a color image, the similarity of each pixel color to wood color or to skin color can be quantified. Many algorithms for face detection based on skin color are available, e.g. [1,11,13,14,30]. Face detection using symmetry has also been considered, e.g. [3,4,11]. Our interest is in the *added value* obtained by performing segmentation *in conjunction* with symmetry detection, rather than as separate processes. Progress in this direction has recently been described in [9].

To maintain the generality of the method presented, we intentionally ignore highly specific and application-dependent cues that can be very useful in particular applications, such as the position and exact shape of facial features in the case of face detection. The algorithm can thus be applied, with minimal changes, to other computer vision problems, where roughly symmetric objects, characterized by some uniformity in an arbitrary measurement space, have to be rapidly detected.

Let D denote an elliptical domain at any location, orientation and scale within a color image I. D is thus characterized by five parameters. Let $S(D)$ denote a measure of the symmetry of the image within D, with respect to the major axis of D, taking color into account. Let $C(D)$ quantify the color-compatibility of D, i.e., the dominance of wood-colored (or skin-colored) pixels within D. Define a functional $F(D) \equiv \mathcal{F}\{S(D), C(D), D\}$ that combines symmetry, color compatibility and size. The global maximum of $F(D)$ corresponds to some elliptical domain D^* in which the image is highly symmetric and exhibits high color compatibility. The operational goal is to efficiently find D^*.

2   Color Compatibility

Identifying the "best" color-space for grouping tasks such as skin segmentation is still controversial. We carried out a modest performance evaluation, using images taken locally and some images from the University of Stirling face database [10].

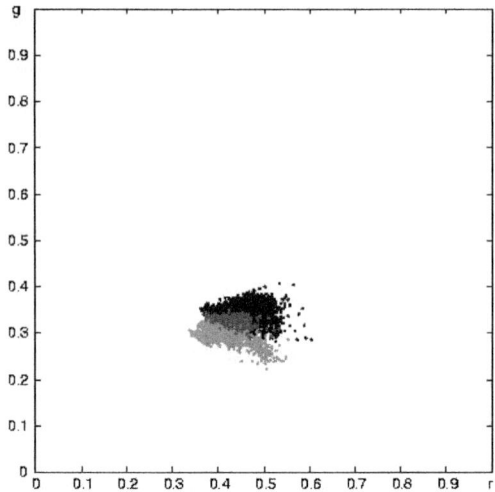

Fig. 1. *Light grey:* A scatter-diagram showing the position in the *rgb* space (normalized *RGB*) of the skin pixels in 35 face images. Some of the images were imported from the Stirling database [10], a few were taken locally. *Black:* The clustering of wood colors, taken from 7 images of objects made of dark and light wood. *Dark grey:* Positions in which skin and wood colors overlap.

We compared the following color-spaces: *RGB*, *YES* [11], *TSV* [13], *rgb* (normalized RGB: *NRGB*) [33], *HSV*, *XYZ*, *L***U***V** and *xyz* [5]. It turned out that *YES*, *rgb* and *TSV* were most useful for skin segmentation, *rgb* yielding the best results in our tests. The *rgb* color space is defined by

$$r = \frac{R}{R+G+B}, g = \frac{G}{R+G+B}, b = \frac{B}{R+G+B} \tag{1}$$

The transformation from *RGB* to *rgb* is nonlinear. All values are normalized by intensity $(R + G + B)$ and $b = 1 - r - g$. Note that skin colors typical to people of different origins, including Asian, African American and Caucasian cluster in the *rgb* color space [33]. Furthermore, the *rgb* color space is insensitive to surface orientation and illumination direction [6]. The light-grey points in Fig. 1 depict the scatter in the *rgb* color-space of skin-pixels from 35 face images. Colors of different wood types also cluster in the *rgb* space (black points). Note the overlap between skin and wood colors (dark grey).

Let $\mathbf{f}(i,j) = [r(i,j), g(i,j)]^T$ denote the normalized color vector at a specific pixel (i, j). We wish to obtain $c(i, j)$, a measure of the similarity of $\mathbf{f}(i, j)$ to a given family of colors, e.g., wood colors or skin colors. The method used is inspired by a skin detection algorithm presented in [11], but we use the *rgb* color-space while [11] uses *YES*. More important, in [11] $c(i, j)$ is a binary function, classifying pixels as either members or non-members of the family, while here intermediate similarity values are accommodated.

Table 1. The mean vector $\boldsymbol{\mu}$ and the covariance matrix $\mathbf{K}$ for skin and wood.

Family	$\boldsymbol{\mu}$	$\mathbf{K}$
Skin	$\begin{pmatrix} 0.41 \\ 0.31 \end{pmatrix}$	$\begin{pmatrix} 9.00\ 0.67 \\ 0.67\ 2.51 \end{pmatrix} \cdot 10^{-4}$
Wood	$\begin{pmatrix} 0.46 \\ 0.35 \end{pmatrix}$	$\begin{pmatrix} 10.2\ -0.6 \\ -0.6\ 2.7 \end{pmatrix} \cdot 10^{-4}$

The class-conditional probability density function of skin-colored pixels can be reasonably modeled by a two dimensional Gaussian [33], where the mean vector $\boldsymbol{\mu}$ and the covariance matrix $\mathbf{K}$ are estimated from an appropriate training set. Our small-scale experiments indicate that a 2-D Gaussian model is suitable for wood-color as well. Equal-height contours of the color-family probability density function are ellipses in the r-g plane, whose centers are all at $\boldsymbol{\mu}$ and whose principal axes depend on $\mathbf{K}$. Table 1 shows the mean vector $\boldsymbol{\mu}$ and the covariance matrix $\mathbf{K}$ obtained for skin and wood from Fig. 1.

The similarity measure $c(i,j)$ is taken as the color-family probability density of $\mathbf{f}(i,j)$, i.e.

$$c(i,j) = \exp\left\{ -\frac{1}{2}[\mathbf{f}(i,j) - \boldsymbol{\mu}]^T \mathbf{K}^{-1}[\mathbf{f}(i,j) - \boldsymbol{\mu}] \right\} \tag{2}$$

Visualizations of $c(i,j)$ are shown in Fig. 2. Given an image domain D, its color compatibility is quantified as

$$C(D) = \frac{1}{||D||} \sum_{(i,j)\in D} c(i,j). \tag{3}$$

3   Color Symmetry Measurement

The mirror-symmetry of a continuous scalar function $f(x,y)$ with respect to the x-axis can be measured [22,23,34] by a reflectional correlation coefficient

$$S_f = \frac{\iint f(x,y)f(x,-y)dx\,dy}{\iint f^2(x,y)dx\,dy}. \tag{4}$$

Note that any function f can be expressed as the sum of a fully symmetric component f_s and a perfectly anti-symmetric component f_{as}; it is easy to show that

$$S_f = \frac{||f_s||^2 - ||f_{as}||^2}{||f_s||^2 + ||f_{as}||^2}. \tag{5}$$

For non-negative functions f, $S_f \in [0,1]$.

Fig. 2. *Top:* Two color images (grey-level versions shown). *Bottom:* The corresponding skin (left) or wood (right) similarity functions $c(i,j)$.

Symmetry measurement with respect to an arbitrary axis t, in a translated and rotated coordinate system (t,s), can be implemented by alignment of the (t,s) system with the (x,y) system, i.e., translation and rotation of the relevant sub-image to a standard position. In this research, local symmetry is measured in *elliptic* domains. This is accomplished by multiplying the relevant sub-image, in the standard position, by an elliptical Gaussian window

$$G(x,y,r_x,r_y) = \frac{1}{2\pi r_x r_y} \, e^{-x^2/2r_x^2} \cdot e^{-y^2/2r_y^2} \, , \tag{6}$$

where (r_x, r_y) are referred to as the effective radii of the elliptic support.

Variations in illumination intensity over the scene distort symmetry measurements based on grey levels. This phenomenon must be taken into consideration in face image analysis, since most face images are taken indoors, with great spatial variability in the illumination intensity. One novel aspect of this research is symmetry measurement of *color* images. By using the *rgb* (normalized *RGB*) color-space, the symmetry measured is that of a vector field of normalized color components. This compensates for spatial intensity variations.

The reflectional color symmetry measure of a color image $\mathbf{f}$ in a domain D is defined as

$$S(D) = \frac{||r||^2 S_r(D) + ||g||^2 S_g(D) + ||b||^2 S_b(D)}{||r||^2 + ||g||^2 + ||b||^2} \tag{7}$$

i.e., the weighted average of the 2-D symmetry values measured in the r, g and b normalized color components with respect to the energy in each component (within D).

Given the image $\mathbf{f}(i, j)$, the measure $S(D)$ of color symmetry in an elliptical domain D is a function of five parameters: the center coordinates of D, the effective radii corresponding to D and the orientation of D, i.e., the angle between its major axis and the x-axis. Observe that $S(D)$ is in itself scale-invariant, reflecting the fact that magnification has no effect on symmetry.

4   Objective Function

As defined, the measures of color compatibility $C(D)$ and color symmetry $S(D)$ within an elliptic domain D are scale invariant. Therefore, the symmetry and color compatibility associated with a tiny symmetric area of the right color will be higher than in a larger support, in which both symmetry are color compatibility are not as perfect. This is an undesirable state of affairs, since in any relevant image one may find many unimportant tiny symmetric regions of the right color, and at the limit each single pixel is perfectly symmetric and uniform in color. Regions of interest for image segmentation are usually much larger. Scale dependence should therefore be built into the objective function. The objective function is also the point of choice for imposing application-specific a-priori knowledge and preferences, possibly expressed via a function $P(D)$. Thus, the objective function takes the general form $F(D) = \mathcal{F}\{S(D), C(D), D, P(D)\}$. The objective function used in this research is of the form

$$F(D) = S^k(D) \cdot C^l(D) \cdot ||D|| \cdot P(D) \tag{8}$$

where k and l are positive integers. $P(D)$ was used, for example, to limit the ratio between the length of the major and minor axes in an elliptic approximation of a human face.

5   Global Optimization

Given an image, the objective function is a highly complex, multimodal function of five parameters: the coordinates of the centroid of the supporting region, its effective radii and its orientation. Maximizing the objective function is an elaborate global optimization problem. Solving this problem by exhaustive search is computationally prohibitive.

We implemented both a conventional genetic search algorithm [20] and a variation of the probabilistic genetic algorithm (PGA) described in [22]. Both

Fig. 3. The suggested algorithm applied as a face detector. Note that, to maintain generality, the method relies only on symmetry and color-fitness: facial features are not used. Grey level versions of the actual color images are shown. *Top-left:* By measuring symmetry in the normalized color channels, large illumination variations can be accommodated. *Top-right:* Since facial features are not used, glasses pose no difficulty other than a slight reduction in color compatibility. *Middle-left:* Added value provided by the color cue. *Middle-right:* Added value brought by the symmetry cue. *Bottom-left:* Asymmetric background. *Bottom-right:* Cluttered background.

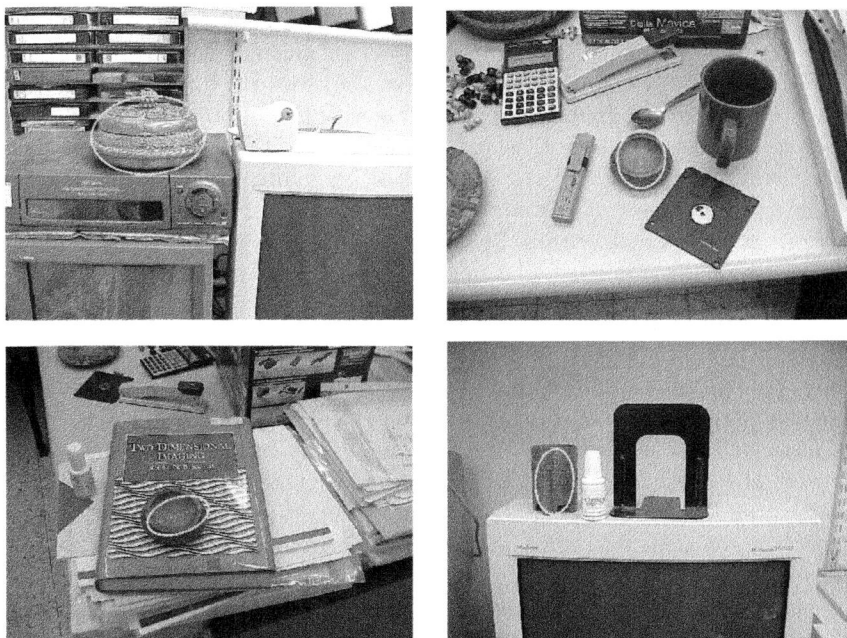

Fig. 4. The suggested algorithm as a detector of man-made wooden objects. Grey level versions of the actual color images are presented.

Fig. 5. Limitations of the suggested algorithm. Grey level versions of the actual color images are presented. *Left:* Convergence to a local maximum. *Right:* Perspective projection leads to skewed symmetry. The chess board is an extreme case in which skewing turns symmetry to anti-symmetry. In this example, parts of the chessboard are sufficiently symmetric locally, but (the image of) the whole chessboard is not symmetric. Accommodating skewed symmetry in the method is straightforward, but would require higher dimensional search.

algorithms perform quite well. The PGA tends to be faster than the standard genetic algorithm in the initial stages, but its final convergence seems to be slower. Typically, only about 3000 evaluations of the objective function are needed to reach the global maximum with either algorithm. Considering that 32 bits are used to describe each hypothesis (7 bits for each of the the location parameters x, y and 6 bits for each of the other three parameters), computing time is reduced by 6 orders of magnitude with The images in Figs. 3-4 demonstrate the performance of the algorithm. Some of its limitations are shown in Fig. 5.

6 Discussion

Towards segmentation from multiple cues, this paper demonstrates the combined use of symmetry (global feature) and color (local property) for detecting regions of interest. Frontal-view face detection and the detection of man-made wooden objects have been used as working examples, but generality has been carefully maintained and the approach is not limited to those applications. One novel aspect of the suggested approach is the measurement of *chromatic* symmetry, thus compensating for illumination variations in the scene. Note that, unlike previous works, symmetry is analyzed *in conjunction* with skin detection rather than sequentially. The integration of the symmetry and color cues takes place in a unified objective function.

Great computational savings are obtained by avoiding exhaustive search. The global optimization method used can be extended [15,19,24] to detect more than one region of interest in the image. Further computational gains can be achieved by caching values of the objective function, thus avoiding unnecessary recomputation. An interesting direction for future research is the extraction of smoothness properties of the objective function. These could lead to global optimization with *guaranteed* convergence [27].

References

[1] T.C. Chang and T.S. Huang, "Facial feature extraction from color images", *Proc. International Conference on Pattern Recognition*, Vol. 1, pp. 39-43, Jerusalem, 1994.
[2] R. Chellappa, C.L. Wilson and S. Sirohey, "Human and machine recognition of faces: A survey", *IEEE Proceedings*, Vol. 83, pp. 705-740, 1995.
[3] A.J. Colmenarez and T.S. Huang, "Frontal view face detection", *SPIE* Vol. 2501, pp. 90-98, 1995.
[4] T. Kondo and H. Yan, "Automatic human face detection and recognition under non-uniform illumination", *Pattern Recognition*, Vol. 32, pp. 1707-1718, 1999.
[5] Y. Ohta, T. Kanade and T. Sakai, "Color information for region segmentation", *Computer Graphics and Image Processing*, Vol. 13, pp. 222-241, 1980.
[6] T. Gevers and A.W.M. Smeulders, "Color-based object recognition", *Pattern Recognition*, Vol. 32, pp. 453-464, 1999.
[7] S.J. McKenna, S. Gong and Y. Raja, "Modelling facial colour and identity with gaussian mixtures", *Pattern Recognition*, Vol. 31, pp. 1883-1892, 1998.

[8] H.A. Rowley, S. Baluja and T. Kanade, "Neural network-based face detection", *IEEE Trans. Pattern Analysis and Machine Intelligence*, Vol. 20, pp. 23-38, 1998.

[9] Q.B. Sun, W.M. Huang and J.K. Wu, "Face detection based on color and local symmetry information", *Proc. 3rd IEEE Int. Conf. on Automatic Face and Gesture Recognition*, pp. 130-135, Nara, Japan, 1998.

[10] The Psychological Image Collection at Stirling (PICS), University of Stirling Psychology Department, http://pics.psych.stir.ac.uk .

[11] E. Saber and A.M. Tekalp, "Frontal-view face detection and facial feature extraction using color, shape and symmetry based cost function", *Pattern Recognition Letters*, Vol. 19, pp. 669-680, 1998.

[12] A. Samal and P.A. Iyengar, "Automatic recognition and analysis of human faces and facial expressions: A survey", *Pattern Recognition*, Vol. 25, pp. 65-77, 1992.

[13] J.C. Terrillon, M. David and S. Akamatsu, "Detection of human faces in complex scene images by use of a skin color model and of invariant fourier-mellin moments", *Proc. 14th International Conference on Pattern Recognition*, pp. 1350-1356, Brisbane, 1998.

[14] H. Wu, Q. Chen and M. Yachida, "Face detection from color images using a fuzzy pattern matching method", *IEEE Trans. Pattern Analysis and Machine Intelligence*, Vol. 21, pp. 557-563, 1999.

[15] D. Beasley, D.R. Bull and R.R. Martin, "A sequential niche technique for multimodal function optimization", *Evolutionary Computation*, Vol. 1, pp. 101-125, 1993.

[16] J. Bigün, "Recognition of local symmetries in gray value images by harmonic functions", *Proc. International Conference on Pattern Recognition*, pp. 345-347, Rome, 1988.

[17] M. Gardner, *The New Ambidextrous Universe - Symmetry and Asymmetry from Mirror Reflections to Superstrings*, Freeman, New York, 1979.

[18] J.M. Gauch and S.M. Pizer, "The intensity axis of symmetry and its application to image segmentation", *IEEE Trans. Pattern Analysis and Machine Intelligence*, Vol. 15, pp. 753-770, 1993.

[19] D.E. Goldberg and J. Richardson, "Genetic algorithms with sharing for multimodal function optimization", *Proc. 2nd Int. Conf. on Genetic Algorithms*, pp. 41-49, Cambridge, Mass., 1987.

[20] J.H. Holland, "Genetic algorithms", *Scientific American*, pp. 44–50, 1992.

[21] M.F. Kelly and M.D. Levine, "Annular symmetry operators: a method for locating and describing objects", *Proc. Int. Conf. on Computer Vision (ICCV)*, pp. 1016-1021, Cambridge, Mass., 1995.

[22] N. Kiryati and Y. Gofman, "Detecting symmetry in grey level images: the global optimization approach", *International Journal of Computer Vision*, Vol. 29, pp. 29-45, 1998.

[23] G. Marola, "On the detection of the axes of symmetry of symmetric and almost symmetric planar images", *IEEE Trans. Pattern Anal. Machine Intell.*, Vol. 11, p.. 104-108, 1989.

[24] B.L. Miller and M.J. Shaw, "Genetic algorithms with dynamic niche sharing for multimodal function optimization", IlliGAL Report No. 95010, University of Illinois, department of general engineering, 1995. Available At *http://gal4.ge.uiuc.edu.*

[25] T.R. Reed and H. Wechsler, "Segmentation of textured images and gestalt organization using spatial/spatial-frequency representations", *IEEE Trans. Pattern Anal. Machine Intell.*, Vol. 12, pp. 1-12, 1990.

[26] D. Reisfeld, H. Wolfson and Y. Yeshurun, "Context free attentional operators: the generalized symmetry transform", *Int. J. Computer Vision*, Vol. 14, pp. 119-130, 1995.

[27] A. Törn and A. Žilinskas, *Global Optimization*, Lecture Notes in Computer Science #350, Springer-Verlag, 1989.

[28] L. Van Gool, T. Moons, D. Ungureanu and E. Pauwels, "Symmetry from shape and shape from symmetry", *Int. J. Robotics Research*, Vol. 14, pp. 407-424, 1995.

[29] H. Weyl, *Symmetry*, Princeton University Press, 1952.

[30] J.G. Wang and E. Sung, "Frontal-view face detection and facial feature extraction using color and morphological operations", *Pattern Recognition Letters*, Vol. 20, pp. 1053-1068, 1999.

[31] A. Ylä-Jääski and F. Ade, "Grouping symmetrical structures for object segmentation and description", *Computer Vision and Image Understanding*, Vol. 63, pp. 399-417, 1996.

[32] H. Zabrodsky, S. Peleg and D. Avnir, "Symmetry as a continuous feature", *IEEE Trans. Pattern Anal. Machine Intell.*, Vol. 17, pp. 1154-1166, 1995.

[33] J. Yang and A. Weibel, "Tracking human faces in real-time", *Technical Report CMU-CS-95-210*, Carnegie Mellon University, 1995.

[34] T. Zielke, M. Brauckmann and W. Von Seelen, "Intensity and edge based symmetry detection with application to car following", *CVGIP: Image Understanding*, Vol. 58, pp. 177-190, 1993.

Pose Estimation Using Geometric Constraints

Gerald Sommer, Bodo Rosenhahn, and Yiwen Zhang

Institut für Informatik und Praktische Mathematik
Christian-Albrechts-Universität zu Kiel
Preußerstrasse 1-9, 24105 Kiel, Germany
{gs,bro,yz}@ks.informatik.uni-kiel.de

Abstract. The paper concerns 2D-3D pose estimation in the algebraic language of kinematics. The pose estimation problem is modeled on the base of several geometric constraint equations. In that way the projective geometric aspect of the topic is implicitly represented and thus, pose estimation is a pure kinematic problem. The authors propose the use of motor algebra to model screw displacements of lines or the use of rotor algebra to model the motion of points. Instead of using matrix based LMS optimization, the development of special extended Kalman filters is proposed. In this paper extended Kalman filters for estimating rotation and translation of several constraints in terms of rotors and motors will be presented. The experiments aim to compare the use of different constraints and different methods of optimal estimating the pose parameters.

1   Introduction

The paper describes the estimation of pose parameters of known rigid objects in the framework of kinematics. The aim is to experimentally verify advantages of extended Kalman filter approaches versus linear least squares optimizations. Pose estimation in the framework of kinematics will be treated as nonlinear optimization with respect to geometric constraint equations expressing the relations between 2D image features and 3D model data.

Pose estimation is a basic visual task. In spite of its importance it has been identified for a long time (see e.g. Grimson [5]), and although there is published an overwhelming number of papers with respect to that topic [8], up to now there is no unique and general solution of the problem. In a general sense, pose estimation can be classified into three categories: 2D-2D, 3D-3D, and 2D-3D. In the first and second category, both the measurement data and the model data are 2D or 3D, respectively. In the third category fall those experiments where measurement data are 2D and model data are 3D. This is the situation we will assume.

An often made assumption is that of rigidity of objects. The wellknown kinematic model of rigid body transformation is a natural one. It consists of rotation and translation. On the other hand, the visual data result from perspective projection, which normally can be modeled using a pinhole camera model.

R. Klette et al. (Eds.): Multi-Image Analysis, LNCS 2032, pp. 153–170, 2001.

In this paper we attend to a pose estimation related to estimations of motion as a problem of kinematics. The problem can be linearly represented in motor algebra [7] or dual quaternion algebra [6]. We are using implicit formulations of geometry as geometric constraints. We will demonstrate that geometric constraints are well conditioned and, thus behave more robust in case of noisy data.

Pose estimation is an optimization problem, formulated in either linear or nonlinear manner, or as either constraint or unconstraint technique. In case of noisy data, which is the standard case in practice, nonlinear optimization techniques are preferred [8]. We will use extended Kalman filters because of their incremental, real-time potential for estimation. In that respect it will be of interest that the estimation error of the fulfillment of the considered geometric constraints keeps a natural distance measure of the considered entities to the actual object frame. Thus, EKF based estimation of geometric constraints permits a progressive scheme of pose estimation.

The paper is organized as follows. In section two we will introduce the motor algebra as representation frame for either geometric entities, geometric constraints, or Euclidean transformations. In section three we introduce the geometric constraints and their changes in an observation scenario. Section four is dedicated to the geometric analysis of these constraints. In section five we will present the EKF approaches for estimating the constraints. In section six we compare the performance of different algorithms for constraint based pose estimation.

2   The Algebraic Frame of Kinematics

In our comparative study we will consider the problem of pose estimation as a kinematic one. In this section we want to sketch the modeling of rigid body motions in the framework of motor algebra, a special degenerate geometric algebra with remarkable advantages.

2.1   The Motor Algebra as Degenerate Geometric Algebra

We introduce the motor algebra as the adequate frame to represent screw transformations in line geometry [7]. This algebra belongs to the family of geometric algebras, a variant of Clifford algebras in which the geometric interpretation of operations is dominantly considered [11].

A geometric algebra $\mathcal{G}_{p,q,r}$ is a linear space of dimension 2^n, $n = p + q + r$, with a rich subspace structure, called blades, to represent so-called multivectors as higher order algebraic entities in comparison to vectors of a vector space as first order entities. A geometric algebra $\mathcal{G}_{p,q,r}$ results in a constructive way from a vector space $\mathbb{R}^n$, endowed with the signature (p, q, r), $n = p + q + r$ by application of a geometric product. The geometric product consists of an outer ($\wedge$) and an inner ($\cdot$) product, whose role is to increase or to decrease the order of the algebraic entities, respectively.

To make it concretely, a motor algebra is the 8D even subalgebra of $\boldsymbol{\mathcal{G}}_{3,0,1}$, derived from $\mathbb{R}^4$, i.e. $n = 4$, $p = 3$, $q = 0$, $r = 1$, with basis vectors γ_k, $k = 1, ..., 4$, and the property $\gamma_1^2 = \gamma_2^2 = \gamma_3^2 = +1$ and $\gamma_4^2 = 0$. Because $\gamma_4^2 = 0$, $\boldsymbol{\mathcal{G}}_{3,0,1}$ is called a degenerate algebra. The motor algebra $\boldsymbol{\mathcal{G}}_{3,0,1}^+$ is of dimension eight and spanned by qualitative different subspaces with the following basis multivectors:

$$
\begin{array}{ll}
\text{one scalar} & : 1 \\
\text{six bivectors} & : \gamma_2\gamma_3, \gamma_3\gamma_1, \gamma_1\gamma_2, \gamma_4\gamma_1, \gamma_4\gamma_2, \gamma_4\gamma_3 \\
\text{one pseudoscalar} & : \boldsymbol{I} \equiv \gamma_1\gamma_2\gamma_3\gamma_4.
\end{array}
$$

Because $\gamma_4^2 = 0$, also the unit pseudoscalar squares to zero, i.e. $\boldsymbol{I}^2 = 0$. Remembering that the hypercomplex algebra of quaternions $\mathbb{H}$ represents a 4D linear space with one scalar and three vector components, it can simply be verified that $\boldsymbol{\mathcal{G}}_{3,0,1}^+$ is isomorphic to the algebra of dual quaternions $\widehat{\mathbb{H}}$, [11]. Each dual quaternion $\widehat{q} \in \widehat{\mathbb{H}}$ is related with quaternions $q_r, q_d \in \mathbb{H}$ by $\widehat{q} = q_r + \boldsymbol{I}q_d$. It is obvious from that isomorphism that also quaternions have a representation in geometric algebra, just as complex and real numbers have. Quaternions correspond to the 4D even subalgebra of $\boldsymbol{\mathcal{G}}_{3,0,0}$, derived from $\mathbb{R}^3$. They have the basis $\{1, \gamma_2\gamma_3, \gamma_3\gamma_1, \gamma_1\gamma_2\}$. The advantage of using geometric algebra instead of diverse hypercomplex algebras is the generality of its construction and, derived from that, the existence of algebraic entities with unique interpretation whatever the dimension of the original vector space.

More important is to remark that the bivector basis of motor algebra constitutes the basis for line geometry using Plücker coordinates. Therefore, motor algebra is extraordinary useful to represent line based approaches of kinematics, also in computer vision.

The motor algebra is spanned by bivectors and scalars. Therefore, we will restrict our scope to that case. Let be $\boldsymbol{A}$, $\boldsymbol{B}$, $\boldsymbol{C} \in \langle\boldsymbol{\mathcal{G}}_{3,0,1}^+\rangle_2$ bivectors and α, $\beta \in \langle\boldsymbol{\mathcal{G}}_{3,0,1}^+\rangle_0$ scalars. Then the geometric product of bivectors $\boldsymbol{A}$, $\boldsymbol{B} \in \langle\boldsymbol{\mathcal{G}}_{3,0,1}^+\rangle_2$, $\boldsymbol{AB}$, splits into $\boldsymbol{AB} = \boldsymbol{A} \cdot \boldsymbol{B} + \boldsymbol{A} \times \boldsymbol{B} + \boldsymbol{A} \wedge \boldsymbol{B}$, where $\boldsymbol{A} \cdot \boldsymbol{B}$ is the inner product, which results in a scalar $\boldsymbol{A} \cdot \boldsymbol{B} = \alpha$, $\boldsymbol{A} \wedge \boldsymbol{B}$ is the outer product, which in this case results in a pseudoscalar $\boldsymbol{A} \wedge \boldsymbol{B} = \boldsymbol{I}\beta$, and $\boldsymbol{A} \times \boldsymbol{B}$ is the commutator product, which results in a bivector $\boldsymbol{C}$, $\boldsymbol{A} \times \boldsymbol{B} = \frac{1}{2}(\boldsymbol{AB} - \boldsymbol{BA}) = \boldsymbol{C}$. Changing the sign of the scalar and bivector in the real and the dual parts of the motor leads to the following variants of a motor

$$
\begin{array}{ll}
\boldsymbol{M} = (a_0 + \boldsymbol{a}) + \boldsymbol{I}(b_0 + \boldsymbol{b}) & \widetilde{\boldsymbol{M}} = (a_0 - \boldsymbol{a}) + \boldsymbol{I}(b_0 - \boldsymbol{b}) \\
\overline{\boldsymbol{M}} = (a_0 + \boldsymbol{a}) - \boldsymbol{I}(b_0 + \boldsymbol{b}) & \widetilde{\overline{\boldsymbol{M}}} = (a_0 - \boldsymbol{a}) - \boldsymbol{I}(b_0 - \boldsymbol{b}).
\end{array}
$$

These versions will be used to model the motion of points, lines and planes.

2.2   Rotors, Translators, and Motors

In a general sense, motors are called all the entities existing in motor algebra. Thus, any geometric entity as points, lines, and planes have a motor representation. We will use the term motor in a more restricted sense to call with it a screw transformation, that is an Euclidean transformation embedded in motor algebra. Its constituents are rotation and translation. In line geometry we represent rotation by a rotation line axis and a rotation angle. The corresponding entity is called a unit rotor, R, and reads as follows

$$R = r_0 + r_1\gamma_2\gamma_3 + r_2\gamma_3\gamma_1 + r_3\gamma_1\gamma_2 = \cos\left(\frac{\theta}{2}\right) + \sin\left(\frac{\theta}{2}\right)n = \exp\left(\frac{\theta}{2}n\right).$$

Here θ is the rotation angle and n is the unit orientation vector of the rotation axis in bivector representation, spanned by the bivector basis. A unit rotor is in geometric algebra a general entity with a spinor structure, representing rotation in terms of a specified plane. It exists in any dimension and it works for all types of geometric objects, just in contrast to rotation matrices, complex numbers or quaternions. Its very nature is that it is composed by bivectors B and that there is an exponential form $R = \pm\exp\left(\frac{1}{2}B\right)$.

If on the other hand, $t = t_1\gamma_2\gamma_3 + t_2\gamma_3\gamma_1 + t_3\gamma_1\gamma_2$ is a translation vector in bivector representation, it will be represented in motor algebra as the dual part of a motor, called translator T with

$$T = 1 + I\frac{t}{2} = \exp\left(\frac{t}{2}I\right).$$

Thus, a translator is also a special kind of rotor.

Because rotation and translation concatenate multiplicatively in motor algebra, a motor M reads

$$M = TR = R + I\frac{t}{2}R = R + IR'.$$

A motor represents a line transformation as a screw transformation. The line L will be transformed to the line L' by means of a rotation R_s around line L_s by angle θ, followed by a translation t_s parallel to L_s. The screw motion equation as motor transformation reads [7], [9]

$$L' = T_s R_s L \widetilde{R}_s \widetilde{T}_s = ML\widetilde{M}.$$

2.3   Motion of Points, Lines, and Planes in Motor Algebra

First, we will introduce the description of the important geometric entities [7].

A point $x \in \mathbb{R}^3$, represented in the bivector basis of $\mathcal{G}_{3,0,1}^+$, i.e. $X \in \mathcal{G}_{3,0,1}^+$, reads $X = 1 + x_1\gamma_4\gamma_1 + x_2\gamma_4\gamma_2 + x_3\gamma_4\gamma_3 = 1 + Ix$.

A line $L \in \mathcal{G}_{3,0,1}^+$ is represented by $L = n + Im$ with the line direction $n = n_1\gamma_2\gamma_3 + n_2\gamma_3\gamma_1 + n_3\gamma_1\gamma_2$ and the moment $m = m_1\gamma_2\gamma_3 + m_2\gamma_3\gamma_1 + m_3\gamma_1\gamma_2$.

A plane $P \in \mathcal{G}_{3,0,1}^+$ will be defined by its normal p as bivector and by its Hesse distance to the origin, expressed as the scalar $d = (x \cdot p)$, in the following way, $P = p + Id$.

Note that the fact of using line geometry does not prevent to define points and planes, just as in point geometry the other entities also are well defined. In case of screw motions $M = T_s R_s$ not only line transformations can be modeled, but also point and plane transformations. These are expressed as follows.

$$X' = 1 + Ix' = M X \widetilde{M} = M(1 + Ix)\widetilde{M} = 1 + I(R_s x \widetilde{R}_s + t_s)$$
$$L' = n' + Im' = M L \widetilde{M} = R_s n \widetilde{R}_s + I(R_s n \widetilde{R}_s{}' + R'_s n \widetilde{R}_s + R_s m \widetilde{R}_s)$$
$$P' = p' + Id' = M P \widetilde{M} = M(p + Id)\widetilde{M} = R_s p \widetilde{R}_s + I((R_s p \widetilde{R}_s) \cdot t_s + d).$$

We will use in this study only point and line transformations because points and lines are the entities of our object models.

3   Geometric Constraints and Pose Estimation

First, we make the following assumptions. The model of an object is given by points and lines in the 3D space. Furthermore we extract line subspaces or points in an image of a calibrated camera and match them with the model of the object. The aim is to find the pose of the object from observations of points and lines in the images at different poses. Figure 1 shows the scenario with respect to observed line subspaces.

We want to estimate the rotation and the translation parameters which lead to the best fit of the model with the extracted line subspaces or points. To estimate the transformations, it is necessary to relate the observed lines in the image to the unknown pose of the object using geometric constraints.

The key idea is that the observed 2D entities together with their corresponding 3D entities are constraint to lie on other, higher order entities which result from the perspective projection. In our considered scenario there are three constraints which are attributed to two classes of constraints:

1. Collinearity: A 3D point has to lie on a line (i.e. a projection ray) in the space
2. Coplanarity: A 3D point or a 3D line has to lie on a plane (i.e. a projection plane).

With the terms projection ray or projection plane, respectively, we mean the image-forming ray which relates a 3D point with the projection center or the infinite set of image-forming rays which relates all 3D points belonging to a 3D line with the projection center, respectively. Thus, by introducing these two entities, we implicitly represent a perspective projection without necessarily formulating it explicitly. Instead, the pose problem is in that framework a purely kinematic problem. A similar approach of avoiding perspective projection equations by using constraint observations of lines has been proposed in [2,3].

In the scenario of figure 1 we describe the following situation: We assume 3D points Y_i, and lines S_i of an object or reference model. Further we extract points and lines in an image of a calibrated camera and match them with the model.

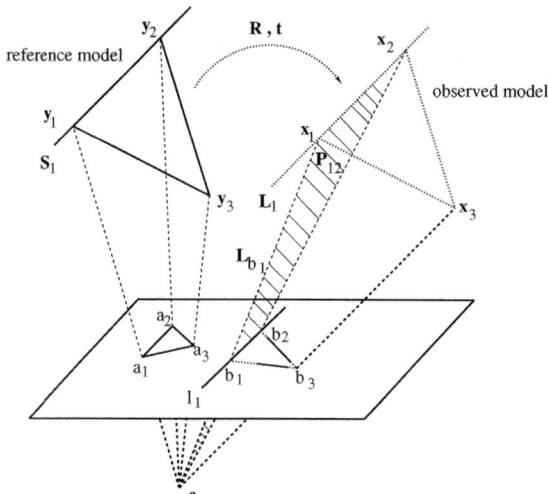

Fig. 1. The scenario. The solid lines at the left hand describe the assumptions: the camera model, the model of the object and the initially extracted lines on the image plane. The dashed lines at the right hand describe the actual pose of the model.

Table 1. The geometric constraints in motor algebra and dual quaternion algebra.

constraint	entities	dual quaternion algebra	motor algebra
point-line	point $X = 1 + Ix$ line $L = n + Im$	$LX - X\overline{L} = 0$	$XL - \overline{L}X = 0$
point-plane	point $X = 1 + Ix$ plane $P = p + Id$	$P\overline{X} - XP = 0$	$PX - \overline{XP} = 0$
line-plane	line $L = n + Im$ plane $P = p + Id$	$LP - P\overline{L} = 0$	$LP + P\overline{L} = 0$

Table 1 gives an overview on the formulations of these constraints in motor algebra, taken from Blaschke [4], who used expressions in dual quaternion algebra. Here we adopt the terms from section 2. The meaning of the constraint equations is immediately clear. They represent the ideal situation, e.g. achieved as the result of the pose estimation procedure with respect to the observation frame. With respect to the previous reference frame these constraints read

$$(MY\widetilde{M})L - \overline{L}(MY\widetilde{M}) = 0$$
$$P(MY\widetilde{M}) - \overline{(MY\widetilde{M})P} = 0$$
$$(MS\widetilde{M})P + \overline{P(MS\widetilde{M})} = 0.$$

These compact equations subsume the pose estimation problem at hand: find the best motor M which satisfies the constraint. With respect to the observer frame those entities are variables of the measurement model of the extended Kalman filter on which the motors act.

4   Analysis of Constraints

In this section we will analyze the geometry of the constraints introduced in the last section in motor algebra. We want to show that the relations between different entities are controlled by their orthogonal distance, the Hesse distance. This intuitive result is not only of importance for formulating a mean square minimization method for finding the best motor satisfying the constraints. But in case of noisy data the error of that task can be immediately interpreted as that Hesse distance.

4.1   Point-Line Constraint

Evaluating the constraint of a point $X = 1 + Ix$ collinear to a line $L = n + Im$ leads to

$$0 = XL - \overline{L}X \doteq I(m - n \times x).$$

Since $I \neq 0$, although $I^2 = 0$, the aim is to analyze the bivector $m - n \times x$. Suppose $X \notin L$. Then, nonetheless, there exists a decomposition $x = x_1 + x_2$ with $X_1 = (1 + Ix_1) \in L$ and $X_2 = (1 + Ix_2) \perp L$. Figure 2 shows the scenario. Then we can calculate

$$\|m - n \times x\| = \|m - n \times (x_1 + x_2)\| = \| - n \times x_2\| = \|x_2\|.$$

Thus, satisfying the point-line constraint means to equate the bivectors m and $n \times x$, respectively making the Hesse distance $\|x_2\|$ of the point X to the line L to zero.

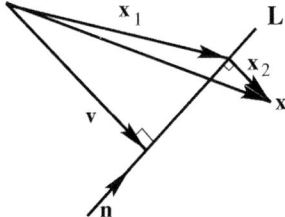

Fig. 2. The line L consists of the direction n and the moment $m = n \times v$. Further, there exists a decomposition $x = x_1 + x_2$ with $X_1 = (1 + Ix_1) \in L$ and $X_2 = (1 + Ix_2) \perp L$, so that $m = n \times v = n \times x_1$.

4.2   Point-Plane Constraint

Evaluating the constraint of a point $X = 1 + Ix$ coplanar to a plane $P = p + Id$ leads to

$$0 = PX - \overline{X}P = I(2d + px + xp) \doteq I(d + p \cdot x).$$

Since $\boldsymbol{I} \neq 0$, although $\boldsymbol{I}^2 = 0$, the aim is to analyze the scalar $d + \boldsymbol{p} \cdot \boldsymbol{x}$. Suppose $\boldsymbol{X} \notin \boldsymbol{P}$. The value d can be interpreted as a sum so that $d = d_{01} + d_{02}$ and $d_{01}\boldsymbol{p}$ is the orthogonal projection of $\boldsymbol{x}$ onto $\boldsymbol{p}$. Figure 3 shows the scenario. Then we

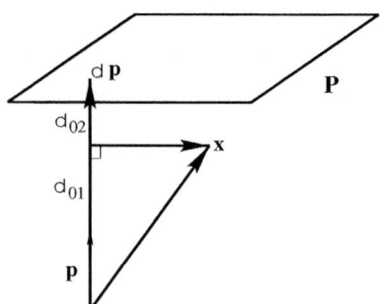

Fig. 3. The value d can be interpreted as a sum $d = d_{01} + d_{02}$ so that $d_{01}\boldsymbol{p}$ corresponds to the orthogonal projection of $\boldsymbol{x}$ onto $\boldsymbol{p}$. That is $d_{01} = -\boldsymbol{p} \cdot \boldsymbol{x}$.

can calculate

$$d + \boldsymbol{p} \cdot \boldsymbol{x} = d_{01} + d_{02} + \boldsymbol{p} \cdot \boldsymbol{x} = d_{01} + \boldsymbol{p} \cdot \boldsymbol{x} + d_{02} = d_{02}.$$

The value of the expression $d + \boldsymbol{p} \cdot \boldsymbol{x}$ corresponds to the Hesse distance of the point $\boldsymbol{X}$ to the plane $\boldsymbol{P}$.

4.3   Line-Plane Constraint

Evaluating the constraint of a line $\boldsymbol{L} = \boldsymbol{n} + \boldsymbol{Im}$ coplanar to a plane $\boldsymbol{P} = \boldsymbol{p} + \boldsymbol{I}d$ leads to

$$0 = \boldsymbol{L}\boldsymbol{P} + \boldsymbol{P}\overline{\boldsymbol{L}} = \boldsymbol{np} + \boldsymbol{pn} + \boldsymbol{I}(2d\boldsymbol{n} - \boldsymbol{pm} + \boldsymbol{mp}) \doteq \boldsymbol{n} \cdot \boldsymbol{p} + \boldsymbol{I}(d\boldsymbol{n} - \boldsymbol{p} \times \boldsymbol{m})$$

Thus, the constraint can be partitioned in one constraint on the real part of the motor and one constraint on the dual part of the motor. The aim is to analyze the scalar $\boldsymbol{n} \cdot \boldsymbol{p}$ and the bivector $d\boldsymbol{n} - (\boldsymbol{p} \times \boldsymbol{m})$ independently. Suppose $\boldsymbol{L} \notin \boldsymbol{P}$. If $\boldsymbol{n} \not\perp \boldsymbol{p}$ the real part leads to

$$\boldsymbol{n} \cdot \boldsymbol{p} = -\|\boldsymbol{n}\|\|\boldsymbol{p}\|\cos(\alpha) = -\cos(\alpha),$$

where α is the angle between $\boldsymbol{L}$ and $\boldsymbol{P}$, see figure 4. If $\boldsymbol{n} \perp \boldsymbol{p}$, we have $\boldsymbol{n} \cdot \boldsymbol{p} = 0$.

Since the direction of the line is independent of the translation of the rigid body motion, the constraint on the real part can be used to generate equations with the parameters of the rotation as the only unknowns. The constraint on the dual part can then be used to determine the unknown translation. In other words, since the motor to be estimated, $\boldsymbol{M} = \boldsymbol{R} + \boldsymbol{I}\boldsymbol{R}\boldsymbol{T} = \boldsymbol{R} + \boldsymbol{I}\boldsymbol{R}'$, is determined in its real part only by rotation, the real part of the constraint allows to estimate the rotor R, while the dual part of the constraint allows to estimate the rotor R'. So it is possible to sequentially separate equations on the unknown rotation from equations on the unknown translation without the limitations, known from the embedding of the problem in Euclidean space [6]. This is very useful, since the two smaller equation systems are easier to solve than one larger equation system.

To analyze the dual part of the constraint, we interpret the moment m of the line representation $L = n + Im$ as $m = n \times s$ and choose a vector s with $S = (1 + Is) \in L$ and $s \perp n$. By expressing the inner product as the anti-commutator product, it can be shown ([1]) that $-(p \times m) = (s \cdot p)n - (n \cdot p)s$. Now we can evaluate

$$dn - (p \times m) = dn - (n \cdot p)s + (s \cdot p)n.$$

Figure 4 shows the scenario. Further, we can find a vector s_1 with $s \parallel s_1$, so

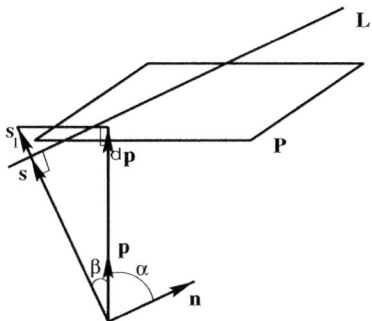

Fig. 4. The plane P consists of its normal p and the Hesse distance d. Furthermore we choose $S = (1 + Is) \in L$ with $s \perp n$.

that

$$0 = d - (\|s\| + \|s_1\|)\cos(\beta).$$

The vector s_1 might also be antiparallel to s. This leads to a change of the sign, but does not affect the constraint itself. Now we can evaluate

$$dn - (n \cdot p)s + (s \cdot p)n = dn - \|s\|\cos(\beta)n + \cos(\alpha)s = \|s_1\|\cos(\beta)n + \cos(\alpha)s.$$

The error of the dual part consists of the vector s scaled by the angle α and the direction n scaled by the norm of s_1 and the angle β.
If $n \perp p$, we will find

$$\|dn - (p \times m)\| = \|dn + (s \cdot p)n - (n \cdot p)s\| = |(d + s \cdot p)|$$

This means, in agreement to the point-plane constraint, that $(d + s \cdot p)$ describes the Hesse distance of the line to the plane.

This analysis shows that the considered constraints are not only qualitative constraints, but also quantitative ones. This is very important, since we want to measure the extend of fulfillment of these constraints in the case of noisy data.

5   The Extended Kalman Filter for Pose Estimation

In this section we want to present the design of EKFs for estimating the pose based on three constraints. Because an EKF is defined in the frame of linear vector algebra, it will be necessary to map the estimation task from any chosen algebraic embedding to linear vector algebra (see e.g. [9]).

5.1   EKF Pose Estimation Based on Point-Line Constraint

In case of point based measurements of the object at different poses, an algebraic embedding of the problem in the 4D linear space of the algebra of rotors $\mathcal{G}_{3,0,0}^{+}$, which is isomorphic to that one of quaternions $\mathbb{H}$, will be sufficient [7,9]. Thus, rotation will be represented by a unit rotor $\boldsymbol{R}$ and translation will be a bivector $\boldsymbol{t}$. A point $\boldsymbol{y_1}$ transformed to $\boldsymbol{x_1}$ reads $\boldsymbol{x_1} = \boldsymbol{R}\boldsymbol{y_1}\tilde{\boldsymbol{R}} + \boldsymbol{t}$. We denote the four components of the rotor as

$$\boldsymbol{R} = r_0 + r_1\sigma_2\sigma_3 + r_2\sigma_3\sigma_1 + r_3\sigma_1\sigma_2.$$

To convert a rotor $\boldsymbol{R}$ into a rotation matrix $\mathcal{R}$, simple conversion rules are at hand:

$$\mathcal{R} = \begin{pmatrix} r_0^2 + r_1^2 - r_2^2 - r_3^2 & 2(r_1r_2 + r_0r_3) & 2(r_1r_3 - r_0r_2) \\ 2(r_1r_2 - r_0r_3) & r_0^2 - r_1^2 + r_2^2 - r_3^2 & 2(r_2r_3 + r_0r_1) \\ 2(r_1r_3 + r_0r_2) & 2(r_2r_3 - r_0r_1) & r_0^2 - r_1^2 - r_2^2 + r_3^2 \end{pmatrix}.$$

In vector algebra, the above point transformation model can be described as

$$\mathbf{x_1} = \mathcal{R}\mathbf{y_1} + \mathbf{t}.$$

The projection ray $\mathbf{L}_{b_1}$ in the point-line equation is represented by Plücker coordinates $(\mathbf{n_1}, \mathbf{m_1})$, where $\mathbf{n_1}$ is its unit direction and $\mathbf{m_1}$ its moment. The point-line constraint equation in vector algebra of $\mathbb{R}^3$ reads

$$\mathbf{f_1} = \mathbf{m_1} - \mathbf{n_1} \times \mathbf{x_1} = \mathbf{m_1} - \mathbf{n_1} \times (\mathcal{R}\mathbf{y_1} + \mathbf{t}) = \mathbf{0}.$$

Let the state vector $\mathbf{s}$ for the EKF be a 7D vector, composed in terms of the rotor coefficients for rotation and translation,

$$\mathbf{s} = (\mathbf{R}^T, \mathbf{t}^T)^T = (r_0, r_1, r_2, r_3, t_1, t_2, t_3)^T.$$

The rotation coefficients must satisfy the unit condition

$$\mathbf{f_2} = \mathbf{R}^T\mathbf{R} - 1 = r_0^2 + r_1^2 + r_2^2 + r_3^2 - 1 = 0.$$

The noise free measurement vector $\mathbf{a_i}$ is given by the actual line parameters $\mathbf{n_i}$ and $\mathbf{m_i}$, and the actual 3D point measurements $\mathbf{y_i}$,

$$\mathbf{a_i} = (\mathbf{n_i}^T, \mathbf{m_i}^T, \mathbf{y_i}^T)^T = (n_{i1}, n_{i2}, n_{i3}, m_{i1}, m_{i2}, m_{i3}, y_{i1}, y_{i2}, y_{i3})^T.$$

For a sequence of measurements $\mathbf{a_i}$ and states $\mathbf{s_i}$, the constraint equations

$$\mathbf{f_i}(\mathbf{a_i}, \mathbf{s_i}) = \begin{pmatrix} \mathbf{f_{1i}} \\ \mathbf{f_{2i}} \end{pmatrix} = \begin{pmatrix} \mathbf{m_i} - \mathbf{n_i} \times (\mathcal{R}_i \mathbf{y_i} + \mathbf{t_i}) \\ \mathbf{R_i}^T \mathbf{R_i} - 1 \end{pmatrix} = 0$$

relate measurements and states in a nonlinear manner. The system model in this static case should be $\mathbf{s_{i+1}} = \mathbf{s_i} + \boldsymbol{\zeta}_i$, where $\boldsymbol{\zeta}_i$ is a vector random sequence with known statistics, $E[\boldsymbol{\zeta}_i] = 0$, $E[\boldsymbol{\zeta}_i^T \boldsymbol{\zeta}_k] = \mathcal{Q}_i \delta_{ik}$, where δ_{ik} is the Kronecker delta and the matrix $\mathcal{Q}_i$ is assumed to be nonnegative definite. We assume that the measurement system is disturbed by additive white noise, i.e., the real observed measurement $\mathbf{a_i'}$ is expressed as $\mathbf{a_i'} = \mathbf{a_i} + \boldsymbol{\eta}_i$.

The vector $\boldsymbol{\eta}_i$ is an additive, random sequence with known statistics, $E[\boldsymbol{\eta}_i] = 0$, $E[\boldsymbol{\eta}_i^T \boldsymbol{\eta}_k] = \mathcal{W}_i \delta_{ik}$, where the matrix $\mathcal{W}_i$ is assumed to be nonnegative definite.

Since the observation equation is nonlinear (that means, the relationship between the measurement $\mathbf{a_i'}$ and state $\mathbf{s_i}$ is nonlinear), we expand $\mathbf{f_i}(\mathbf{a_i}, \mathbf{s_i})$ into a Taylor series about the $(\mathbf{a_i'}, \hat{\mathbf{s}}_{i/i-1})$, where $\mathbf{a_i'}$ is the real measurement and $\hat{\mathbf{s}}_{i/i-1}$ is the predicted state at situation i. By ignoring the second order terms, we get the linearized measurement equation

$$\mathbf{z_i} = \mathcal{H}_i \mathbf{s_i} + \boldsymbol{\xi}_i,$$

where

$$\mathbf{z_i} = \mathbf{f_i}(\mathbf{a_i'}, \hat{\mathbf{s}}_{i/i-1}) - \frac{\partial \mathbf{f_i}(\mathbf{a_i'}, \hat{\mathbf{s}}_{i/i-1})}{\partial \mathbf{s_i}} \hat{\mathbf{s}}_{i/i-1}$$

$$= \begin{pmatrix} \mathbf{m_i'} - \mathbf{n_i'} \times (\hat{\mathcal{R}}_{i/i-1} \mathbf{y_i'} + \hat{\mathbf{t}}_{i/i-1}) \\ \hat{\mathbf{R}}_{i/i-1}^T \hat{\mathbf{R}}_{i/i-1} - 1 \end{pmatrix} + \mathcal{H}_i \hat{\mathbf{s}}_{i/i-1}.$$

The measurement matrix $\mathcal{H}_i$ of the linearized measurement $\mathbf{z_i}$ reads

$$\mathcal{H}_i = -\frac{\partial \mathbf{f_i}(\mathbf{a_i'}, \hat{\mathbf{s}}_{i/i-1})}{\partial \mathbf{s_i}} = \begin{pmatrix} \mathcal{C}_{\mathbf{n_i'}} \mathcal{D}_{\hat{\mathcal{R}} \mathbf{y'}} & \mathcal{C}_{\mathbf{n_i'}} \\ \mathcal{D}_\mathbf{R} & \mathbf{0}_{1 \times 3} \end{pmatrix},$$

where

$$\mathcal{D}_\mathbf{R} = \frac{\partial(\hat{\mathbf{R}}_{i/i-1}^T \hat{\mathbf{R}}_{i/i-1} - 1)}{\partial \mathbf{R_i}} = \begin{pmatrix} -2\hat{r}_{(i/i-1)0} & -2\hat{r}_{(i/i-1)1} & -2\hat{r}_{(i/i-1)2} & -2\hat{r}_{(i/i-1)3} \end{pmatrix},$$

$$\mathcal{D}_{\hat{\mathcal{R}} \mathbf{y'}} = \frac{\partial(\hat{\mathcal{R}}_{i/i-1} \mathbf{y_i'})}{\partial \mathbf{R_i}} = \begin{pmatrix} d_1 & d_2 & d_3 & d_4 \\ d_4 & -d_3 & d_2 & -d_1 \\ -d_3 & -d_4 & d_1 & d_2 \end{pmatrix},$$

$$d_1 = 2(\hat{r}_{(i/i-1)0}y'_{i1} + \hat{r}_{(i/i-1)3}y'_{i2} - \hat{r}_{(i/i-1)2}y'_{i3}),$$
$$d_2 = 2(\hat{r}_{(i/i-1)1}y'_{i1} + \hat{r}_{(i/i-1)2}y'_{i2} + \hat{r}_{(i/i-1)3}y'_{i3}),$$
$$d_3 = 2(-\hat{r}_{(i/i-1)2}y'_{i1} + \hat{r}_{(i/i-1)1}y'_{i2} - \hat{r}_{(i/i-1)0}y'_{i3}),$$
$$d_4 = 2(-\hat{r}_{(i/i-1)3}y'_{i1} + \hat{r}_{(i/i-1)0}y'_{i2} + \hat{r}_{(i/i-1)1}y'_{i3}).$$

The 3×3 matrix $\boldsymbol{C}_{\mathbf{n}'_i}$ is the skew-symmetric matrix of $\mathbf{n}'_i$. For any vector $\mathbf{y}$, we have $\boldsymbol{C}_{\mathbf{n}'_i}\mathbf{y} = \mathbf{n}'_i \times \mathbf{y}$ with

$$\boldsymbol{C}_{\mathbf{n}'_i} = \begin{pmatrix} 0 & -n'_{i3} & n'_{i2} \\ n'_{i3} & 0 & -n'_{i1} \\ -n'_{i2} & n'_{i1} & 0 \end{pmatrix}.$$

The measurement noise is given by

$$\boldsymbol{\xi}_i = -\frac{\partial \mathbf{f}_i(\mathbf{a}'_i, \hat{\mathbf{s}}_{i/i-1})}{\partial \mathbf{a}_i}(\mathbf{a}_i - \mathbf{a}'_i) = \frac{\partial \mathbf{f}_i(\mathbf{a}'_i, \hat{\mathbf{s}}_{i/i-1})}{\partial \mathbf{a}_i}\boldsymbol{\eta}_i$$

$$= \begin{pmatrix} \boldsymbol{C}_{\hat{\mathbf{x}}_{i/i-1}} & \mathbf{I}_{3\times3} & -\boldsymbol{C}_{\mathbf{n}'_i}\hat{\boldsymbol{\mathcal{R}}}_{i/i-1} \\ \mathbf{0}_{1\times3} & \mathbf{0}_{1\times3} & \mathbf{0}_{1\times3} \end{pmatrix}_{4\times9} \boldsymbol{\eta}_i,$$

where $\mathbf{I}_{3\times3}$ is a unit matrix and $\boldsymbol{C}_{\hat{\mathbf{x}}_{i/i-1}}$ is the skew-symmetric matrix of $\hat{\mathbf{x}}_{i/i-1}$ with

$$\hat{\mathbf{x}}_{i/i-1} = \hat{\boldsymbol{\mathcal{R}}}_{i/i-1}\mathbf{y}'_i + \hat{\mathbf{t}}_{i/i-1}.$$

The expectation and the covariance of the new measurement noise $\boldsymbol{\xi}_i$ are easily derived from that of $\mathbf{a}'_i$ as

$$E[\boldsymbol{\xi}_i] = \mathbf{0} \text{ and } E[\boldsymbol{\xi}_i^T \boldsymbol{\xi}_i] = \boldsymbol{\mathcal{V}}_i = \left(\frac{\partial \mathbf{f}_i(\mathbf{a}'_i, \hat{\mathbf{s}}_{i/i-1})}{\partial \mathbf{a}_i}\right)\boldsymbol{\mathcal{W}}_i\left(\frac{\partial \mathbf{f}_i(\mathbf{a}'_i, \hat{\mathbf{s}}_{i/i-1})}{\partial \mathbf{a}_i}\right)^T.$$

The EKF motion estimation algorithms based on point-plane and line-plane constraints can be derived in a similar way.

5.2 EKF Pose Estimation Based on Point-Plane Constraint

The projection plane $\mathbf{P}_{12}$ in the point-plane constraint equation is represented by $(d_1, \mathbf{p}_1)$, where d_1 is its Hesse distance and $\mathbf{p}_1$ its unit direction. The point-plane constraint equation in vector algebra of $\mathbb{R}^3$ reads

$$d_1 - \mathbf{p}_1^T(\boldsymbol{\mathcal{R}}\mathbf{x}_1 + \mathbf{t}) = 0.$$

With the measurement vector $\mathbf{a}_i = (d_i, \mathbf{p}_i^T, \mathbf{y}_i^T)^T$ and the same state vector $\mathbf{s}$ as above, the measurement $\mathbf{z}_i$ of linearized measurement equation reads

$$\mathbf{z}_i = \begin{pmatrix} d'_i - \mathbf{p}_i'^T(\hat{\boldsymbol{\mathcal{R}}}_{i/i-1}\mathbf{y}'_i + \hat{\mathbf{t}}_{i/i-1}) \\ \hat{\boldsymbol{\mathcal{R}}}_{i/i-1}^T\hat{\boldsymbol{\mathcal{R}}}_{i/i-1} - 1 \end{pmatrix} + \boldsymbol{\mathcal{H}}_i\hat{\mathbf{s}}_{i/i-1}.$$

The measurement matrix $\mathcal{H}_i$ of the linearized measurement $\mathbf{z}_i$ now reads

$$\mathcal{H}_i = \begin{pmatrix} \mathbf{p_i}^T \mathcal{D}_{\hat{R}\mathbf{y}'} & \mathbf{p_i}^T \\ \mathcal{D}_\mathbf{R} & \mathbf{0}_{1\times3} \end{pmatrix}.$$

The measurement noise is given by

$$\xi_i = \begin{pmatrix} 1 & -(\hat{\mathcal{R}}_{i/i-1}\mathbf{y}_i' + \hat{\mathbf{t}}_{i/i-1})^T & -(\mathbf{p_i}'^T \hat{\mathcal{R}}_{i/i-1}) \\ 0 & \mathbf{0}_{1\times3} & \mathbf{0}_{1\times3} \end{pmatrix}_{2\times7} \eta_i.$$

5.3   EKF Pose Estimation Based on Line-Plane Constraint

Using the line-plane constraint, the reference model entity in $\mathcal{G}_{3,0,1}^+$ [9,7] is the Plücker line $S_1 = n_1 + Im_1$. This line transformed by a motor $M = R + IR'$ reads

$$L_1 = MS_1\widetilde{M} = Rn_1\tilde{R} + I(Rn_1\tilde{R'} + R'n_1\tilde{R} + Rm_1\tilde{R}) = u_1 + Iv_1.$$

We denote the 8 components of the motor as

$$M = r_0 + r_1\gamma_2\gamma_3 + r_2\gamma_3\gamma_1 + r_3\gamma_1\gamma_2 + I(r_0' + r_1'\gamma_2\gamma_3 + r_2'\gamma_3\gamma_1 + r_3'\gamma_1\gamma_2).$$

The line motion equation can be equivalently expressed by vector form,

$$\mathbf{u_1} = \mathcal{R}\mathbf{n_1} \text{ and } \mathbf{v_1} = \mathcal{A}\mathbf{n_1} + \mathcal{R}\mathbf{m_1},$$

with

$$\mathcal{A} = \begin{pmatrix} a_{11} & a_{12} & a_{13} \\ a_{21} & a_{22} & a_{23} \\ a_{31} & a_{32} & a_{33} \end{pmatrix},$$

$$a_{11} = 2(r_0'r_0 + r_1'r_1 - r_2'r_2 - r_3'r_3), \quad a_{12} = 2(r_3'r_0 + r_2'r_1 + r_1'r_2 + r_0'r_3),$$
$$a_{13} = 2(-r_2'r_0 + r_3'r_1 - r_0'r_2 + r_1'r_3), \ a_{21} = 2(-r_3'r_0 + r_2'r_1 + r_1'r_2 - r_0'r_3),$$
$$a_{22} = 2(r_0'r_0 - r_1'r_1 + r_2'r_2 - r_3'r_3), \quad a_{23} = 2(r_1'r_0 + r_0'r_1 + r_3'r_2 + r_2'r_3),$$
$$a_{31} = 2(r_2'r_0 + r_3'r_1 + r_0'r_2 + r_1'r_3), \quad a_{32} = 2(-r_1'r_0 - r_0'r_1 + r_3'r_2 + r_2'r_3),$$
$$a_{33} = 2(r_0'r_0 - r_1'r_1 - r_2'r_2 + r_3'r_3).$$

The line-plane constraint equation in vector algebra of $\mathbb{R}^3$ reads

$$\begin{pmatrix} \mathbf{f_1} \\ \mathbf{f_2} \end{pmatrix} = \begin{pmatrix} \mathbf{p_1}^T\mathbf{u_1} \\ d_1\mathbf{u_1} + \mathbf{v_1} \times \mathbf{p_1} \end{pmatrix} = \begin{pmatrix} \mathbf{p_1}^T(\mathcal{R}\mathbf{n_1}) \\ d_1\mathcal{R}\mathbf{n_1} + (\mathcal{A}\mathbf{n_1} + \mathcal{R}\mathbf{m_1}) \times \mathbf{p_1} \end{pmatrix} = \mathbf{0}.$$

We use the 8 components of the motor as the state vector for the EKF,

$$\mathbf{s} = (r_0, r_1, r_2, r_3, r_0', r_1', r_2', r_3')^T$$

and these 8 components must satisfy both the unit and orthogonal conditions:

$$f_3 = r_0^2 + r_1^2 + r_2^2 + r_3^2 - 1 = 0,$$
$$f_4 = r_0r_0' + r_1r_1' + r_2r_2' + r_3r_3' = 0.$$

The 10D noise free measurement vector $\mathbf{a_i}$ is given by the true plane parameters d_i and $\mathbf{p_i}$, and the true 6D line parameters $(\mathbf{n_i}, \mathbf{m_i})$,

$$\mathbf{a_i} = (d_i, \mathbf{p_i}^T, \mathbf{n_i}^T, \mathbf{m_i}^T)^T = (d_i, p_{i1}, p_{i2}, p_{i3}, n_{i1}, n_{i2}, n_{i3}, m_{i1}, m_{i2}, m_{i3})^T.$$

The new measurement in linearized equation reads

$$\mathbf{z_i} = \begin{pmatrix} \mathbf{p'_i}^T(\hat{\mathcal{R}}_{i/i-1}\mathbf{n'_i}) \\ d'_i\hat{\mathcal{R}}_{i/i-1}\mathbf{n'_i} + (\hat{\mathcal{A}}_{i/i-1}\mathbf{n'_i} + \hat{\mathcal{R}}_{i/i-1}\mathbf{m'_i}) \times \mathbf{p'_i} \\ \hat{\mathbf{R}}_{i/i-1}^T\hat{\mathbf{R}}_{i/i-1} - 1 \\ \hat{\mathbf{R}}_{i/i-1}^T\hat{\mathbf{R}}'_{i/i-1} \end{pmatrix} + \mathcal{H}_i\hat{\mathbf{s}}_{i/i-1}.$$

The measurement matrix $\mathcal{H}_i$ of the linearized measurement $\mathbf{z_i}$ reads

$$\mathcal{H}_i = \begin{pmatrix} -\mathbf{p'_i}^T\mathcal{D}_{\hat{\mathcal{R}}\mathbf{n'}} & \mathbf{0}_{1\times 4} \\ -d'_i\mathcal{D}_{\hat{\mathcal{R}}\mathbf{n'}} + \mathcal{C}_{\mathbf{p'_i}}(\mathcal{D}_{\hat{\mathcal{A}}\mathbf{n'}} + \mathcal{D}_{\hat{\mathcal{R}}\mathbf{m'}}) & \mathcal{C}_{\mathbf{p'_i}}\mathcal{D}_{\hat{\mathcal{R}}\mathbf{n'}} \\ \mathcal{D}_{\mathbf{R}} & \mathbf{0}_{1\times 4} \\ \mathcal{D}_{\mathbf{R'}} & \frac{1}{2}\mathcal{D}_{\mathbf{R}} \end{pmatrix},$$

where $\mathcal{D}_{\hat{\mathcal{R}}\mathbf{n'}} = \dfrac{\partial(\hat{\mathcal{R}}_{i/i-1}\mathbf{n'_i})}{\partial\mathbf{R}_i}$, $\mathcal{D}_{\hat{\mathcal{R}}\mathbf{m'}} = \dfrac{\partial(\hat{\mathcal{R}}_{i/i-1}\mathbf{m'_i})}{\partial\mathbf{R}_i}$, $\mathcal{D}_{\hat{\mathcal{A}}\mathbf{n'}} = \dfrac{\partial(\hat{\mathcal{A}}_{i/i-1}\mathbf{n'_i})}{\partial\mathbf{R}_i}$,

$\mathcal{D}_{\mathbf{R'}} = \dfrac{\partial(\hat{\mathbf{R}}_{i/i-1}^T\hat{\mathbf{R}}'_{i/i-1})}{\partial\mathbf{R}_i}$ and $\frac{1}{2}\mathcal{D}_{\mathbf{R}} = \dfrac{\partial(\hat{\mathbf{R}}_{i/i-1}^T\hat{\mathbf{R}}'_{i/i-1})}{\partial\mathbf{R}'_i}$.

The 3×3 matrix $\mathcal{C}_{\mathbf{p'_i}}$ is the skew-symmetric matrix of $\mathbf{p'_i}$. The measurement noise is given by

$$\boldsymbol{\xi}_i = \begin{pmatrix} 0 & \mathbf{n'_i}^T\hat{\mathcal{R}}_{i/i-1} & \mathbf{p'_i}^T\hat{\mathcal{R}}_{i/i-1} & \mathbf{0}_{1\times 3} \\ \hat{\mathcal{R}}_{i/i-1}\mathbf{n'_i} & \mathcal{C}_{\hat{\mathbf{v}}_i} & d'_i\hat{\mathcal{R}}_{i/i-1} - \mathcal{C}_{\mathbf{p'_i}}\hat{\mathcal{A}}_{i/i-1} & -\mathcal{C}_{\mathbf{p'_i}}\hat{\mathcal{R}}_{i/i-1} \\ \mathbf{0}_{2\times 3} & \mathbf{0}_{2\times 3} & \mathbf{0}_{2\times 3} & \mathbf{0}_{2\times 3} \end{pmatrix} \boldsymbol{\eta}_i$$

where $\mathcal{C}_{\hat{\mathbf{v}}_i}$ is skew-symmetric matrix of $\hat{\mathbf{v}}_i$, and $\hat{\mathbf{v}}_i$ is defined as

$$\hat{\mathbf{v}}_i = \hat{\mathcal{A}}_{i/i-1}\mathbf{n'_i} + \hat{\mathcal{R}}_{i/i-1}\mathbf{m'_i}.$$

Having linearized the measurement models, the EKF implementation is straightforward and standard. Further implementation details will not be repeated here [10,9,12]. In next section, we will denote the EKF as **RtEKF**, if the state explicitly uses the rotor components of rotation **R** and of translation **t**, or **MEKF**, if the components of motor **M** are used.

6   Experiments

In this section we present some experiments with real images. The aim of the experiments is to study the performance of the algorithms for pose estimation based on geometric constraints. We expect that both the special constraints and the algorithmic approach of using them may influence the results.

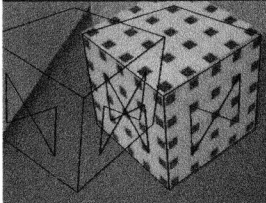

Fig. 5. The scenario of the experiment: The calibration of an object model is performed and the 3D object model is projected on the image. Then the camera moved and corresponding line segments are extracted.

Table 2. The experiment 1 results in different qualities of derived motion parameters, depending on the used constraints and algorithms to evaluate their validity.

no.	$\mathcal{R}$ — t	Constraint		Experiment 1		Error
1	RtEKF — RtEKF	XL-XL	$\mathcal{R} = \begin{pmatrix} 0.987 & 0.089 & -0.138 \\ -0.117 & 0.969 & -0.218 \\ 0.115 & 0.231 & 0.966 \end{pmatrix}$		$t = \begin{pmatrix} -58.21 \\ -217.26 \\ 160.60 \end{pmatrix}$	5.2
2	SVD — MAT	XL-XL	$\mathcal{R} = \begin{pmatrix} 0.976 & 0.107 & -0.191 \\ -0.156 & 0.952 & -0.264 \\ 0.154 & 0.287 & 0.945 \end{pmatrix}$		$t = \begin{pmatrix} -60.12 \\ -212.16 \\ 106.60 \end{pmatrix}$	6.7
3	RtEKF — RtEKF	XP-XP	$\mathcal{R} = \begin{pmatrix} 0.987 & 0.092 & -0.133 \\ -0.118 & 0.973 & -0.200 \\ 0.111 & 0.213 & 0.970 \end{pmatrix}$		$t = \begin{pmatrix} -52.67 \\ -217.00 \\ 139.00 \end{pmatrix}$	5.5
4	RtEKF — MAT	XP-XP	$\mathcal{R} = \begin{pmatrix} 0.986 & 0.115 & -0.118 \\ -0.141 & 0.958 & -0.247 \\ 0.085 & 0.260 & 0.962 \end{pmatrix}$		$t = \begin{pmatrix} -71.44 \\ -219.34 \\ 124.71 \end{pmatrix}$	3.7
5	SVD — MAT	XP-XP	$\mathcal{R} = \begin{pmatrix} 0.979 & 0.101 & -0.177 \\ -0.144 & 0.957 & -0.251 \\ 0.143 & 0.271 & 0.952 \end{pmatrix}$		$t = \begin{pmatrix} -65.55 \\ -221.18 \\ 105.87 \end{pmatrix}$	5.3
6	SVD — MAT	LP-XP	$\mathcal{R} = \begin{pmatrix} 0.976 & 0.109 & -0.187 \\ -0.158 & 0.950 & -0.266 \\ 0.149 & 0.289 & 0.945 \end{pmatrix}$		$t = \begin{pmatrix} -66.57 \\ -216.18 \\ 100.53 \end{pmatrix}$	7.1
7	MEKF — MEKF	LP-LP	$\mathcal{R} = \begin{pmatrix} 0.985 & 0.106 & -0.134 \\ -0.133 & 0.969 & -0.208 \\ 0.107 & 0.229 & 0.969 \end{pmatrix}$		$t = \begin{pmatrix} -50.10 \\ -212.60 \\ 142.20 \end{pmatrix}$	2.9
8	MEKF — MAT	LP-LP	$\mathcal{R} = \begin{pmatrix} 0.985 & 0.106 & -0.134 \\ -0.133 & 0.968 & -0.213 \\ 0.108 & 0.228 & 0.968 \end{pmatrix}$		$t = \begin{pmatrix} -67.78 \\ -227.73 \\ 123.90 \end{pmatrix}$	2.7
9	SVD — MAT	LP-LP	$\mathcal{R} = \begin{pmatrix} 0.976 & 0.109 & -0.187 \\ -0.158 & 0.950 & -0.266 \\ 0.149 & 0.289 & 0.945 \end{pmatrix}$		$t = \begin{pmatrix} -80.58 \\ -225.59 \\ 93.93 \end{pmatrix}$	6.9

In our experimental scenario we positioned a camera two meters in front of a calibration cube. We focused the camera on the calibration cube and took an image. Then we moved the camera, focused the camera again on the cube and took another image. The edge size of the calibration cube is 46 cm and the image size is 384×288 pixel. Furthermore, we defined on the calibration cube a 3D object model. Figure 5 shows the scenario. In the left images the calibration is performed and the 3D object model is projected on the image. Then the camera is moved and corresponding line segments are extracted. In these experiments we actually selected certain points by hand and from these the depicted line segments are derived and, by knowing the camera calibration by the cube of the first image, the actual projection ray and projection plane parameters are computed.

For the first experiment we show in table 2 the results of different algorithms for pose estimation. In the second column of table 2 EKF denotes the use of the EKFs derived in section 5, MAT denotes matrix algebra, SVD denotes the singular value decomposition of a matrix. In the third column the used constraints,

point-line (XL), point-plane (XP) and line-plane (LP) are indicated. The fourth
column shows the results of the estimated rotation matrix $\mathcal{R}$ and the translation vector $\mathbf{t}$, respectively. The translation vectors are shown in mm. The fifth
column shows the error of the equation system. Since the error of the equation
system describes the Hesse distance of the entities, the value of the error is an
approximation of the squared average distance of the entities. It is easy to see,
that the results obtained with the different approaches are all very close to each
other, though the implementation leads to totally different calculations and algorithms. Furthermore the EKF's perform more stable than the matrix solution
approaches.

The visualization of some errors is done in figure 6. We calculated the motion
of the object and projected the transformed object in the image plane. The
extracted line segments are overlayed in addition. Figure 6 shows the results of
nos. 5, 3, 7 and 8 of table 2, respectively.

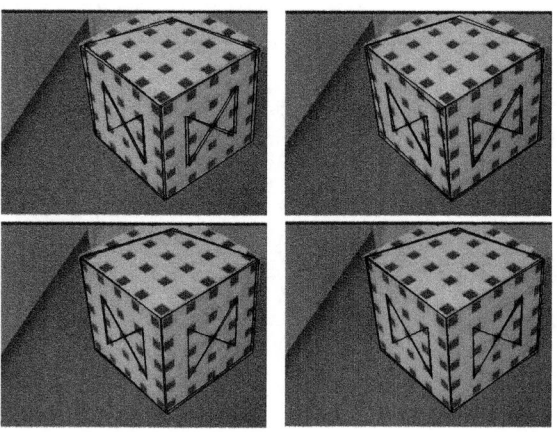

Fig. 6. Visualization of some errors. The results of nos. 5, 3 7 and 8 of table 2 are
visualized respectively.

In a second experiment we compare the noise sensitivity of the Kalman filters
and of the matrix solution approaches for pose estimation. The experiment is
organized as follows. We took the point correspondences of the first experiment
and estimated both $\mathcal{R}$ and $\mathbf{t}$. Then we added a Gaussian noise error on the
extracted image points. The error varied from 0 to 16 pixels in 0.25 steps and
we estimated $\mathcal{R}'$ and $\mathbf{t}'$ for each step. Then we calculated the error between
$\mathcal{R}'$ and $\mathcal{R}$ and between $\mathbf{t}'$ and $\mathbf{t}$. The results are shown in figure 7. Since $\mathcal{R}$
and $\mathcal{R}'$ are rotation matrices, the absolute value of the error differs in the range
$0 \leq \epsilon_{\mathcal{R}} \leq 1$. The error of the translation vector is evaluated in mm. So the error
of the translation vector differs by using the matrix solution approach at around
$0 \leq \epsilon_{\mathbf{t}} \leq 10$ cm, while using the Kalman filter the corresponding range is $0 \leq
\epsilon_{\mathbf{t}} \leq 6$ cm. The matrix based solutions look all very similar. Compared with the

EKF results they are very sensitive to noise and the variances between the noise steps are very high. The results are in agreement with the well known behavior of error propagation in case of matrix based rotation estimation. The EKF based solutions perform all very stable and the behavior of the different constraints are also very similar. This is a consequence of the estimators themselves and of the fact that the concatenation of rotors is more robust than that of rotation matrices. It is obvious, that the results of these experiments are affected by the method to obtain the entities in the image. In this experiment we selected certain points directly by hand and derived from these the line subspaces. So the quality of the line subspaces is directly connected to the quality of the point extraction. For comparison purposes between the algorithms this is necessary and reasonable. But for real applications, since the extraction of lines is more stable than that of points, the XP or LP algorithms should be preferred.

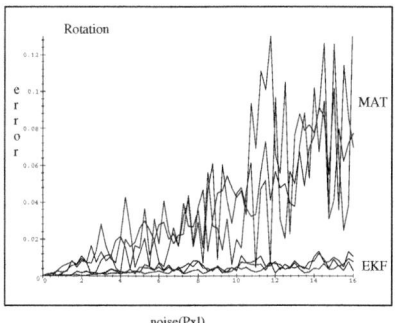 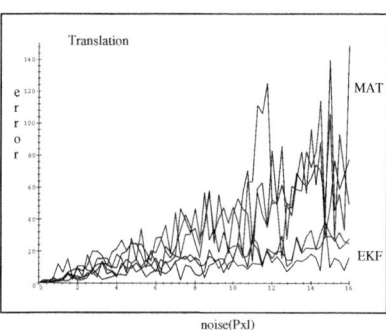

Fig. 7. Performance comparison of different methods in case of noisy data. With increasing noise the EKF performs with more accurate and more stable estimates than the matrix based methods.

7   Conclusions

In this paper we describe a framework for 2D-3D pose estimation. The aim of the paper is to compare several pose modeling approaches and estimation methods with respect to their performance. The main contribution of the paper is to formulate 2D-3D pose determination in the language of kinematics as a problem of estimating rotation and translation from geometric constraint equations. There are three such constraints which relate the model frame to an observation frame. The model data are either points or lines. The observation frame is constituted by lines or planes. Any deviations from the constraint correspond the Hesse distance of the involved geometric entities. From this starting point as a useful algebraic frame for handling line motion, the motor algebra has been introduced. The estimation procedure is realized as extended Kalman filters (EKF).

The paper presents EKFs for estimating rotation and translation for each constraint model in different algebraic frames. The experiments show advantages of that representation and of the EKF approaches in comparison to normal matrix based LMS algorithms, all applied within the context of constraint based pose estimation.

References

[1] C. Perwass and J. Lasenby. A novel axiomatic derivation of geometric algebra. *Technical Report CUED/F - INFENG/TR.347, Cambridge University Engineering Department*, 1999.

[2] Shevlin F. Analysis of orientation problems using Plücker lines. *International Conference on Pattern Recognition, Brisbane*, 1: 685–689, 1998.

[3] Horaud R., Phong T.Q. and P.D. Tao. Object pose from 2-d to 3-d point and line correspondences. *International Journal of Computer Vision*, 15: 225–243, 1995.

[4] Blaschke W. Mathematische Monographien 4, Kinematik und Quaternionen. *Deutscher Verlag der Wissenschaften*, Berlin, 1960.

[5] Grimson W. E. L. Object Recognition by Computer. *The MIT Press, Cambridge, MA*, 1990.

[6] Daniilidis K. Hand-eye calibration using dual quaternions. *Int. Journ. Robotics Res*, 18: 286–298, 1999.

[7] Bayro-Corrochano E. The geometry and algebra of kinematics. *In Sommer G., editor, Geometric Computing with Clifford Algebra. Springer Verlag*, to be published, 2000.

[8] Carceroni R. L. and C. M. Brown. Numerical methods for model-based pose recovery. *Techn. Rept. 659, Comp. Sci. Dept., The Univ. of Rochester, Rochester, N. Y.*, August 1998.

[9] Zhang Y., Sommer G., and E. Bayro-Corrochano. The motor extended Kalman filter for dynamic rigid motion estimation from line observations. *In G. Sommer, editor, Geometric Computing with Clifford Algebra. Springer Verlag*, to be published, 2000.

[10] Sommer G., Rosenhahn B. and Zhang Y. Pose estimation using geometric constraints. *Techn. Rept. 2003, Institut für Informatik und Praktische Mathematik Christian-Albrechts-Universität zu Kiel*, 2000.

[11] Hestenes D., Li H. and A. Rockwood. New algebraic tools for classical geometry. *In Sommer G., editor, Geometric Computing with Clifford Algebra. Springer Verlag*, to be published, 2000.

[12] Zhang, Z. and O. Faugeras. 3D Dynamic Scene Analysis. *Springer Verlag*, 1992.

The Fusion of Image and Range Flow

John L. Barron and Hagen Spies

[1] Dept. of Computer Science, University of Western Ontario
London, Ontario, Canada, N6A 5B7
barron@csd.uwo.ca
[2] Interdisciplinary Center for Scientific Computing
University of Heidelberg, INF 368, 69121 Heidelberg, Germany
Hagen.Spies@iwr.uni-heidelberg.de

Abstract. We present quantitative results for computing local least squares and global regularized range flow using both image and range data. We first review the computation of local least squares range flow and then show how its computation can be cast in a global Horn and Schunck like regularization framework [15]. These computations are done using both range data only and using a combination of image and range data [14]. We present quantitative results for these two least squares range flow algorithms and for the two regularization range flow algorithms for one synthetic range sequence and one real range sequence, where the correct 3D motions are known a priori. We show that using both image and range data produces more accurate and more dense range flow than the use of range flow alone.

1 Introduction

We can use image sequences to compute optical flow in a local least squares calculation, for example, Lucas and Kanade [8], or in a global iterative regularization, for example, Horn and Schunck [5]. In addition to the use of image intensity data, it is possible to use densely sampled range sequences [17] to compute range flow. Range data (for example from a Biris range sensor [3]) consists of 2D arrays of the 3D coordinates (in millimeters) of a scene, i.e. the 3D X, Y and Z values, plus the grayvalue intensity at those same points. Since our range sensor acquires images under orthographic projection we can only compute **image flow** (orthographic optical flow) rather than perspective optical flow, although the same algorithms can be used in both cases. Just as optical/image flow can be computed from time-varying image data [1], range flow can be computed from time varying range data [17]. The Biris range sensor is based on active triangularization using a laser beam and on a dual aperture mask. It has a reported depth accuracy of about 0.1mm for objects at a distance of 250mm [3]. This paper investigates the computation of range flow on one synthetic range sequence and on one real range sequence made with a Biris range sensor using regularization on both range and/or intensity derivatives. We

R. Klette et al. (Eds.): Multi-Image Analysis, LNCS 2032, pp. 171–189, 2001.
© Springer-Verlag Berlin Heidelberg 2001

also show how local and global optical flow computations can be extended into 3D, allowing the calculation of dense accurate range flow fields, often when the number of individual range velocities is sparse.

Although the work reported here was performed with Biris range sensor data, there is no reason why our algorithms could not be used with other sources of time-varying depth information, such as depth maps from stereo [16] or motion and structure [6] algorithms. Here we assume locally rigid objects (although both of our sequences have globally rigid objects). Instead of computing camera motion parameters and overall scene motion, we are interested in computing the range flow, i.e. the 3D velocity, at each point the depth data is sampled at. Towards this end, we start with the range constraint equation of [6,16,17].

2D optical flow methods have recently been generalized into the 3D domain. Chaudhury et al. [4] formulated at 3D optical flow constraint, using I_x, I_y, I_z and I_t derivatives. Thus they have a time-varying volume of intensity where all 4 derivatives can be computed. A lot of this work has been medically motivated, for example, to compute 3D flow for CT, MRI and PET datasets [11,12,18,7]. Since range flow is computed with respect to a moving 3D surface, derivative data in the Z dimension is not available, resulting in different constraint equations for range data and for 3D optical flow.

The basic algorithms used in this paper have been reported in more detail elsewhere:

1. Quantitative flow analysis using the Lucas and Kanade least squares calculation and the Horn and Schunck regularization were reported in [1].
2. The computation of full range flow (and its two types of normal flow) in a total least squares framework was reported in [13]. Here, the range flow calculation is reformulated in in a least squares framework [2].
3. The direct regularization was presented in [15] for a number of different sequences, including a real sequence made from the 3D motion of a growing caster oil bean leaf using a Biris range sensor.
4. The computation of range flow from both intensity and range data in both a total least squares framework (as opposed to a least squares framework used here) and a regularization framework is reported in [14].

We examine the quantitative performance of these algorithms on two intensity/range sequences: a synthetic sequence where the range and intensity data was error-free, yielding good flows and a real sequence where both the range and intensity data are poor. In the later case, we also know the true 3D velocity and are thus able to quantitatively analyze the flow. The results are quite good when the combined intensity and range data are taken into account, especially when one considers that the range structure is very poor at most locations (the surfaces are planar).

2   2D Image Flow

The well known motion constraint equation:

$$I_x u + I_y v + I_t = 0 \qquad (1)$$

forms the basis of most optical flow algorithms. I_x, I_y and I_t in equation (1) are the x, y and t intensity derivatives while $v = (u, v)$ is the image velocity (or optical flow) at pixel (x, y), which is an approximation of the local image motion. Equation (1) is 1 equation in 2 unknowns and manifests the *aperture problem*. Raw normal velocity (the component of image velocity normal to the local intensity structure) can be totally expressed in terms of derivative information:

$$v_{rn} = \frac{-I_t(I_x, I_y)^T}{I_x^2 + I_y^2} \tag{2}$$

while tangential velocity, v_t cannot, in general, be recovered.

To solve for v we need to impose an additional constraint. An example of a local constraint is to assume that locally all image velocities are the same. For example, Lucas and Kanade [8] use a least squares computation to integrate local neighbourhoods of normal image velocities into full image velocities. For a $n \times n$ neighbourhood, they solve a $n \times 2$ linear system of equations $A_{n\times2}v = B_{n\times1}$ as

$$v = (A^T A)^{-1} A^T B, \tag{3}$$

where A has entries I_{xi} and I_{yi} in the ith row and B has entries $-I_{ti}$ in the ith row. We perform eigenvector/eigenvalue analysis on $A^T A$ using routines in [9]. Eigenvalue ($\lambda_0 \leq \lambda_1$) and corresponding eigenvector ($\hat{e}_0$ and $\hat{e}_1$) decomposition of the symmetric matrix $A^T A$ yields least squares full image velocity, if both $\lambda_0 > \tau_{D1}$ and $\lambda_1 > \tau_{D1}$, or least squares normal image velocity, $v_{ln} = v \cdot \hat{e}_1$, if $\lambda_1 > \tau_{D1}$ but $\lambda_0 \leq \tau_{D1}$. On the other hand, Horn and Schunck [5] impose a global smoothness constraint on the optical flow field and minimize:

$$\int \int (I_x u + I_y v + I_t)^2 + \alpha^2 (u_x^2 + u_u^2 + v_x^2 + v_y^2) \partial x \partial y. \tag{4}$$

We can minimize this functional using Euler-Lagrange equations (with $\nabla^2 u$ and $\nabla^2 v$ approximated as $\bar{u} - u$ and $\bar{v} - v$ respectively) as;

$$\underbrace{\begin{bmatrix} (\alpha^2 + I_x^2) & I_x I_y \\ I_x I_y & (\alpha^2 + I_y^2) \end{bmatrix}}_{A} \begin{bmatrix} u \\ v \end{bmatrix} = \begin{bmatrix} (\alpha^2 \bar{u} - I_x I_t) \\ (\alpha^2 \bar{v} - I_y I_t) \end{bmatrix}, \tag{5}$$

yielding the Gauss Seidel iterative equations:

$$\begin{bmatrix} u^{n+1} \\ v^{n+1} \end{bmatrix} = A^{-1} \begin{bmatrix} (\alpha^2 \bar{u}^n - I_x I_t) \\ (\alpha^2 \bar{v}^n - I_y I_t) \end{bmatrix}. \tag{6}$$

3   3D Range Flow

Biris range data consists not only of 3D coordinate (X, Y, Z) data of an environmental scene but also intensity data for each of those environmental points.

The motion constraint equation can easily be extended into the range constraint equation [17] in 3D:

$$Z_X U + Z_Y V + W + Z_t = 0, \qquad (7)$$

where $\boldsymbol{V} = (U, V, W)$ is the 3D range velocity and Z_X, Z_Y and Z_t are spatio-temporal derivatives of the depth coordinate Z. Raw normal velocity can also be computed directly from Z derivatives as

$$\boldsymbol{V}_{rn} = \frac{-Z_t(Z_X, Z_Y, 1)}{Z_X^2 + Z_Y^2 + 1}. \qquad (8)$$

For a $n \times n$ neighbourhood, we can solve a $n \times 3$ linear system of equations $A_{n \times 3} \boldsymbol{V} = B_{n \times 1}$ as

$$\boldsymbol{V} = (A^T A)^{-1} A^T B, \qquad (9)$$

where A has entries Z_{Xi}, Z_{Yi} and 1 in the ith row and B has entries $-Z_{ti}$ in the ith row. Alternatively to this least squares computation a total least squares approach may be used [13]. The eigenvalues ($\lambda_0 \leq \lambda_1 \leq \lambda_2$) and their corresponding eigenvectors ($\hat{e}_0$, $\hat{e}_1$ and $\hat{e}_2$) can be computed from the 3×3 symmetric matrix $A^T A$ and then used to compute least squares full range velocity, $\boldsymbol{V}_F$, when $\lambda_0, \lambda_1, \lambda_2 > \tau_{D2}$, an estimate of least squares line normal velocity, $\boldsymbol{V}_L$, when $\lambda_1, \lambda_2 > \tau_{D2}$, $\lambda_0 \leq \tau_{D2}$ and an estimate of the least squares plane normal velocity, $\boldsymbol{V}_P$, when $\lambda_2 > \tau_{D2}$, $\lambda_0, \lambda_1 \leq \tau_{D2}$. The terms line and plane normal range velocity are motivated by the fact that these types of normal velocity always occur on lines or planes on the 3D surface. That is:

$$\boldsymbol{V}_F = (\boldsymbol{V} \cdot \hat{e}_0)\hat{e}_0 + (\boldsymbol{V} \cdot \hat{e}_1)\hat{e}_1 + (\boldsymbol{V} \cdot \hat{e}_2)\hat{e}_2 \qquad (10)$$
$$\boldsymbol{V}_L = (\boldsymbol{V} \cdot \hat{e}_1)\hat{e}_1 + (\boldsymbol{V} \cdot \hat{e}_2)\hat{e}_2 \qquad (11)$$
$$\boldsymbol{V}_P = (\boldsymbol{V} \cdot \hat{e}_2)\hat{e}_2. \qquad (12)$$

Of course $\boldsymbol{V}$ is $\boldsymbol{V}_F$. This computational scheme breaks down if $A^T A$ cannot be reliably inverted as then we cannot compute $\boldsymbol{V}$ as required in equations (10) to (12). Below we outline how to compute line and planar normal flow when $A^T A$ is nearly singular. We can rewrite the eigenvalue/eigenvector equation, $A^T A \hat{e}_i = \lambda_i \hat{e}_i$, as

$$A^T A \begin{bmatrix} \hat{e}_0 \\ \hat{e}_1 \\ \hat{e}_2 \end{bmatrix} = A^T A R = \begin{bmatrix} \lambda_0 & 0 & 0 \\ 0 & \lambda_1 & 0 \\ 0 & 0 & \lambda_2 \end{bmatrix} R, \qquad (13)$$

where $R = [\hat{e}_0, \hat{e}_1, \hat{e}_2]^T$. Thus we can rewrite (9) as:

$$\begin{bmatrix} \lambda_0 & 0 & 0 \\ 0 & \lambda_1 & 0 \\ 0 & 0 & \lambda_2 \end{bmatrix} \boldsymbol{V}' = B', \qquad (14)$$

where $\boldsymbol{V}' = (U', V', W') = R^T \boldsymbol{V}$ and $B' = (b'_0, b'_1, b'_2)^T = R^T A^T B$. If λ_0 is small, $\lambda_0 \leq \tau_{D2}$, $\lambda_1, \lambda_2 > \tau_{D2}$, we are dealing with a line normal velocity,

$\boldsymbol{V}_L = (U_L, V_L, W_L)$. Then the 2nd and 3rd equations of (14) give two equations that define constraint planes that the normal velocity must lie in. The line normal is given by the point on their intersecting line with minimal distance from the origin. The direction of this line is given by $\hat{e}_0 = \hat{e}_1 \times \hat{e}_2$, which yields a third equation. The system of equations to be solved is:

$$V\prime = e_{10}U_L + e_{11}V_L + e_{12}W_L = \frac{b_1'}{\lambda_1} \tag{15}$$

$$W\prime = e_{21}U_L + e_{21}V_L + e_{22}W_L = \frac{b_2'}{\lambda_2} \tag{16}$$

$$e_{01}U_L + e_{01}V_L + e_{02}W_L = 0. \tag{17}$$

If both λ_0 and λ_1 are less than τ_{D2} then we can only compute planar normal range flow. In this case, we have one constraint:

$$e_{20}U_P + e_{21}V_P + e_{22}W_P = \frac{b_2'}{\lambda_2}. \tag{18}$$

The plane normal flow is the point on this plane with minimal distance from the origin:

$$\boldsymbol{V}_P = \frac{\frac{b_2'}{\lambda_2}}{e_{20}^2 + e_{21}^2 + e_{22}^2} \begin{bmatrix} e_{20} \\ e_{21} \\ e_{22} \end{bmatrix} = \frac{b_2'}{\lambda_2} \begin{bmatrix} e_{20} \\ e_{21} \\ e_{22} \end{bmatrix}. \tag{19}$$

Since $A^T A$ is a real, positive semi-definite, symmetric matrix, eigenvalue/eigenvector decomposition always yields real positive eigenvalues.

4   Least Squares Image-Range Flow

We note that if we compute derivatives of intensity with respect to X and Y, rather than x and y (the projection of X and Y on the sensor grid) the motion constraint equation becomes:

$$I_X U + I_Y V + I_t = 0, \tag{20}$$

where U and V are the first two components of range flow. Since a Biris sensor's images are made under orthographic projection we use standard optical flow as image flow. (U, V) can then be recovered by a least squares calculation. They are the first two components of range flow and are orthographic image velocity (which we call image flow). If we use equations of the form in (20) and (7) whenever intensity and/or depth derivatives reliably available, we obtain a least squares linear system of equations for U, V and W in terms of the spatio-temporal intensity and depth derivatives. We require at least one equation of the form in equation (7) be present to constrain the W parameter. We use β to weigh the contribution of the depth and intensity derivatives in the computation of (U, V, W) so that they are of equal influence. We solve for (U, V, W) using least squares as outlined above, checking the eigenvalues against a third threshold, τ_{D3}.

5   Direct Regularized Range Flow

We can compute regularized range flow directly using the spatio-temporal derivatives of Z by minimizing

$$\int\int\int\int (Z_X U + Z_Y V + W + Z_t)^2 + \alpha^2 (U_X^2 + U_Y^2 + U_Z^2 +$$

$$V_X^2 + V_Y^2 + V_Z^2 + W_X^2 + W_Y^2 + W_Z^2) \partial X \partial Y \partial Z \partial t. \qquad (21)$$

We can write the Euler-Lagrange equations using the approximations $\nabla^2 U = U_{XX} + U_{YY} + U_{ZZ} \approx \bar{U} - U$, $\nabla^2 V = V_{XX} + V_{YY} + V_{ZZ} \approx \bar{V} - V$ and and $\nabla^2 W = W_{XX} + W_{YY} + W_{ZZ} \approx \bar{W} - W$ respectively as:

$$\underbrace{\begin{bmatrix} (\alpha^2 + Z_X^2) & Z_X Z_Y & Z_X \\ Z_X Z_Y & (\alpha^2 + Z_Y^2) & Z_Y \\ Z_X & Z_Y & (\alpha^2 + 1) \end{bmatrix}}_{A} \begin{bmatrix} U \\ V \\ W \end{bmatrix} = \begin{bmatrix} (\alpha^2 \bar{U} - Z_X Z_t) \\ (\alpha^2 \bar{V} - Z_Y Z_t) \\ (\alpha^2 \bar{W} - Z_t) \end{bmatrix}. \qquad (22)$$

The Gauss Seidel equations then become:

$$\begin{bmatrix} U^{n+1} \\ V^{n+1} \\ W^{n+1} \end{bmatrix} = A^{-1} \begin{bmatrix} (\alpha^2 \bar{U}^n - Z_X Z_t) \\ (\alpha^2 \bar{V}^n - Z_Y Z_t) \\ (\alpha^2 \bar{W}^n - Z_t) \end{bmatrix}. \qquad (23)$$

6   Combined Range Flow from Intensity and Range Derivatives

It is possible to compute V using both intensity and range derivatives via equations (1) and (7) and the same smoothness term given in equation (21). We regularize:

$$\int\int\int\int (Z_X U + Z_Y V + W + Z_t)^2 + \beta^2 (I_X U + I_Y V + I_t)^2$$

$$+\alpha^2 (U_X^2 + U_Y^2 + U_Z^2 + + V_X^2 + V_Y^2 + V_Z^2 +$$

$$W_X^2 + W_Y^2 + W_Z^2) \partial X \partial Y \partial Z \partial t, \qquad (24)$$

The Euler-Lagrange equations are

$$A \begin{bmatrix} U \\ V \\ W \end{bmatrix} = \begin{bmatrix} \alpha^2 \bar{U} - Z_X Z_t - \beta^2 I_X I_t \\ \alpha^2 \bar{V} - Z_Y Z_t - \beta^2 I_Y I_t \\ \alpha^2 \bar{W} - Z_t - \beta^2 I_t \end{bmatrix}, \qquad (25)$$

where A is

$$\begin{bmatrix} Z_X^2 + \beta^2 I_X^2 + \alpha^2 & Z_X Z_Y + \beta^2 I_X I_Y & Z_X \\ Z_X Z_Y + \beta^2 I_X I_Y & Z_Y^2 + \beta^2 I_Y^2 + \alpha^2 & Z_Y \\ Z_X & Z_Y & 1 + \alpha^2 \end{bmatrix}. \qquad (26)$$

The Gauss Seidel equations are then

$$\begin{bmatrix} U^{n+1} \\ V^{n+1} \\ W^{n+1} \end{bmatrix} = A^{-1} \begin{bmatrix} \alpha^2 \bar{U}^n - Z_X Z_t - \beta^2 I_X I_t \\ \alpha^2 \bar{V}^n - Z_Y Z_t - \beta^2 I_Y I_t \\ \alpha^2 \bar{W}^n - Z_t - \beta^2 I_t \end{bmatrix}. \tag{27}$$

The matrix A^{-1} only has to be computed once in equations (23) and (27), existence of the inverse is guaranteed by the Sherman-Morrison-Woodbury formula [15].

7   Differentiation

The use of a good differential kernel is essential to the accuracy of both image and range flow calculations. We use the balanced/matched filters for prefiltering and differentiation proposed by Simoncelli [10]. A simple averaging filter $[\frac{1}{4}, \frac{1}{2}, \frac{1}{4}]$ was used to slightly blur the images before prefiltering/differentiation. The prefiltering kernel's coefficients were $(0.0356976, 0.2488746, 0.4308557, 0.2488746$ and $0.0356976)$ while the differential kernel's coefficients were $(-0.107663, -0.282671, 0.0, 0.282671$ and $0.107663)$. For example, to compute I_x, we first convolve the prefiltering kernel in the t dimension, then convolve the prefiltering kernel on that result in the y dimension and finally convolve the differentiation kernel in the x dimension on that result. We assume a uniform sampling of the Z data in X and Y; in general, this is not true (but is true for our data).

8   Error Measurement

We report 2D error for image flow and 3D error for range flow using relative magnitude error (as a percentage) and angle error (in degrees). $\boldsymbol{V}_c$ is the correct image/range flow and $\boldsymbol{V}_e$ is the estimated or computed image/range flow in the equations below. For magnitude error we report:

$$\psi_M = \frac{|\,||\boldsymbol{V}_c||_2 - ||\boldsymbol{V}_e||_2\,|}{||\boldsymbol{V}_c||_2} \times 100\%, \tag{28}$$

while for angle error we report:

$$\psi_A = \arccos(\hat{V}_c \cdot \hat{V}_e). \tag{29}$$

For line normal range flow we compute an estimated correct line flow as:

$$\boldsymbol{V}_{Lc} = (\boldsymbol{V}_c \cdot \hat{e}_1)\hat{e}_1 + (\boldsymbol{V}_c \cdot \hat{e}_2)\hat{e}_2. \tag{30}$$

Of course $\hat{e}_1$ and $\hat{e}_2$ have error in themselves as they are computed from the least squares integration matrix. We then report magnitude and angle error as given in equations (28) and (29). Finally, for planar normal range flow we can only compute the planar magnitude error:

$$\psi_{P3D} = \frac{\left| \boldsymbol{V}_c \cdot \hat{V}_P - ||\boldsymbol{V}_P||_2 \right|}{||\boldsymbol{V}_P||_2} \times 100\%, \tag{31}$$

as the direction of the computed and estimated correct plane flow are always the same (the direction of the eigenvector corresponding to the largest eigenvalue). We also examine ϕ_{abs}, the average absolute error:

$$\phi_{abs} = \sum^{N} ||\boldsymbol{V}_c \cdot \hat{V}_P||_2 - ||\boldsymbol{V}_P||_2 \tag{32}$$

9 Synthetic Range Flow Results

To test our algorithms, we made a synthetic range sequence where we know the correct 3D translation (0.4,0.6,0.9 units/frame), allowing quantitative error analysis. In Figure 1a we show the depth map synthetically generated while Figure 1b shows the corresponding image data. Each line in the depth map has a Gaussian profile - this is made by simply rotating the coordinates into the line and then applying the appropriate exponential function. The motion in Z is done afterwards by simply adding the appropriate motion, thus W is globally constant for this sequence. The image data was made by simply overlaying two sinusoids with perpendicular orientations with the correct XY motion, thus $\boldsymbol{V} = (U, V, W)$ is globally constant.

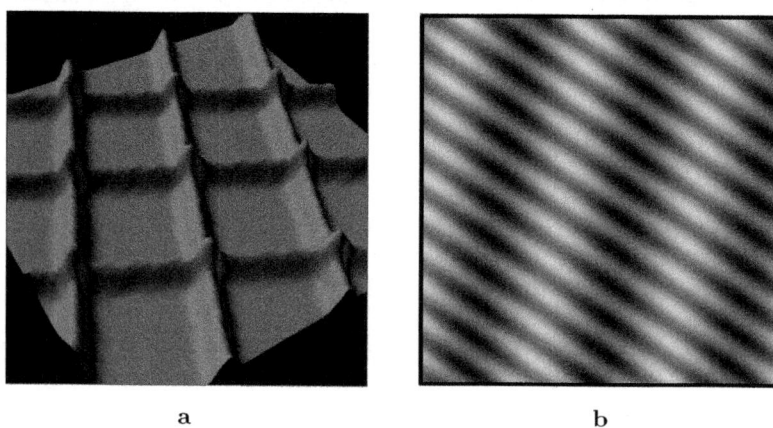

a   b

Fig. 1. Synthetic depth map without texture and (b) a sinusoid texture.

Figure 2a through 2e show the computed XY and XZ full, line and planar range flow for this sequence (section 3) while Table 1 gives their quantitative magnitude (percentage) and direction (angle) error measures. We use the projected correct flow in the direction of computed eigenvectors as "correct" line and plane flow. These are good estimates of correct plane range flow but not so good for line flow.

Figures 3a,b shows the computed Horn and Schunck and Lucas and Kanade flow fields (section 2) for the two image sequences while Table 2 shows their quantitative error. The local least squares image-range flow results (section 4) are

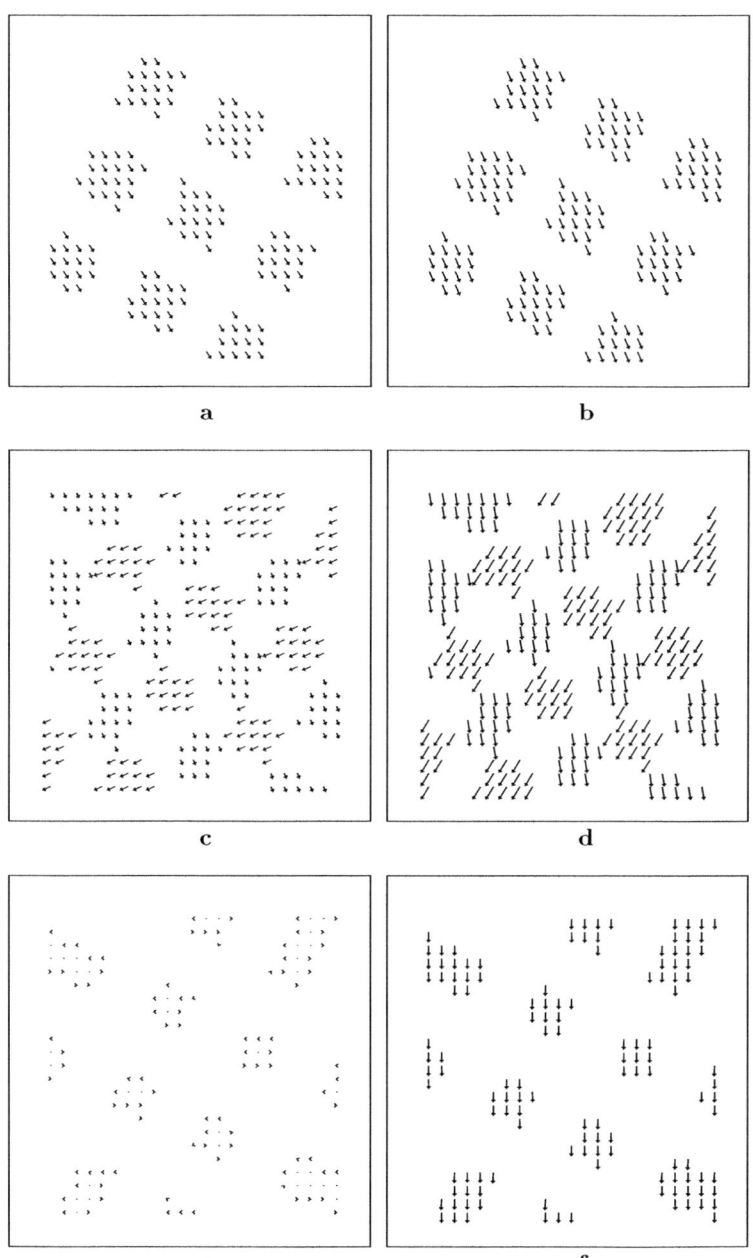

Fig. 2. The computed XY and XZ components of full ((a) and (b))), line ((c) and (d)) and planar ((e) and (f)) range flow for the synthetic sequence.

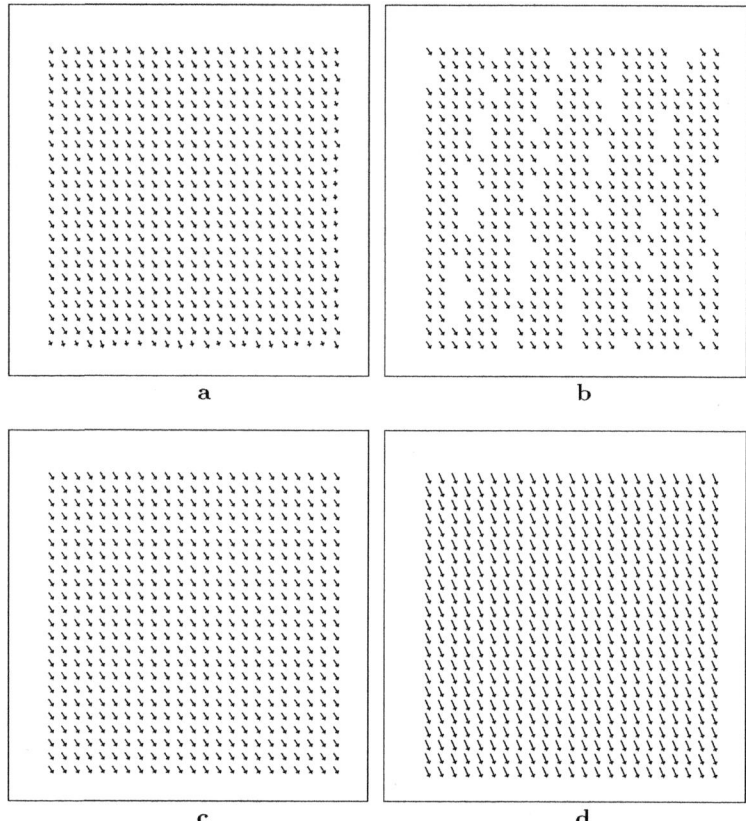

Fig. 3. The   image flow computed using (a) Horn and Schunck method (1000 iterations) and (b) Lucas and Kanade's method ($\tau_{D1} = 1.0$) for the synthetic sequence. Flows (c) and (d) show the XY and XZ components of range flow for the synthetic sequence computed using the least squares image-range flow calculation.

also shown in Table 2 and Figures 3c,d. These range flow results are quite good, better than Horn and Schunck image flow. This is quite remarkable, considering that we are computing 100% dense 3D range flow (compared with 100% dense 2D image flow). Table 3 shows the magnitude and angle results for the Direct (section 5) and Combined (section 6) regularization methods for 1000 iterations. Results for the Combined regularization are the best (but not as good as the Least Squares optical-range calculation). These results indicate that using both image and range data is the best way to recover accurate 3D velocity fields. We used $\alpha = \beta = 1.0$ for all regularizations.

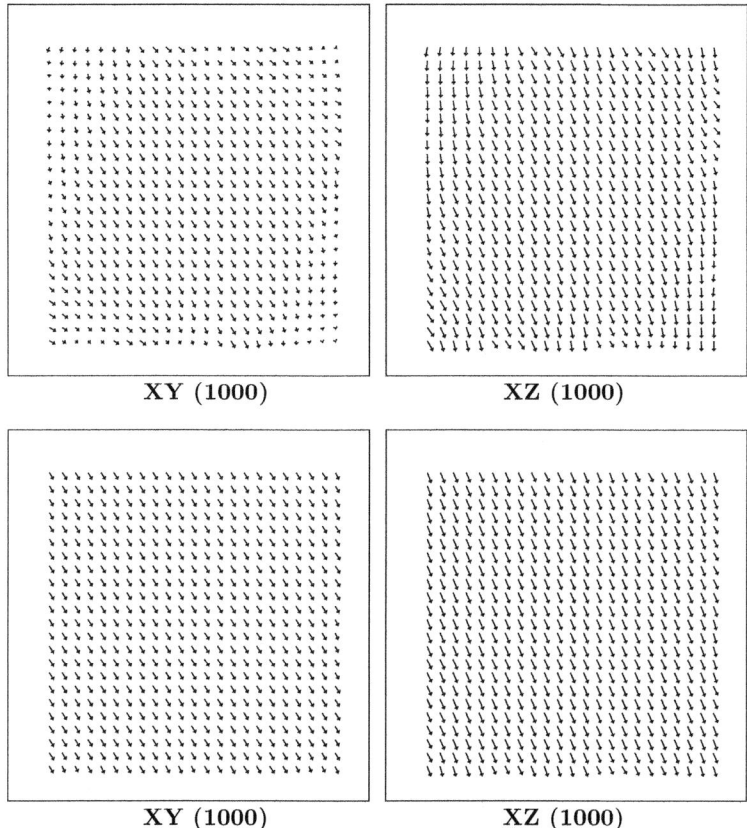

Fig. 4. The computed XY and XZ components of Direct and Combined Regularized Range Flow for 1000 iterations.

10   Real Range Flow Results

We also have one real range sequence which we made in 1997 at NRC in Ottawa[1]. Each image of this sequence is 454×1024 and was made by moving a scene (consisting of some boxes wrapped in newspaper) a set of fixed equal distances on a linear positioner and after each movement, taking intensity and range images. Thus, the correct 3D translation $(0.095377, 1.424751, 0.087113)$ mm/frame is known, allowing quantitative error analysis. NRC's Biris range sensor was also mounted on another linear positioner and at each time three sets of four overlapping (intensity and X, Y and Z) images were acquired. These images are then manually viewed and joined into one larger image (some partially overlaid data was discarded). A sheet of white paper was also imaged and used to correct the

---

[1] Thanks to Luc Cournoyer at NRC for helping us make this data.

(a)   **(b)**

Fig. 5. (a) The smoothed subsampled intensity image for frame 25 of the NRC sequence and (b) its corresponding depth (Z) image.

Table 1. Direction and magnitude error of the computed full, line and plane range velocities wrt the estimated "correct" full, line and range flow for the synthetic range sequence.

Full Range Velocity ($\tau_{D2} = 0.2$)	
ϕ_M	$0.045\% \pm 0.005\%$
ϕ_A	$0.007° \pm 0.012°$
Density	33.68%
Line Normal Range Velocity ($\tau_{D2} = 0.2$)	
ϕ_M	$11.24\% \pm 10.73\%$
ϕ_A	$21.89° \pm 0.80°$
Density	41.21%
Plane Normal Range Velocity ($\tau_{D2} = 0.2$)	
ϕ_{P3D}	$4.78\% \pm 2.56\%$
ϕ_{abs}	0.75 ± 1.69
Density	25.11%

intensity images by rescaling their intensities so that all intensities were white and then rescaling the acquired images by these same factors.

In retrospect, if we were to make these images again, we would not use only planar surfaces, as only plane range flow can be recovered there. Sparse

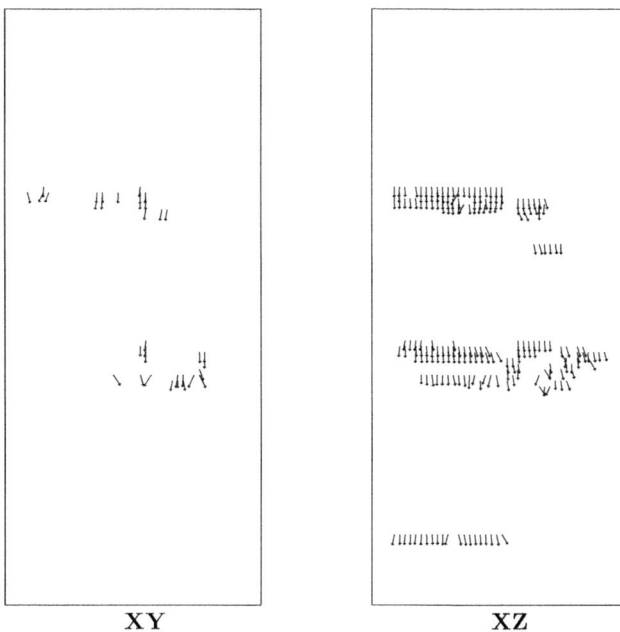

Fig. 6. The computed XY components of full and line range flow for the NRC sequence.

Table 2. Direction and magnitude error of the computed Horn and Schunck image flow (for 1000 iterations), Lucas and Kanade image flow (for $\tau_{D1} = 1.0$) and for the 3D range flow computed via the least squares optical-range flow algorithm (for $\tau_{D3} = 0.2$) for the synthetic range sequence.

Horn and Schunck XY Flow (1000 iterations)	
ϕ_M	$0.27\% \pm 0.88\%$
ϕ_A	$0.07° \pm 0.24°$
Density	100%
Lucas and Kanade XY Flow ($\tau_{D1} = 1.0$)	
ϕ_M	$0.0004\% \pm 0.0006\%$
ϕ_A	$0.0057° \pm 0.0113°$
Density	81.86%
Least Squares Image-Range 3D Flow ($\tau_{D2} = 0.2$)	
ϕ_M	$0.048\% \pm 0.005\%$
ϕ_A	$0.007° \pm 0.012°$
Density	100.0%

full and line flow can be recovered, but only at the boxes' corners and edges. Nevertheless, we were able to compute some meaningful and dense full range flow fields using our regularization algorithms. To attenuate the effects of noise artifacts and to improve computational time we used level 1 of the Gaussian

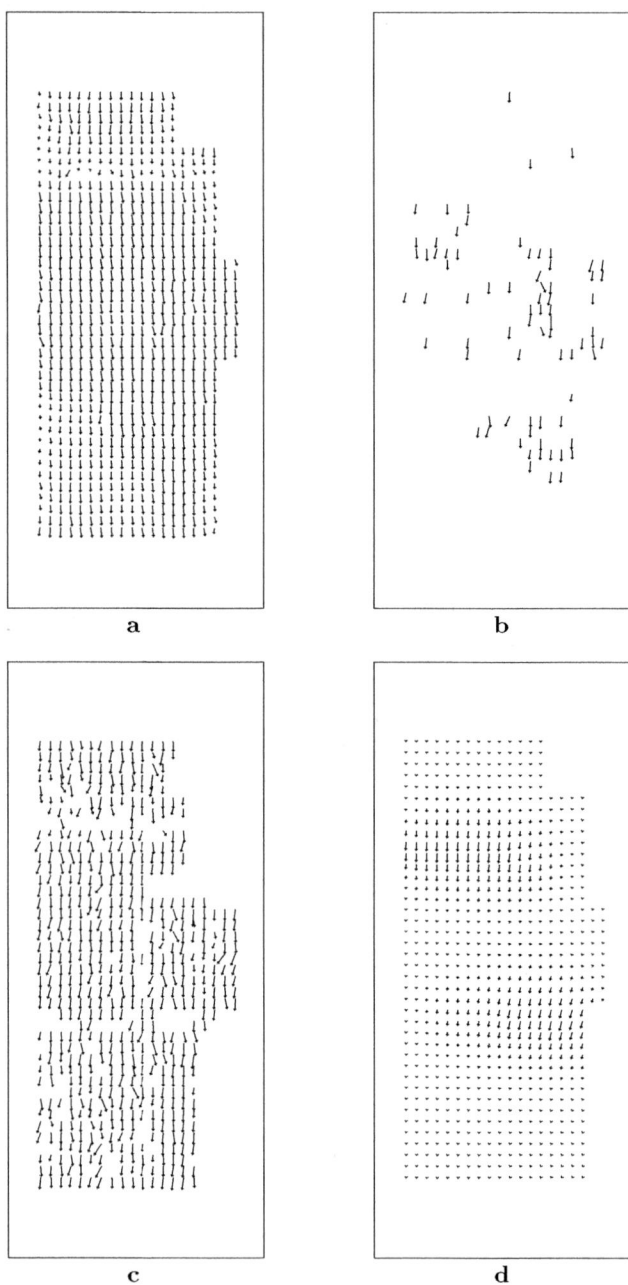

Fig. 7. The image flow computed using (a) Horn and Schunck method (1000 iterations) and (b) Lucas and Kanade's method ($\tau_{D1} = 1.0$ on the NRC sequence. Flows (c) and (d) show the XY components of range flow computed using the direct image-range flow calculation and direct regularization.

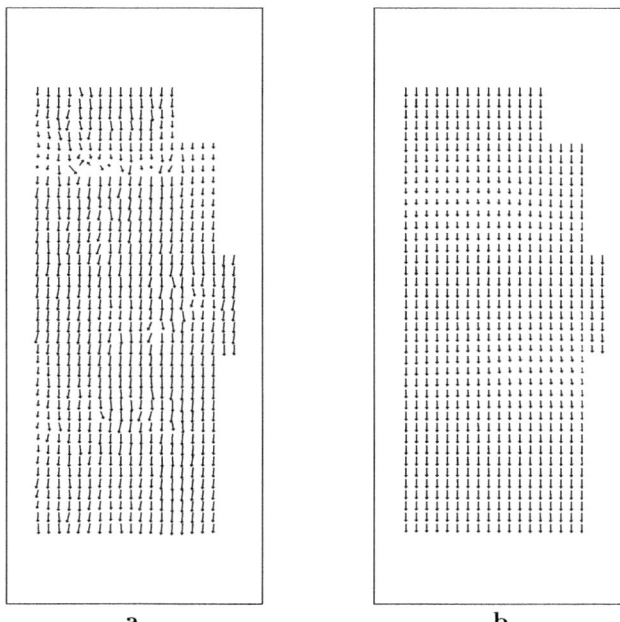

a   b

Fig. 8. (a) Combined regularization XY flow for 1000 iterations and (b) direct regularization with 1000 iterations initialized with combined regularization with 1000 iterations regularization for the NRC sequence.

Table 3. Direction and magnitude error of the computed flow via the Direct and Combined regularization algorithms for 1000 iterations for the synthetic sequence.

Direct Regularization (1000 iterations)	
ϕ_M	$7.26\% \pm 8.96\%$
ϕ_A	$6.69° \pm 8.34°$
Combined Regularization (1000 iterations)	
ϕ_M	$1.45\% \pm 3.44\%$
ϕ_A	$0.83° \pm 1.96°$

pyramid to compute all flows (3D Gaussian smoothing with a standard deviation of 1.0 and the subsampling in the X and Y dimensions by 2). Figure 5a shows one intensity image in the sequence while 5b shows its depth (Z) map (scaled into an image). Since we used level 1 of the Gaussian pyramid our correct known translation is halved. Because there are intensity patterns on the surfaces (the printed newspaper text) and there is slight distortion in parameter estimation caused by the local intensity variation, the Z values vary slightly according to the surfaces' intensity and one is able to read some text in the Z images (see Figure (5b)). The top and bottom parts and some of the right side of the image in Figure (5a) are part of the linear positioner setup; one cannot obtain good derivative values here and to increase computational accuracy and speed we masked out these parts of the image in our flow calculations. To show fully recovered range flow fields we need to show both XY and XZ flow fields; however since the X and Z flow components are only about 6% of the Y component for this sequence, the XZ flows are quite small relative to the XY flows and due to space limitations are not shown here. Figure 6 shows the computed XY full and line range flows (section 3). The plane flows are quite small and not shown here. Table 4 give the quantitative results for these full, line normal and plane normal fields. Because the plane normal flow is so small we just give its absolute error.

Figures 7a,b shows the image flows recovered by Horn and Schunck's algorithm (1000 iterations) and Lucas and Kanade's algorithm ($\tau_{D1} = 1.0$) (section (2)) while Figures 7c shows the XY flow using our least squares computation on the intensity and range derivatives. Table 5 show the magnitude and direction errors for these flows.

Table 4. Direction and magnitude error of the computed full, line and plane range velocities wrt the estimated "correct" full, line and range flow for the NRC real range sequence.

Full Range Flow ($\tau_{D2} = 0.2$)	
ψ_M	21.76% $\pm$ 23.36%
ψ_A	22.66° $\pm$ 14.53°
Density	1.04%
Line Normal Range Flow ($\tau_{D2} = 0.2$)	
ϕ_M	15.88% $\pm$ 21.83%
ϕ_A	36.41° $\pm$ 22.42°
Density	18.06%
Plane Normal Range Flow ($\tau_{D2} = 0.2$)	
ϕ_{abs}	0.20 $\pm$ 3.25
Density	28.34%

Figures 7d and 8a show the regularized XY range flow fields for the direct (section (5)) and combined (section (6)) algorithms for 1000 iterations while Table 6 shows their magnitude and angle errors. We used $\alpha = 10.0$ and $\beta = 1.0$ for all the regularizations. For direct regularization, overall results are poor because most of the image only has plane flow information, the regions surrounding full flow have good velocities. Results improve with more iterations. The combined regularized flows are the best, these use both intensity and range derivative data and yield dense flow. We report one last experiment: we use the flow after 1000 iterations of the combined regularization algorithm to initialize the direct regularization algorithm (also 1000 iterations). The flow is shown in Figure 8b and the error in Table 6. 71.75% of the flow had 10% or less magnitude error (average magnitude error of 4.29% $\pm$ 2.51% and average angle error of 0.24° $\pm$ 1.64°). This was the best result of all the NRC flows. This use of an initial set of non-zero ve-

Table 5. Direction and magnitude error of the computed Horn and Schunck image flow (for 1000 iterations), Lucas and Kanade image flow (for $\tau_{D1} = 1.0$) and for the 3D range flow computed via the least squares optical-range flow algorithm (for $\tau_{D3} = 0.2$) for the NRC range sequence.

Horn and Schunck XY Flow (1000 iterations)	
ϕ_M	$10.33\% \pm 12.47\%$
ϕ_A	$3.48° \pm 5.53°$
Density	82.67%
Lucas and Kanade XY Flow ($\tau_{D1} = 1.0$)	
ϕ_M	$10.51\% \pm 10.073\%$
ϕ_A	$9.68° \pm 5.57°$
Density	8.11%
Least Squares Image-Range 3D Flow ($\tau_{D3} = 0.2$)	
ϕ_M	$13.80\% \pm 12.50\%$
ϕ_A	$14.04° \pm 5.94°$
Density	65.25%

locities in the initialization step of regularization seems to be one way to obtain dense accurate flow for the NRC sequence.

Table 6. Direction and magnitude error of the direct and combined regularized flow for 1000 iterations for the NRC sequence. Also shown are the error results when the combined regularized flow is used to initialize the direct regularization. The density of all flow fields (due to masking) is 82.68%.

Direct Regularization (1000 iterations)	
ϕ_M	$39.97\% \pm 24.52\%$
ϕ_A	$7.84° \pm 3.97°$
Combined Regularization (1000 iterations)	
ϕ_M	$15.46\% \pm 20.06\%$
ϕ_A	$16.50° \pm 13.08°$
Direct Regularization (1000 iterations) initialized by Combined Regularization (1000 iterations)	
ϕ_M	$9.76\% \pm 9.19\%$
ϕ_A	$5.88° \pm 2.97°$

11   Conclusions

We have shown the computation of full, line normal and plane normal range flow on a synthetic intensity/range sequence. Our computation was in a least squares framework [2]; total least squares is used in [13,15,14] and we are currently investigating the difference. Line normal flow was the most difficult flow to compute accurately for this sequence.

The NRC sequence is perhaps the most difficult type of range sequence to analyze; most of the surfaces are planar with little or no full or line normal velocity. The direct regularization algorithm were only able to compute full flow in the vicinity of this full and line normal flow. The combined regularization used both intensity and range data to obtain full flow everywhere. The usefulness of combining the two types of data should not be in doubt; its flow was better than that with the use of range data alone and, of course, image flow, by itself cannot be used to recover the 3rd component of range flow. When we initialized direct regularization with combined regularized flow, we obtain the best results.

Acknowledgements. We gratefully acknowledge financial support from NSERC (National Science and Engineering Research Council of Canada) and the DFG (Deutsche Forschungsgemeinschaft) research unit "Image Sequence Analysis to Investigate Dynamic Processes".

References

[1] J. L. Barron, D. J. Fleet, and S. S. Beauchemin. Performance of optical flow techniques. *IJCV*, 12(1):43–77, 1994.

[2] J.L. Barron and H. Spies. Quantitative regularized range flow. In *Vision Interface VI2000*, pages 203–210, May 2000.

[3] J.-A. Beraldin, S.F. El-Hakim, and F. Blais. Performance evaluation of three active vision systems built at the national research council of canada. In *Conf. on Optical 3D Measurement Techniques III*, pages 352–361, October 1995.

[4] K. Chaudhury and R. Mehrota amd C. Srinivasan. Detecting 3d flow. In *Proc. IEEE Int. Conf. Robotics and Automation*, volume 2, pages 1073–1078, May 1994.

[5] B. K. P. Horn and B. G. Schunck. Determining optical flow. *Artificial Intelligence*, 17:185–204, 1981.

[6] B.K.P. Horn and J.G. Harris. Rigid body motion from range image sequences. *CVGIP: Image Understanding*, 53(1):1–13, January 1991.

[7] Gregory J. Klien and Ronald H. Huesman. A 3d optical approach to addition of deformable pet volumes. In *IEEE Nonrigid and Articulated Motion Workshop*, pages 136–143, June 1997.

[8] B. D. Lucas and T. Kanade. An iterative image-registration technique with an application to stereo vision. In *Image Understanding Workshop*, pages 121–130. DARPA, 1981. (see also IJCAI81, pp674-679).

[9] W.H. Press, B.P. Flannery, S.A. Teukolsky, and W. T. Vetterling. *Numerical Recepes in C: The art of scientific computing*. Cambridge University Press, 1988.

[10] E.P. Simoncelli. Design of multi-dimensional derivative filters. In *IEEE Int. Conf. Image Processing*, volume 1, pages 70–793, 1994.

[11] S.M. Song and R.M. Leahy. Computation of 3d velocity fields from 3d cine ct images of a human heart. *IEEE Trans. Medical Imaging*, 10(1):295–306, 1991.

[12] S.M. Song, R.M. Leahy, D.P Boyd, and B.H. Brundage. Determining cardiac velocity fields and intraventricular pressure distribution from a sequence of ultrafast ct cardiac images. *IEEE Trans. Medical Imaging*, 13(2):386–397, 1994.

[13] H. Spies, H. Haußecker, B. Jähne, and J.L.Barron. Differential range flow estimation. In *21.Symposium fur Mustererkennung, DAGM '1999*, pages 309–316. Springer, September 15-17th 1999. Bonn, Germany.

[14] H. Spies, B. Jähne, and J.L. Barron. Dense range flow from depth and intensity data. In *Int. Conf. on Pattern recognition ICPR2000*, September 2000.

[15] H. Spies, B. Jähne, and J.L. Barron. Regularised range flow. In *European Conference on Computer Vision ECCV2000*, June 2000.

[16] Richard Szeliski. Estimating motion from sparse range data without correspondence. In *ICCV '88*, pages 207–216, 1988.

[17] M. Yamamoto, P. Boulanger, J. Beraldin, and M. Rioux. Direct estimation of range flow on deformable shape from a video rate range camera. *IEEE Transactions on Pattern Analysis and Machine Intelligence*, 15(1):82–89, January 1993.

[18] Z. Zhou, C.E. Synolakis, R.M. Leahy, and S.M. Song. Calculation of 3d internal displacement fields from 3d x-ray computer tomographic images. *Proc. R. Soc. Lond. A*, 449(1937):537–554, 1995.

Knowledge-Based Concepts for the Fusion of Multisensor and Multitemporal Aerial Images

Claus-Eberhard Liedtke and Stefan Growe

Institute of Communication Theory and Signal Processing, University of Hannover
Appelstr. 9A, D-30167 Hannover, Germany
{liedtke,growe}@tnt.uni-hannover.de

Abstract. The increasing amount of remotely sensed imagery from multiple platforms requires efficient analysis techniques. The leading idea of the presented work is to automate the interpretation of multisensor and multitemporal remote sensing images by the use of common prior knowledge about landscape scenes. In addition the system can use specific map knowledge of a GIS, information about sensor projections and temporal changes of scene objects. Prior expert knowledge about the scene content is represented explicitly by a semantic net. A common concept has been developed to distinguish between the semantics of objects and their visual appearance in the different sensors considering the physical principle of the sensor and the material and surface properties of the objects. A flexible control system is used for the automated analysis, which employs mixtures of bottom up and top down strategies for image analysis dependent on the respective state of interpretation. The control strategy employs rule based systems and is independent of the application. The system permits the fusion of several sensors like optical, infrared, and SAR-images, laser-scans etc. and it can be used for the fusion of images taken at different instances of time. Sensor fusion can be achieved on a pixel level, which requires prior rectification of the images, on feature level, which means that the same object may show up differently in different sensors, and on object level, which means that different parts of an object can more accurately be recognized in different sensors. Results are shown for the extraction of roads from multisensor images. The approach for a multitemporal image analysis is illustrated for the recognition and extraction of an industrial fairground from an industrial area in an urban scene.

1   Introduction

The recognition of complex patterns and the understanding of complex scenes from remotely sensed data requires in many cases the use of multiple sensors and views taken at different time instances. For this purpose sensors such as optical, thermal, radar (SAR), and range sensors are used. In order to automate the processing of these sensor signals new concepts for sensor fusion are needed. In the following a novel approach to the automated multisensor analysis of aerial images is described, which results in a symbolic description of the observed scene content. The symbolic description is represented by a semantic net.

R. Klette et al. (Eds.): Multi-Image Analysis, LNCS 2032, pp. 190–200, 2001.

Due to the great variety of scenes to be interpreted a modern system for image analysis should be adaptable to new applications. This flexibility can be achieved by a knowledge based approach where the application dependent knowledge is strictly separated from the control of information processing. In the literature various approaches to image interpretation have been presented. Most interpretation systems like SPAM [5] and SIGMA [4] use a hierarchic control and construct the objects incrementally using multiple levels of detail. Inspired by ERNEST [1] the presented system AIDA formulates prior knowledge about the scene objects with semantic nets. In the following the system architecture is described and a common concept for the interpretation of images from multiple sensors is presented.

2   Knowledge Based Interpretation

For the automatic interpretation of remote sensing images the knowledge based system AIDA [3] [8] has been developed. The prior knowledge about the objects to be extracted is represented explicitly in a knowledge base. Additional domain specific knowledge like GIS data can be used to support the interpretation process. From the prior knowledge hypotheses about the appearance of the scene objects are generated which are verified in the sensor data. An image processing module extracts features that meet the constraints given by the expectations. It returns the found primitives - like polygons or line segments- to the interpretation module which assigns a semantic meaning to them, e.g. *river* or *road* or *building*. The system finally generates a symbolic description of the observed scene. In the following the knowledge representation and the control scheme of AIDA is described briefly.

2.1   Representation of Knowledge

For the explicit representation of prior knowledge a semantic net has been chosen. Semantic nets are directed acyclic graphs and they consist of nodes and links in between. The nodes represent the objects expected to appear in the scene while the links of the semantic net form the relations between these objects. The properties of nodes and edges can be described by attributes.

Two classes of *nodes* can be distinguished: the *concepts* are generic models of the object and the instances are realizations of their corresponding concepts in the observed scene. Thus, the prior knowledge is formulated consisting of concepts. During interpretation a symbolic scene description is generated consisting of instances. The object properties are described by *attributes* attached to the nodes. They contain an attribute value which is measured bottom-up in the data and an attribute range which represents the expected attribute value. The range is predefined and/or calculated during the interpretation. For each attribute a value and range computation function has to be defined. A judgement function computes the compatibility of the measured value with the expected range.

The *relations* between the objects are described by links forming the semantic net. The specialization of objects is described by the *is-a* relation introducing

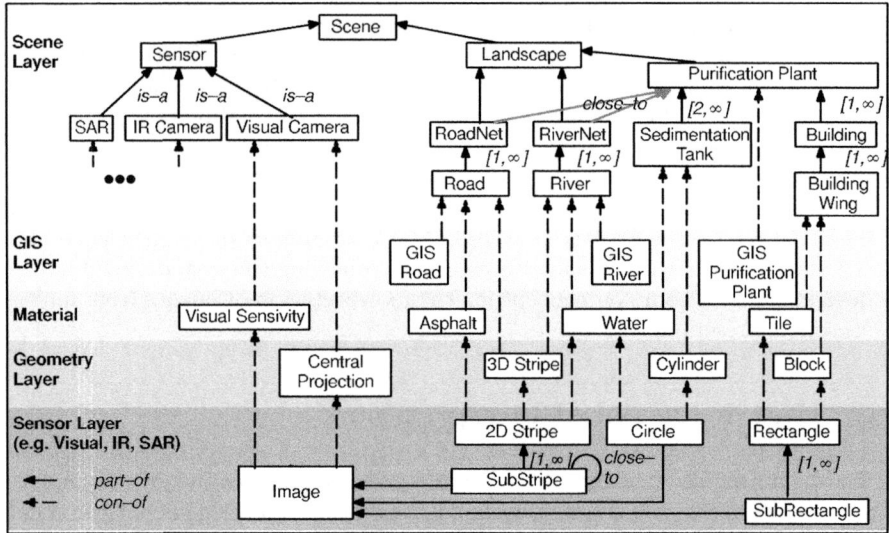

Fig. 1. Simplified semantic net representing the generic landscape model and its relation to the sensor image.

the concept of inheritance. Along the *is-a* link all attributes, edges and functions are inherited to the more special node which can be overwritten locally. Objects are composed of parts represented by the *part-of-link*. Thus the detection of an object can be reduced to the detection of its parts. The transformation of an abstract description into its more concrete representation in the data is modelled by the *concrete-of* relation, abbreviated *con-of*. This relation allows to structure the knowledge in different conceptual layers like for example a *scene layer*, a *geometry-* and *material layer* and a *sensor layer* in Fig. 1. Topological relations provide information about the kind and the properties of neighbouring objects. For this purpose *attributed relations* (*attr-rel*) are introduced. In contrast to other edges this relation has attributes which can be used to constrain the properties of the connected nodes. For example a topological relation *close-to* can restrict the position of an object to its immediate neighbourhood. The initial concepts which can be extracted directly from the data are connected via the *data-of* link to the primitives segmented by image processing algorithms.

2.2   Processing Control

To make use of the knowledge represented in the semantic net control knowledge is required that states how and in which order scene analysis has to proceed. The control knowledge is represented explicitly by a set of rules. For example the rule for instantiation changes the state of an instance from *hypothesis* to *complete instance*, if all subnodes which are defined as obligatory in the concept net have been completely instantiated. If an obligatory subnode could not be detected, the parent node becomes a *missing instance*.

An inference engine determines the sequence of rule executions. Whenever ambiguous interpretations occur they are treated as competing alternatives and are stored in the leaf nodes of a search tree. Each alternative is judged by comparing the measured object properties with the expected ones. The judgement calculus models imprecision by fuzzy sets and considers uncertainties by distinguishing the degrees of necessity and possibility. The judgements of attributes and nodes are fused to one numerical figure of merit for the whole interpretation state. The best judged alternative is selected for further investigation. Using a mixed top-down and bottom-up strategy the system generates model-driven hypotheses for scene objects and verifies them consecutively in the data. Expectations about scene objects are translated into expected properties of image primitives to be extracted from the sensor data. Suitable image processing algorithms are activated and the semantic net assigns a semantic meaning to the returned primitives.

2.3   Knowledge Base for the Interpretation of Aerial Images

For an object recognition only those features are relevant which can on the one hand be observed by the sensor and on the other hand give a cue for the presence of the object of interest. Hence the knowledge base contains only the necessary and visible object classes and properties. The network language described above is used to represent the prior knowledge by a semantic net. In Fig. 1 part of a generic model for the interpretation of remote sensing data in a landscape scene containing a purification plant is shown. It is divided into the *3D scene layer* and the *2D image layer*. The *3D scene layer* is split into a *semantic layer* and a *physical layer*, here a *geometry-* and a *material layer*. If a geo-information system (GIS) is available and applicable an additional *GIS layer* can be defined representing the scene specific knowledge from the GIS. The *2D image layer* contains the *sensor layers* adapted to the current sensors and the *data layer*.

For the objects of the 2D image domain general knowledge about the sensors and methods for the extraction and grouping of image primitives like lines and regions is needed. The primitives are extracted by image processing algorithms and they are stored in the semantic net as instances of concepts like *2D-Stripe* or *Rectangle*. Due to the variety of possible regions they have to be grouped according to perceptual criteria like compactness, size, shape etc. The sensor layer can be adapted to the current sensor type like optical camera, SAR, range sensor, etc. For a multisensor analysis the layer is duplicated for each new sensor type to be interpreted assuming that each object can be observed in all the images (see Fig. 1). All information of the 2D image domain is given related to the image coordinate system. As each transformation between image and scene domain is determined by the sensor type and its projection parameters the transformations are modelled explicitly in the semantic net by the concept *Sensor* and its specializations for the different sensor types.

The knowledge about inherent and sensor independent properties of objects is represented in the 3D scene domain which is subdivided into the physical, the GIS and the semantic layer. The physical layer contains the geometric and radiometric material properties as basis for the sensor specific projection. Hence it forms the interface to the sensor layer(s). The semantic layer represents the most abstract layer where the scene objects with their symbolic meanings are stored. The semantic net eases the formulation of hierarchical and topological relations between objects. Thus it is possible to describe complex objects like a purification plant as a composition of sedimentation tanks and buildings, which are close to a river and are connected by roads to the road net or an industrial site as a composition of halls close to each other and parking lots. The symbolic objects are specified more concrete by their geometry. In conjunction with the known sensor type the geometrical and radiometrical appearance of the objects in the image can be predicted. This prediction can be improved if GIS data of the observation area is available. Though the GIS may be out of date it represents a partial interpretation of the scene providing semantic information. Hence the GIS objects are connected directly with the objects of the semantic layer (Fig. 1).

3   Interpretation of Multisensor Images

The automatic analysis of multisensor data requires the fusion of the data. The presented concept to separate strictly the sensor independent knowledge of the 3D scene domain from the sensor dependent knowledge in the 2D image domain eases the integration and simultaneous interpretation of images from multiple sensors. New sensor types can be introduced by simply defining another specialization of the *Sensor* node with the corresponding geometrical and radiometrical transformations. According to the images to be interpreted the different sensor layers (SAR, IR, Optical, Range) are activated.

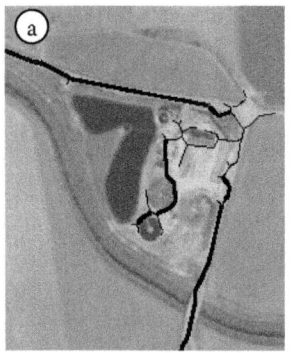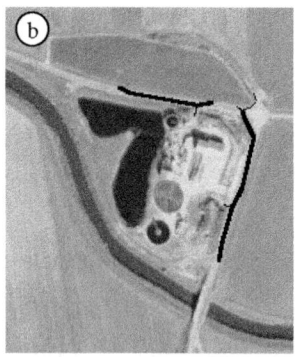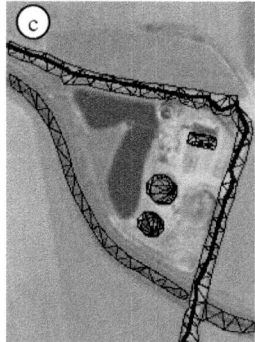

Fig. 2. Rejected (thin line) and accepted (wide line) road features from a) visual and b) infrared image with c) fusion result. Each object (road, river, building, sedimentation tank) is approximated by a polygon mesh to model geometry.

The interpretation distinguishes the following types of sensor fusion:

Sensor selection: The object can be extracted completely using only one sensor. For example, rivers show up clearly in infrared images (Fig. 2b) due to their cold temperatures.

Composite feature: This fusion type exploits several *con-of* links to combine redundant sensors. The extraction of the feature from only one sensor is erroneous like the road extraction from the visual sensor or infrared sensor alone. Hence the extraction combines the measured feature properties to improve the road detection (see Fig. 2).

Composite object: The object is composed of several complementary parts, indicated by *part-of* links, which can be extracted from different sensors. The purification plant in Fig. 2c consists of sedimentation tanks and buildings (Fig. 1). The complex task of detecting a purification plant is simplified to the extraction of the buildings from the visual and the sedimentation tank from the infrared image. Furthermore, the plant has a road access and is located *close-to* a river to drain off cleaned water.

Composite context: The object may be only detectable in a certain context. For example, the roads in urban areas are usually accompanied by building rows along their sides which show up as bright lines in a SAR image. In Fig. 3 only those segmented dark stripes in the aerial image are interpreted as roads which are supported by parallel bright lines in the SAR image.

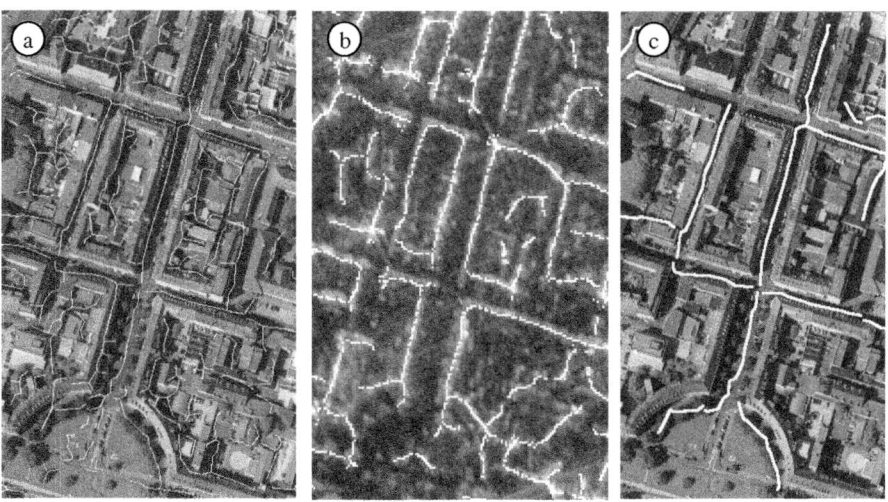

Fig. 3. The segmented lines, i.e. road candidates in the visual image (a) must be accompanied by parallel lines as hint for buildings in the SAR image (b) to verify a road hypothesis (c).

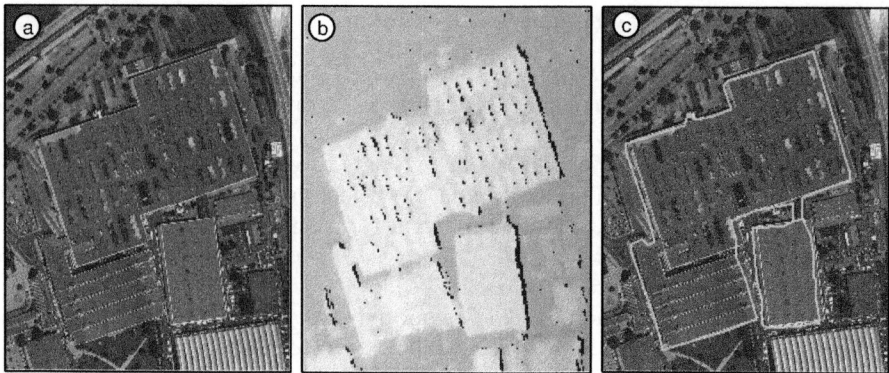

Fig. 4. Images from an airborne optical sensor (a) and range sensor (b) serving as input. (c) Segmentation results for the extraction of halls representing an intermediate step during the scene interpretation.

If a GIS is available the object location can be constrained further. However, the GIS may be out of date and incomplete. Hence the GIS is used to hypothesize an initial scene description to be tested in the remote sensing data. The use of a GIS is described in [9].

For the application of an industrial town scene, here the industrial fairground in Hanover/Germany, the advantages of a multisensor image analysis based on composite feature fusion is illustrated in Fig. 4. In this case an aerial photo (Fig. 4a) and a range image (Fig. 4b) are used. Taking only the aerial image the flat buildings roofs cannot be differentiated from the streets and the parking lots. Using only the range image the walkways for pedestrians cannot be differentiated from the parking lots containing cars. If both images are analyzed simultaneously the buildings can be clearly separated from the street level by their elevation as is shown in Fig. 4c and the walkways can be differentiated from the parking lots by the recognition of regular pattern of rows of cars. Other examples for the fusion of multisensor images are given in [6] and [7].

4   Interpretation of Multitemporal Images

Currently the system is being extended for the interpretation of multitemporal images. Applications like change detection and monitoring require the analysis of images from different acquisition times. By comparing the current image with the latest interpretation derived from the preceding image changes in land use and new construction sites can be detected. In the following the necessary extensions to a multitemporal analysis with the system AIDA are described and illustrated on the application of recognizing an industrial fairground.

4.1   Extension of the Knowledge Based System

The easiest way to generate a prediction for the current image from an existing scene interpretation is to assume that nothing has changed during the elapsed time. But in many cases humans have knowledge about possible or at least probable temporal changes. Hence the knowledge about possible state transitions between two time steps should be exploited in order to increase the reliability of the scene interpretation.

Temporal changes can be formulated in a so called *state transition graph* where the nodes represent the temporal states and the edges model the state transitions. To integrate the graph in a semantic net the states are represented by concept nodes which are connected by a new relation: the *temporal relation.* For each temporal relation a transition probability can be defined. As states can either be stable or transient the corresponding state transitions differ in their transition time which can also be specified for the temporal relation. For the exploitation of the temporal knowledge a time stamp is attached to each node of the semantic net which documents the time of its instantiation. As normally no knowledge about the temporal changes of geometrical objects is available the state transition diagram is part of the scene layer (compare Fig. 5). In contrast to hierarchical relations like *part-of* or *con-of* the start and end node of temporal relations may be identical - forming a loop - to represent that the state stays unchanged over the time.

During the interpretation process the state transition diagram is used by a new inference rule. Analysis starts with the first image of the given sequence marked with time stamp t_1. If a state of the state transition diagram can be instantiated completely, the temporal knowledge is used to hypothesize one or more possible successors of this state for the next image in the chronological order (time stamp t_2). The system selects all successor states that can be reached within the elapsed time $t_2 - t_1$ according to the transition times defined in the temporal relations. States which are multiple selected due to loops in the transition diagram are eliminated. The possible successor states are sorted by decreasing probability so that the most probable state is investigated first. All hypotheses are treated as competing alternatives represented in separate leaf nodes of the search tree (see Chap. 2.2). Starting with the alternative of the highest probability the hypotheses for the successor state are either verified or falsified in the current image. For continuous monitoring the time stamps of the instances can be used to remove the old nodes of t_1.

4.2   Recognition of an Industrial Fairground

An industrial fairground is an example for a complex structure detectable by a multitemporal image interpretation only. Using a single image it would be classified as an industrial area consisting of a number of halls. But during several weeks of the year some unusual activity can be observed: exhibition booths are constructed, visitors pour to the site, and the booths are dismantled again. This knowledge about observable events can be exploited for the automatic extraction of a fairground and formulated in a semantic net (see Fig. 5). The different states of a fairground are represented by the concepts *FairInactivity*, *FairConstruction*, *FairActive*, and *FairDismantling*. The states representing the actual fair like the construction-state, the active-state and the dismantling-state are transient compared to the FairInactivity-state which is valid most of the year. Therefore transition times of four to eight days are defined for the corresponding temporal relations and the node *FairInactivity* is looped back to itself.

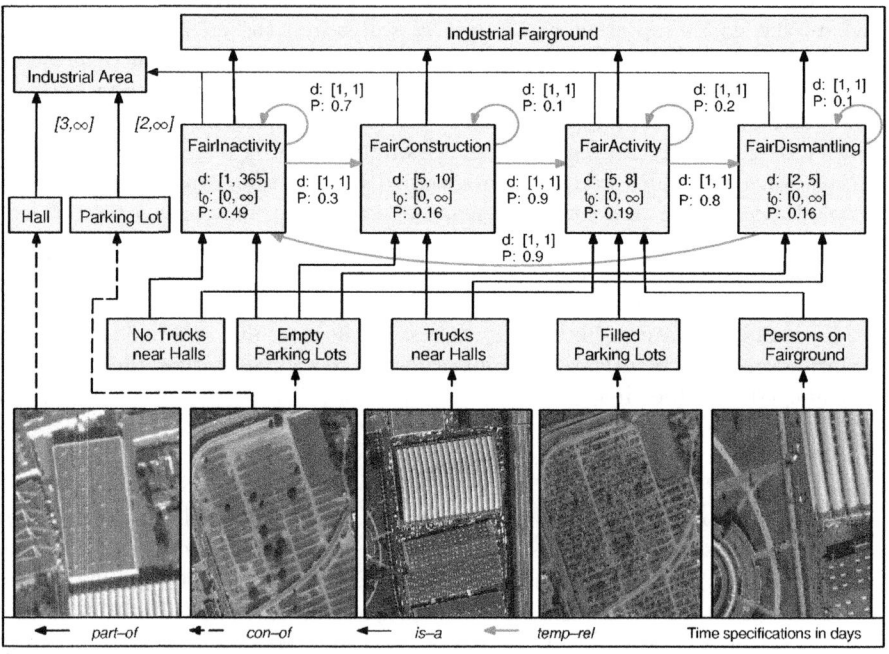

Fig. 5. Semantic net for the detection of an industrial fairground with integrated state transition graph.

The analysis starts with the first image looking for an *Industrial Area*. In the given example the system searches for at least three halls and two parking lots. If the *Industrial Area* can be instantiated completely the system tries to refine the interpretation by exchanging the *Industrial Area* by a more special concept. There are four possible specializations (*FairInactivity* to *FairDismantling*) and the search tree splits into four leaf nodes. Each hypothesis is tested in the image data. A construction or dismantling phase is characterized by trucks near the halls which keep the equipment for the booths. Hence the system searches for bright rectangles close to the halls. An active fair can be recognized by parking lots filled with cars and - if the image accuracy is sufficient - by persons walking on the fairground.

If one of the four states can be verified the temporal inference is activated. The system switches to the next image in the sequence and generates hypotheses for the successor state. According to the elapsed time and considering the transition times all possible successors are determined. If for example the time step between the two images was two weeks, it is possible that *FairInactivity* follows immediately after *FairActive* omitting the dismantling phase. All hypothesized successor states are represented in separate leaf nodes and are treated as competing alternatives. Having found hints for all obligatory states a complete instance of *Industrial Fairground* can be generated and the interpretation goal is reached. The presented approach is currently being tested for a sequence of five aerial images of the Hanover fairground. First results are documented in [2].

5   Conclusions

A knowledge based scene interpretation system called AIDA was presented, which uses semantic nets, rules, and computation methods to represent the knowledge needed for the interpretation of remote sensing images. Controlled by an adaptable interpretation strategy the knowledge base is exploited to derive a symbolic description of the observed scene in form of an instantiated semantic net. If available the information of a GIS database is used as partial interpretation increasing the reliability of the generated hypotheses. The system is employed for the automatic recognition of complex structures from multisensor images. Different paradigms for multisensoral and multitemporal sensor fusion can be used enabling the recognition of complex structures like street nets or in this example a purification plant. The use of knowledge about temporal changes improves the generation of hypotheses for succeeding time instances and allows for example the extraction of complex structures like an industrial fairground. In another application a detailed interpretation of moorland areas was accomplished.

The knowledge based scene interpretation system AIDA is a promising approach in the field of image understanding, because it provides a common concept for the use of multisensor and multitemporal information in connection with machine accessible prior knowledge about the scene content.

References

[1] Kummert, F., Niemann, H., Prechtel, R., Sagerer, G.: "Control and explanation in a signal understanding environment", *Signal Processing*, Vol. 32, No. 1-2, May 1993.

[2] Growe, S.: "Knowledge Based Interpretation of Multisensor and Multitemporal Remote Sensing Images", *Joint EARSeL/ISPRS Workshop on 'Fusion of Sensor Data, Knowledge Sources and Algorithms for Extraction and Classification of Topographic Objects'*, Valladolid, Spain, 3-4 June 1999.

[3] Liedtke, C.-E., Bückner, J., Grau, O., Growe, S., T-njes, R.: "AIDA: A System for the Knowledge Based Interpretation of Remote Sensing Data", *3rd. Int.. Airborne Remote Sensing Conference and Exhibition*, Copenhagen, Denmark, July 1997.

[4] Matsuyama, T., Hwang, V.S.-S., "SIGMA : A Knowledge-Based Aerial Image Understanding System", *Plenum Press*, New York 1990.

[5] McKeown, D. M. Jr., Harvey, W. A. Jr., McDermott, J., "Rule-Based Interpretation of Aerial Imagery", *IEEE Trans. on Pattern Analysis and Machine Intelligence*, Vol. PAMI-7, No. 5, pp. 570-585, Sept. 1985.

[6] Toenjes, R., Growe, S., "Knowledge Based Road Extraction from Multisensor Imagery", *ISPRS Symposium "Object Recognition and Scene Classification from Multispectral and Multisensor Pixels"*, Columbus, Ohio, USA, July 1998.

[7] Toenjes, R., Liedtke, C.-E.,"Knowledge Based Interpretation of Aerial Images Using Multiple Sensors", *EUSIPCO-98 Conference on Signal Processing*, Island of Rhodes, Greece, September 1998.

[8] Toenjes, R., Growe, S., Bückner, J., Liedtke, C.-E.: "Knowledge Based Interpretation of Remote Sensing Images Using Semantic Nets", In: *Photogrammetric Engineering and Remote Sensing (PERS)*, July 1999.

[9] Toenjes, R., 1999b. "Wissensbasierte Interpretation und 3D-Rekonstruktion von Landschaftsszenen aus Luftbildern", Fortschritt-Berichte VDI, Reihe 10, Nr. 575, VDI-Verlag, Düsseldorf

Ellipsoidal Bias in Learning Appearance-Based Recognition Functions

Josef Pauli and Gerald Sommer

Christian-Albrechts-Universität zu Kiel
Institut für Informatik und Praktische Mathematik
Preußerstraße 1–9, D-24105 Kiel
{jpa,gs}@ks.informatik.uni-kiel.de

Abstract. We present an approach for learning appearance-based recognition functions, whose novelty is the sparseness of necessary training views, the exploitation of constraints between the views, and a special treatment of discriminative views. These characteristics reflect the trade-off between efficiency, invariance, and discriminability of recognition functions. The technological foundation for making adequate compromises is a combined use of principal component analysis (PCA) and Gaussian basis function networks (GBFN). In contrast to usual applications we utilize PCA for an ellipsoidal interpolation (instead of approximation) of a small set of seed views. The ellipsoid enforces several biases which are useful for regularizing the process of learning. In order to control the discriminability between target and counter objects the coarse manifold must be fine-tuned locally. This is obtained by dynamically installing weighted Gaussian basis functions for discriminative views. Using this approach, recognition functions can be learned for objects under varying viewing angle and/or distance. Experiments in numerous real-world applications showed impressive recognition rates.

1 Introduction

Famous physiologists (e.g. Hermann von Helmholtz) insisted on the central role of learning in visual processes [2]. For example, object recognition is based on adequate a priori information which can be acquired by learning in the actual environment. The statistical method of principal component analysis (PCA) has been used frequently for this purpose, e.g. by Turk and Pentland for recognition of faces [8], or by Murase and Nayar for recognition of arbitrary objects [3]. The most serious problem in using PCA for recognition is the daring assumption of *one* multi-dimensional Gaussian distribution of the vector population, which is not true in many realistic applications. Consequently, approaches of *nonlinear dimension reduction* have been developed, in which the input data are clustered and local PCA is applied for each cluster, respectively. The resulting architecture is a Gaussian basis function network which approximates the manifold more accurately by a combination of local multi-dimensional Gaussian distributions [6]. However, large numbers of training views are required for approximating the Gaussians. Furthermore, the description length has increased which makes

R. Klette et al. (Eds.): Multi-Image Analysis, LNCS 2032, pp. 201–213, 2001.

the recognition function less efficient in application. Our concern is to reduce the effort of training and description by discovering and incorporating *invariances* among the set of object views.[1] Apart from characteristics of efficiency and invariance, the major criterion for evaluating a recognition function is the discriminability, i.e. the capability to discriminate between the target object and counter objects. Similar views stemming from different objects are of special interest for learning reliable recognition functions. This principle is fundamental for the methodology of *support vector machines*. At the border between neighboring classes a small set of critical elements must be determined from which to construct the decision boundary [9]. Although the border elements play a significant role it would be advantageous to additionally incorporate a statistical approximation of the distribution of training samples. Our approach takes special care for counter (critical) views but also approximates the distribution of all training views.

2   Foundation for Object Recognition

For the purpose of object recognition we construct an implicit function f^{im}, which approximates the manifold of appearance patterns under different viewing conditions.

$$f^{im}(\boldsymbol{A}, \boldsymbol{Z}) = 0 \tag{1}$$

Parameter vector $\boldsymbol{A}$ specifies a certain version subject to the type of the function, and measurement vector $\boldsymbol{Z}$ is the representation of an appearance pattern. In terms of the *Lie group theory of invariance* [4], the manifold of realizations of $\boldsymbol{Z}$ is the *orbit* of a *generator function* whose *invariant features* are represented in $\boldsymbol{A}$. Function f^{im} must be learned such that equation (1) holds more or less for patterns of the target object and clearly not holds for patterns of counter situations. Solely small deviations from the ideal orbit are accepted for target patterns and large deviations are expected for counter patterns. The degree of deviation is controlled by a parameter ψ.

$$|\, f^{im}(\boldsymbol{A}, \boldsymbol{Z})\,| \le \psi \tag{2}$$

The function f^{im} can be squared and transformed by an exponential function in order to obtain a value in the *unit interval*.

$$f^{Gi}(\boldsymbol{A}, \boldsymbol{Z}) := exp\left(-f^{im}(\boldsymbol{A}, \boldsymbol{Z})^2\right) \tag{3}$$

If function f^{Gi} yields value 0, then vector $\boldsymbol{Z}$ is infinite far away from the orbit, else if function f^{Gi} yields value 1, then vector $\boldsymbol{Z}$ belongs to the orbit. Equation (1) can be replaced equivalently by

$$f^{Gi}(\boldsymbol{A}, \boldsymbol{Z}) = 1 \tag{4}$$

---

[1] Our work in [5] replaces the concept of *invariance* realistically by the concept of *compatibility*.

For reasons of consistency, we also use the exponential function to transform parameter ψ into ζ in order to obtain a threshold for *proximities*, i.e. $\zeta := exp\left(-\psi^2\right)$. With this transformations, we replace equation (2) equivalently by

$$f^{Gi}(\boldsymbol{A}, \boldsymbol{Z}) \geq \zeta \qquad (5)$$

3   Concept of Canonical Frames and Ellipsoid Basis Function

Learning a recognition function requires the estimation of parameter vector $\boldsymbol{A}$ based on measurement vectors $\boldsymbol{Z}$. However, for an appearance-based approach to recognition the input space is high-dimensional as it consists of patterns, and frequently, also the parameter vector is high-dimensional. Consequently, first we project the high-dimensional space in a low-dimensional subspace (so-called *canonical frame*), and then we do the learning therein. The construction of canonical frames is based on so-called *seed images* which are representative for the object. The learning procedure is based on a *coarse-to-fine strategy* in which the *coarse* part does the subspace construction and is responsible for global aspects in the manifold of patterns. The subsequent refinement step treats local aspects in the manifold by taking more specific object views or counter situations into account, i.e. so-called *validation views*.

We impose three requirements to canonical frames. First, the implicit function will be defined in the canonical frame and should have a simpler description than in the original frame. Second, equation (4) must hold perfectly for all seed images which are represented as vector $\boldsymbol{Z}$, respectively. Therefore, the parameters $\boldsymbol{A}$ are invariant features of the set of all seed images. Third, the implicit function should consider generalization biases as treated in the theory of Machine Learning [10, pp. 349-363]. For example, according to the *enlarge-set bias* and the *close-interval bias*, the implicit function must respond continuous around the seed vectors and must respond nearly invariant along certain courses between successive seed images (in the space of images). The *minimal-risk bias* avoids hazardous decisions by preferring low degrees of generalization.

An appropriate canonical frame together with a definition of the implicit function can be constructed by principal component analysis (PCA). Remarkably, we use PCA for *interpolating* a small set of seed images by a hyper-ellipsoid function. As all seed images are equal significant we avoid approximations in order not to waste essential information. Based on the covariance matrix of the seed images, we take the normalized eigenvectors as basis vectors. The representation of a seed image in the canonical frame is by *Karhunen-Loéve expansion (KLE)*. Implicit function f^{im} is defined as a hyper-ellipsoid in normal form with the half-lengths of the ellipsoid axes defined dependent on the eigenvalues of the covariance matrix, respectively. As a result, the seed vectors are located on the orbit of this hyper-ellipsoid, and invariants are based on the half-lengths of the ellipsoid axes.

4   Construction of Canonical Frame and Ellipsoid Basis Function

Let $\Omega := \{X_i^s | X_i^s \in R^m; i = 1, \cdots, I\}$ be the vectors representing the seed images of an object. Based on the mean vector X^c the *covariance matrix* $\mathcal{C}$ is obtained by

$$\mathcal{C} := \frac{1}{I} \cdot \mathcal{M} \cdot \mathcal{M}^T \; ; \quad \mathcal{M} := (X_1^s - X^c, \cdots, X_I^s - X^c) \tag{6}$$

We compute the eigenvectors $e_1, \cdots, e_I$ and eigenvalues $\lambda_1, \cdots, \lambda_I$ (in decreasing order). The lowest eigenvalue is equal to 0 and therefore the number of relevant eigenvectors is at most $(I - 1)$ (this statement can be proved easily). The I original vectors of Ω can be represented in a coordinate system which is defined by just $(I - 1)$ eigenvectors $e_1, \cdots, e_{I-1}$ and the origin of the system. KLE defines the projection/representation of a vector X in the $(I - 1)$-dimensional eigenspace.

$$\hat{X} := (\hat{x}_1, \cdots, \hat{x}_{I-1})^T := (e_1, \cdots, e_{I-1})^T \cdot (X - X^c) \tag{7}$$

Based on PCA and KLE we introduce the $(I - 1)$-dimensional hyper-ellipsoid function.

$$f^{im}(A, Z) := \left(\sum_{l=1}^{I-1} \frac{\hat{x}_l^2}{\kappa_l^2} \right) - 1 \tag{8}$$

Measurement vector $Z := \hat{X}$ is defined according to equation (7). Parameter vector $A := (\kappa_1, \cdots, \kappa_{I-1})^T$ contains parameters κ_l, which are taken as half-lengths of the ellipsoid axes in normal form and are defined as

$$\kappa_l := \sqrt{(I - 1) \cdot \lambda_l} \tag{9}$$

For the special case of assigning the KLE-represented seed vectors to Z, respectively, we can prove that equation (1) holds perfectly for all seed vectors.[2] All seed vectors are located on the orbit of the hyper-ellipsoid defined above, and therefore, the half-lengths are an *invariant description* for the set of seed vectors. The question of interest is twofold, (i) why use ellipsoid interpolation, and (ii) why use PCA for constructing the ellipsoid?

Ad (i): The hyper-ellipsoid considers the enlarge-set and the close-interval biases, as demonstrated in the following. Let us assume three points X_1^s, X_2^s, X_3^s in 2D, visualized as black disks in the left diagram of Figure 1. The 2D ellipse through the points is constructed by PCA. The right diagram of Figure 1 shows a constant value 1 when applying function f^{Gi} (as defined in equations (8) and (3)) to all orbit points of the ellipse. Therefore the generalization comprises all points on the ellipse (close-interval bias). The degree of generalization can be increased furthermore by considering the threshold ζ and accepting for f^{Gi} small deviations from 1. The relevant manifold of points is enlarged, as shown by the dotted band around the ellipse in Figure 1 (enlarge-set bias).

---

[2] The proof is given in the Appendix.

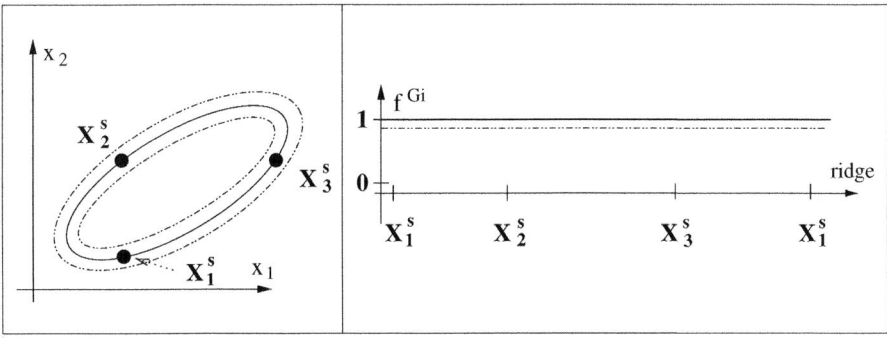

Fig. 1. (Left) Input space with three particular points from which a 2D ellipse is defined by PCA, small deviations from this ellipse are constrained by an inner and an outer ellipse; (Right) Result of function f^{Gi} along the ellipse, which is constant 1, accepted deviations are indicated by horizontal lines with offset $\mp\zeta$.

Ad (ii): In general, more than I points are necessary for fitting a unique $(I-1)$-dimensional hyper-ellipsoid. PCA determines the first principal axis by maximizing the variances which are obtained by an orthogonal projection of the sample points on hypothetical axes, respectively. Actually, this is the constraint which makes the fitting unique. Figure 2 shows two examples of ellipses fitting the same set of three points, the left one was determined by PCA, and the right one was fitted manually. As expected, the variance on the right is lower than on the left, which is measured along the dashed axes, respectively. Exemplary, it is also observed in the figure that the maximum variance (on the left) implies a minimal size of the ellipsoid. The size of the ellipsoid manifold correlates with the degree of generalization, and therefore, PCA produces moderate generalizations by avoiding large ellipsoids (minimal-risk bias).

5   Fine Approximation Based on Validation Views

The manifold defined by the hyper-ellipsoid must be refined in order to consider the discriminability criterion of recognition functions. We take an *ensemble of validation views* $\boldsymbol{X}_j^v$ into account (different from the ensemble of validation views) which in turn is subdivided into two classes. The first class $\mathcal{X}^{vp}$ (positive) of validation views is taken from the target object additionally and the second class $\mathcal{X}^{vn}$ (negative) is taken from counter objects or situations. Depending on certain results of applying the implicit function f^{Gi} to these validation views we specify spherical Gaussians and combine them appropriately with the implicit function. The purpose is to obtain a modified orbit which includes target views and excludes counter views.

For each validation view $\boldsymbol{X}_j^v \in \mathcal{X}^{vp} \cup \mathcal{X}^{vn}$ the function f^{Gi} yields a *measurement of proximity* η_j to the hyper-ellipsoid orbit.

$$\eta_j := f^{Gi}(\boldsymbol{A}, \boldsymbol{X}_j^v) \tag{10}$$

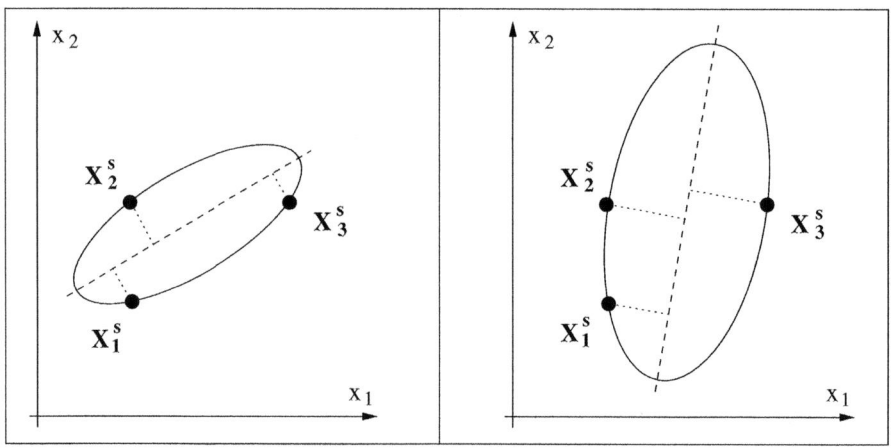

Fig. 2. Ellipses fitted through three points; (Left) Ellipse determined by PCA, showing first principal axis, determined by maximizing the variance; (Right) Ellipse determined manually with less variance along the dashed axis.

For $\eta_j = 0$ the view X_j^v is far away from the orbit, for $\eta_j = 1$ the view belongs to the orbit. There are *two cases* for which it is reasonable to modify the implicit function. *First*, maybe a view of the target object is too far away from the orbit, *i.e.* $X_j^v \in \mathcal{X}^{vp}$ and $\eta_j \leq \varsigma$. *Second*, maybe a view of a counter situation is too close to the orbit, *i.e.* $X_j^v \in \mathcal{X}^{vn}$ and $\eta_j \geq \varsigma$. In the first case the modified function should yield a value near to 1 for validation view X_j^v, and in the second case should yield a value near to 0. Additionally, we would like to reach generalization effects in the local neighborhood (in the space of views) of the validation view. The modification of the implicit function takes place by locally putting a spherical Gaussian f_j^{Gs} into the space of views, then multiplying a weighting factor to the Gaussian, and finally adding the weighted Gaussian to the implicit function. The mentioned requirements are reached with the following parameterizations. The center vector of the Gaussian is defined as X_j^v.

$$f_j^{Gs}(X) := exp\left(-\frac{1}{\tau} \cdot \|X - X_j^v\|\right) \tag{11}$$

For the two cases we define the weighting factor w_j dependent on η_j.

$$w_j := \begin{cases} 1 - \eta_j & : \quad \text{first case (target pattern too far away from orbit)} \\ -\eta_j & : \quad \text{second case (counter pattern too close to orbit)} \end{cases} \tag{12}$$

The additive combination of implicit function and weighted Gaussian yields a new function for which the orbit has changed, and in particular meets the requirements for the validation view $X = X_j^v$. In both cases, the Gaussian value is 1, and the specific weight plays the role of an increment respective decrement to obtain the final outcome 1 for the case $X_j^v \in \mathcal{X}^{vp}$ respective 0 for vector

$\boldsymbol{X}_j^v \in \mathcal{X}^{vn}$. The coarse-to-fine strategy of learning can be illustrated graphically (by recalling and modifying Figure 1). The course of proximity values obtained along the ellipse is constant 1 (see Figure 3, left and right), and along a straight line passing the ellipse perpendicular, the course of proximity values is a Gaussian (see left and middle).

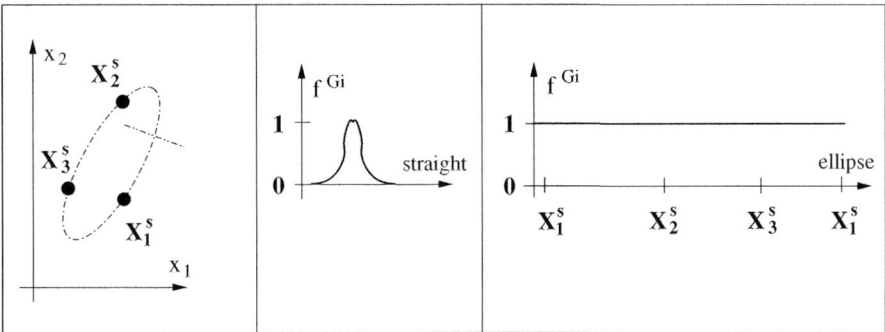

Fig. 3. (Left) Ellipse through three seed vectors and perpendicular straight line across the ellipse; (Middle) Gaussian course of proximity values along the straight line; (Right) Constant course of proximity values along the ellipse.

The first example considers a counter vector, *i.e.* $\boldsymbol{X}_2^v \in \mathcal{X}^{vn}$, which is too near to the ellipse. A Gaussian f_2^{Gs} is defined with $\boldsymbol{X}_2^v$ as center vector, and weight w_2 defined by η_2. Based on the additive combination of implicit function and weighted Gaussian the value decreases locally around point $\boldsymbol{X}_2^v$. Figure 4 (left and middle) shows the effect along the straight line passing through the ellipse, i.e. the summation of the two dashed Gaussians results in the bold curve. Figure 4 (left and right) shows the effect along the ellipse, i.e. the constancy is disturbed locally, which is due to diffusion effects originating from the added Gaussian.

The second example considers an additional view from the target object, *i.e.* $\boldsymbol{X}_3^v \in \mathcal{X}^{vp}$, which is far off the ellipse orbit. The application of f^{Gi} at $\boldsymbol{X}_3^v$ yields η_3. A Gaussian is defined with vector $\boldsymbol{X}_3^v$ taken as center vector, and the weighting factor w_3 is defined by $(1 - \eta_3)$. The combination of implicit function and weighted Gaussian is constant 1 along the course of the ellipse (for this example), and additionally the values around $\boldsymbol{X}_3^v$ are increased according to a Gaussian shape (see Figure 5).

6   Construction of Recognition Functions

The recognition function f^{rc} is defined as sum of implicit function and linear combination of Gaussians.

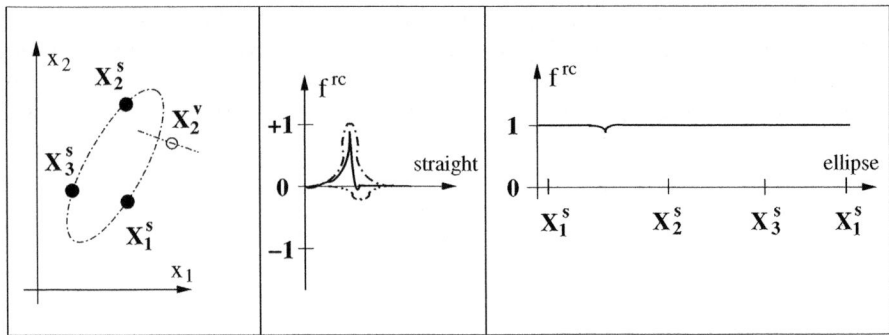

Fig. 4. (Left) Ellipse through three seed vectors and perpendicular straight line through a counter vector located near to the ellipse; (Middle) Along the straight line the positive Gaussian course of proximity values is added with the shifted negative Gaussian originating from the counter vector, such that the result varies slightly around 0; (Right) Along the ellipse the values locally decrease at the position near the counter vector.

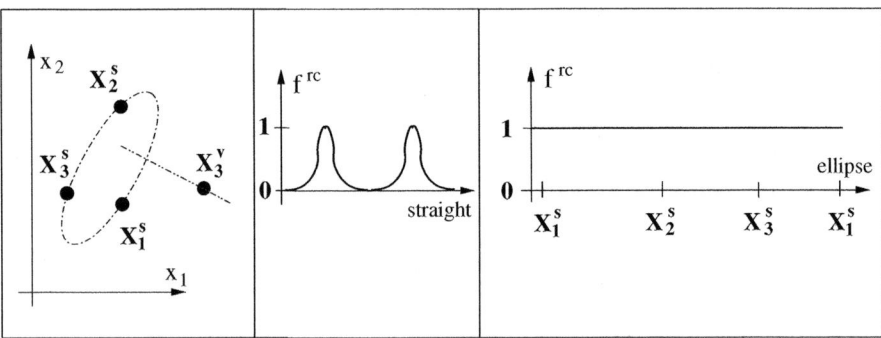

Fig. 5. (Left) Ellipse through three seed vectors and perpendicular straight line through a further target vector located far off the ellipse; (Middle) Along the straight line the positive Gaussian course of proximity values is added with the shifted positive Gaussian originating from the target vector, such that the result describes two shifted Gaussians; (Right) Along the ellipse the values are constant 1.

$$f^{rc}(\boldsymbol{X}) := f^{Gi}(\boldsymbol{A}, \boldsymbol{X}) + \sum_{j=1}^{J} w_j \cdot f_j^{Gs}(\boldsymbol{X}) \qquad (13)$$

Vector $\boldsymbol{X}$ represents an unknown view which has to be recognized. Parameter vector $\boldsymbol{A}$ is determined during the coarse approximation phase, and the set of Gaussians is constructed during the fine approximation phase. Factor τ for specifying the extent of the Gaussians is obtained by the *Levenberg-Marquardt algorithm* [7, pp. 683-688].

This coarse-to-fine strategy of learning can be applied to any target object which we would like to recognize. If $k \in \{1, \cdots, K\}$ is the index for a set of target objects, then recognition functions f_k^{rc}, with $k \in \{1, \cdots, K\}$, can be learned as above. The final decision for classifying an unknown view X is by looking for the maximum value computed from the set of recognition functions f_k^{rc}, $k \in \{1, \cdots, K\}$.

$$k^* := \arg \max_{k \in \{1, \cdots, K\}} f_k^{rc}(X) \qquad (14)$$

For taking images under controlled viewing conditions, i.e. viewing angle or distance, the camera can be mounted on a robot arm and moved in any desired pose. The simplest strategy for selecting seed views is a regular discretization of the space of possible viewing poses. The selection of validation views may be done in a similar way, but considering pose offsets for views of the target objects and also taking images from counter situations. Several improvements for these strategies are conceivable, and the most important one concerns the treatment of validation views. For example, the fine approximation phase may be performed iteratively by checking for every validation view the necessity for modifying the emerging recognition function. Actually, we must install a new Gaussian only in the case of facing a recognition error according to the decision criterion given in equation (14). Every validation view is considered as a candidate, and only if the view is critical then the refinement may take place *dynamically*. This sophisticated strategy reduces the description length of the recognition function. Other interesting work has been reported belonging to the paradigm of *active learning* in which random or systematic sampling of the input domain is replaced by a *selective sampling* [1]. This paper doesn't focus on this aspect.

7   Experiments with the Coarse-to-Fine Strategy of Learning

The primary purpose is to obtain a recognition function for a target object of three-dimensional shape, which can be rotated arbitrary and can have different distances from the camera. According to this, both the gray value structure and the size of the target pattern varies significantly. Three objects are considered which look similar between each other, *i.e.* integrated circuit, chip carrier, bridge rectifier. Figure 6 shows a subset of three images from each object, respectively. Different sets of seed and validation ensembles will be used for learning. Exemplary, we only present the recognition results for the integrated circuit. A set of 180 testing images is taken which differs from the training images in offset values of the rotation angle and in the size of the patterns, as shown by three overlays in Figure 7.

We determine recognition results, first by using a 1-nearest-neighbor approach, second by applying a coarse manifold approximation, and third compare them with those recognition results obtained from our coarse-to-fine strategy of learning. The approaches have in common that in a first step a testing pattern is projected into three canonical frames (CFs), which are the eigenspaces of

Fig. 6. Three seed images from three objects, respectively.

Fig. 7. Overlay between a training image and three testing images.

the three objects, respectively. The second step of the approaches is the characteristic one. In the first approach (CF_{1NN}, $1NN$ for 1-Nearest-Neighbor) the recognition of a testing view is based on the proximity to all seed views from all three objects, and the relevant seed view determines the relevant object. In the second approach (CF_{ELL}, ELL for proximity to ELLipsoids) the recognition of a testing view is based on the proximity to the three hyper-ellipsoids defined in the canonical frames, respectively. In the third approach (CF_{EGN}, EGN for proximity to *E*llipsoids extended with *G*aussian *N*etworks), the recognition of a testing view is based on a refinement of the coarse approximation of the pattern manifold by considering counter views with a network of GBFs, *i.e.* our favorite coarse-to-fine approach of learning. For validation views we simply take the seed views of the other objects, respectively. The decision for recognition is based on equation (14).

We make experiments with different numbers of seed views and thus obtain canonical frames of different dimensionality. Exemplary, 6, 12, 20, and 30 seed views are used which give dimension 5, 11, 19, and 29 of the canonical frames (denoted by NS_1, NS_2, NS_3, NS_4, respectively, NS for *N*umber of *S*eed views). Table 1 shows the results, i.e. the numbers of recognition errors, when applying the three approaches and taking four different dimensions into account. Approach CF_{ELL} clearly surpasses CF_{1NN}, and our favorite approach CF_{EGN} is clearly better than the other two. The course of recognition errors of CF_{EGN}, by increasing the dimension, shows the classical conflict between over-generalization and over-fitting. That is, the number of errors decreases significantly when increasing the dimension from NS_1 to NS_2, and remains constant or even increases when increasing the dimension further from NS_2 to NS_3 or to NS_4. Therefore, it is convenient to take the dimension NS_2 for the recognition function as compromise, which is both reliable and efficient. Qualitatively, all our experiments showed similar results (we omit to present them in this paper).

Table 1. Recognition errors for a testing set which consists of 180 elements. The approaches of object recognition have been trained alternatively with 6, 12, 20, or 30 seed vectors, for the CF_{EGN} approach we take into account additionally 12, 24, 40, or 60 validation vectors.

Errors	NS_1	NS_2	NS_3	NS_4
CF_{1NN}	86	59	50	49
CF_{ELL}	32	3	14	18
CF_{EGN}	24	1	2	3

According to the last row in Table 1 a slight increase of the number of recognition errors occurs when raising the number of seed views beyond a certain threshold, e.g. 20 or 30 seed views in our experiments. Therefore, the advantage of considering generalization biases (mentioned in Section 3) is weakened to a certain extent. This undesired finding is due to the fact that each new seed view will lead to an additional dimension and thus will cause a redefinition of the canonical frame. The generalization induced by the higher dimensional hyper-ellipsoid may become more and more hazardous.

A more sophisticated approach is needed which increases the dimension on the basis of several (instead of just one) additional seed views. However, the purpose of this work has been to demonstrate the advantageous role of generalization biases in neural network learning, which is obtained by combining Gaussian basis funtion networks with hyper-ellipsoidal interpolations.

8   Discussion

The work presented a learning paradigm for appearance-based recognition functions. Principal component analysis (PCA) and Gaussian basis function networks (GBFN) are combined for dealing with the trade-off between efficiency, invariance, and discriminability. PCA is used for incorporating generalization biases which is done by a hyper-ellipsoid interpolation of seed views. GBFN is responsible for making the recognition function discriminative which is reached by a dynamic installation of weighted Gaussians for critical validation views. The combined set of training views is sparse which makes the learning procedure efficient and also results in a minimal description length. Apart from that, the discriminability of the learned recognition functions is impressive.

The presented learning paradigm is embedded in our methodology of developing Robot Vision systems. It works in combination with Active Vision strategies, i.e. we must exploit the agility of a camera in order to constrain the possible camera-object relations and thus reduce the complexity of the manifold. Specifically controlled camera movements enable the incorporation of further constraints, e.g. space-time correlations, log-polar invariants, which make the manifold construction more sophisticated.

We may extend the iterative learning procedure such that also canonical frames are constructed dynamically. This would be in addition to the dynamic installation of Gaussians. The purpose is to find a compromise between the dimension of canonical frames and the number of Gaussians, i.e. keep the product of both numbers as low as possible to reach minimum description length. The mentioned concept is a focus of future work.

Appendix

Let a hyper-ellipsoid be defined according to Section 4.

Theorem   *All seed vectors $\boldsymbol{X}_i^s \in \Omega, i \in \{1, \cdots, I\}$ are located on the hyper-ellipsoid.*

Proof. There are several $(I - 1)$-dimensional hyper-ellipsoids which interpolate the set Ω of vectors, respectively. PCA determines the principal axes $\boldsymbol{e}_1, \cdots, \boldsymbol{e}_{I-1}$ of a specific hyper-ellipsoid which is subject to maximization of projected variances along candidate axes. For the vectors in Ω we determine the set $\hat{\Omega}$ of KLE-transformed vectors $\hat{X}_i := (\hat{x}_{i,1}, \cdots, \hat{x}_{i,I-1})^T$, $i \in \{1, \cdots, I\}$. All vectors in $\hat{\Omega}$ are located on a normal hyper-ellipsoid with constant Mahalanobis distance h form the origin. With the given definition for the half-lengths we can show that h is equal to 1, which will prove the theorem.

For the vectors in $\hat{\Omega}$ the variance v_l along axis $\boldsymbol{e}_l$, $l \in \{1, \cdots, I - 1\}$ is given by $v_l := \frac{1}{I} \cdot (\hat{x}_{1,l}^2 + \cdots + \hat{x}_{I,l}^2)$. The variances v_l are equal to the eigenvalues λ_l. For each vector $\hat{X}_i$ we have the equation $\frac{\hat{x}_{i,1}^2}{\kappa_1^2} + \cdots + \frac{\hat{x}_{i,I-1}^2}{\kappa_{I-1}^2} = h$, because the vectors are located on a normal hyper-ellipsoid. Replacing κ_l^2 in the equation by the expression $\frac{I-1}{I} \cdot \left(\hat{x}_{1,l}^2 + \cdots + \hat{x}_{I,l}^2 \right)$ yields the following equation $\frac{I}{I-1} \cdot \left(\frac{\hat{x}_{i,1}^2}{\hat{x}_{1,1}^2 + \cdots + \hat{x}_{I,1}^2} + \cdots + \frac{\hat{x}_{i,I-1}^2}{\hat{x}_{1,I-1}^2 + \cdots + \hat{x}_{I,I-1}^2} \right) = h$. Summing up all these equations for $i \in \{1, \cdots, I\}$ yields the equation $\frac{I}{I-1} \cdot (I-1) = I \cdot h$, which results in $h = 1$.

q.e.d.

References

[1] Cohn, D., Atlas, L., Ladner, R.: Improving generalization with active learning. Machine Learning **15** (1994) 201-221
[2] Dayan, P., Hinton, G., Neal, R., Zemel, R.: The Helmholtz machine. Neural Computation **7** (1995) 889-904
[3] Murase, H., Nayar, S.: Visual learning and recognition of 3D objects from appearance. International Journal of Computer Vision **14** (1995) 5-24
[4] Papathomas, T., Julesz, B.: Lie differential operators in animal and machine vision. In Simon, J.: From Pixels to Features. Elsevier Science Publishers (1989) 115-126
[5] Pauli, J.: Development of Camera-Equipped Robot Systems. Christian-Albrechts-Universität zu Kiel, Institut für Informatik und Praktische Mathematik, Technical Report **9904** (2000)
[6] Poggio, T., Girosi, F.: Networks for approximation and learning. Proceedings of the IEEE **78** (1990) 1481-1497
[7] Press, W., Teukolsky, S., Vetterling, W.: Numerical Recipes in C. Cambridge University Press (1992)
[8] Turk, M., Pentland, A.: Eigenfaces for recognition. Journal of Cognitive Neuroscience **3** (1991) 71-86
[9] Vapnik, V.: The Nature of Statistical Learning Theory. Springer-Verlag (1995)
[10] Winston, P.: Artificial Intelligence. Addison-Wesley Publishing Company (1992)

Scene Change Detection Based on Audio-Visual Analysis and Interaction

Sofia Tsekeridou, Stelios Krinidis, and Ioannis Pitas

Department of Informatics, Aristotle University of Thessaloniki
Box 451, 54006 Thessaloniki, Greece
{sofia,skrinidi,pitas}@zeus.csd.auth.gr

Abstract. A scene change detection method is presented in this paper, which analyzes both auditory and visual information sources and accounts for their inter-relations and coincidence to semantically identify video scenes. Audio analysis focuses on the segmentation of the audio source into three types of semantic primitives, i.e. silence, speech and music. Further processing on speech segments aims at locating speaker change instants. Video analysis attempts to segment the video source into shots, without the segmentation being affected by camera pans, zoom-ins/outs or significantly high object motion. Results from single source segmentation are in some cases suboptimal. Audio-visual interaction achieves to either enhance single source findings or extract high level semantic information. The aim of this paper is to identify semantically meaningful video scenes by exploiting the temporal correlations of both sources based on the observation that semantic changes are characterized by significant changes in both information sources. Experimentation has been carried on a real TV serial sequence composed of many different scenes with plenty of commercials appearing in-between. The results are proven to be rather promising.

1 Introduction

Content-based video parsing, indexing, search, browsing and retrieval have recently grown to active research topics due to the enormous amount of unstructured video data available nowadays, the spread of its use as a data source in many applications and the increasing difficulty in its manipulation and retrieval of the material of interest. The need for content-based indexing and coding has been foreseen by ISO/MPEG that has introduced two new standards: MPEG-4 and MPEG-7 for coding and indexing, respectively [1].

In order to efficiently index video data, one must firstly semantically identify video scenes. The term *scene* refers to one or more successive shots combined together because they exhibit the same semantically meaningful concept, e.g. a scene that addresses the same topic although many shots may be involved. The term *shot* denotes a sequence of successive frames that corresponds to a single camera start and end session. Scene characterization should be content- and search-dependent. The task of semantic scene identification is rather tedious and no automatic approaches have been reported to date. Usually, low-level pro-

R. Klette et al. (Eds.): Multi-Image Analysis, LNCS 2032, pp. 214–225, 2001.

cessing of the visual data is initially undertaken. Shot boundary detection, i.e., temporal segmentation, is performed and analysis of detected shots follows [2,3, 4]. Results are enhanced and higher level semantic information can be extracted when other information sources are analyzed, such as aural or textual ones [5, 6,7,8]. It is evident that semantic characterization can only be achieved with annotator intervention or by imposing user-defined interaction rules and domain knowledge.

A scene change detection method is presented in this paper which analyzes both auditory and visual sources and accounts for their inter-relations and synergy to semantically identify video scenes. The audio source is analyzed and segmented into three types of semantic primitives: silence, speech and music. Further analysis on speech parts leads to the determination of speaker change instants, without any knowledge on the number or the identity of speakers and without any need for a training process. The video source is processed by a combination of two shot boundary detection methods based on color frame and color vector histogram differences in order to efficiently detect shot boundaries even under various edit effects and camera movement. Combination of the results extracted from single information sources leads to grouping a number of successive shots into a scene according to whether they are in-between two successive speaker change instants or the same music segment accompanies them, or there are long duration silence segments before and after them. If further speaker alternation is attempted, such scenes can also be partially identified as commercials or events or dialogue scenes. In Sect. 2, the tools for low-level audio analysis and segmentation are summarized, while in Sect. 3, video segmentation into shots is reported. In Sect. 4, scene identification by combining both aural and visual information based on interaction rules is presented. Simulation results on a TV serial sequence of around 15 min duration containing many commercials are reported in Sects. 5. Finally, conclusions are drawn in Sect. 6.

2   Audio Analysis

Audio analysis aims at segmenting the audio source into three types of semantic primitives: silence, speech and music. Further processing on speech segments attempts to locate speaker change instants. Segmentation and speaker change identification are achieved by low-level processing methods. In the sequel, the term *audio frame* refers to the shortest in duration audio part used in short-time audio analysis, whereas the term *segment* refers to a group of a variable number of successive frames pre-classified to one of the three predefined audio types.

Initially, silence detection is performed to identify silence periods and discard them from subsequent analysis. Silence frames are audio frames of only background noise with a relatively low energy level and high zero crossing rate (ZCR) compared to other audio signal types. In order to distinguish silence from other audio signal types, the average magnitude M_t and zero crossing rate Z_t functions of an M-sample audio frame $x_t(n)$, $n = 0, \ldots, M-1$, are exploited [9]:

$$M_t = \sum_{k=0}^{M-1} |x_t(k)| \tag{1}$$

$$Z_t = \frac{1}{2M} \sum_{k=1}^{M} |\mathrm{sgn}(x_t(k)) - \mathrm{sgn}(x_t(k-1))| \tag{2}$$

$t = 0, .., N-1$, where N is the total number of audio frames. Non-overlapping audio frames of 10msec duration are employed. A convenient approach to robust speech-silence discrimination is end point detection [9], which determines the beginning and end of words, phrases or sentences so that subsequent processing is applied only on these segments. Average magnitude and ZCR thresholds are chosen relative to the background noise characteristics of an apriori known audio interval, its average magnitude and ZCR functions being $M_{t,n}$ and $Z_{t,n}$ respectively. The average magnitude thresholds used by endpoint detection are set equal to:

$$M_{thr,up} = E[M_t]$$
$$M_{thr,low} = \max(M_{t,n}) \tag{3}$$

The ZCR threshold is set equal to: $Z_{thr} = \max(Z_{t,n})$. Such a threshold selection proves to be robust and endpoint detection is satisfactorily performed. Boundaries of words, phrases or entire sentences are well estimated, a useful outcome that is subsequently exploited for audio segmentation and characterization.

Music detection is further performed to discriminate speech from music. Music segments are audio parts having significant high frequency content, high ZCR, different periodicity, compared to speech segments (voiced parts), and usually long duration. The latter is attributed to the fact that music does not usually exhibit silence periods between different successive parts leading to a long audio segment. Thus, in order to distinguish speech from music, four criteria are used: an energy measure, the ZCR, a correlation measure in the frequency domain that attempts to detect periodicity, and, finally, segment duration. Energy, M_t, and ZCR, Z_t, values are evaluated by (1) and (2), respectively, on audio frames of 10 msec duration located inside the current segment S_i, $i = 1, \ldots, N_S$, where N_S is the total number of detected segments other than silence ones. Subsequently, segment-based mean values and variances of M_t and Z_t are estimated, i.e.:

$$\mu_{M_{S_i}} = E[M_t | t \in S_i] \qquad \mu_{Z_{S_i}} = E[Z_t | t \in S_i]$$
$$\sigma^2_{M_{S_i}} = E[(M_t - \mu_{M_{S_i}})^2] \quad \sigma^2_{Z_{S_i}} = E[(Z_t - \mu_{Z_{S_i}})^2] \tag{4}$$

Their quotient is considered more discriminative for recognizing music from speech:

$$QM_{S_i} = \frac{\mu_{M_{S_i}}}{\sigma^2_{M_{S_i}}} \tag{5}$$

$$QZ_{S_i} = \frac{\mu_{Z_{S_i}}}{\sigma^2_{Z_{S_i}}} \tag{6}$$

Because both long-term (segment-based) energy and ZCR mean values are higher for music than speech. Besides, due to the existence of voiced and unvoiced parts in speech, long-term variance values of speech segments are expected to be higher than musical ones. In order to take advantage of the long duration periodicity of music, a frequency-based correlation metric C_t is defined between the magnitude spectrums of successive non-overlapping audio frames of 30msec located in segment S_i, $i = 1, \ldots, N_S$:

$$C_t = \frac{1}{M} \sum_{k=0}^{M-1} |\mathcal{F}(x_t(k))| \cdot |\mathcal{F}(x_{t-1}(k))| \tag{7}$$

where $\mathcal{F}(.)$ denotes the Fourier transform operator. If the signal is periodic, x_t and x_{t-1} will have almost identical spectra, thus leading to a high correlation value. Correlation is performed in frequency due to the fact that the Fourier transform remains unaffected by time shifts. In the case of music, C_t is expected to attain constantly large values within S_i. On the other hand, speech, characterized by both periodic (voiced) and aperiodic (unvoiced) parts, will have alternating high and low values of C_t within S_i. Thus, segment-based mean values of C_t, $\mu_{C_{S_i}} = E[C_t | t \in S_i]$ are considered to be adequately discriminative for detecting music. $\mu_{C_{S_i}}$ is expected to be higher for music segments than speech ones. Finally, the segment duration d_{S_i}, $i = 1, \ldots, N_S$, is also employed. Each of the metrics QM_{S_i}, QZ_{S_i}, $\mu_{C_{S_i}}$ and d_{S_i} are individually good discriminators of music. Global thresholding with thresholds:

$$T_M = E[QM_{S_i}] + \frac{\max(QM_{S_i}) - \min(QM_{S_i})}{2} \tag{8}$$

$$T_Z = \frac{7}{8} E[QZ_{S_i}] \tag{9}$$

$$T_C = 2E[\mu_{C_{S_i}}] \tag{10}$$

$$T_d = 5\text{sec} \tag{11}$$

respectively, leads to individual but suboptimal detection of music segments. Combination of these results in order to enhance music detection is based on the validity of the expression:

$$((QM_{S_i} > T_M) \text{ OR } (d_{S_i} > T_d)) \text{ OR } ((QZ_{S_i} > T_Z) \text{ AND } (\mu_{C_{S_i}} > T_C)) \tag{12}$$

If (12) is true for a segment S_i, then this segment is considered to be a music segment. Otherwise, it is declared as a speech segment. It is noted that audio segments, that may contain both speech and music, are expected to be classified according to the most dominant type.

Speech segments are further analyzed in an attempt to locate speaker change instants. In order to do that, low-level feature vectors are firstly extracted from voiced pre-classified frames only [9], located inside a speech segment. Voiced-unvoiced discrimination is based on the fact that unvoiced speech sounds exhibit significant high frequency content in contrast to voiced ones. Thus, the energy distribution of the frame signal is evaluated in the lower and upper frequency bands (the boundary is set at 2kHz with a sampling rate of 11kHz). High to low energy ratio values greater than 0.25 imply unvoiced sounds, that are not processed further. For audio feature extraction in voiced frames, the speech signal is initially pre-emphasized by an FIR filter with transfer function $H(z) = 1 - 0.95z^{-1}$. Speech frames are used of 30msec duration each with an overlap of 20msec with each other. Each frame is windowed by a Hamming window of size M. Finally, the mel-frequency cepstrum coefficients (MFCC), $\mathbf{c} = \{c_k, k \in [1,p]\}$, are extracted per audio frame [10]. p is the dimension of the audio feature vector. The aim now is to locate speaker change instants used later on for enhancing scene boundary detection. In order to do that, firstly feature vectors of successive K speech segments $S_{K_0}, \ldots, S_{K_0+K}$, are grouped together to form sequences of feature vectors of the form [11]:

$$ X = \{\underbrace{\mathbf{c}_1, \ldots, \mathbf{c}_{L_{S_{K_0}}}}_{S_{K_0}}, \underbrace{\mathbf{c}_1, \ldots, \mathbf{c}_{L_{S_{K_1}}}}_{S_{K_0+1}}, \ldots, \underbrace{\mathbf{c}_1, \ldots, \mathbf{c}_{L_{S_{K_0+K}}}}_{S_{K_0+K}}\} \quad (13) $$

Grouping is performed on the basis of the total duration of the grouped speech segments. This is expected to be equal or greater than 2sec, when assuming that only one speaker is talking. Consecutive sequences X and Y of feature vectors of the form (13), with Y composed of K' speech segments and defined by:

$$ Y = \{\underbrace{\mathbf{c}_1, \ldots, \mathbf{c}_{L_{S_{K_0+K+1}}}}_{S_{K_0+K+1}}, \ldots, \underbrace{\mathbf{c}_1, \ldots, \mathbf{c}_{L_{S_{K_0+K+K'}}}}_{S_{K_0+K+K'}}\} \quad (14) $$

are considered, having a common boundary at the end of S_{K_0+K} and the beggining of S_{K_0+K+1}. The similarity of these two sequences is investigated by firstly evaluating their mean vectors, μ_X, μ_Y, and their covariance matrices, Σ_X, Σ_Y, and then defining the following distance metric:

$$ D_t(X,Y) = (\mu_X - \mu_Y)\Sigma_X^{-1}(\mu_X - \mu_Y)^T + (\mu_Y - \mu_X)\Sigma_Y^{-1}(\mu_Y - \mu_X)^T \quad (15) $$

D_t is evaluated for the next pairs of sequences X, Y, until all speech segments have been used. The immediate next pair is constructed by shifting the X sequence by one segment, i.e. starting at S_{K_0+1}, and re-evaluating numbers K and K', so that the constraint on total duration is met. This approach is based on the observation that a speaker can be sufficiently modeled by the covariance matrix of feature vectors extracted from his utterances. Furthermore, the covariance matrices evaluated on feature vectors coming from utterances of the same speaker are expected to be identical. Adaptive thresholding follows to locate speaker change instants. Local mean values on a $1d$ temporal window W of size N_W are obtained, without considering the value of D_t at the current location t_0:

$$ D_m = E[D_t|_{t \in W, t \neq t_0}]. \quad (16) $$

D_{t_0} is examined to specify whether it is the maximum value of those ones inside the temporal window (possibility of a speaker change instant at t_0). If this is the case and $D_{t_0}/D_m \geq \epsilon$, where ϵ is a constant controlling the strictness of thresholding, a speaker change instant is detected at t_0. Speaker change instants are a clue for shot or even scene breaks. The method may be further investigated to identify speaker alternation and identify dialogue shots/scenes.

3   Video Analysis

Video analysis involves the temporal segmentation of the video source into shots. Shot boundary detection is performed by combining distance metrics produced by two different shot boundary detection methods. Such a dual mode approach is expected to lead to enhanced shot boundary detection results even under significant camera or object movement or camera effects, thus overcoming the drawbacks of the single modalities in some cases.

The first method estimates color frame differences between successive frames. Color differences, $FD(t)$, are defined by:

$$FD_t = \frac{1}{3N_X \times N_Y} \sum_{\mathbf{x}} ||\mathbf{I}(\mathbf{x};t) - \mathbf{I}(\mathbf{x};t-1)||_1 \qquad (17)$$

where $\mathbf{I}(\mathbf{x};t) = [I_r(\mathbf{x};t)I_g(\mathbf{x};t)I_b(\mathbf{x};t)]^T$ represents the vector-valued pixel intensity function composed of the three color components: $I_r(\mathbf{x};t)$, $I_g(\mathbf{x};t)$ and $I_b(\mathbf{x};t)$. By $||.||_1$ the L_1-vector norm metric is denoted. $\mathbf{x} = (x,y)$ spans the spatial dimensions of the sequence (each frame is of size $N_X \times N_Y$) whereas t spans its temporal one. Frame differencing is computationally intensive but seldom any limitations on the processing time are imposed when the task is performed off-line. In order to detect possible shot breaks, the adaptive thresholding approach used for detecting speaker change instants in Sect. 2 is adopted. Such window-based thresholding offers the means of adaptive thresholding according to local content and proves flexible and efficient in gradual camera movements, significantly abrupt object or camera movements, and simple edit effects as zoom-ins and outs (no false positives, over-segmentation is avoided). Abrupt changes are directly recognised.

The second method evaluates color vector histograms of successive frames and computes their bin-wise differences. Summation over all bins leads to the metric that is used for shot break detection. Histogram-based methods are robust to camera as well as to object motion. Furthermore, color histograms are invariant under translation and rotation about the view axis and change only slowly under change of view angle, change in scale, and occlusion. However, histograms are very sensitive to shot illumination changes. To overcome this problem and make the method more robust, our approach operates in the HLS color space and ignores luminance information. Thus, instead of using HLS vector histograms (3-valued vector histograms), the method uses HS vector ones (2-valued vector histograms). Luminance conveys information only about illumination intensity changes, while all color information is found in the hue and saturation domain. Usually, hue contains most of the color information. Saturation is examined and used to determine which regions of the image are achromatic. In order to evaluate HS vector histograms, the hue range $[0°, 360°]$ is divided in 32 equally-spaced bins h_i, $i = 1, \ldots, 32$, and the saturation range $[0, 1]$ in 8 equally-spaced bins s_j, $j = 1, \ldots, 8$. Vector bins are constructed by considering all possible pairs of the scalar hue and saturation bins, leading thus to a total number of 256 vector bins $\mathbf{hs}_k = (h_i, s_j)$, $k = 1, \ldots, 256$. Such an approach translates to a 256 uniform color quantization for each frame. The color vector bin-wise histogram $H(\mathbf{hs}_k; t)$ for frame t is computed by counting all pixels having hue and saturation values lying inside the considered vector bin $\mathbf{hs}_k$ and dividing by the total number of frame pixels. The histogram differences, HD_t, are then computed for every frame pair $(t - 1, t)$, by:

$$HD_t = \frac{1}{N_X \times N_Y} \sum_{k=1}^{256} ln(||H(\mathbf{hs}_k; t) - H(\mathbf{hs}_k; t - 1)||_1) \qquad (18)$$

where k is the vector bin index. By $|| \cdot ||_1$, the L_1-vector norm metric is denoted. Each frame is of size $N_X \times N_Y$ and t is a temporal spatial dimension of the sequence. Histogram differencing is computationally intensive. In order to detect possible shot breaks, our approach firstly examines the validity of the expression:

$$2 * E[HD_t] \leq \frac{max(HD_t) - min(HD_t)}{2}. \qquad (19)$$

If it is true, then the sequence is composed by a unique shot without any shot breaks. In the opposite case, the adaptive thresholding technique introduced for detecting speaker change instants is also employed here, leading to efficient shot break detection. Abrupt changes are directly recognized, but the method is also satisfactorily efficient with smooth changes between different shots.

However, both frame difference and color vector histogram based methods, employed separately, exhibit limited performance, than when combined together. Thus, fusion of single case outcomes is proposed. Specifically, the difference metrics (17) and (18) are multiplied to lead to an overall metric:

$$OD_t = FD_t \cdot HD_t \qquad (20)$$

that is adaptively thresholded later on for shot cut detection. Despite its simplicity, such multiplication amplifies peaks of the single case metrics, possibly corresponding to shot cuts, while it lowers significantly the remaining values. The same adaptive thresholding method is employed here as well, leading to enhanced detection compared to the single case approaches. Strong object motion or significant camera movement, edit effects, like zoom ins-outs, and in some cases dissolves (dominant in commercials) are dealt with. Over-segmentation never occurs.

4   Audio-Visual Interaction: Scene Boundary Detection and Partial Scene Identification

Our aim is to group successive shots together into semantically meaningful scenes based on both visual and aural clues and using interaction rules. Multimodal interaction can serve two purposes: (a) enhance the "content findings" of one source by using similar content knowledge extracted from the other source(s), (b) offer a more detailed content description about the same video instances by combining the content descriptors (semantic primitives) of all data sources based on interaction rules and coincidence concepts. Temporal coincidence due to the temporal nature of video data is a very convenient tool for multimodal interaction.

The combination of the results extracted from the single information sources leads to the grouping of a number of successive shots into a scene according to a number of imposed constraints and interaction rules. It is noted here that, given the results of the presented aural and visual segmentation algorithms, only scene boundaries are determined, while scene charecterization, e.g dialogue scene, can only be partially performed in some cases. Further analysis on those and on additional rules may lead to overall scene characterization. Shot grouping into scenes and scene boundary determination is performed in our case when the same audio type (music or speaker) characterizes successive shots. Partial scene identification is done according to the following concepts:

- commercials are identified by their background music and the many, short in duration, shots that they have.
- dialogue scenes can be identified by the high speaker alternation rate exhibited inside the scene.

5   Simulation Results

Experimentation has been carried on several real TV sequences having many commercials in-between, containing many shots, characterized by significant edit effects like zoom-ins/outs and dissolves, abrupt camera movement and significant motion inside single shots. We shall present here a representative case of a video sequence of approximately 12 min duration that has been digitized with a frame rate of 25fps at QCIF resolution. The audio track is a mixture of silence, speech, music and, in some cases, miscellaneous sounds. The audio signal has been sampled at 11kHz and each sample is a 16bit signed integer. In the sequel, firstly the performance of the various aural and visual analysis tools presented in Sects. 2 and 3 will be investigated. Then, scene change detection will be examined and partial scene characterization will be attempted.

In order to evaluate the performance of the audio segmentation techniques, the following performance measures have been defined:

- Detection ratio: the % ratio of the total duration of correctly detected instances versus that of the actual ones,
- False alarm ratio: the % ratio of the total duration of falsely detected instances versus that of the actual ones,
- False rejection ratio: the % ratio of the total duration of missed detections versus that of the actual ones,

focusing initially on the performance of the aural analysis tools. Thus, silence detection exhibits a remarkable performance of 100% detection ratio and 0% false rejection ratio, achieving to locate entire words, phrases or sentences. Rare occasions of unvoiced speech frames being classified as silence frames have only been observed leading to a false alarm ratio of 3.57%. There was no case of silence being classified as any other kind of audio types searched for. Music detection exhibits 96.9% detection ratio, 3.1% false rejection ratio, because some music segments of short duration are being confused as speech. It has 7.11% false alarm ratio, because it confuses some speech segments as music ones. On the other hand, speech detection is characterized by 86.2% detection ratio, 13.8% false rejection ratio and 2.4% false alarm ratio by mistaking music segments as speech. Finally, speaker change instant detection attains a suboptimal performance mainly attributed to the fact that covariance matrices and their inverse ones are insufficiently evaluated given a limited number of feature vectors extracted from 2sec duration segments. However, the use of bigger audio segments would imply that the same speaker is speaking during a longer duration, which would be long in many cases. Speaker change instants are evaluated with a detection accuracy of 62.8%. We have 30.23% false detections, while missed detections are of a percentage of 34.89%. Enhancement of this method may be achieved by simultaneously considering other similarity measures as well, as shown in [11]. Despite, however, of the suboptimal performance of speaker change instants detection, their use during audio-visual interaction for scene boundary detection leads to a satisfactory outcome, in combination with the other segmentation results.

In order to evaluate the performance of the visual segmentation methods, that is, the shot boundary detection methods presented in Sect. 3, the following performance criteria are used [2]:

$$\text{Recall} = \frac{\text{relevant correctly retrieved shots}}{\text{all relevant shots}} = \frac{N_c}{N_c + N_m} \tag{21}$$

$$\text{Precision} = \frac{\text{relevant correctly retrieved shots}}{\text{all retrieved shots}} = \frac{N_c}{N_c + N_f} \tag{22}$$

where N_c denotes the number of correctly detected shots, N_m is the number of missed ones and N_f is the number of falsely detected ones. For comparison purposes and to illustrate the strength of combining different methods and fusing results, the above criteria are also measured for the single shot detection methods presented in Sect. 3. Results for the single cases as well as the combined one are presented in Table 1. Adaptive thresholding that leads to the decision about shot boundaries is performed using two different lengths for the local windows: $W = 3$ and $W = 5$. It can be observed that the combined method attains the best results for $W = 5$. No false detections are made and the missed ones are rather few even under dissolve camera effects. The color vector histogram difference method is inferior in performance compared to the color frame difference method because histograms do not account for spatial color localization. However, the histogram approach is better under illumination changes. To illustrate the discriminative power of all temporal difference metrics considered

Table 1. Recall and Precision values achieved by the Shot Boundary Detection methods.

Method	$W = 3$		$W = 5$	
	Recall	Precision	Recall	Precision
Color Frame Difference	0.7047	0.5866	0.8456	0.7975
Color Vector Histogram Difference	0.3356	0.2155	0.5705	0.4271
Combined Method	0.9329	0.9858	0.9396	1.0

in the shot cut detection methods, i.e., the color frame difference metric FD_t, the color vector histogram difference metric HD_t and the combined difference metric OD_t, Fig. 1 is given, where parts of these temporal difference metrics are shown. One can easily observe how more easily distinguishable are peaks in the third plot, even in parts of the video sequence where a lot of action and movement is dominant, and how less varying are the rest values.

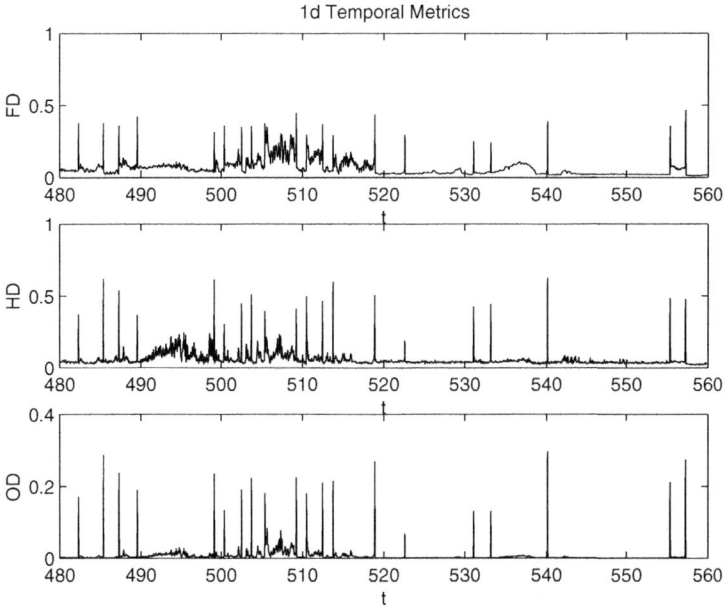

Fig. 1. Evaluated $1d$ temporal difference metrics: FD_t (top plot), HD_t middle plot, OD_t bottom plot, for a certain temporal part of the input sequence.

Finally, the performance of the method according to scene boundary determination is investigated. The sequence under study contains 18 different scenes being either dialogue ones, or action ones, or commercials or the serial logo displays. During boundary detection, those shots that exhibit the same speaker speaking or the same music part are combined together into a scene. The boundaries of the scenes are further extended according to shot boundaries. For example, if the same speaker is found to be speaking during frames 100 and 200, while shot boundaries have been detected to exist to frames 85 and 223, then scene boundaries are further extended to those, based on the enhanced performance of our shot boundary detection. Cases have been observed that extent scene boundaries to even a different speaker or music segment. Thus, dialogues may be identified if the speaker changing points in a scene are rather high. Results show that 13 out of 18 scenes are correctly detected, 12 are false detections (an actual scene is recognized as more than one due to the non-overlapping of speaker boundaries, music boundaries and shot boundaries), while 5 scene boundaries are missed. The performance is good considering that simple rules are imposed for scene boundary detection. Further investigation for scene characterization as well as incorporation of other analysis tools to define more semantic primitives and enhancement of methods attaining a suboptimal performance will be undertaken.

6   Conclusions

Content analysis and indexing systems offer a flexible and efficient tool for further video retrieval and browsing, especially now that distributed digital multimedia libraries have become essential. When such tasks combine semantic information from different data sources (auditory, visual, textual) through multimodal interaction concepts, enhanced scene cut detection and identification is possible. In this paper, a scene boundary detection method has been presented that attains promising performance. Both aural and visual sources are analyzed and segmented. The audio types used are speech, silence and music. Video segmentation into shots is performed by a remarkably efficient method that combines metrics used by the two distinct approaches. Interaction of the single source segmentation results leads to the determination of scene boundaries and the partial scene characterization.

References

[1] P. Correia and F. Pereira, "The role of analysis in content-based video coding and indexing", *Signal Processing, Elsevier*, vol. 66, no. 2, pp. 125–142, 1998.

[2] A. Del Bimbo, *Visual Information Retrieval*, Morgan Kaufmann Publishers, Inc., San Francisco, California, 1999.

[3] M.R. Naphade, R. Mehrotra, A.M. Ferman, J. Warnick, T.S. Huang, and A.M. Tekalp, "A high-performance shot boundary detection algorithm using multiple cues", in *Proc. of 1998 IEEE Int. Conf. on Image Processing*, Chicago, Illinois, USA, 4-7 Oct. 1998, vol. 1, pp. 884–887.

[4] N. Dimitrova, T. McGee, H. Elenbaas, and J. Martino, "Video content management in consumer devices", *IEEE Trans. on Knowledge and Data Engineering*, vol. 10, no. 6, pp. 988–995, 1998.

[5] R. Lienhart, S. Pfeiffer, and W. Effelsberg, "Scene determination based on video and audio features", in *Proc. of 1999 IEEE Int. Conf. on Multimedia Computing and Systems*, Florence, Italy, 1999, pp. 685–690.

[6] C. Saraceno and R. Leonardi, "Identification of story units in audio-visual sequences by joint audio and video processing", in *Proc. of 1998 IEEE Int. Conf. on Image Processing*, Chicago, Illinois, USA, 4-7 Oct. 1998, vol. 1, pp. 363–367.

[7] C. Saraceno, "Video content extraction and representation using a joint audio and video processing", in *Proc. of 1999 IEEE Int. Conf. on Acoustics, Speech and Signal Processing*, 15-19 Mar. 1999, vol. 6, pp. 3033–3036.

[8] S. Tsekeridou and I. Pitas, "Audio-visual content analysis for content-based video indexing", in *Proc. of 1999 IEEE Int. Conf. on Multimedia Computing and Systems*, Florence, Italy, 1999, vol. I, pp. 667–672.

[9] L. Rabiner and R.W. Schafer, *Digital Processing of Speech Signals*, Englewood Cliffs, N.J.: Prentice Hall, 1978.

[10] S.B. Davis and P. Mermelstein, "Comparison of parametric representations for monosyllabic word recognition in continuously spoken sentences", *IEEE Trans. on Acoustics, Speech and Signal Processing*, vol. 28, no. 4, pp. 357–366, 1980.

[11] P. Delacourt and C. Wellekens, "Audio data indexing: Use of second-order statistics for speaker-based segmentation", in *Proc. of 1999 IEEE Int. Conf. on Multimedia Computing and Systems*, Florence, Italy, 1999, vol. II, pp. 959–963.

Implicit 3D Approach to Image Generation: Object-Based Visual Effects by Linear Processing of Multiple Differently Focused Images

Kiyoharu Aizawa[1], Akira Kubota, and Kazuya Kodama[2]

[1] University of Tokyo, Bunkyo-ku, Tokyo, 113-8656, Japan
aizawa@hal.t.u-tokyo.ac.jp
[2] National Institute of Informatics, Chiyoda-ku, Tokyo, 101-8430, Japan

Abstract. A new image generation scheme is introduced. The scheme linearly fuses multiple images, which are differently focused, into a new image in which objcets in the scene is applied arbitrary linear processing such as focus(blurring), enhancement, extraction, shifting etc,. The novelty of the work is that it does not require any segmentation to produce visual effects on objects in the scene. It typically uses two images for the scene: in one of them, the foreground is in focus and the background is out of focus, in the other image, vice versa. A linear imaging model is introduced, based on which an identity equation is derived between the original images and the desired image in which the object in the scene is selectively visually manipulated, and the desired image is directly produced from the original images. A linear filter is derived based on the principle. The two original images which are applied linear filters are added and result in the desired image. Various visual effects are examined such as focus manipulation, motion blur, enhancement, extraction, shifting etc,. A special camera is also introduced, by which synchronized three differently focused video can be captured, and dynamic scene can also handled by the scheme. Realtime implementation using the special camera for processing moving scenes is described, too.

1 Introduction

Real images are manipulated to enhance the reality of the images in applications such as post-production and computer graphics. For example, image based rendering (IBR), that is, generation of novel images from a given set of reference images is intensively investigated in the field of computer graphics. View interpolation [1], view morphing[2], light field rendering [3] are among the IBR techniques. IBR usually generates new views of the object from a given set of images captured at different positions. The technique we propose in this paper is a novel IBR technique that manipulates visual effects such as focusing, enhancement etc. which are selectively applied to the objects in the scene.

Producing visual effect to the object in the image is usually handled by segmenting an image into different objects which are then applied special effects

R. Klette et al. (Eds.): Multi-Image Analysis, LNCS 2032, pp. 226–237, 2001.

and integrated into a new image. Such manipulation of visual effects needs segmentation that is hard to be automated, and the user has to manually correct
the segmentation.

We propose a novel approach to manipulation of visual effects which is very
different from the intuitive one described above. The proposed scheme uses multiple (typically two) differently focused images captured at the fixed position.
By fusing the multiple images, it generates visual effects which are selectively
applied to a object in the scene. For instance, one of the two originally acquired
images has the foreground object in focus and the background object out of
focus, while the other vice versa. Our proposed scheme arbitrarily manipulate
visual effects on objects in the scene only by linear filtering. It can produce
visual effects selectively onto the foreground or background. The visual effects
achievable are linear operation such as focusing, blurring, enhancement, shifting
etc,. The scheme only needs linear spatial invariant filtering and it generates the
target image from the original images. It is notable that it does not need any
segmentation nor 3D modeling, although it generates object-based visual effects.
In our previous work [8,9], we have shown the principle based on iterative reconstruction. In this paper, we show reconstruction by using linear filters which
are uniquely determined.

So call image fusion [4] has been used to merge multiple images such as
those from various type of image sensors. Image fusion can also fuse differently
focused images into an all focused image, but it can not handle object based
special effects. The proposed method in this paper differs from the conventional
image fusion because it is able to achieve object-based special effects.

Differently-focused images have been used for depth from focus and depth
from defocus, in the field of computer vision that computes the depth of the
scene (ex. [5,6]). Our proposal also makes use of differently-focused images, but
it differs because it is aimed at image generation, and not at depth computation.

The linear imaging model has been also used to represent transparently overlapped images such as a view through glass window which has reflection. Separation of differently focused overlapped transparent images was formulated based
on the linear imaging model, and a linear filtering approach was investigated [7].
Its formulation is the same as our approach. But, we deal with usual scene, not
limited in transparent scene, and moreover we can generate object-based various
effects, which includes extraction of objects.

2   Arbitrarily Focused Image Generation

2.1   A Linear Imaging Model

For the time being, we concentrate on the manipulation of focus among the
operations which are achievable. For simplicity, we describe our proposed method
for the case when we use two differently focused images.

Suppose a scene consists of foreground and background objects. We define
$f_1(x)$ and $f_2(x)$ as foreground and background texture, respectively. The two
differently focused images which are acquired are defined as $g_1(x)$ and $g_2(x)$. In

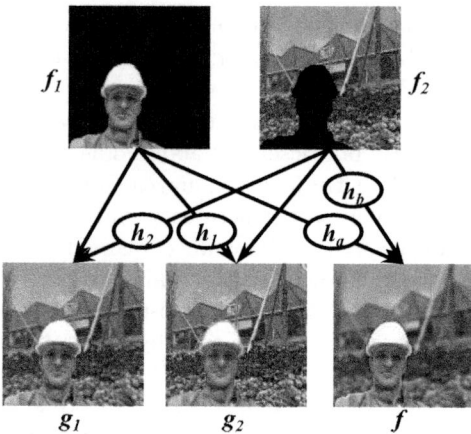

Fig. 1. Image formation by a linear imaging model

$g_1(x)$, the foreground is in focus and the background is out of focus. In $g_2(x)$, the background is in focus and the foreground is out of focus. Then, assuming a linear imaging model shown in fig.1, $g_1(x)$ and $g_2(x)$ are formed as follows:

$$\begin{cases} g_1(x) = f_1(x) + h_2 * f_2(x) \\ g_2(x) = h_1 * f(x) + f_2(x). \end{cases} \tag{1}$$

In g_1, f_1 is in focus and f_2 is out of focus. In g_2, vice versa. h_1 and h_2 are the blurring functions applied to f_1 and f_2 in g_2 and g_1, respectively. * represents the convolution. The amount of blur of h_1 and h_2 are caused by the optics of the camera and the depths of the objects.

Focusing can be manipulated by changing the blurring functions applied to f_1 and f_2. Then, if the blurring functions h_a and h_b are applied to f_1 and f_2, respectively, we are able to generate a new image f with focusing that is different to the originals, g_1 and g_2. The equation of f is given by:

$$f(x) = h_a * f_1(x) + h_b * f_2(x) \tag{2}$$

In eq.(2), h_a and h_b are arbitrarily controllable, which can differ from h_1 and h_2. When $h_a = h_b = \delta(x)$, f is an all focused image. ($\delta(x)$ is the delta function such that $\delta(x) = 1$ if $x = 0$, $\delta(x) = 0$ otherwise.) When we set $h_a = \delta(x)$ and vary h_b, f has a variably blurred background while keeping the foreground in focus.

In order to reconstruct f, usual thinking is to segment the foreground f_1 and the background f_2 in the original images, then to apply visual effects on them and fuse them. However, precise segmentation is difficult and presents a serious barrier to automating the processing.

In this proposal, we take a different approach. From the equations in eq.(1), we obtain the following equations:

$$\begin{cases} h_1 * g_1(x) - g_2(x) = (h_1 * h_2 - \delta) * f_2(x) \\ h_2 * g_2(x) - g_1(x) = (h_1 * h_2 - \delta) * f_1(x). \end{cases} \tag{3}$$

Convolving these two equations with h_b and h_a, respectively, then adding the corresponding sides of the resulting two equations, and finally using eq.(2) results in the equation given below because convolutions with h_a, h_b and $(h_1 * h_2 - 1)$ are interchangeable.

$$(h_b * h_1 - h_a) * g_1(x) + (h_a * h_2 - h_b) * g_2(x) = (h_1 * h_2 - \delta) * f(x). \quad (4)$$

The above equation excludes f_1 and f_2, and is an identity between g_1, g_2 and f. The blurring functions, h_a and h_b, are controlled by the user. The blurring functions, h_1 and h_2, occur when the images g_1 and g_2 are acquired, which can be estimated by pre-processing of either image processing-based estimation or camera parameter based determination. The only unknown in eq. (4) is $f(x)$. Therefore, by solving the linear equation (4), $f(x)$ is obtained directly.

There are two ways to solve the linear equation (4). One is the iterative approach and the other is inverse filtering approach. In our previous paper [9], iterative approach was utilized. In this paper, we introduce a linear inverse filtering solution which leads to more accurate and faster processing.

2.2   Reconstruction by Linear Filtering

We introduce inverse filters applied to the acquired image to obtain an arbitrarily focused image $f(x)$. Firstly, we take Fourier transform(FT) of the imaging models to represent them in Fourier domain. The FT of eq.(1) are expressed by

$$G_1 = F_1 + H_2 F_2$$
$$G_2 = H_1 F_1 + F_2$$

where $G_i, H_i, F_i(i = 1, 2)$ indicates the Fourier transform of g_i, h_i, f_i respectively. Similarly, the FT of eq.(2) is expressed by

$$F = H_a F_1 + H_b F_2. \quad (5)$$

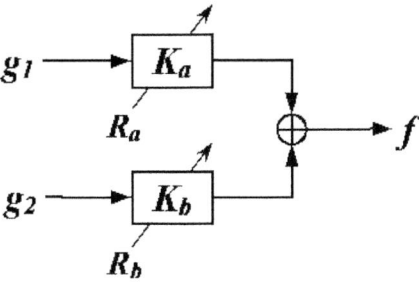

Fig. 2. Reconstruction of arbitrarily focused image from two differently focused images using inverse filters

Secondly, we solve eq.(5) for F_1 and F_2, and then find F by substituting the solution for eq.(5). We assume that the blurring function h_i is either gaussian or cylndrical. According to whether $(1 - H_1H_2)$ is zero or not, we solve eq.(5) as follows:

(i) $1 - H_1H_2 \neq 0$
In all the frequency component except DC component, $H_1H_2 \neq 1$ is satisfied. In this case, the F can be given by the filtering below.

$$F = \frac{H_a - H_bH_1}{1 - H_1H_2}G_1 + \frac{H_b - H_aH_2}{1 - H_1H_2}G_2 \qquad (6)$$

(ii) $1 - H_1H_2 \neq 0$
The DC component of F can not be obtained because the denominator of the above equation is zero at DC. This means the DC component is what we call *ill-conditioned* in the sense of general image restoration problems. However, in our specific problem of reconstruction of arbitrarily focal images using two differently focused images, we can find the DC component of F by taking the limit of the filters of G_1 and G_2 in eq.(6) at the DC. Applying l'Hospital's theorem, we obtain the limit value at the DC for both cases of gaussian and cylindrical PSFs as follows:

$$\lim_{\xi,\eta \to 0} \frac{H_a - H_bH_1}{1 - H_1H_2} = \frac{R_1^2 + R_b^2 - R_a^2}{R_1^2 + R_2^2} \qquad (7)$$

$$\lim_{\xi,\eta \to 0} \frac{H_b - H_aH_2}{1 - H_1H_2} = \frac{R_2^2 + R_a^2 - R_b^2}{R_1^2 + R_2^2} \qquad (8)$$

where ξ and η are horizontal and vertical frequency and R_i $(i = 1, 2, a, b)$ are the blur radiuses.

From the results above, the desired image F can be obtained as

$$F = K_aG_1 + K_bG_2 \qquad (9)$$

where K_a and K_b are the linear filters represented in the frequency domain, which are expressed by

$$K_a(\xi, \eta) = \begin{cases} \dfrac{R_1^2 + R_b^2 - R_a^2}{R_1^2 + R_2^2}, & \text{if } \xi = \eta = 0 \\[2ex] \dfrac{H_a - H_bH_1}{1 - H_1H_2}, & \text{otherwise} \end{cases} \qquad (10)$$

$$K_b(\xi, \eta) = \begin{cases} \dfrac{R_2^2 + R_a^2 - R_b^2}{R_1^2 + R_2^2}, & \text{if } \xi = \eta = 0 \\[2ex] \dfrac{H_b - H_aH_2}{1 - H_1H_2}, & \text{otherwise.} \end{cases} \qquad (11)$$

R_1 is the radius of the blur circle of the foreground when background is in focus. R_2 is that of the background when the foreground is in focus. R_1 and R_2 can be estimated by our previously proposed pre-processing method [10,9]. R_a and R_b are the parameters chosen by the user. H_i ($i = 1, 2, a, b$) are determined by the blur radiuses and the property of PSFs. Thus, the FT of the linear filters can be uniquely determined and the desired image F (in frequency domain) can be directly reconstructed using linear filtering (eq.(9)). The diagram of the reconstruction is shown in fig.2. Note that no segmentation is required in this method. Finally, by applying the inverse FT to F, we obtain the desired image f.

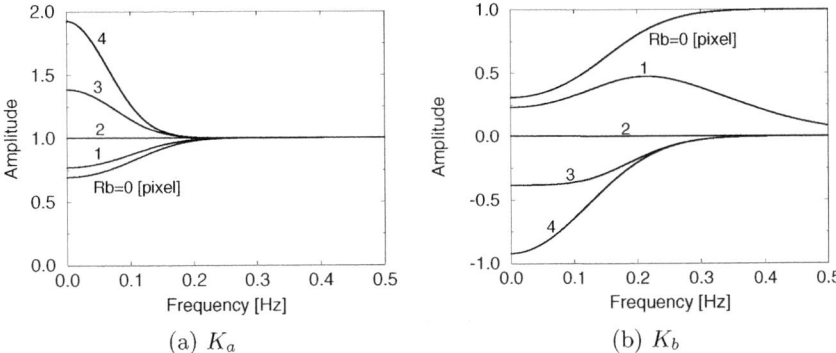

(a) K_a (b) K_b

Fig. 3. Frequency characteristics of the inverse filters ($R_1 = 3$, $R_2 = 2$, $R_a = 0$)

Frequency characteristics of the linear filters K_a and K_b are shown in fig.3 when R_1 and R_2 are 3 and 2 pixels, respectively, changing R_b from 0 to 4 pixels while R_a is constantly 0 pixel. The generated images are such that the background is variably blurred while the foreground is kept in focus. The figure 3 shows the case in which the blurring PSFs (h_is) are gaussian. Note that a noise amplification, which is generally a critical issue, does not occur as large as an general inverse filtering method may have, because the characteristics at higher frequency converge to 1.

3   Experiments for Real Images

For the experiments using real images, we need to pay attention to the two things listed below which are required for pre-processing.

(1) Blurring parameters R_1 of h_1 and R_2 of h_2 should be estimated because they are not known.
(2) Image sizes of g_1 and g_2 should be made equal because the different focus makes the image view slightly different.

There are two ways to obtain these parameters; one is fully image processing based estimation and the other is camera parameter based determination. In the image processing based estimation, discrepancies in the size and the blurring between the two images are detected by image processing, in which hierarchical

(a)The near in focus (g_1)   (b)The far in focus (g_2)

Fig. 4. Real images used for experiments

matching is applied to size difference estimation, and Rs of h_1 and h_2 are estimated by coarse to fine way. The hierarchical registration taking into account the discrepancies of size, position and rotation is described in detail in our paper [10,9].

In the camera parameter based determination, camera characteristics such as discrepancies of image size vs focal length and blurring vs focal length are measured using test charts placed at various depths, and put into a look-up-table in advance. Because the discrepancies of the size and the blurring between the two images are uniquely determined by the camera focal length, they are obtained just by the focal length parameters when the images are taken.

We use real images of fig.4 (a)(b) for experiments. Using the pre-processing fully based on image processing, image g_2 is slightly enlarged. The blurring R_2 of the far object in g_1 and the blurring R_1 of the near object in g_2 are estimated that $R_1 = 4.73, R_2 = 4.77$.

After the pre-processing, we can generate arbitrarily focused images from the acquired images by filtering. Some are shown in fig.5: 5(a) shows the all-focused image in which both the far and the near are in focus ($R_a = R_b = 0pixels$). In 5(b) the near object is slightly blurred ($R_a = 2, R_b = 0pixels$); compared to the original fig.5(b), the near object is slightly restored while keeping the far objects in focus. 5(c), the far objects are much blurred ($R_a = 0, R_b = 10pixels$); compared to fig.5(a), the background is much blurred while keeping the near object in focus.

As shown in the figures, the proposed method for manipulation of the focusing works well for real images. Again, the method does not need any segmentation. Our proposal is based on the linear imaging model which assumes depth of the scene changes stepwise. The real scene never satisfy this assumption. In fact, the scene of the experiments are obviously not two planar layers. Although the model is rough approximation, it is verified that the method can obtain satisfactory results.

(a)All-focused image   (b)near object is slightly blurred.

(c)background is much blurred.

Fig. 5. Various arbitrarily focused synthesis images by linear filtering

4   Various Manipulations

Because the operation h_a and h_b can be any liner processing, we can achieve
various manipulation of visual effects on objects in a image by the same way.
For example, enhancement, shifting, extraction, etc. Among them, a result of
enhancement is shown in fig.6. If h_a is enhancement filtering, the object f is
selectively enhanced. As shown in fig.6. Only the near object is enhanced while
the background is kept the same as that of the all focused image. The difference
is clearly visible on the textures of the object. Example of shifting and extraction
are shown in our paper [9].

5   Real-Time Implementation

To implement the the proposed technique to the scenes of moving objects for
a real-time system, it is required to capture multiple differently focused image
at the same time. We have developed a special camera which can acquire three

Fig. 6. Enhancement of a object

differently focused video for the same scene called the multi-focus video camera. With this multi-focus video camera, we have built a real-time system of arbitrarily focused moving images.

5.1 Multi-focus Video Camera

Fig.7 illustrates structure of the multi-focus video camera. The light beam from the objects passes the lens and then it is divided into three directions by the beam splitter. Focal lengths can be adjusted by moving each CCD camera at the beam axis.

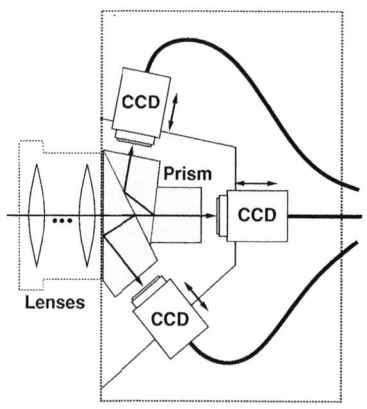

(b) Multifocus camera

(a) Structure of multi-focus video camera

Fig. 7. Multi-focus video camera

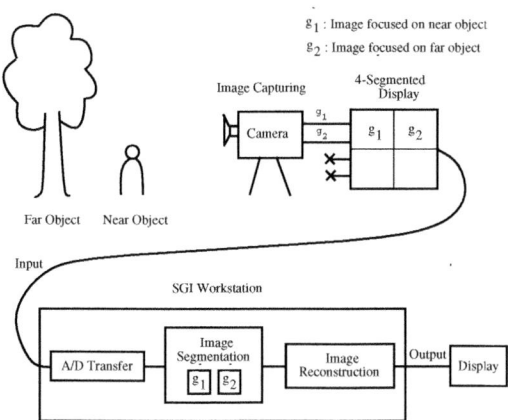

Fig. 8. Diagram of the real-time arbitrarily focused moving images system

5.2 Real-Time Arbitrarily Focused Moving Images System

As illustrated in fig. 8, the system consists of multi-focus video camera, 4-segmented display, and SGI workstation Onyx R10000 (195 MHz). By using multi-focus video camera, we capture two differently focused images; one is focused on the near object and the other one is focused on the far objects. The two images are integrated into one image using 4-segmented display, so that both images can be inputed to the workstation exactly at the same time. Then, the workstation processes the input images, generates an arbitrarily focused image and displays the result. In this system, we also can adjust the focal lengths of the synthesis images in real-time.

5.3 Experimental Results

Fig. 9 shows the experimental results of the real-time system. Fig. 9(a)(b) are the input video images, i.e. near-focused images and far-focused images, and fig. 9(c) is the synthesis video images. Here, at the beginning of the experiment foreground and background objects are in focus, then the background objects are blurred gradually while keeping the foreground object in focus. For image size of 128×128 pixels, the real-time system can generate arbitrarily focused moving images at around 3 frames/second.

In reconstruction using iterative approach[9], the processing time depends on the blur radii, such that the processing time increases when the blur radii become larger. It is not favorable for a real-time system, because the system will have different speed rates when the user change the synthesis image's parameters. But, by using linear filtering approach, we can have a faster processing and the problem mentioned above can be settled.

(a) Near-focused   (b) Far-focused   (c) Arbitrarily
    image   image   focused image

Fig. 9. Samples of arbitrarily focused moving images

6   Conclusion

In this paper, we show a novel approach to producing object-based visual effects. We show spatially invariant linear filtering applied to two differently focused images generates various visual effects selectively produced on objects in the scene. As long as the visual effect is linear processing, the method can produce such object-based effects. Again, the method does not need any segmentation.

In order to apply the proposed technique to the scene of moving objects, it is required to capture multiple differently focused images at the same time. We developed a special camera which can acquire three differently focused video for the same scene, and the realtime implementation using the camera.

References

[1] E.Chen, Lance Williams, View intepolation for image synthesis, Proc. SIG-GRAPH'93, pp.279-288, 1993

[2] S.M.Seitz, C.R.Dyer: Toward image-based scene representation using view morphing, Proc. ICPR'96 pp.84-89, 1996

[3] M.Levoy, P.Hanrahan: Light field rendering, Proc. SIGGRAPH'96, pp.31-42, 1996

[4] P.Burt and R .Kolczynski : Enhanced Image Capture Through Fusion, ICCV93 pp.173-182

[5] T.C.Nguyen and T.S.Huang : Image Blurring Effects Due to Depth Discontinuities: Blurring that Creates Emergent Image Details, ECCV92, pp.347-362, 1992

[6] Subbaro, M. & Surya, G. Depth from defocusing: A spatial domain approach, Int. J. of Computer Vision. Vol.13, No.3, pp.271-294. 1994

[7] Y.Y.Cshechner, N.Kiryati, R.Basri, Separation of transparent layers using focus, ICCV98, pp.1061-1066, 1998

[8] K.Kodama, K.Aizawa, M.Hatori: Acuisition of an all-focused image by the use of multiple differently focused images, IEICE Trans. Vol.J80-D-II, No.9, pp.2298-2307, 1997 (in Japanese)

[9] K.Aizawa, K.Kodama and A.Kubota: Producing object based special effects by fusing multiple differently focused, IEEE Trans. CSVT, 3D special issue, Vol.10, No.2, pp.323-330, March 2000

[10] A.Kubota, K.Kodama, K.Aizawa: Registration and blur estimation methods for multiple differently focused images, Vol.II pp.447-451, IEEE ICIP99

[11] A.Kubota, K.Aizawa: Inverse filters for generation of arbitrarily focused images SPIE VCIP2000, Vol.4067 pp.1633-1641, June 2000

Content-Based Image Retrieval Using Regional Representation

Kap Luk Chan[1], Xuejian Xiong, Fan Liu, and Ricky Purnomo

School of Electrical and Electronic Engineering,
Nanyang Technological University
Nanyang Avenue, Singapore 639798
[1]eklchan@ntu.edu.sg

Abstract. Representing general images using global features extracted from the entire image may be inappropriate because the images often contain several objects or regions that are totally different from each other in terms of visual image properties. These features cannot adequately represent the variations and hence fail to describe the image content correctly. We advocate the use of features extracted from image regions and represent the images by a set of regional features. In our work, an image is segmented into "homogeneous" regions using a histogram clustering algorithm. Each image is then represented by a set of regions with region descriptors. Region descriptors consist of feature vectors representing color, texture, area and location of regions. Image similarity is measured by a newly proposed Region Match Distance metric for comparing images by region similarity. Comparison of image retrieval using global and regional features is presented and the advantage of using regional representation is demonstrated.

1 Introduction

Image databases have been generated for applications such as criminal identification, multimedia encyclopedia, geographic information systems, online applications for art articles, medical image archives and trademark. The volume of these databases is expanding drastically. Effective image indexing and retrieval techniques then become ever more important and critical to facilitate people searching for information from large image databases.

It is generally agreed that image retrieval based on image content is more rational and desirable. There has been intensive research activity in Content-Based Image Retrieval ($CBIR$) systems [1], [2], [3], [5], [8], [14], [16], [18], [24]. Many $CBIR$ methods use features extracted from the entire image. However, for general images depicting a variety of scene domains, such global features will show their limits in representing the image content correctly because the images often contain several objects or regions that are totally different from each other in terms of visual image properties. Hence, we advocate the use of features extracted from image regions and an image is represented by a set of regions. The regions may be obtained by segmenting the image using color, texture or any

R. Klette et al. (Eds.): Multi-Image Analysis, LNCS 2032, pp. 238–250, 2001.

other image properties. Various image properties in a region are then extracted to represent that region. These properties are represented as feature vectors, which are used as the region descriptor. Finally, the entire image is represented by a set of such regions with region descriptors consisting of extracted image features. In the present work, an image is segmented into "homogeneous" color regions using a histogram clustering algorithm. Each image is then represented by a feature set consisting of region descriptors. The region descriptors are made up of feature vectors representing color, texture, area and location of regions. Image similarity is measured by the Region Match Distance (RMD) which is defined based on the Earth Mover's Distance (EMD) adopted for regions. A comparison of image retrieval using global features and regional features is presented which demonstrates the advantage of using regional representation.

The rest of the paper is organized as follows. Section 2 discusses the image representation issue. Section 3 describes a content-based image retrieval system using regional representation. In section 4, experimental results are presented to show the comparison between using global features and the regional features for retrieval. Finally, in section 5, the present work is concluded and the future work is proposed.

2   Image Representation: Global vs. Regional

Content-based image retrieval methods that use features extracted from the entire image can be considered as a global approach. Using global features has some weaknesses when dealing with general images which often contain several objects or regions that are totally different from each other, and each object has its own set of attributes (see Figure 1). The global features cannot reflect the variation of image properties among regions and thus fail to describe the image content correctly. Nevertheless, global feature extraction is much more straight forward and fast. In many situations, global features are sufficient to achieve acceptable image retrieval performance.

church   flower   street   airplane

Fig. 1. Images containing different objects of interests

In our work, we propose to use regional representation of image, and retrieval is based on region similarity. The overall image similarity is determined from region similarity by adopting the Earth Mover's Distance proposed in [20]. This can be seen as a step towards higher level descriptions of an image. In the ideal case where a region corresponds to an object, the representation of the image is then in terms of objects. The image can then be represented by their perceptual organization. This is a step closer to image representation by image semantics.

Recently, some research work in this area has been reported. Methods such as RRD [6], CPC[9], MCAG[19], and CRT[22] are proposed to represent color images. Most of them are based on global color histogram with added spatial domain information. Strictly speaking, these are not really region-based features. In our approach, the features are extracted from image regions. Also, this region-based image representation is believed more similar to the process in human perception. For example, a human often observes an image with a focus of attention. The focus is usually on the object(s) of interests, such as building, flower, and airplane shown in Figure 1. As a result, a human groups images according to the object(s) of interests. He/She will also hope to retrieve images based on these objects. A region-based description allows us to search images based on objects or regions, thus enabling the focus of attention. Global image description can still be achieved by a collection of local regional descriptions to allow search by the entire image content. Motivated by the above considerations, a region-based image retrieval approach using features of regions is developed.

3   Content-Based Image Retrieval System Based on Regional Representation

Developing a region-based image retrieval ($RBIR$) system involves the following main tasks: (i) image segmentation by some chosen criteria; (ii) feature extraction from regions; (iii) construction of region feature sets; (iv) determining similarity between query feature set and the target image feature set. Tasks (i) - (iii) are needed to construct the indexing system for $RBIR$. This is an off-line process. In the on-line process, a query image is presented and all the tasks are performed. The l most similar images are retrieved in descending order of similarity, where l can be specified by the user. The overview of the $RBIR$ system is illustrated in Figure 2.

3.1   Region Extraction

Image segmentation partitions an image into some "meaningful" regions which are assumed to be homogeneous in some sense, such as brightness, color, texture and etc. In this work, a color-spatial space histogram clustering segmentation algorithm is used [12]. It is well-known that most existing image segmentation algorithms cannot produce consistent segmentation for the image of the same scene captured under different illumination conditions and also may not produce consistent and accurate region boundary. This has discouraged many researchers to consider image segmentation as a pre-processing step in their $CBIR$ system. We believe these problems can be alleviated by proper choice of segmentation criteria and by placing more emphasis on large regions.

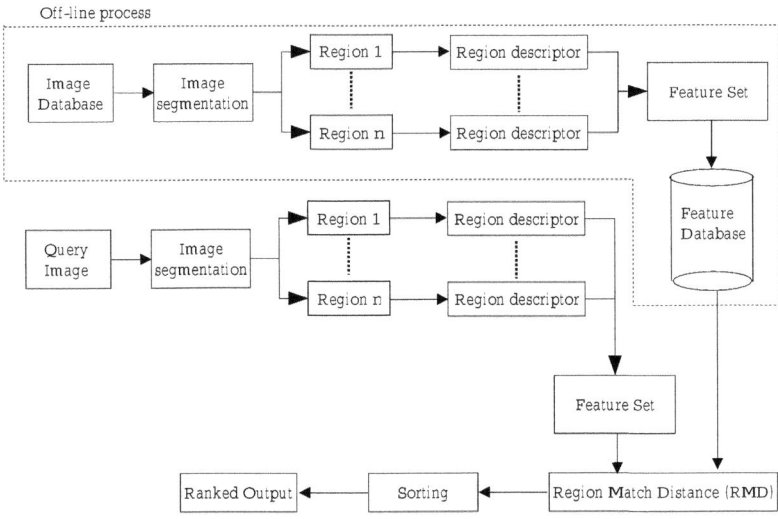

Fig. 2. The region-based image retrieval system

Due to the difference between human perception of colors and computer's perception of colors by the three primaries RGB, equal changes in the RGB space do not necessarily result in equal noticeable changes in the human perception [4], [13]. Hence, we transform the color pixel from RGB space to the CIE-Lab color space in which the perceived differences between individual nearby colors correspond to the Euclidean distances between the color space coordinates. In this color space, the L correlated with brightness, a with redness-greenness and b with yellowness-blueness.

The segmentation of the color image is then performed in this perceptually uniform CIE-Lab color space. The coordinates of each pixel are appended into the Lab color space to include the spatial information. As a result, a color-spatial feature space is constructed. This space is quantized to produce the histogram space on which the clustering algorithm operates. Too coarse quantization will lead to incomplete segmentation while too fine quantization will result in over-segmentation, both of which can adversely affect the retrieval performance. Through experimentation, quantization level for the 5 dimensional histogram space is $L = 4$, $a = b = 25$, and $X = Y = 5$. The image regions are then formed by the clusters obtained from the histogram space clustering algorithm. Hole-filling operation is performed to remove small regions within large regions.

After image segmentation, R largest regions are selected such that $\sum_{i=1} s_i = ws$, where s_i represents the pixel number in ith region, s represents the total number of pixels in an image, while w is the percentage threshold. In this work, $w = 0.95$, i.e. the first R larger regions altogether covering up to 95% of image area are taken. Thus R sub-images can be formed, each of which contains only one "homogeneous" region (see examples in Figure 3).

Fig. 3. Examples of region extraction by color image segmentation

3.2   Regional Representation

Many visual properties can be used to characterize an image region. The commonly used visual properties are color, texture and shape. In the present work, color and texture are used to represent regions in the images. Shape will be considered in future. The next question is how to represent color and texture properties of a region. Typical approaches use single color, color pairs, color mean, and color histogram to index the color information contained in the images. Each approach has different advantages and disadvantages. Over the past decades numerous approaches for the representation of textured images have been proposed [11], [15]. Here, we follow the work reported in [21], in which a 3-level wavelet decomposition was used to derive texture features from the wavelet transformed coefficients. In retrieval by regions, the locations of the regions and their sizes can be important. This is because "more important" regions are usually found near the center of an image. Also, the size of a region can be a criterion when defining similarities. Hence, the following image properties are extracted from regions:

Color feature:

– **Color mean**: Color mean is a basic image feature. It is considered to be less effective in representing images. If this mean is used to represent a homogeneous color region, it is then meaningful. Let c_j denotes the color value of a pixel, m_{ci} $(i = 0, ..., n)$ denotes mean value of color c of the ith region Ω_i respectively, then

$$m_{ci} = \frac{\sum_{j \in \Omega_i} (c_j)}{p}, (j = 1, ..., p) \tag{1}$$

where p represents the number of pixels in the ith region. The color value here is a vector $(L, a, b)^T$

– **Color histogram**: Color histogram represents of the color distributions of a region. This regional color feature can be obtained by quantizing the L, a, b, the color space into bins. The quantization level was set to $q_l = 2$, $q_a = 9$, $q_b = 9$. Thus the following color feature vector consisting 162 elements is defined,

$$\mathbf{f_c} = (h_1, h_2, ..., h_{162})^T \tag{2}$$

where h_i $(i = 1, ..., 162)$ represent the normalized histogram value for ith bin of the *Lab* color histogram respectively.

Wavelet texture feature: A three-level wavelet decomposition using "Daub4" wavelet is performed in the L, a, and b images. Means and standard deviations of the approximation coefficients, the horizontal, vertical and diagonal detail coefficients at each level are used to construct the wavelet feature vector [25]. This feature vector has $3 \times 2 \times 4 \times 3 = 72$ dimension:

$$\mathbf{f_w} = (\alpha_1, \alpha_2, ..., \alpha_{72})^T \tag{3}$$

Region Location: The location of the region is represented by a bounding box which is subdivided into 3×3 sub-boxes. These sub-boxes represents a region location vector (RLV) of 9 elements, and the elements represent top-left, top-middle, top-right, middle-left, middle-middle, middle-right, bottom-left, bottom-middle, and bottle-right regions respectively. The RLV is defined as follows.

$$\mathbf{l_w} = (l_1, l_2, l_3, l_4, l_5, l_6, l_7, l_8, l_9)^T \tag{4}$$

The value for each element is defined as the ratio between the area of the region falling in the location represented by this element to the whole area of the region.

$$l_i = \frac{area\_in\_location\_i}{area\_of\_region} (i = 1, 2, ..., 9) \tag{5}$$

AreaVector: An *AreaVector* for each image is defined to reflect the area distribution among its regions. Each element in the vector is the ratio of the area of a region to that of the entire image. For example, if an image is segmented into three regions, the *AreaVector* of it will contain three elements with each is the ratio between the area of one region and the area of the whole image.

$$AreaVector = [r_1, r_2, ..., r_R], \quad r_i = \frac{area\_of\_region\_i}{area\_of\_image}, \quad (i = 1, 2, ..., R) \quad (6)$$

It is clear that $\sum r_i = 1$, $(i = 1, 2, ..., R)$. Each element of *AreaVector* will reflect the importance of the region to the whole image in terms of area.

FeatureSet **Construction:** Now the regions have been represented by feature vector for color or texture and *RLV* for region location. A *FeatureSet* representing the whole image can be constructed based on these region descriptors and the *AreaVector*. For an image with R regions, the *FeatureSet* will be:

$$FeatureSet = \{\mathbf{f_1}, \mathbf{l_{w1}}, r_1; \mathbf{f_2}, \mathbf{l_{w2}}, r_2; ...; \mathbf{f_R}, \mathbf{l_{wR}}, r_R\} \quad (7)$$

where $\mathbf{f_i}$, $(i = 1, 2, .., R)$ are the *RLV* for region i which may be color mean, color histogram, or wavelet texture feature; $\mathbf{l_{wi}}$, $(i = 1, 2, .., R)$ are the *RLV* for region i; r_i, $(i = 1, 2, ..., R)$ are the *AreaVector* element for region i.

3.3   Regional Similarity Measurement

In this work, a distance measure - the Region Match Distance (RMD), which is based on the Earth Mover's Distance (EMD), for matching two feature sets is proposed. The EMD is a distance measure proposed in [20]. It aims to measure similarity between two variable-size descriptions of two distributions. Basically, it reflects the minimal cost that must be paid to transform one distribution into the other one. The EMD has many desirable properties. It is more robust in comparison to other histogram matching techniques for measuring two distributions, in that it suffers from no arbitrary quantization problems due to the fixed binning of the latter. Also, it allows for partial match between any two distributions. This makes the EMD very appealing for matching two images where there may not be equal number of regions in these two images. A maximal match is sought.

From EMD to RMD: An image can be viewed as a distribution over the two dimensional spatial domain. After the segmentation, only the prominent regions are extracted from the original distribution and are used to form the *FeatureSet*. In the *FeatureSet*, each region is represented by a single point in the relative feature-location coordinate system, together with a weight - an element in the *AreaVector* of the image - that denotes the size of that region. By using the EMD, to compute the distance between two feature sets is to emulate one

FeatureSet with the other one in terms of their *AreaVector* match. The *RMD* is proposed based on this idea. It reflects the minimal work needed in matching the two image distributions.

Definition of RMD: The RMD is computed based on the solution to the traditional transportation problem as in the EMD [7]. First, we need to define an elementary distance between two regions, called the Region Distance(RD):

$$rd = \|v_q - v_d\|/w_{ol} \tag{8}$$

where v_q is a feature vector of a region from the query and v_d is a feature vector of a region from an image in the database.

Here w_{ol} is a weight which reflects the location overlap of two regions. It is defined as follows: let l_{wq}, l_{wd} are sets of RLV for the query image and the image from the database respectively,

$$w_{ol} = \sum_{i=1}^{i=9} min(l_{qi}, l_{di}) \tag{9}$$

where $l_{qi} \in l_{wq}$, $l_{di} \in l_{wd}$, $(i = 1, 2, .., 9)$.

Using w_{ol} as the weight for RD means the more two regions overlap, the smaller the distance. Then, let Φ, Ψ represent the sets of regions from two images P and Q, we define the RMD between the two distribution as:

$$RMD(P,Q) = \min_{C} \frac{\sum_{i\in\Phi}\sum_{j\in\Psi} c_{ij}d_{ij}}{\sum_{i\in\Phi}\sum_{j\in\Psi} c_{ij}} \tag{10}$$

where $c_{ij}(i \in \Phi, j \in \Psi)$ is the amount of "flow" from region i in the first image to region j in the second image, C is the set of all permissible flow c_{ij}, and d_{ij} is the RD between region i of one image and region j of another image. "Flow" here is a measure of how many parts of one region that can be transformed/matched into another region, which can be measured in terms of absolute size of the region (number of pixels) or area of the region relative to the whole image.

The solution for RMD is obtained by solving the transportation problem to obtain the combination of c_{ij} such that the RMD equation above is minimized. In other words, it matches the regions in the two images by pairing such that the overall dissimilarity measure between the two images is as small as possible. The values of c_{ij} is subject to the following constraints:

$$c_{ij} \geq 0 \ ; \ i \in \Phi, \ j \in \Psi \tag{11}$$

$$\sum_{j\in\Psi} y_j \leq \sum_{i\in\Phi} x_i \tag{12}$$

$$\sum_{i\in\Phi} c_{ij} = y_j \ ; \ j \in \Psi \tag{13}$$

$$\sum_{j\in\Psi} c_{ij} \leq x_i \ ; \ i \in \Phi \tag{14}$$

where $y_j \in Y(j \in \Psi)$, $x_i \in X(i \in \Phi)$, X, Y are *Area Vectors* for the two images.

The first constraint above maintains that the flow is unidirectional, from i to j, to avoid negative minimal value caused by a flow from the opposite direction. The next constraint specifies that the bigger image, i.e. the image with more regions, is always considered as the "supplier" of flow. This allows for partial matches between images of unequal region numbers, and maintains the symmetrical relation that $RMD(P, Q) = RMD(Q, P)$. The last two conditions require that all parts of the "consumer"(smaller image) must be matched to a flow, while the flow from the supplier cannot exceed the number of parts/pixels it can provide. These also mean that the smaller image has to be fully emulated by the larger image, but not vice versa.

Thus the RMD extends the distance between two images to distance between two sets of regions even when the two sets are of different sizes. It can reflect the notion of nearness without the quantization problems that other histogram matching techniques have. Also it allows for partial match between two images naturally. The characteristics of RMD is similar to EMD.

An example of image pair matching using the RMD: An example of the matching process for two images containing three and two regions respectively are illustrated in figure 4. In the figure, f_{ij} is the feature vector for jth region of image i ($i = 1, 2; j = 1, 2, 3$). $y_j(j \in \Psi)$, $x_i(i \in \Phi)$ are Area Vectors for the two images respectively. $d_{ij}, (i = 1, 2, 3; j = 1, 2)$ are the RDs between region ith of image 1 and jth region of image 2. Assume that regions 1 and 3 in image 1 are similar to regions 1 and 2 in image 2 respectively, which means that d_{11} and d_{32} are small. Therefore, to minimize the RMD equation, the flows c_{11} and c_{32} should be chosen to be as big as possible; that is, as many pixels as possible are matched between the two region pairs. Any unmatched pixels will be matched with other unmatched pixels in the next most similar region. This means that the RMD will be smaller when the matched regions are of similar size as well; an image with a big red region and a small blue one when compared with an image comprising a small red region and a big blue one will yield a relatively big RMD. Also, bigger regions tend to dominate in similarity comparison because they contribute more flow.

Based on the principles and constraints of the RMD, the image 1 is always the one with more regions. It can be either the query image or a candidate target image. The selected feature vectors of a region in image 1 is compared with another feature vector of a region in image 2 to determine the region-wise similarity according to visual features and the region overlap, i.e. the RDs. The overall image similarity is therefore determined by the RMD which requires maximal similarity over all the matched regions. The computation of RMD involves an optimization process and hence takes much longer time than computing the RDs.

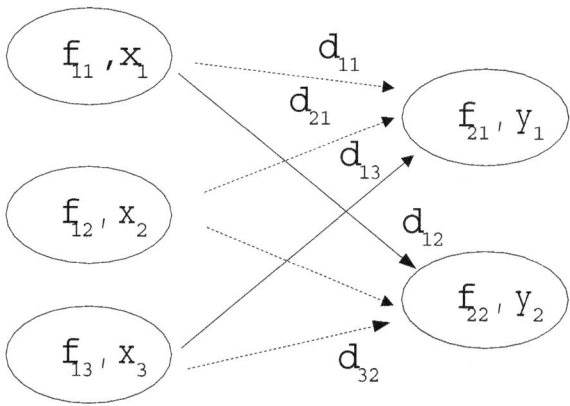

Fig. 4. The matching of an image pair by regions using RMD

4   Experiments

Image retrieval is performed using color mean, color histogram, wavelet feature as region feature respectively. In order to make a comparison with global content representation, the popular global color histogram feature is also used.

Each image in the image database is first segmented into a number of homogeneous regions by color. Each region is represented using color and texture attributes as described in Section 3.2. Thus, three kinds of feature databases, i.e. color mean feature, region color histogram feature, and the wavelet feature, are constructed. Obviously, if every image is segmented into one region, the global feature database can also be generated. As a result, the comparison of Image Retrieval using Global and Regional Feature can be done. The global feature is defined by the color histogram known as the global color histogram.

In the experiment, the Average Retrieval Rate(ARR) proposed in [10] is used to evaluate the effectiveness and accuracy. ARR is defined as the average percentage number of images retrieved from a particular class, given a sample image of that class. Given that ω represents the number of classes experimented on, n_i $(i = 1...\omega)$ represents the number of image retrieved for the sample image of ith class, r_i $(i = 1...\omega)$ represents the number of images retrieved correctly for that image,

$$ARR = \sum(r_i)/\sum(n_i) \qquad (15)$$

The retrieval experiments are performed on images coming from ten classes of a scaled down Corel Stock Photos image database (see Table 1). The ten classes are considered to be the most typical kinds of natural images in the database. They represent grass and animals, sunset, star and sky, building, sky and plane, green scene, lake, sea creature and sea floor, flowers and cars respectively. Some of these images are shown in Figure 5. For each class, 10 images are randomly selected as the query of that class, thus a total of 100 test images. 8 most similar images ($n_i = 8$) are retrieved for each of them according to selected features. The experiment results are tabulated in Table 1. The number in the table is the average number of images retrieved correctly for certain class, i.e. the average of r_i.

Table 1. Performance evaluation by ARR

image class	color mean	region histogram	wavelet feature	global histogram
grass & animals	7	4.5	5.5	5
sunset	5	3.5	6	3.5
stars & sky	6.5	5	3	5.5
building	6	4	6.5	5.5
sky and planes	6.5	4.5	6.5	6
forest scene	7	5.5	5.5	6
lake	4.5	2	4.5	3.5
underwater world	3	2.5	4.5	2.5
flowers	6	5.5	6	5.5
cars	5.5	3	5	5.5
Overall ARR	**71.3%**	**50%**	**68.5%**	**60.6%**

The results in these experiments show that the region-based approach produce better performance than the global histogram based method when using the color mean features and wavelet texture features. Region color histogram seems not suitable because the images have already been segmented into homogeneous regions in terms of color. So the histogram of region does not contain too much useful information while color quantization may also introduce other errors in adverse. The color mean is a good invariant feature for representing the color information of the region. On the other hand the wavelet features are not invariant and hence produce lower ARR than the color mean.

In our experiments, the images are grouped into classes by human observers largely based on image semantics. This explains the overall low ARRs. However, image classification itself is an issue. Studies on relevance feedback for the training of CBIR system may lead to a better way of classifying image databases.

5 Conclusions and Future Work

In this paper, $CBIR$ using regional representation is advocated. Features extracted from an image region are used to represent that region and an image is represent by a feature set of regional feature vectors. Together with the region location vector and area vector, the content of the image can then be better described. The Region Match Distance(RMD), which is based on the Earth Mover's Distance, is proposed to measure the similarity between the two feature sets representing two images. The experimental results shows that using

Fig. 5. Examples of some of the scaled down experimental images and their pre-classification (each row forms an image class)

regional representation is better than using global representation. It also shows the importance of using invariant features for region-based image retrieval. Future work will address the feature invariance issues, the similarity metrics, and linking of the high-level perceptual concepts to the low-level features.

References

[1] S. Belongie, C. Carson, H. Greenspan, and J. Malik. Color- and texture-based image segmentation using em and its application to content-based image retrieval. In *Proceedings of theSixth International Conference on Computer Vision*, pages 675–682, 1998.

[2] C. Carson, S. Belongie, H. Greenspan, and J. Malik. region-based image querying. In *Proceedings IEEE Workshop on Content-Based Access of Image and Video Libraries*, pages 42–49, 1997.

[3] Chad Carson, Megan Thomas, Serge Belongie, Joseph M. Hellerstein, and Jitendra Malik. Blobworld: A system for region-based image indexing and retrieval. In *the Third International Conference on Visual Information Systems*, June 1999.

[4] Kap Luk Chan and Han Wang. Reading resistor by color image processing. In *Proceedings of SPIE*, volume 3185, pages 157–169, 1997.

[5] Shih-Fu Chang. content-based indexing and retrieval of visual information. *IEEE Signal Processing Magazine*, 14(4):45–48, July 1997.

[6] L. Cinque, F. Lecca, S. Levialdi, and S. Tanimoto. Retrieval of image using rich region description. In *Fourteeth International Conference on Pattern Recognition*, volume 1, pages 899–901, 1998.

[7] Hillier Frederick S. and Lieberman Gerald J. Introduction to Mathematical Programming. *McGraw-Hill*, 1995.

[8] M. Flickner, H. Sawheny, Wayne Niblack, J. Ashley, Q. Huang, Byron Dom, M. Gorkani, J. Hafner, D. Lee, D. Petkovic, D. Steele, and P. Yanker. Query by image and video content: the qbic system. *Computer*, 28(9), Sept 1995.

[9] Theo Gevers and Armold W.M. Smeulders. Content-based image retrieval by viewpoint-invariant color indexing. *Image Vision Computation*, 17, 1999.

[10] Yihong Gong. Intelligent Image Databases, Towards Advanced Image Retrieval. In *Kluwer Academic Publishers*, 1998.

[11] A. K. Jain and F. Farrokhnia. Unsupervised texture segmentation using Gabor filters. *Pattern Recognition*, 24(12), 1991.

[12] Alireza Khotanzad and Abdelmajid Bouarfa. Image segmentation by a parallel non-parametric histogram clustering algorithm. *Pattern Recognition*, 23, 1990.

[13] Michael Kliot and Ehud Rivlin. Invariant-based shape retrieval in pictorial database. *Computer Vision and Image Understanding*, August 1998.

[14] W. Y. Ma and B. S. Manjunath. netra: a toolbox for navigating large image database. In *Proceedings of the International Conference on Image Processing*, volume 1, pages 568 –571, 1997.

[15] B. S. Manjunath and W. Y. Ma. Texture features for browsing and retrieval of image data. *IEEE Transactions on Pattern Analysis and Machine Intelligence*, 18(8):837–842, 1996.

[16] Swarup Medasani and Raghu Krishnapuram. A fuzzy approach to content-based image retrieval. In *Proceedings of the IEEE International Conference on Multimedia Computing and Systems*, pages 964–968, 1999.

[17] B. M. Mehtre, M. S. Kankanhalli, A. D. Narasimhalu, and G. C. Man. Color matching for image retrieval. *Pattern Recognition Letters*, 16, 1995.

[18] Virginia E. Ogle and Michael Stonebraker. Chabot: retrieval from a relational database of images. *Computer*, 28(9), Sept 1995.

[19] In Kyu Park, Dong Yun, and Sang UK Lee. Color image retrieval using hybrid graph representation. *Image Vision Computation*, 17, 1999.

[20] Yossi Rubner, Carlo Tomasi, and Leonidas J. Guibas. A metric for distributions with applications to image databases. In *Proceedings of the sixth IEEE International Conference on Computer Vision*, 1998.

[21] J. R. Smith, *Integrated Spatial and Feature Image Systems: Retrieval, Analysis and Compression*. PhD thesis, Columbia University, 1997.

[22] John R. Smith and Chung-Sheng Li. Decoding image semantics using composite region templates. In *IEEE workshop on content-based access of image and video libraries*, pages 1286–1303, June 1998.

[23] M. Swain and D. Ballard. Color indexing. *International Journal of Computer Vision*, 7(1):11–32, 1991.

[24] B. Verma, P. Sharma, S. Kulkarni, and H. Selvaraj. An intelligent on-line system for content based image retrieval. In *Proceedings of the Third International Conference on Computational Intelligence and Multimedia Applications (ICCIMA)*, pages 273 –277, 1999.

[25] Changliang Wang, Kap Luk Chan, and Stan Z Li. Spatial-frequency analysis for color image indexing and retrieval. In *The Fifth International Conference on Control, Automation, Robotics and Vision (ICARCV'98)*, pages 1461–1465, 1998.

Integration of Photometric Stereo and Shape from Occluding Contours by Fusing Orientation and Depth Data

Chia-Yen Chen[1] and Radim Šára[2]

[1] Centre for Image Technology and Robotics, Tamaki Campus
University of Auckland, Auckland, New Zealand
yen@citr.auckland.ac.nz
[2] Centre for Machine Perception, Faculty of Electrical Engineering
Czech Technical University, Prague, Czech Republic
sara@waltz.felk.cvut.cz

Abstract. In this paper, we have investigated the fusion of surface data obtained by two different surface recovery methods. In particular, we have fused the depth data obtainable by shape from contours and local surface orientation data obtainable by photometric stereo. It has been found that the surface obtained by fusing orientation and depth data is able to yield more precision when compared with the surfaces obtained by either type of data alone.

1 Introduction

Current surface recovery methods have their respective advantages and drawbacks. For example, while it is possible to obtain accurate measurements using structured lighting, the process can be extremely time consuming. Photometric stereo offers fast and dense recovery of the local surface orientations, but the depth values that are calculated by the integration [2,4,5,6] of recovered normals may be inaccurate with respect to the true depth values.

To construct a new shape recovery method that can be more robust, efficient and versatile than existing methods, we fuse the data obtained by shape recovery methods that have complementary characteristics. From previous work [1], we have decided to construct a new shape recovery method by the fusion of depth and orientation data, which are respectively obtained by shape from occluding contours and photometric stereo method. These two methods have been chosen on the basis that shape from contours is able to provide reliable measurements, but unable to recover surface cavities that are occluded from the camera by the contours of the object. Conversely, photometric stereo provides dense orientation information over the surface, but the depth measurements obtained by integration of the surface orientations are relatively scaled to the actual depth values. Therefore, the integration of these two methods may be able to yield results with higher precision than either one of the methods is able to achieve.

We have approached the task in the following steps. Firstly, we generate the synthetic surfaces and simulate the orientation and depth data as would be obtained by the shape recovery methods. From the simulated data, we calculate the weighting functions for

R. Klette et al. (Eds.): Multi-Image Analysis, LNCS 2032, pp. 251–269, 2001.

the different types of data. The fusing of orientation and depth data is then performed according to the weights for the orientation and depth data. Finally, we compare the surfaces obtained by fusion of data, as well as the surfaces obtained by photometric stereo and shape from contours, to evaluate the performance of the fusion method.

The block diagram in Fig. 1 shows the steps involved in the integration of photometric stereo and shape from contours by fusing orientation and depth data.

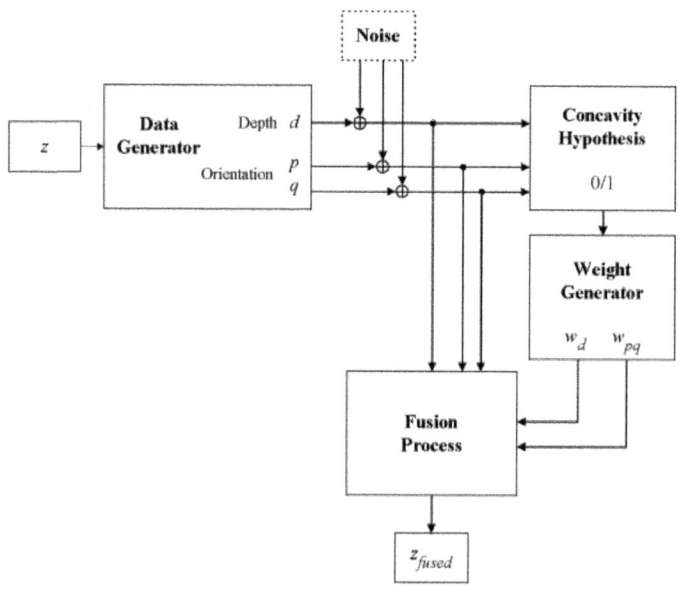

Fig. 1. Block diagram for the integration of shape recovery methods using fusion of depth and orientation data.

In Fig. 1, z represent the original, known surface function. The data generator extracts the surface depth values d, and orientation components p and q from z. Noise is added to extracted depth and orientation values to simulate the effect of obtaining depth and orientation data respectively using shape from contours and photometric stereo. The simulated depth and orientation data are put through the concavity hypothesis to determine the locations where cavities are likely to occur. The weight generator produces weights for depth w_d and orientation w_{pq} data according to the outcome of the concavity hypothesis. The fusion process combines the depth and orientation data according to w_d and w_{pq} to generate the fused surface z_{fused}.

There are two objectives for this work. The first objective is to determine whether fusion of the two kinds of data is able to provide more precision than either one of these methods. This will be achieved by comparing the recovered surfaces with the true surfaces. The second objective is to determine whether there are any observable artifacts in the region where different data are fused. The surface recovered by fusion of data will be examined to achieve this objective.

2   Generation of Surfaces

We have used *MatLab* for the generation of the surfaces. Each of the generated surfaces has a concave region which is occluded by a neighbouring region on the surface. Such surface cavity will not be recovered by shape from contours, yet the surface orientations within the cavity can be recovered by photometric stereo.

Two types of surfaces were used in this work. The first surface is generated by addition of Gaussian functions, such that the surface is C^2 continuous. It is an example of most general surfaces. The second surface, z_2, is a polyhedral surface generated by intersecting five planar surfaces. It is an example of a simple surface, such as the surface from a man-made object. Figure 2 shows the surfaces z_1 and z_2.

We have used both the continuous and polyhedral surfaces to evaluate the performance of the fusing method in different cases.

3   Simulation of Orientation and Depth Data

The surface orientations as obtained by photometric stereo are provided by the partial derivatives of the surfaces.

The surface normals are calculated by approximating the derivatives of the original surfaces z_1 and z_2 with respect to the horizontal and vertical directions. For each surface, z_i, the local derivatives in the horizontal and vertical directions, respectively indexed by x and y, are given by

$$\frac{\Delta z_i(x,y)}{\Delta x} = \frac{z_i(x+1,y) - z_i(x,y)}{\Delta x} \tag{1}$$

$$\frac{\Delta z_i(x,y)}{\Delta y} = \frac{z_i(x,y+1) - z_i(x,y)}{\Delta y} \tag{2}$$

For our surfaces, Δx and Δy are both 0.05 units.

The orientation data are further simulated by adding random noise, N, to the derivatives. The resultant orientation data in the x and y directions are respectively given by

$$p_i(x,y) = \frac{\Delta z_i(x,y)}{\Delta x} + \alpha \cdot N(x,y), \tag{3}$$

$$q_i(x,y) = \frac{\Delta z_i(x,y)}{\Delta y} + \alpha \cdot N(x,y). \tag{4}$$

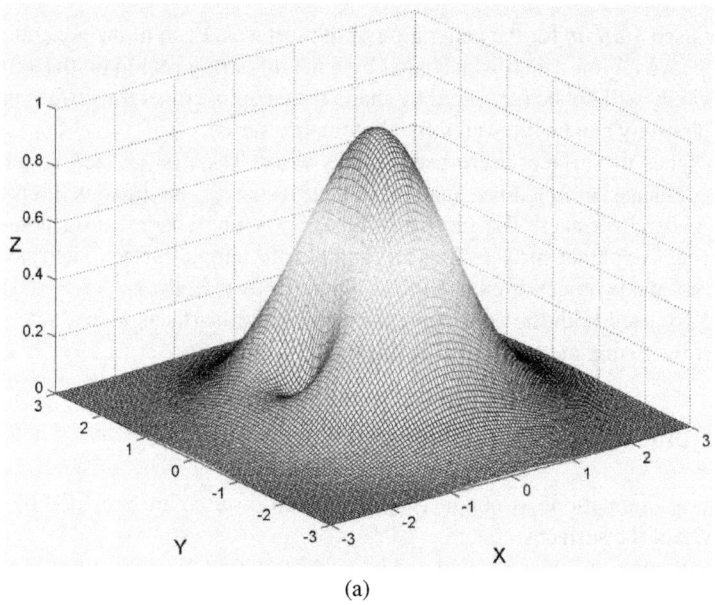

(a)

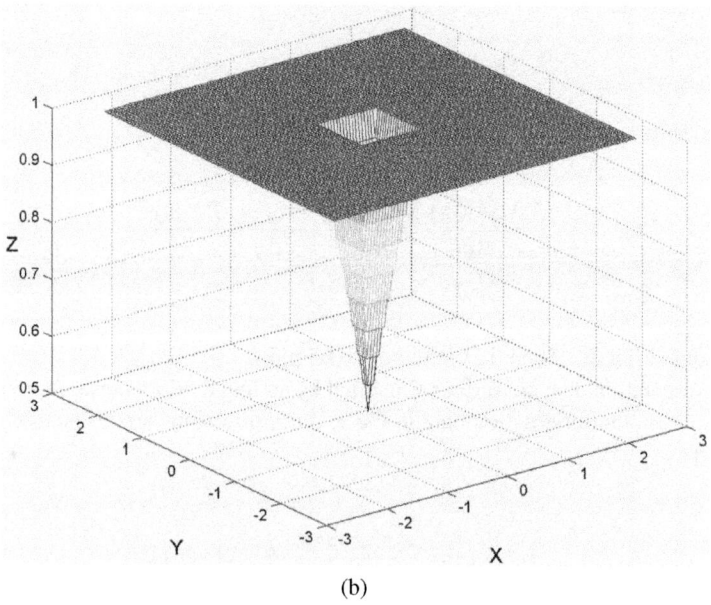

(b)

Fig. 2. (a) Surface z_1 and (b) surface z_2.

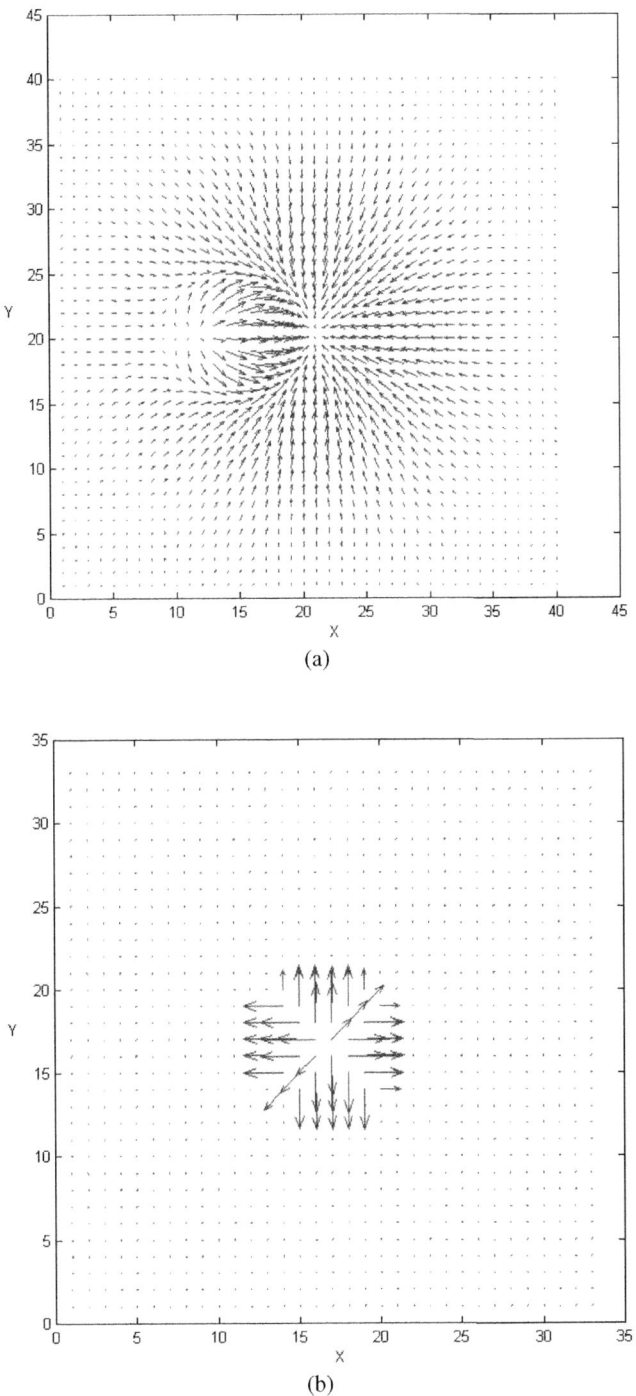

(a)

(b)

Fig. 3. Simulated photometric stereo orientation data for surfaces (a) z_1 and (b) z_2.

The simulated photometric stereo results for surfaces z_1 and z_2 are shown as needle maps in Fig. 3.

The amplitude of the original surfaces can be used directly as the depth values obtained by shape from contours, except for concave regions on surfaces. The reason is that shape from contours is unable to recover cavities that are occluded from the viewing direction by other regions of the surface. Therefore, to simulate the depth data as obtained by shape from contours, we need to take into account the method's inability to recover surface cavities.

The surfaces are discretised into a given number of layers. For each layer, a convex polygon for the surface contour is drawn. The layers are then piled up again and the convex polygons are joined to form the surface, z_{conv}. Random noise N is added to further simulate the depth data obtained by shape from contours, given by

$$z_d(x, y) = z_{conv}(x, y) + \alpha \cdot N(x, y). \tag{5}$$

The obtained surface z_d has a developable patch covering the cavity on the original surface, as would be expected when shape from contours is used to recover the surface. The simulated surfaces are given in Fig. 4. Figure 4(a) and (b) respectively show the depth data for z_1 and z_2 as might be obtained by shape from contours(). From the figures, it can be seen that the cavities have been covered with developable patches.

4   Detection of Concave Regions

The compatibility of depth data obtained using shape from contours and orientation data obtained using photometric stereo is used to detect the region of cavity on the surface to be recovered. The detected concave regions are used to determine the contribution of depth and orientation data in the fusion process.

There are two possible approaches to compare the input data; either by using the depth values, or the surface orientations. In this work, the surface orientations have been used for the comparison of input data since they are easier to obtain. With the approach, partial derivatives are used to provide the surface normals for the surface recovered by shape from contours.

A cross section at $y = 0$, from surface z_1 is shown in Fig. 5. Surface z_1 is represented by the solid line, and the surface normals obtained by photometric stereo are plotted on z_1. The surface recovered by shape from contours is represented by the dotted line, and the surface normals calculated from the surface recovered by shape from contours are plotted on the dotted line.

From Fig. 5, it can be seen that the orientations of surface normals along the left column ($x = 1.25$) differ significantly, whereas the orientations of the surface normals are quite similar along the right column ($x = 1.66$). The difference of surface normals in the left column is caused by the occurrence of a cavity. One way of calculating the angle between the two orientation vectors is to use the dot product of the surface normals.

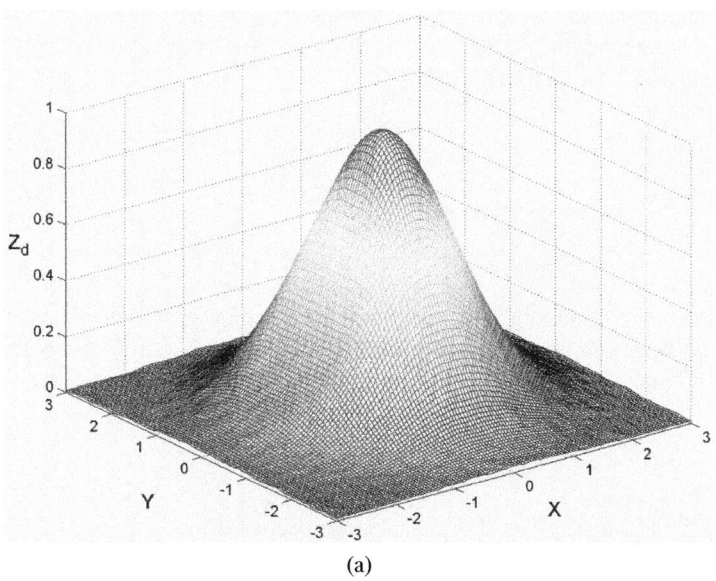

(a)

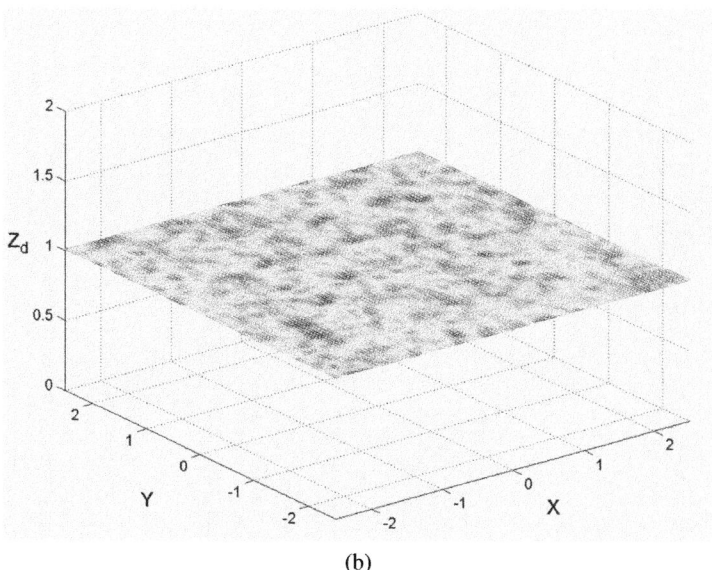

(b)

Fig. 4. Simulated shape from contours depth data for surfaces (a) z_1 and (b) z_2.

Therefore, the dot products of the normals can be used to indicate the discrepancies between these two types of data.

The discrepancies caused by noise also need to be taken into account when determining the compatibility of the data. In this work, the compatibility function between the data is a binary function given by

$$c(x,y) = \begin{cases} 1 & : \quad n_{psm} \cdot n_{sfc} < t, \\ 0 & : \quad otherwise \end{cases} \tag{6}$$

where t is the thresholding value that has been chosen such that the data discrepancies caused by noise can be avoided. The vectors n_{psm} and n_{sfc} respectively represent the surface normals obtained by photometric stereo and shape from contours.

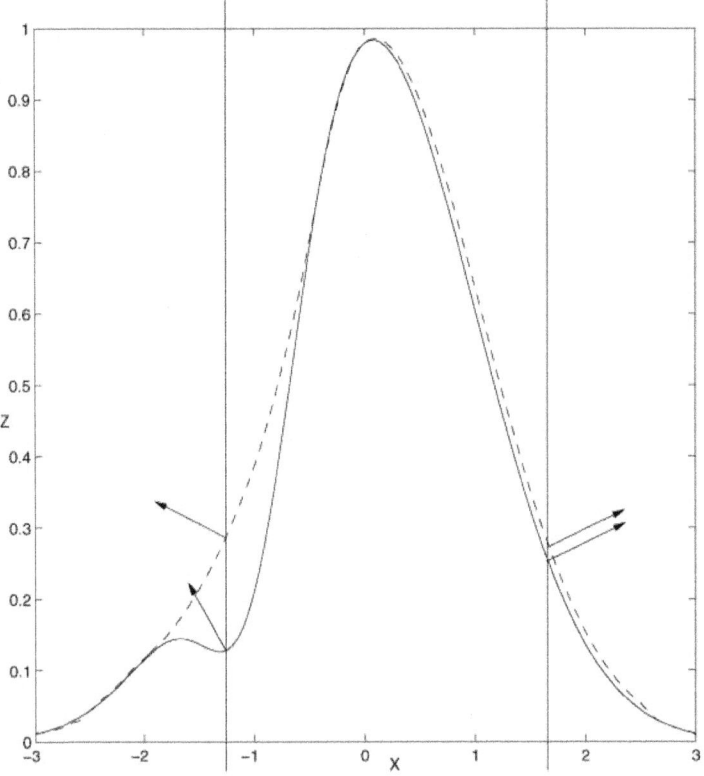

Fig. 5. Cross section and surface normals of original surface and surface obtained by shape from contours.

In Fig. 6, white pixels represent regions where the data are compatible, and black pixels represent regions where the data are incompatible. From the figures, it can be seen that the general shape of the cavities have been detected for both surfaces. However, note that for some points, the surface orientations within the cavity do agree with the surface orientations for the developable patch. Noise added to simulated data has also caused the data to disagree outside the cavity. Therefore, the compatibility function will need to be improved further to enable more accurate detection of concave regions.

5   Calculation of Weights for Fusing Data

In this step, we determine the contribution of the depth and orientation data towards the final result based on the computed data compatibility. This is a crucial step in the fusion of data, since suitable choice of weights enables the fusion of the complementing data to be performed in such a way that the surface given by fusion yields higher accuracy than surfaces given by either method alone.

The depth data obtained by shape from contours are reliable except in concave regions. Therefore, the data weighting functions are computed based on the data compatibility function, $c(x, y)$, which indicates region of cavity. In this work, the weighting function for the depth data,

$$w_d(x, y) = \begin{cases} 1 & : \quad c(x, y) = 1 \\ 0 & : \quad c(x, y) = 0 \end{cases} \tag{7}$$

is the same as the compatibility function, which is 1 when the data are compatible, and 0 when the data are incompatible. The values are thus defined because the depth data are not reliable within concave regions, where the depth and orientation data are likely to be incompatible.

The weighting function for the orientation data,

$$w_{pq}(x, y) = \begin{cases} 1 & : \quad c(x, y) = 0 \\ 0 & : \quad c(x, y) = 1 \end{cases} \tag{8}$$

has values of 0 in regions where the data are compatible and 1 where the data are incompatible, since the orientation data obtained by photometric stereo are more reliable than the depth data obtained by shape from contours within surface cavities.

The weighting functions are selected such that the unknown surface will generally be recovered from the depth values obtained by shape from contours, except for the concave regions, where the surface will be recovered according to the surface orientations obtained by photometric stereo.

The weighting functions may also take on values other than 1 or 0 to adjust the contributions of depth and orientation data towards the fusion process.

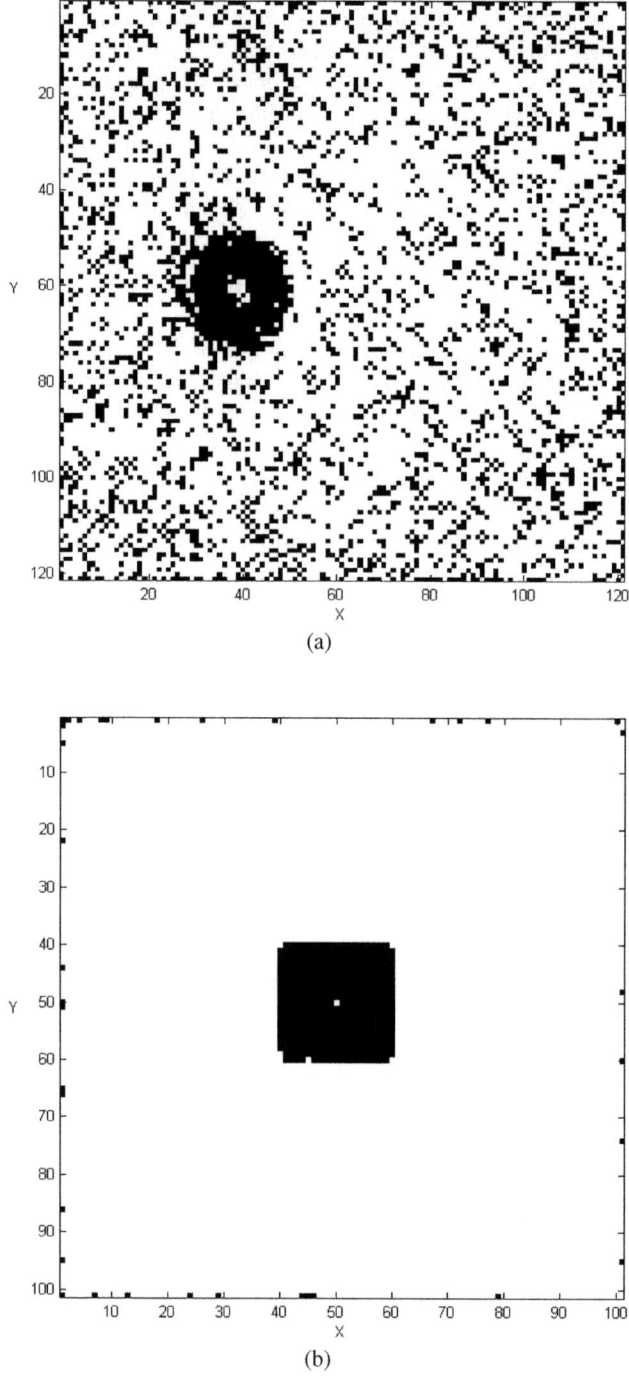

Fig. 6. Computed data compatibilities for (a) z_1 and (b) z_2.

6   Fusion of Data

The fusion algorithm is implemented according to the work by D. Terzopoulos [3,9]. It reconstructs the unknown C^2 continuous function z by combining the depth and orientation data with respect to certain weighting functions. The input parameters are d, the depth data, p and q, the horizontal and vertical orientation data, as well as w_d and w_{pq}, the weighting functions for depth and orientation data. In this work, the depth data, d, are the noise corrupted depth values obtained using shape from contours. The orientation data, p and q, are the noise corrupted orientation data obtained by photometric stereo.

The fusion algorithm minimises the error function

$$E(z) = E_d(z, d, p, q) + E_m(z) + E_t(z),\tag{9}$$

where

$$E_d(z, d, p, q) = w_d \cdot S_d \sum_u \sum_v |z - d|^2 + w_{pq} \cdot S_{pq} \sum_u \sum_v |\frac{\delta z}{\delta u} - p|^2 + |\frac{\delta z}{\delta v} - q|^2\tag{10}$$

$$E_m(z) = S_m \iint (\frac{\delta z}{\delta u})^2 + (\frac{\delta z}{\delta v})^2 \, du dv\tag{11}$$

$$E_t(z) = \iint [\frac{\delta^2 z}{\delta u^2}\frac{\delta^2 z}{\delta v^2} - (\frac{\delta^2 z}{\delta u \delta v})^2] \, du dv.\tag{12}$$

In the above formula, E_d is the data error function, which specifies how well the unknown surface z conforms to the input depth and orientation data at discrete grid positions. The second term, E_m, represents the membrane function. It specifies that the surface z should be continuous. The third term, E_t, represents the thin-plate function, which specifies that the surface z should have small changes in its curvature, that is, the surface should be smooth, with no sudden peaks. The values S_d, S_{pq}, and S_m are the coefficients of the depth error, orientation error and the continuity constraint, respectively. These values can be assigned by the designer of the algorithm. In our case, the coefficients have all been set to 1.

The conjugate gradient descend method is used to iteratively minimise the error function, such that the result is obtained when the value of the error function is at its minimum. The error function is convex, so that the algorithm will always converge to the global minimum [7].

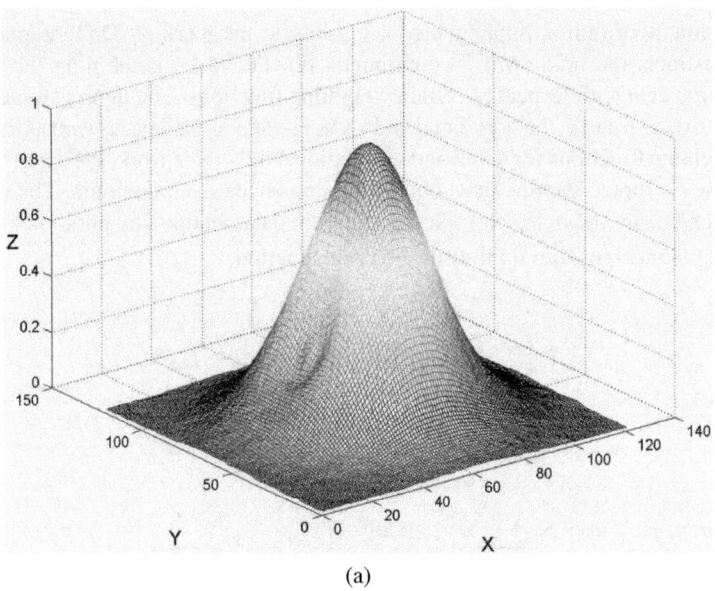

(a)

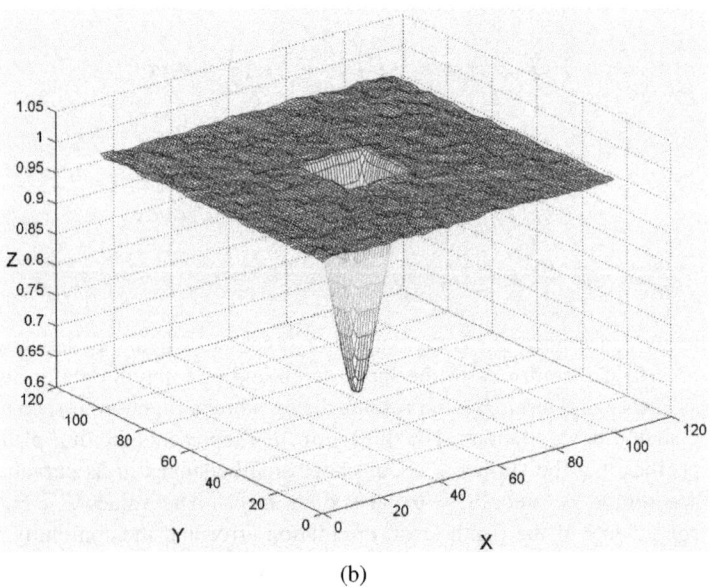

(b)

Fig. 7. Fused surfaces for (a) z_1 and (b) z_2.

7 Results

After applying the fusion algorithm to the two different types of data, we obtained the surfaces as shown in Fig. 7

Figure 7(a) shows the surface obtained by fusion of orientation and depth data for surface z_1. The shape and amplitude of the recovered surface conform well to the original surface. Also notice that there are no visible artifacts along the cavity boundary in the resultant surface.

The surface recovered by fusion of data for surface z_2 is shown in Fig. 7(b). The recovered surface also retains the general shape of the original surface, but the amplitude of the recovered surface differs slightly from the original surface. There are also no artifacts on the fused surface along the cavity boundary. In fact, the recovered surface is a continuous surface, whereas the original surface has discontinuous folds along the cavity boundary and within the concave region. The reason is that the fusion method assumes that the unknown function z has to be C^2 continuous, hence the sharp folds of the original surface are not recovered.

From Fig. 7(a), it can be seen that the recovered cavity is not as deep as the cavity on the original surfaces. The result can be more clearly examined in Figs. 8 and 9.

Figure 8(a) shows cross sections at $y = 0$ of the true surface z_1, the surfaces recovered by simulating shape from contours and photometric stereo, and the fused surface. Figure 9(a) shows the same for surface z_2. With reference to the figures, it can be seen that the surfaces recovered by shape from contours, z_{sfc}, have good conformity to the original surfaces in most regions, except for the cavities. Whereas the surfaces recovered by photometric stereo, z_{psm}, conform to the original surfaces quite well in the concave regions, but suffer from the effect of cumulated errors towards the positive x direction. The surfaces obtained by fusion, z_{fused}, lie between the surfaces recovered by photometric stereo and shape from contourshave the combined advantages from both methods. Like the surface recovered by shape from contours, the surface recovered by fusion conforms to the original surface quite well in most regions. But unlike z_{sfc}, z_{fused} has a cavity in the concave region, even though the cavity is less emphasised when compared to the original surface. The insufficient depth of the recovered cavity is a major source of error in the surface recovered from fusion. The shallower cavity is partly due to the fact that the weighting functions are binary, thus the contribution from each type of data is either 0 or 1. The smoothness constraint of the recovered surface is another cause for the insufficiently recovered cavity.

Figure 8(b) shows the sum of absolute errors along the y direction between z_1 and surfaces acquired using different methods. Figure 9(b) shows the errors for surface z_2. From the figures, it can be seen that the errors from z_{sfc} are fairly constant, apart from the concave regions. While z_{psm} appears to conform to the true surfaces quite well in the selected cross sections, the larger error magnitudes indicate that it is more erroneous over all, for surfaces z_1 and z_2. The cumulative errors for z_{psm} can also be easily observed, as the errors increase towards the positive x direction. The errors for z_{fused} are similar to the errors from z_{sfc} for regions without cavities. Therefore, z_{fused} is generally less erroneous than z_{psm}. On the other hand, z_{fused} recovers cavities to certain extent, hence the errors in the cavity regions are less than that of z_{sfc}.

Overall, from Figs. 8 and 9, it can be seen that the surface recovered from fusion of depth and orientation data gives better result than the surfaces obtained by either depth or orientation data alone.

8   Evaluation

In this section, the recovered surfaces are compared with the ground truth to evaluate the accuracy of each method.

The error function is given by $e = z - \tilde{z}$, where z is the surface obtained by fusion of original, un-corrupted data, and $\tilde{z}$ is the surface recovered from simulated data, which are corrupted by noise.

For surface z_1,

Table 1. Errors between z_1 and surfaces recovered using different methods.

(%)	Fused	SFC	PSM
$min\,|e|$	0.0005	0.0018	0.0000
$max\,|e|$	16.5979	19.3352	7.8308
$mean\,|e|$	1.5120	1.5617	2.5173
RMS	1.5630	1.8562	1.7958

For surface z_2,

Table 2. Errors between z_2 and surfaces recovered using different methods.

(%)	Fused	SFC	PSM
$min\,|e|$	1.1752	1.1769	0.0070
$max\,|e|$	24.9002	101.5993	15.4209
$mean\,|e|$	2.3244	3.5532	5.3134
RMS	1.1657	8.5130	3.6062

It can be seen from the tables that the surfaces recovered by fusing of data are more accurate than the surfaces recovered by either shape from contours or photometric stereo alone.

9   Discussion

In this work, we have tested the fusion method, as well as photometric stereo and shape from contours on two different types of surfaces. The first surface is a C^2 continuous surface constructed from Gaussian functions. The second surface is a polyhedral surface constructed from planar patches. The C^2 continuous surface is an example of general surfaces, and the polyhedral surface is an example of simple surfaces.

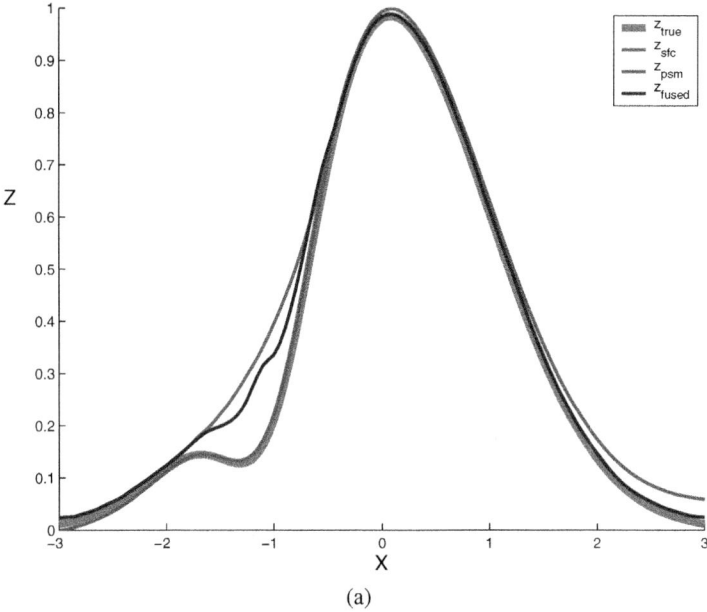

(a)

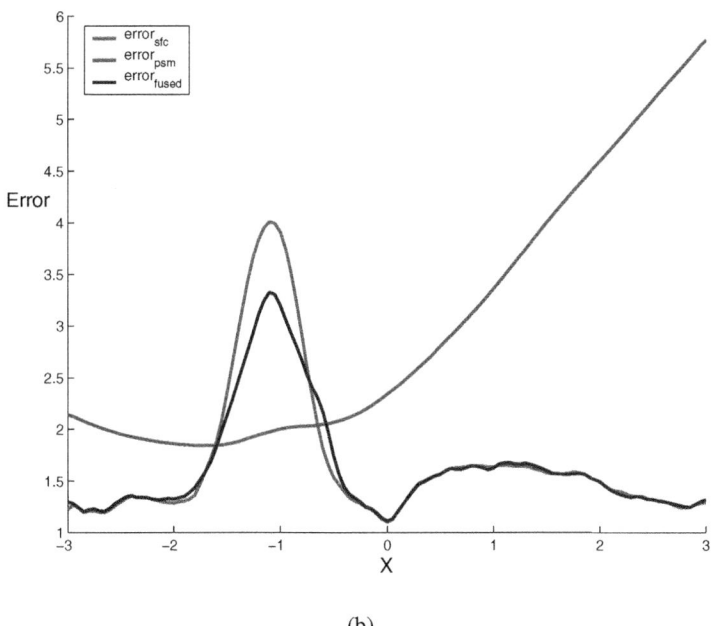

(b)

Fig. 8. Cross sections of (a) resultant surfaces and (b) error, for surface z_1.

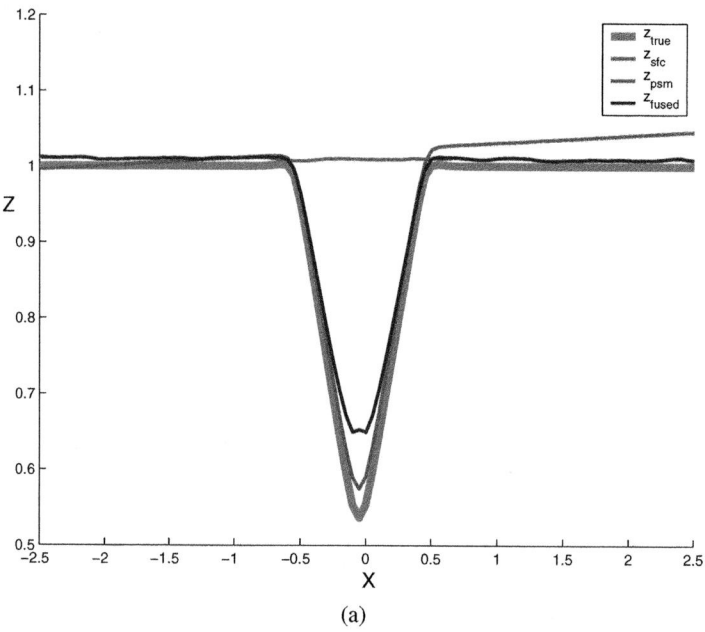

(a)

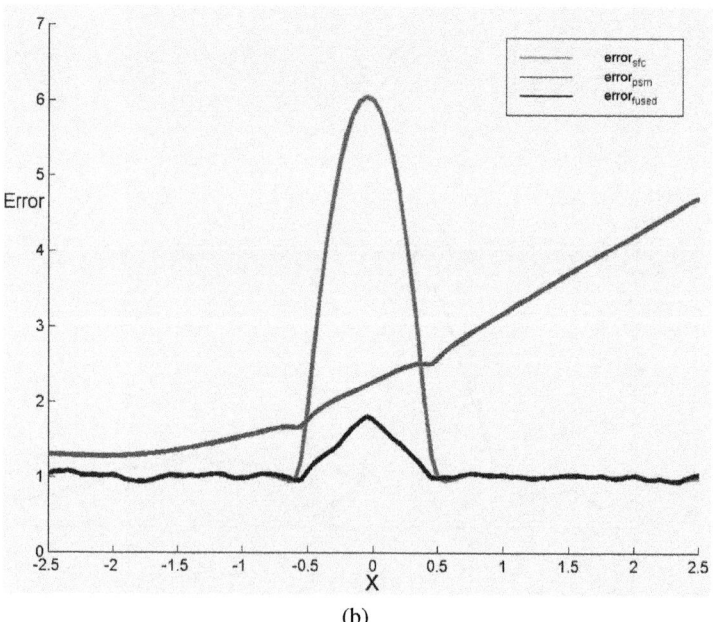

(b)

Fig. 9. Cross sections of (a) resultant surfaces and (b) error, for surface z_2.

The depth and orientation data are obtained by simulating the results as would be obtained by shape from contours and photometric stereo. The depth data recovered by shape from contours are simulated by discretising surface heights at fixed grid positions, which introduces errors into the simulated depth values. The orientation data recovered by photometric stereoare simulated by approximating the partial derivatives with the differences in surface height between adjacent positions at discrete grid positions. Since the approach provides approximate partial derivatives, errors are thus introduced into the orientation data. Apart from the errors introduced by the discretisation of data, random noises were further added to the simulated data.

Once the orientation and depth data have been obtained, they are used to calculate the data compatibility function. The main purpose of the compatibility function is to determine the concave region on the surface. In this work, the compatibility of the different data is based on the dot product of the surface normals calculated from photometric stereo and shape from contours. However, the compatibility function calculated by this approach is unable to provide all of the points that lie within the concave region, since at some positions within the cavity, the surface normals obtained by photometric stereo agree with the normals obtained by shape from contours. Furthermore, positions that do not lie within the cavity may also be determined as a cavity point, simply because of the introduced noise. One way to improve the detection of cavities is to take the compatibilities of neighbouring positions into consideration. For example, if the neighbours of a point are all incompatible, yet the point itself is compatible, then it is highly possible that the point lies within the cavity. The same approach can be taken to eliminate points that do not lie within the cavity.

Alternatively, the compatibility function can be given as the confidence with which different types of data agree and has continuous rather than binary values. In which case, the confidence can be indicated by the differences between two types of data, as well as the compatibility of neighbouring positions.

The weighting functions are calculated according to the data compatibility function. The data weighting functions should be constructed such that the unknown surface will generally be recovered from the depth data provided by shape from contours, since shape from contours provides reliable dimensions of the object. However, the unknown surface needs to be recovered according to the surface orientation data in cavity regions, because photometric stereo is able to recover orientation data within the cavities where shape from contours is unable to. In this work, we have used binary weighting functions for the purpose of evaluation. But such inflexibility of weighting values has caused the recovered cavities to be shallower than the original cavities. One approach to improve the result is to increase the orientation data weighting function in the concave region. However, more generally, the weighting function can be made to vary continuously with respect to the data compatibility. For example, the depth weighting function may vary proportionally to the data compatibility, such that the weight increases as the confidence in data compatibility increases. The orientation data weighting function may vary inversely with the data compatibility, and with higher values in the concave regions to emphasis the recovered cavities.

The orientation and depth data, as well as the respective weights are given to the fusion algorithm to recover the unknown surface. The fusion algorithm has assumed that the unknown surface is C^2 continuous, which might not always be the case, as can be seen from the smoothing of the folds in the recovered surface for the simple surface z_2. The coefficients of the different constraining error functions have all been set to 1 in this work. These values may need adjustment to lessen the effect of the continuity or smoothness constraints.

10   Future Work

Our next task is to apply the fusion method on data obtained using shape from contours and photometric stereo, rather than simulated data. The errors contained in the recovered orientation and depth data cause difficulties in the fusion of real data. Therefore, the functions involved in data fusion will need to be more robust and resistant to errors. The data compatibility function requires improvement to provide reliable cavity detection in spite of the noisy data. The weighting functions may need to take the variance of the input data into consideration to avoid emphasising erroneous data. The error functions used in the fusion algorithm also need to be modified to handle real data. Furthermore, if the variances of the errors are known, they can be incorporated into the fusion process to compensate for the errors in the fused result.

Since the fused surface generally conforms with the original surface apart from the cavity regions, it may be possible to refine the fused surface by inputting the fused surface into the fusion algorithm to be combined with the orientation data. Alternative orientation and depth weights can be calculated by comparing the fused surface with the orientation and depth data. The process of fusion may be repeated to further refine the resultant surface.

11   Conclusion

This work is a preliminary step towards the integration of photometric stereo and shape from occluding contours. In this work, we have performed fusion on simulated surface data and acquired more accurate surface recovery for different types of surfaces. The data being fused are the orientation and depth data obtained by simulating the photometric stereo method and the shape from contours, respectively.

Our first objective is to determine if surface obtained by fusing orientation and depth data is more accurate than surface obtained by either type of data alone. This has been achieved by quantitatively comparing the surfaces recovered from simulated data with the surface obtained from original data. It has been found that the surfaces recovered by fusion is more accurate than the surfaces recovered by either photometric stereo or shape from contours.

The second objective is to see if there are any observable artifacts along the cavity boundary where different types of data are fused. A sharp transition of different types of data occur along the cavity boundary, since the surface orientations obtained by photometric stereo is used to complement the inability to recover cavities in shape from contours. By examining the surface recovered by fusion, it has been found that there are no observable artifacts along the cavity boundary, where the transition from one type of data to the other occurs.

We have proposed a method for determining the reliability of the depth and orientation data respectively obtained by shape from contours and photometric stereo. The fusion process is performed by combining portions of orientation and depth data that have been determined to be reliable.

In the experiment, the shape from contours method is able to provide accurate depth recovery of the surface except for the concave regions. The maximum error occurs in the concave regions since the cavity cannot be recovered from the contours alone. On the other hand, the photometric stereo method is able to recover the surface cavities with accuracy, but the surface recovered from the orientations alone is more erroneous overall, as indicated by the mean errors.

The results of our simulated experiment are encouraging. From the evaluations, it has been seen that The surface recovered by fusing depth and orientation data is more accurate than the surfaces recovered using either depth or orientation data alone.

Finally, we discussed some modifications for the procedures involved in fusing orientation and depth data, such that the fusion method may be applied on real data. Possible future work for improving result obtained by fusion of orientation and depth data have also been discussed.

References

[1] C.Y. Chen, K. Schlüns and R. Klette: Comparative 3D shape recovery for archaeological artefacts. *Proc. of IASTED International Conference on Applied Modelling and Simulation* (1999) 577–582.

[2] R. Frankot, R. Chellappa: A method for enforcing integrability in shape from shading algorithms. *IEEE Trans. on Pattern Analysis and Machine Intelligence* **PAMI-10** (1988) 439–451.

[3] W. Grimson: *A computational theory of visual surface interpolation.* **B298** (1982) 395–427.

[4] R. Klette, K. Schlüns: Height data from gradient fields. *Proc. SPIE* **Vol. 2908** (1996) 204–215.

[5] R. Klette, R. Kozera and K. Schlüns,: Shape from shading and photometric stereo methods. *CITR Technical Report* **CITR-TR-20** (1998).

[6] R. Klette, K. Schlüns, A. Koschan: *Computer Vision: Three-dimensional Data from Images.* Springer, Singapore (1998).

[7] R. Szeliski: Fast surface interpolation using hierarchical basis functions. *IEEE Trans. on Pattern Analysis and Machine Intelligence* **12-6** (1990) 513–528.

[8] J. Stoker: *Differential Geometry.* New York (1989) 74–94.

[9] D. Terzopoulos: Multi-level reconstruction of visual surfaces. *Massachusetts institute of technology artificial intelligence laboratory* (1982).

Visual Sign Language Recognition

Eun-Jung Holden and Robyn Owens

Department of Computer Science and Software Engineering,
The University of Western Australia,
35 Stirling Hway, Crawley, W.A. 6009, Australia
{eunjung, robyn}@cs.uwa.edu.au

Abstract. Automatic gesture recognition systems generally require two separate processes: a motion sensing process where some motion features are extracted from the visual input; and a classification process where the features are recognised as gestures. We have developed the Hand Motion Understanding (HMU) system that uses the combination of a 3D model-based hand tracker for motion sensing and an adaptive fuzzy expert system for motion classification. The HMU system understands static and dynamic hand signs of the Australian Sign Language (Auslan). This paper presents the hand tracker that extracts 3D hand configuration data with 21 degrees-of-freedom (DOFs) from a 2D image sequence that is captured from a single viewpoint, with the aid of a colour-coded glove. Then the temporal sequence of 3D hand configurations detected by the tracker is recognised as a sign by an adaptive fuzzy expert system. The HMU system was evaluated with 22 static and dynamic signs. Before training the HMU system achieved 91% recognition, and after training it achieved over 95% recognition.

1 Introduction

Deaf communities in Australia use a sign language called Auslan. Signers use a combination of hand movements, which change in shape and location relative to the upper body, and facial expressions. Auslan is different from American Sign Language or indeed any other sign language, though it is related to British Sign Language. As is the case in other countries, Auslan has rules of context and grammar that are separable from the spoken language of the community, in this case English. Despite the effort to educate the deaf community to master the written form of the spoken language, there is still a vast communication barrier between the deaf and aurally unaffected people, the majority of whom do not know sign language.

Thus, there is a need for a communication bridge between Auslan and spoken English and a means whereby unaffected people can efficiently learn sign language. An automated communication tool must translate signs into English as well as translate English into signs. Sign to English translation could be achieved by using a visual gesture recognition system that must recognise the motion of the whole upper body, including facial expressions. As an initial step towards

R. Klette et al. (Eds.): Multi-Image Analysis, LNCS 2032, pp. 270–287, 2001.

building such system, we developed a framework for the Hand Motion Understanding (HMU) system that understands one-handed Auslan signs. The HMU system uses a combination of 3D tracking of hand motion from visual input and an adaptive fuzzy expert system to classify the signs. Previously, these techniques have not been used for gesture recognition and they are presented in this paper. Automated gesture recognition has been an active area of research in human-computer interaction applications and sign language translation systems. The gesture recognition may be performed in two stages: the motion sensing, which extracts useful motion data from the actual motion input; and the classification process, which classifies the movement data as a sign. Current vision-based gesture recognition systems [1] [2] [3] extract and classify 2D hand shape information in order to recognise gestures. The representation of 3D hand postures or 3D motion by using 2D characteristic descriptors from a single viewpoint, has its inherent limitations. In order to overcome these limitations, Watanabe and Yachida [4] approximate 3D information by using an eigenspace constructed from multiple input sequences that are captured from many directions, without reconstructing 3D structure. The idea of a vision-based sign recognition system that uses 3D hand configuration data was previously suggested by Dorner [5]. She developed a general hand tracker that extracts 26 DOFs of a single hand configuration from the visual input as a first step towards an American Sign Language (ASL) recognition system. She used a colour-coded glove for easier extraction of hand features. Regh and Kanada [6], on the other hand, developed a hand tracker that extracts 27 DOFs of a single hand configuration from unadorned hand images. Both trackers were developed as a motion sensing device, and have not been tested to recognise meaningful gestures. The HMU system [7] recognises Auslan hand signs by using the 3D model-based hand tracking technique to previous approaches. While the HMU system employs a similar tracking technique, our tracker handles occlusion of fingers to some degree, and uses a simpler hand model with only 21 DOFs. The 3D hand tracker produces the kinematic configuration changes as motion data, which are similar to data obtained from Virtual Reality (VR) gloves. In the existing VR-based gesture recognition systems, the 3D motion data are classified by either using neural networks [8] [9] or Hidden Markov Models [3] [10]. Sign language signs are very well-defined gestures, where the motion of each sign is explicitly understood by both the signer and the viewer. However, the motion of signers varies slightly due to individual physical constraints and personal interpretation of the signing motion. We have earlier proposed a classification technique [11] that is capable of imposing expert knowledge of the input/output behaviour on the system yet also supports data classification over a range of errors in the motion sensing process or slight individual hand movement variations. This is achieved by using an adaptive fuzzy expert system. The HMU system employs this technique to classify the 3D hand kinematic data extracted from the visual hand tracker as signs.

2   Overview of the HMU System

The HMU system recognises static and dynamic hand signs by dealing with "fine grain" hand motion, such as the kinematic configuration changes of fingers. A signer wears a colour-coded glove and performs the sign commencing from a specified starting hand posture, then proceeds on to a static or dynamic sign. A colour image sequence is captured through a single video camera and used as input to the HMU system. The recognition is performed by using the combination of a 3D tracker and an adaptive fuzzy expert classifier. The recognition process is illustrated in Figure 1.

The 3D model-based hand tracker extracts a 3D hand configuration sequence (each frame containing a set of 21 DOF hand parameters) from the visual input. Then, the adaptive fuzzy expert system classifies the 3D hand configuration sequence as a sign. This paper presents the techniques used in the hand tracker and the classifier, and its performance evaluation for the recognition of 22 static and dynamic signs. Our system achieved a recognition rate of over 95%, and demonstrated that the tracker computes the motion data with an accuracy that is sufficient for effective classification by the fuzzy expert system. Throughout this paper, a hand posture refers to a 3D hand configuration. Thus a static sign may be recognised by a hand posture only, while a dynamic sign is recognised by 3D hand motion that consists of changes of hand postures and 3D locations during the course of signing.

3   The HMU Hand Tracker

The hand tracker uses a 3D model-based tracking technique, where given a sequence of 2D images and a 3D hand model, the 3D hand configurations captured in the images are sequentially recovered by processing a sequence of 2D images. The hand tracker consists of three components:

- The **3D Hand model**, which specifies a mapping from 3D hand posture space, which characterises all possible spatial configurations of the hand, to 2D image feature space which represents the hand in an image.
- The **feature measurement** that extracts the necessary features from images.
- The **state estimation**, which makes corrections to the 3D model state in order to fit the model state to the 3D posture appearing in the 2D image. Throughout the sequence of 2D images, incremental corrections are made to the 3D model.

3.1   Hand Model

A hand is modelled as a combination of 5 finger mechanisms (totalling 15 DOFs) each attached to a wrist base of 6 DOFs. The model represents a kinematic chain that describes the hand configuration, where a model state encodes the hand posture by using the 21 DOFs, as illustrated in Figure 2.

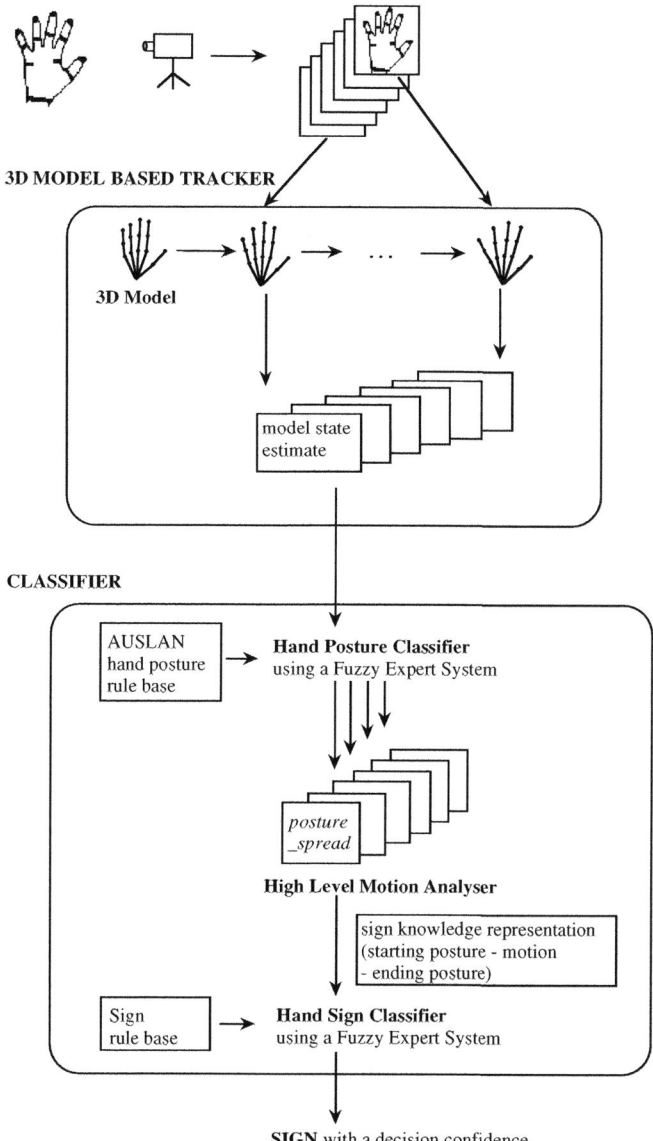

Fig. 1. Structure of the HMU system. The HMU hand tracker extracts 3D hand configuration data from the images, then the HMU classifier recognises them as a sign.

Each of F1, F2, F3 and F4 finger mechanisms has 3 DOFs, which consist of 2 DOFs for the MCP (Meta Carpo Phalangeal) joint, and 1 DOF for the PIP (Proximal Inter Phalangeal) joint. F0 also has 3 DOFs, which consist of 2

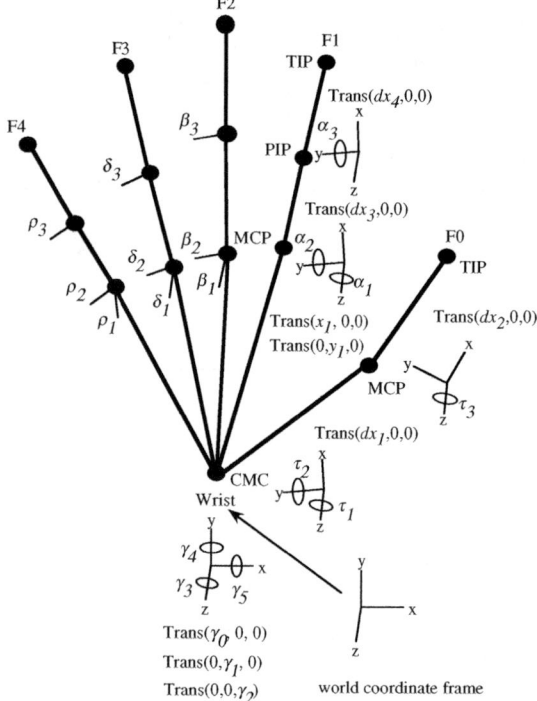

Fig. 2. Hand model used in the HMU hand tracker. The base coordinate frame for each joint and their transformation through rotations and translations are illustrated.

DOFs for the CMC (Carpo Meta Carpal) joint, and 1 DOF for the MCP joint. Thus the model describes the transformation between attached local coordinate frames for each finger segment, by using the Denavit-Hartenberg (DH) representation, which is a commonly used representation in the field of robotics [16]. For example, the transformation matrix for the wrist segment, describing the position and orientation of the wrist frame relative to some world coordinate frame may be calculated as follows:

$$T_{origin}^{wrist} = Trans(\gamma_0,0,0) \cdot Trans(0,\gamma_1,0) \cdot Trans(0,0,\gamma_2) \cdot$$
$$Rot(z,\gamma_3) \cdot Rot(y,\gamma_4) \cdot Rot(x,\gamma_5).$$

For the other segments of F1, and similarly for F2, F3 and F4, we have

$$T_{wrist}^{MCP} = Trans(x_1,0,0) \cdot Trans(0,y_1,0)$$
$$Rot(z,\alpha_3) \cdot Rot(y,\alpha_2),$$
$$T_{MCP}^{PIP} = Trans(dx_3,0,0) \cdot Rot(y,\alpha_3), \text{and}$$
$$T_{PIP}^{TIP} = Trans(dx_4,0,0).$$

For the segments of F0, we have

$$T_{wrist}^{CMC} = Rot(z, \tau_1) \cdot Rot(y, \tau_2),$$

$$T_{CMC}^{MCP} = Trans(dx_1, 0, 0) \cdot Rot(z, \tau_3), \text{and}$$

$$T_{MCP}^{TIP} = Trans(dx_2, 0, 0).$$

Thus, the hand state encodes the orientation of the palm (three rotation and three translation parameters) and the joint angles of the fingers (three rotation parameters for each finger and the thumb).

4   Feature Measurement

In order to locate the joint positions of the hand in images, a well-fitted cotton glove is used and the joint markers are drawn with fabric paints, as shown in Figure 3. The feature measurement process performs rapid marker detection by colour segmentationand determines the corresponding joints between the marker locations and the joints in the model.

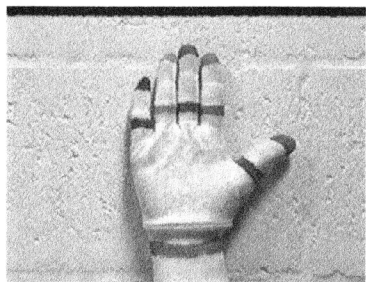

Fig. 3. Colour coded glove. Ring-shaped markers are applied at the wrist (in green), the PIP and TIP joints of four fingers (fluorescent orange for F1, green for F2, violet for F3, and magenta for F4), and the MCP joint and TIP of the thumb (in blue). Semi-ring-shaped markers are used for the MCP joints of fingers (in yellow).

However imposter or missing markers arise when marker areas are split or disappear entirely, and are usually caused by finger occlusions. The tracker computes the marker size, and if a sudden change in size (or a disappearance) occurs from the previous frame, it assumes the marker is partially occluded and regards it as a missing marker. The HMU tracker deals with the missing marker problem by predicting the location of the missing marker. This is achieved by using the changes of the 3D model state estimates of the 5 previous frames in order to predict the 3D model state (for all parameters of the model) that may appear in the image, and generating the predicted joint positions by projecting this state onto the image. Kalman filtering is used for the prediction. Figure 4 illustrates the prediction process.

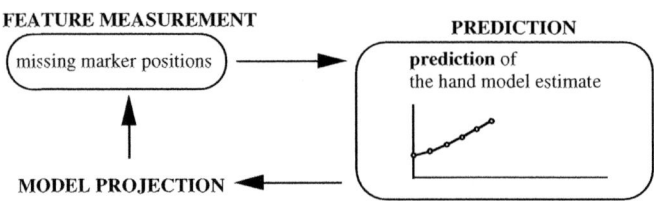

Fig. 4. Prediction of the missing marker. The tracker uses a limited case of Kalman filtering to predict the state estimate based on the previous estimates, which is then projected onto an image in order to find a predicted location of the missing marker.

4.1   The State Estimation

Given a 2D image and the 3D initial model state (the current estimate in our system), the state estimation calculates the 3D parameter corrections that need to be applied to the model state to fit the posture appearing in the image. The state estimation process is shown in Figure 5.

The parameter corrections are calculated by minimising the Euclidean distances between the image features (that are extracted by the feature measurement process), and the projected features of the predicted model state (that are calculated from the model projection process). State estimation employs Lowe's object tracking algorithm [12], which uses a Newton-style minimisation approach where the corrections are calculated through iterative steps, and in each step the model moves closer to the posture that is captured in the image.

Parameters. We define the parameter vector to be,

$$\tilde{\alpha} = (\alpha_1, \alpha_2, \cdots \alpha_n)^T,$$

where n is the total number of parameters. The wrist model consists of 6 parameters (that is, the x, y, and z translation parameters and the 3 rotation parameters for the wrist). A finger uses 3 rotation parameters as previously shown in Figure 2.

Projected Features. The projection of the ith joint onto an image is a function of the hand state $\tilde{\alpha}$, and is given by

$$\tilde{p}_i(\tilde{\alpha}) = \begin{pmatrix} p_{ix}(\tilde{\alpha}) \\ p_{iy}(\tilde{\alpha}) \end{pmatrix}.$$

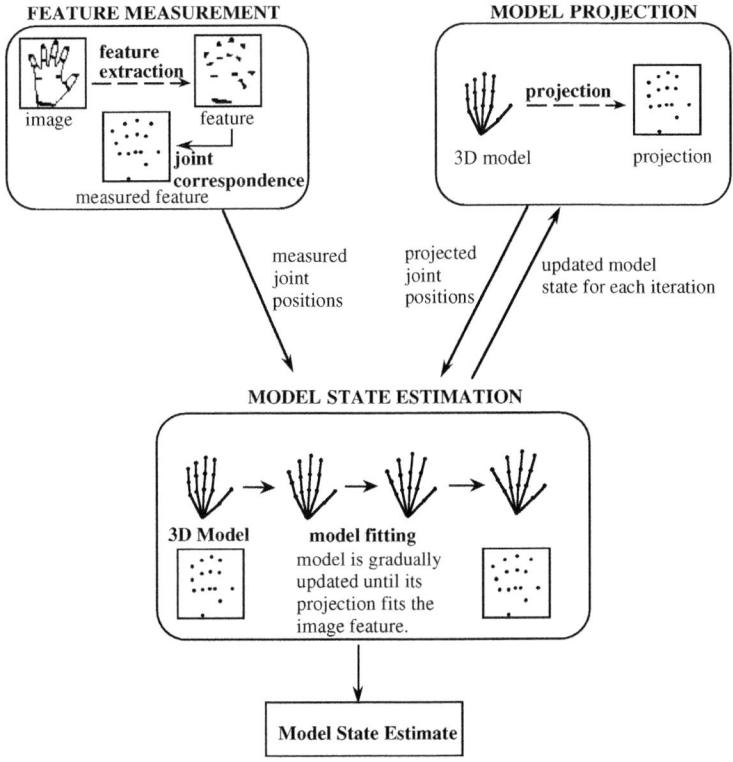

Fig. 5. One cycle of state estimation. All model parameters are corrected iteratively in order to fit the model to the posture appearing in the image.

For the whole hand, these vectors are concatenated into a single vector, and for convenience we define $q_1(\tilde{\alpha}) = p_{1x}(\tilde{\alpha})$, $q_2(\tilde{\alpha}) = p_{1y}(\tilde{\alpha})$, etc. Thus,

$$\tilde{q}(\tilde{\alpha}) = \begin{pmatrix} p_{1x}(\tilde{\alpha}) \\ p_{1y}(\tilde{\alpha}) \\ \vdots \\ p_{kx}(\tilde{\alpha}) \\ p_{ky}(\tilde{\alpha}) \end{pmatrix} = \begin{pmatrix} q_1(\tilde{\alpha}) \\ q_2(\tilde{\alpha}) \\ \vdots \\ q_{m-1}(\tilde{\alpha}) \\ q_m(\tilde{\alpha}) \end{pmatrix} ,$$

where k is the total number of joints (thus $m = 2k$).

Tracking the palm or a finger requires 3 joints. Palm tracking uses the wrist and the knuckles of F1 and F4, whereas finger tracking uses the knuckle, PIP and TIP of the finger.

Error Vector. The measured joint locations are the joint positions, which are obtained by the feature extraction process from an image. As with the projected joints, the measured feature locations are concatenated into a single vector, $\tilde{g}$, and then the error vector describing the difference between the projected and measured joint positions is defined by

$$\tilde{e} = \tilde{q}(\tilde{\alpha}) - \tilde{g}.$$

Implementation of Lowe's Algorithm. We compute a vector of corrections $\tilde{c}$ to be subtracted from the current estimate for $\tilde{\alpha}$, the model parameter vector, on each iteration. This correction vector is computed using Newton's method as follows:

$$\tilde{c} = \tilde{\alpha}^{(i)} - \tilde{\alpha}^{(i+1)}.$$

Using Lowe's algorithm, the tracker solves the following normal equation to obtain the correction vector $\tilde{c}$:

$$(J^T J + \lambda W^T W)\tilde{c} = J^T \tilde{e} + \lambda W^T W \tilde{s},$$

where J is the Jacobian matrix of $\tilde{q}$, defined by

$$\frac{d\tilde{q}(\tilde{\alpha})}{d\tilde{\alpha}} = \begin{pmatrix} \frac{\partial q_1(\tilde{\alpha})}{\partial \alpha_1} & \cdots & \frac{\partial q_m(\tilde{\alpha})}{\partial \alpha_1} \\ \vdots & \ddots & \vdots \\ \frac{\partial q_1(\tilde{\alpha})}{\partial \alpha_m} & \cdots & \frac{\partial q_m(\tilde{\alpha})}{\partial \alpha_m} \end{pmatrix}.$$

The matrix W is a normalised identity matrix whose diagonal elements are inversely proportional to the standard deviation σ_i of the change in parameter α_i from one frame to the next, that is $W_{ii} = \frac{1}{\sigma_i}$, s_i is the desired default value for parameter α_i, and λ is a scalar weight.

The above equation is driven to minimise the difference between the measured error and the sum of all the changes in the error resulting from the parameter corrections. The stabilisation technique uses the addition of a small constant to the diagonal elements of $J^T J$ in order to avoid the possibility of J being at or near a singularity. This is similar to the stabilisation technique often used in other tracking systems [6].

In this algorithm, the standard deviation of parameter changes in consecutive frames represents the limit on the acceleration of each parameter from frame to frame. For translation parameters, a limit of up to 50 pixels (within the image size of 256×192) is used as the standard deviation, but for rotational parameters, ranges from $\pi/2$ up to $\pi/4$, depending on the finger joint, are used as standard deviation. The scalar λ can be used to increase the weight of stabilisation whenever divergence occurs, but a constant scalar of 64 is used in the HMU system to stabilise the system throughout the iterations. For each frame of the sequence, the correction vector is calculated and the model state is updated iteratively until the error vector is small, at which point the measured hand shape is close to the projected hand model. Thus for each frame of the input sequence, the hand tracker generates a hand state vector that consists of 21 DOFs representing the hand configuration.

5   The HMU Classifier

The HMU classifier recognises the 3D configuration sequence that was extracted from the hand tracker as a sign. A frame in the 3D hand configuration sequence will be referred to as a kinematic data set, and an example of the set is defined as *kin_pos*.

From the previously shown Figure 2, *kin_pos* is a vector of 15 finger joint angles (3 DOFs in the MCP and PIP joints of each of the five fingers). Note that even though the tracker recovers 21 DOFs of the hand, the 6 parameters of the wrist translation and orientation are not used for sign classification at this stage of the development. The adaptive fuzzy expert classifier relies on the sign rules that use the following knowledge representation.

5.1   Knowledge Representation

In the HMU system, a sign is represented by a combination of:

- a starting hand posture;
- motion information that describes the changes that occurred during the movement, such as the number of wiggles in a finger movement; and
- an ending hand posture.

The starting and ending hand postures are defined by using Auslan basic hand postures [13]. The HMU system uses 22 postures that are a subset of Auslan basic hand postures and their variants. Fuzzy set theory [15] is applied to all posture and motion variables to provide imprecise and natural descriptions of the sign. Postures are represented by the following variables.

- Finger digit flex variables are defined for all of F0 (**d_F0**), F1 (**d_F1**), F2 (**d_F2**), F3 (**d_F3**), and F4 (**d_F4**). The states of **d_F0** may be straight (**st**), slightly flexed (**sf**), or flexed (**fx**). The states of the other digit flex variables may be straight (**st**) or flexed (**fx**). An example of F0 digit flex variable states and their default fuzzy membership distributions are shown in Figure 6.
- Finger knuckle flex variables are defined for F1 (**k_F1**), F2 (**k_F2**), F3 (**k_F3**) and F4 (**k_F4**), and the states may be straight (**st**) or flexed (**fx**).
- Finger spread variables (**FS**) represent the degree of yaw movement of the MCP joints of F1, F2, F3 and F4, and the states may be **closed** or **spread**.

In the sign knowledge representation, motion is represented by the number of directional changes (wiggles) in the movement of finger digits, finger knuckles, and finger spreading. We assume 5 states are possible: no wiggle (**nw**), very small wiggle (**vsw**), small wiggle (**sw**), medium wiggle (**mw**), and large wiggle (**lw**). Note that a state of a posture or motion variable is defined by a state name, "_", followed by the variable name. For example, a flexed digit of F1 is **fx_d_F1**, and no wiggle motion in an F0 digit flex would be represented as **nw_d_F0**. An example sign representation is illustrated in Figure 7.

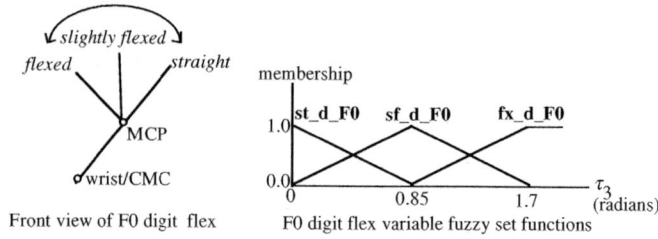

Fig. 6. F0 digit flex variable states, and their default fuzzy membership distributions. A triangular distribution function has been used for all fuzzy membership distributions in our sign representation.

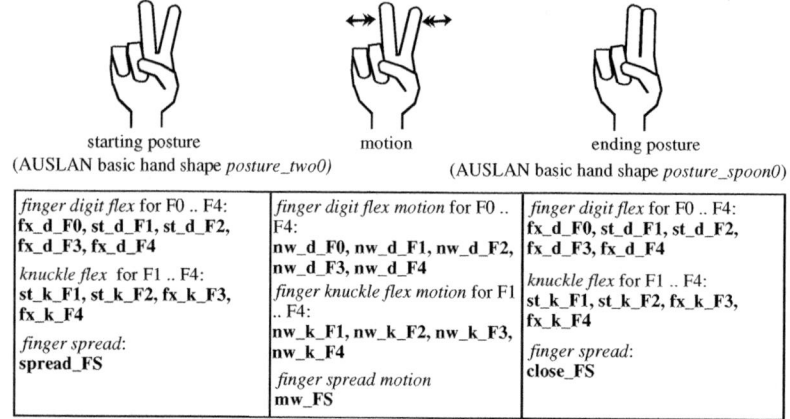

finger digit flex for F0 .. F4: **fx_d_F0, st_d_F1, st_d_F2, fx_d_F3, fx_d_F4**	*finger digit flex motion* for F0 .. F4: **nw_d_F0, nw_d_F1, nw_d_F2, nw_d_F3, nw_d_F4**	*finger digit flex* for F0 .. F4: **fx_d_F0, st_d_F1, st_d_F2, fx_d_F3, fx_d_F4**
knuckle flex for F1 .. F4: **st_k_F1, st_k_F2, fx_k_F3, fx_k_F4**	*finger knuckle flex motion* for F1 .. F4: **nw_k_F1, nw_k_F2, nw_k_F3, nw_k_F4**	*knuckle flex* for F1 .. F4: **st_k_F1, st_k_F2, fx_k_F3, fx_k_F4**
finger spread: **spread_FS**	*finger spread motion* **mw_FS**	*finger spread*: **close_FS**

Fig. 7. Graphical description of *sign_scissors* and its corresponding sign representation.

5.2 Classification

The classification is performed through three stages. Firstly, the classifier analyses each frame of the hand configuration sequence, and recognises the basic hand postures. Secondly, it determines the starting and ending postures as well as the motion that occurred in between. Then thirdly, a sign is recognised. The recognition of both basic hand postures and signs is performed by the fuzzy inference engine that also generates an output confidence, or Rule Activation Level (RAL). This is shown in Figure 8.

5.3 Adaptive Engine

Fuzzy set theory allows the system to tolerate slight tracker errors or movement variations. However, the fuzzy expert system may produce a low decision confi-

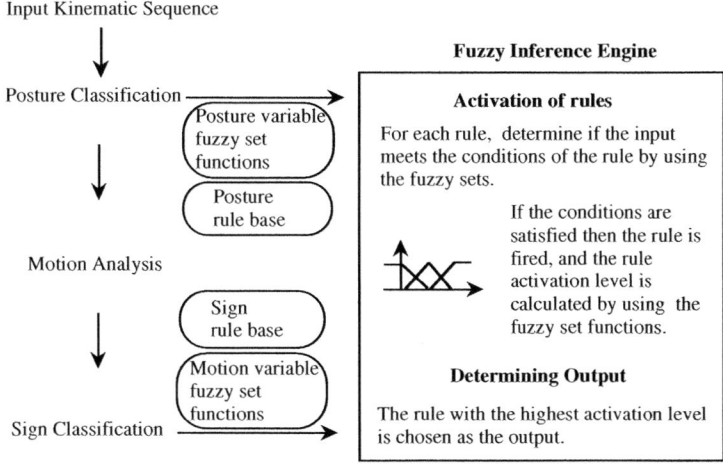

Fig. 8. Sign Classification using the fuzzy inference engine.

dence (RAL), or fail if the input lies near or outside the boundary of the fuzzy set. Therefore, we made our fuzzy system adaptive. In the HMU classifier, dynamic adjustments to the individual fuzzy distributions are performed under a supervised learning paradigm. The adaptive engine modifies fuzzy set regions by slightly narrowing or widening the region depending upon whether the system's response was above or below expectation, respectively [14]. As the training data are entered, the system classifies them into output signs and their corresponding RALs. Then according to the output, the fuzzy regions are modified.

6   Sign Recognition

The input image sequence always starts with a specified posture, *posture_flat0*, which appears in Figure 9. The hand then moves to the starting posture of the sign and performs the sign until it reaches the ending posture of the sign.

6.1   Signs Used in the Evaluation

The HMU system stores the 22 postures that are illustrated in Figure 9, and 22 signs that consist of 11 static signs and 11 dynamic signs as shown in Figure 10. Signs consist of actual Auslan signs as well as artificial signs that use various combinations of the basic hand postures and motion.

   One signer recorded the image sequences, wearing the colour-coded glove and signing under the fluorescent lighting of a normal office environment.

   For evaluation, 44 motion sequences that consist of two sub-sequences for each of the 22 signs were recorded by using a single video camera. To enable a fair test to be conducted, half of the recorded sequences were used for testing,

posture_flat0   posture_flat1   posture_flat2   posture_spread0

posture_ten0   posture_good0   posture_good1   posture_point0

posture_hook0   posture_spoon0   posture_two0   posture_two1

posture_gun0   posture_eight0   posture_bad0   posture_mother0

posture_three0   posture_four0   posture_ambivalent0   posture_animal0

posture_ok0   posture_queer0

Fig. 9. Illustrations of Auslan basic hand postures used in the evaluation.

and the other half were used for training of the HMU classifier. One sequence for each sign was randomly selected, producing the total of 22 sequences as a test set. The remaining 22 sequences were used as a training set.

6.2   Recognition Results

Prior to training, the system correctly recognised 20 out of the 22 signs. After training, for the same test set, the system recognised 21 signs. For all failed cases, the system did not produce false output. Figure 11 illustrates the results by showing the sign RAL for each of the recognised signs before and after training.

Given the complexity of extracting and recognising 3D hand configuration data from the visual input, the HMU system achieved a very high recognition rate. Recognition results of *sign_dew* are shown in Figure 12. The tracker result is graphically shown under each image frame, and the posture recognition results before (b/t) and after (a/t) training are shown. Note that only every third frame is shown, and each posture and sign recognition result is accompanied by a RAL. The adaptive engine aims to modify the fuzzy set functions in order to improve the system's behaviour by adjusting the acceptable range of variations in hand configuration data when classifying the signs. Thus the training should make appropriate adjustments to all fuzzy set regions in order to achieve an improved

sign	starting posture	intermediate postures	ending posture
point	point0		point0
ambivalent	ambivalent0		ambivalent0
queer	queer0		queer0
good	good0		good0
gun	gun0		gun0
ok	ok0		ok0
two	two0		two0
four	four0		four0
dark	two1		two1
hook	hook0		hook0
spoon	spoon0		spoon0
dew	point0		spread0
ten	ten0		spread0
good_animal	good0		animal0
have	spread0		ten0
spread	flat2		spread0
fist_bad	ten0		bad0
good_spoon	good0		spoon0
flicking	ok0		spread0
queer_flicking	queer0		spread0
scissors	two0	spoon0 two0	spoon0
quote	two0	two1 two0	two1

Fig. 10. Signs used in the evaluation of the HMU system. Note that to perform a sign, the hand moves from the specified starting posture to possibly intermediate postures until it reaches the ending posture.

recognition rate, higher RALs, as well as producing fewer posture outputs for each sequence.

A close observation shows that the tracker produces quite significant errors (up to 45 degrees) for either the MCP or the PIP joint flex angles for some motion sequences. This has caused the confusion between two close postures, *posture_spoon0* and *posture_two0*, resulting in the failure of *sign_scissors* after training (*sign_scissors* use both of *posture_two0* and *posture_spoon0* as subpostures during its execution). The overall recognition results, however demonstrate that the HMU tracker has generated hand configuration data with an acceptable range of errors for training of the system, by making the system more selective in recognition of postures. This is shown in the recognition of the signs that were not recognised before training but were recognised after training, and the reduction in the posture outputs by an average of 10.7%. Figure 13 shows a recognition result of *sign_good_animal*, which was not recognised before training, but successfully recognised after training.

sign	before training			after training		
	success	RAL	no. of pos. outputs	success	RAL	no. of pos. outputs
point	√	0.79	87	√	0.79	81
ambivalent	√	0.45	37	√	0.45	37
queer	√	0.51	27	√	0.51	16
good	√	0.83	33	√	0.83	32
gun	√	0.71	13	√	0.71	13
ok	√	0.71	40	√	0.71	26
two	√	0.82	19	√	0.82	15
four	√	0.81	38	√	0.8	38
dark	√	0.71	24	√	0.71	21
hook	√	0.58	47	√	0.58	47
spoon	√	0.8	19	√	0.8	19
dew	√	0.5	78	√	0.5	67
ten	√	0.32	49	√	0.32	44
good_animal	–	–	(41)*	√	0.6	36*
have	√	0.63	54	√	0.63	53
spread	√	0.58	67	√	0.53	67
fist_bad	√	0.37	38	√	0.28	36
good_spoon	–	–	(63)*	√	0.58	56*
flicking	√	0.27	34	√	0.26	32
queer_flicking	√	0.46	118	√	0.46	83
scissors	√	0.63	205*	–	–	(193)*
quote	√	0.41	96	√	0.41	79

number of signs	number of sequences per sign	total number of test sequence
22	1	22

Recognition results		
	before training	after training
number of success	20	21
success rate (%)	91	95
av. reduction rate for the posture outputs after training (%)	10.7	

Fig. 11. Evaluation Results. A √ in the 'success' column indicates that the sign is recognised correctly, and a dash indicates that no output is produced. An asterisk in the 'no. of pos. output' column indicates the figure that is not included in calculating the average reduction rate for the posture outputs after training (only the signs that were recognised before and after training are used for the calculation).

7   Conclusion

The HMU system successfully recognised various 'fine-grain' hand movements by using a combination of the 3D hand tracker as a low-level motion sensing device and the fuzzy expert as a high-level motion understanding system. The tracker

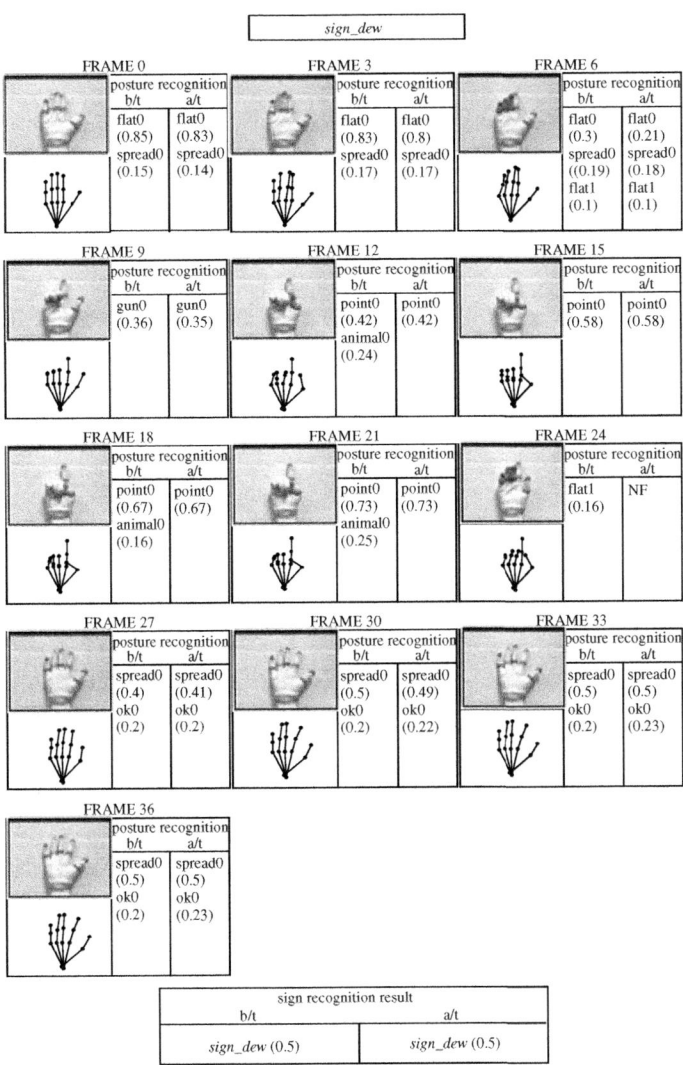

Fig. 12. Recognition result of *sign_dew* before and after training.

analyses a sequence of images to produce the changes of 21 DOFs of the hand including the orientation and trajectory of the hand (on the wrist base). This is achieved by employing a computer vision-based feature extraction technique and robotics-based 3D model manipulation. The hand configuration data are then classified by the fuzzy expert system, where the sign knowledge is defined by high-level, natural language-like descriptions of the hand movement using fuzzy logic. To build an automated communication tool between the deaf and the unaffected, we are continuing our research. The system not only needs to un-

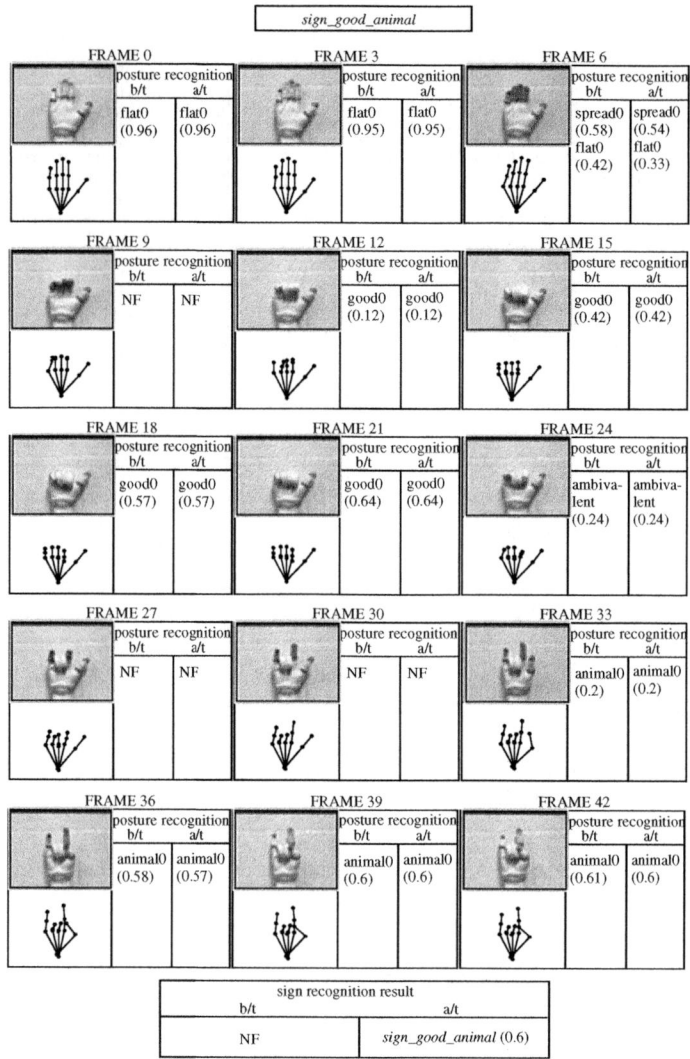

Fig. 13. Recognition result of *sign_good_animal* before and after training.

derstand fine-grain hand gestures, but also the hand trajectory, facial expression and lipreading. Thus the current projects include the development of the following systems: The facial expression recognition system recognises emotions using the facial muscle movement appearing in the visual input in order to provide an additional clue to sign recognition. The lipreading system visually recognises the signer's speech in cases where the signer uses a combination of speech and signing, as often occurs in deaf education systems. The lipreading system detects the mouth contour and inner mouth appearance to recognise English phonemes.

The 3D head tracker recognises the 3D head orientation while signing. This is useful in facial expression recognition and lipreading systems to deal with the 2D feature detection while the signer moves the head in 3D.

Acknowledgments. We would like to thank Geoffrey Roy for his contribution to early parts of this work, and Michael Arbib for his feedback on this paper. This project is supported by the Australian Research Council (ARC).

References

[1] Tamura, S., Kawasaki, S.: Recognition of sign language motion images. Pattern Recognition **21(4)** (1988) 343-353

[2] Davis, J., Shah, M.: Visual gesture recognition. IEE Proceedings - Vision, Image, and Signal Processing (1994) 101-106

[3] Starner, T., Pentland, A.: Real-Time American sign language recognition using desk and wearable computer based video. IEEE Transactions on Pattern Analysis and Machine Intelligence **20(12)** (1998).

[4] Watanabe, T., Yachida, M.: Real time gesture recognition using eigenspace from multi input image sequences. Proceedings of The Third International Conference on Automatic Face and Gesture Recognition (1998) 428-433.

[5] Dorner, B.: Chasing the colour glove: Visual hand tracking, Master's dissertation, Department of Computer Science, Simon Fraser University(1994)

[6] Regh, J., Kanade, T.: DigitEyes: Vision-based human hand tracking, Technical Report CMU-CS-93-220, School of Computer Science, Carnegie Mellon University (1993)

[7] Holden, E.J.: Visual Recognition of Hand Motion, PhD thesis, University of Western Australia(1997)

[8] Fels, S. S., Hinton, G. E.: Glove-Talk: A neural network interface between a data-glove and a speech synthesizer. IEEE Transactions on Neural Networks **4(1)** (1993) 2-8

[9] Vamplew, P., Adams, A.: Recognition and anticipation of hand motions using a recurrent neural network. Proceedings of IEEE International Confference on Neural Networks **3** (1995) 2904-2907

[10] Liang R. H., Ouhyoung, M.: Real time continuous gesture recognition system for sign language. Proceedings of The Third International Conference on Automatic Face and Gesture Recognition (1998) 558-565

[11] Holden, E. J., Roy, G. G., Owens, R.: Hand movement classification using an adaptive fuzzy expert system. International Journal of Expert Systems **9(4)** (1996) 465-480

[12] Lowe, D.G.: Fitting parameterized three dimensional models to images. IEEE Transactions on Pattern Analysis and Machine Intelligence **13(5)** (1991) 441-450

[13] Johnston, T.A.: Auslan Dictionary: A dictionary of the sign language of the Australian deaf community, Deafness Resources, Australia, (1989)

[14] Cox, E.: Adaptive fuzzy systems. IEEE Spectrum February (1993) 27-31

[15] Zadeh, L. A.: Fuzzy sets. Information Control **8**(1965) 338-353

[16] Yoshikawa, T.: Foundation of Robotics Analysis and Control, The MIT press, Cambridge, Massachusetts (1990)

Author Index

Lecture Notes in Computer Science

For information about Vols. 1–1962
please contact your bookseller or Springer-Verlag